T0366352

Further praise for Exotic Options and Hybrids

"This book brings a practitioner's prospective into an area that has seen little treatment to date. The challenge of writing a logical, rigorous, accessible and readable account of a vast and diverse field that is structuring of exotic options and hybrids is enthusiastically taken up by the authors, and they succeed brilliantly in covering an impressive range of products."

Vladimir Piterbarg, Head of Quantitative Research, Barclays

"What is interesting about this excellent work is that the reader can measure clearly that the authors are sharing a concrete experience. Their writing approach and style bring a clear added value to those who want to understand the structuring practices, Exotics pricing as well as the theory behind these."

Younes Guemouri, Chief Operating Officer, Sophis

"The book provides an excellent and compressive review of exotic options. The purpose of using these derivatives is well exposed, and by opposition to many derivatives' books, the authors focus on practical applications. It is recommended to every practitioner as well as advanced students looking forward to work in the field of derivatives."

Dr Amine Jalal, Vice President, Equity Derivatives Trading, Goldman Sachs International

"*Exotic Options and Hybrids* is an exceptionally well written book, distilling essential ingredients of a successful structured products business. Adel and Mohamed have summarized an excellent guide to developing intuition for a trader and structurer in the world of exotic equity derivatives."

Anand Batepati, Structured Products Development Manager, HSBC, Hong Kong

"A very precise, up-to-date and intuitive handbook for every derivatives user in the market."

Amine Chkili, Equity Derivatives Trader, HSBC Bank PLC, London

"*Exotic Options and Hybrids* is an excellent book for anyone interested in structured products. It can be read cover to cover or used as a reference. It is a comprehensive guide and would be useful to both beginners and experts. I have read a number of books on the subject and would definitely rate this in the top three."

Ahmed Seghrouchni, Volatility Trader, Dresdner Kleinwort, London

"A clear and complete book with a practical approach to structured pricing and hedging techniques used by professionals. *Exotic Options and Hybrids* introduces technical concepts in an elegant manner and gives good insights into the building blocks behind structured products."

Idriss Amor, Rates and FX Structuring, Bank of America, London

About the authors

MOHAMED BOUZOUBAA is an experienced practitioner in the world of derivatives, and is currently Head of Derivatives Trading and Structuring at CDG Capital. His professional expertise spans the spectrum of topics in exotic options and hybrids having held positions in Equity Derivatives Sales at Société Générale in Paris, as a Risk and Fund Management expert at Sophis specializing in the risks involved in equity, credit and fixed income derivatives, and as a derivatives structurer at Bear Stearns/JP Morgan Chase in London and Equity Structured Products Manager at First Gulf Bank in Dubai. Mohamed holds masters degrees in Financial Engineering and in Applied Mathematics.

ADEL OSSEIRAN is a mathematician by training. His work as a financial practitioner in derivative pricing includes working in front office roles as a quantitative analyst and as a derivatives structurer in London. He studied Mathematics at the University of Oxford and to PhD level in Financial Mathematics at Imperial College London.

The book is accompanied by a website
www.exotic-options-and-hybrids.com
which features extended resources, forums and an interactive zone.

"An intermediate to advanced comprehensive treatment of derivative products, from the simplest options to the most complex ones. It provides a good theoretical grounding and some practical insights as well as very relevant examples. This book will become a reference for practitioners."

Stephane Junod, ex-Head of Hybrids Trading and Structuring at Citigroup in London, Head of the Global Hedging Units, Zurich Insurance, Zurich

"Striking an outstanding balance between theory and (good) practice, this comprehensive book is very informative, smart and useful. From vanilla option pricing and hedging to exotic options, complex structured products and sophisticated dynamic strategies, readers will learn and enjoy most of what is required of an option-oriented financial engineer. A valuable addition to an already well stocked pack."

Professor Patrice Poncet, Sorbonne University and ESSEC Business School

"This is a new and different book about structured products. Readers get detailed coverage of all major types of structured notes across all types of assets. This guide is a practical reference and a great complement to anybody's financial library."

Mimoun Nadir, Head of Exotic Equity Derivatives, Calyon, Paris

"Exotic Options and Hybrids is a refreshing book about getting the reader familiar with modern structured products and the rational behind their creation. More importantly, the emphasis on revealing the embedded risks will be well appreciated by anyone interested in structuring, pricing or trading these products."

Abdelkerim Karim, Head of Equity Structured Products, Nomura, London

"Mohamed Bouzoubaa and Adel Osseiran, highly regarded senior structurers, have come up with a thorough study of exotic options and hybrids, covering the subject from all possible structuring, pricing and trading angles, both from theoretical and practical standpoints. An essential and exciting read for financial professionals and students."

Bruno Pannetier, former Head of Structured Products at CIC, former Senior Managing Director and Co-Global Head of Equity and Hybrid Structuring at Bear Stearns, Division Director and Head of Structuring at Macquarie Bank

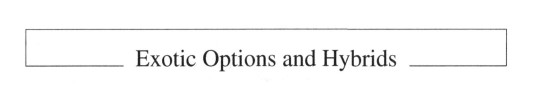

Exotic Options and Hybrids

For other titles in the Wiley Finance series
please see www.wiley.com/finance

Exotic Options and Hybrids

A Guide to Structuring, Pricing and Trading

Mohamed Bouzoubaa and Adel Osseiran

A John Wiley and Sons, Ltd., Publication

To my parents
Chakib and Fadia
MB

To the memory of my grandfather
Adil
AO

Contents

List of Symbols and Abbreviations

$\mathbf{1}$	Indicator function
ATM	At the money
ATMF	At the money forward
bp	Basis point, equal to 1% of 1%
EUR	Euro
GBP	Great Britain pound
ITM	In the money
JPY	Japanese yen
K	The strike of a specified option
MTM	Marked-to-market
$\mathcal{N}$	Normal cumulative distribution function
OTC	Over the counter
OTM	Out of the money
ρ	Correlation
q	Dividend yield of a specified asset
r	Risk-free rate of interest
$S(t)$	Price of asset S at time t
$S_i(t)$	Price of asset S_i at time t (multi-asset case)
σ	The volatility of a specified asset
T	Maturity of an option
USD	United States dollar

Preface

Toxic waste. . .it is a sad day when derivatives are described as toxic waste. Are these financial products really so, particularly those of exotic nature, or is it in fact people's grasp and usage of them that is the source of toxicity? While the use of derivatives increased in recent years at astounding rates, the crash of 2008 has revealed that people's understanding of them has not rivalled their spread. *Exotic Options and Hybrids* covers a broad range of derivative structures and focuses on the three main parts of a derivative's life: the structuring of a product, its pricing and its hedging. By discussing these aspects in a practical, non-mathematical and highly intuitive setting, this book blasts the misunderstandings and the stigma, and stands strong as the only book in its class to make these *exotic* and complex concepts truly accessible.

We base *Exotic Options and Hybrids* on a realistic setting from the heart of the business: inside a derivatives operation. Working from the assumption that one has a range of correctly implemented models, and the ability to trade a set of basic financial instruments, a client's need for a tailored financial product then raises these questions: How does one structure this product, correctly price it for the sale, and then hedge the resulting position until its maturity? Following a risk-centred approach, *Exotic Options and Hybrids* is a well-written, thoroughly researched and consistently organized book that addresses these points in a down-to-earth manner.

The book contains many examples involving time series and scenarios for different assets, and while hypothetical, all are carefully designed so as to highlight interesting and significant aspects of the business. Adoptions of real trades are examined in detail. To further illuminate payoff structures, their introduction is accompanied by payoff diagrams, scenario analyses involving figures and tables of paths, plus lifelike sample term sheets. By first understanding the investor's point of view, readers learn the methodology to structure a new payoff or modify an existing one to give different exposures. The names of various products can sometimes vary from one side of the industry to another, but those attributed to the products discussed in this book are commonly accepted to a great extent. Next, the reader learns how to spot where the risks lie to pave the way for sound valuation and hedging of the products. Models are de-mystified in separately dedicated sections, but their implications are alluded to throughout the book in an intuitive and non-mathematical manner.

Exotic Options and Hybrids is the first book to offer insights into the structuring, pricing and trading of modern exotic and hybrid derivatives, without complicating matters with the use of maths. The applications, the strengths and the limitations of various models are highlighted, in relevance to the products and their risks, rather than the model implementations. Readers can thus understand how models work when applied to pricing and hedging, without getting lost in the mathematical dwellings that shape related texts. While previous texts are heavily technical, others do not offer enough exposure, if any, to the more advanced and modern structures. The multitude of structures covered in *Exotic Options and Hybrids* is quite comprehensive, and encompasses many of the most up-to-date and promising products, including hybrid derivatives and dynamic strategies.

The book is formed of four parts, each containing related chapters which evolve in increasing degrees of complexity in the structures. Readers will be continuously stimulated by more advanced topics, and because of this breakdown the book can be read from front to back without loss of interest. Alternatively, readers can jump straight to a specific chapter because the book is self-contained and references to earlier chapters and sections within the book are explicitly clear. Furthermore, movement between the various angles of analysis of a specific product or concept is transparent, leaving readers free to focus on one aspect, or to read an entire treatment of a subject.

The first two chapters lay the foundations and explain not only the basic blocks of derivatives but also the setup and people involved in the creation, pricing and hedging of exotic structures. Chapters 3 to 7 define vanilla options, the risks involved in trading them and the different tools one can use to measure them. The second part of the book deals with the concept of dispersion which is of key importance in the world of exotic options. Chapters 10 and 11 focus on barrier options and digitals that are very much used in the conception of structured products. Chapters 13 to 16 constitute the third part of the book and present cliquets and related structures, mountain range options, and volatility derivatives, all of which are considered to be slightly more advanced exotic products.

After completing the discussion of exotic structures based upon equities, we move to hybrid derivatives. These chapters allow us to draw on many of the points made earlier in the book regarding correlation, dispersion and volatility, and provide a transparent insight into the world of hybrid derivatives. The first two of the four chapters on hybrids discuss the key asset classes: interest rates, commodities, foreign exchange, inflation and credit. For each asset class we look at the markets individually and gain insight into the nature of each, the various underlyings, vanilla instruments, skews and smiles and a brief look at some popular exotics in each. These are followed by a chapter that discusses the structuring of hybrid derivatives and explains how to construct meaningful combinations of the various asset classes. The last chapter on hybrids discusses the pricing intricacies of these instruments, starting from each asset class and then modelling combinations thereof. Chapter 21, the final chapter, deals with thematic indices and dynamic strategies. These assets are very different from the traditional structured products presented throughout the book, and constitute the new generation of advanced investment solutions.

We strongly believe that attentive readers of this book will learn many valuable insights in to all facets of the business of structured products. *Exotic Options and Hybrids* appeals to all the parties involved in the creation, pricing and hedging of the simplest to the most complex products. Once the heart of the business and its technical features are deeply assimilated, readers should be well equipped to contribute their own stone to the world of structured products.

Part I
Foundations

1
Basic Instruments

Concentrate all your thoughts on the task at hand. The sun's rays do not burn until brought to a focus.

Alexander Graham Bell

1.1 INTRODUCTION

We begin the book by first reviewing the basic set of financial instruments. These are either building blocks of derivatives or impact their valuation. A derivative is a financial instrument *derived* from another asset. It can also be derived from a set of events, an index or some condition, and in all cases we refer to these as the underlying asset(s) of the derivative. The set of financial instruments discussed in this introductory chapter fall into two categories: they are either *exchange traded* or *over the counter*. Exchange-traded products, also referred to as *listed*, are standardized products that are traded on an exchange which acts as the intermediary. Futures contracts are an example of exchange-traded contracts. Over-the-counter products, on the other hand, are privately agreed directly between two parties, without the involvement of an exchange. This includes almost all swaps and exotic derivatives.

We first look at interest rates and explain the differences between the various types. These include LIBOR, which is not only the most common floating rate used in swap agreements but also a reference rate that can be used to compute the present value of a future amount of money. We also introduce the different discounting methods, which are of prime importance in the valuation of derivatives. Within the topic of fixed income, we define the essential debt instruments known as zero coupon bonds.

This chapter also provides the basics of equity and currency markets. The features of stocks are defined as well as the parameters impacting their future price. We discuss how a currency can be viewed as a stock asset; we then define the importance and uses of indices and exchange-traded funds in trading strategies. Forward and futures contracts are also described in this chapter.

To round out the review of financial instruments we discuss swaps, which are agreements that occupy a central and crucial position in the over-the-counter market; the most commonly traded swap being the interest rate swap. After defining swaps' features and trading purposes, we introduce cross-currency swaps that are used to transform a loan from one currency to another. Finally, we present the features of total return swaps, which can replicate the performances of assets such as equities or bonds.

1.2 INTEREST RATES

Interest rates represent the premium that has to be paid by a borrower to a lender. This amount of money depends on the credit risk – that is, the risk of loss due to a debtor's non-payment of his duty, on the interest and/or the principal, to the lender as promised. Therefore, the higher the credit risk, the higher the interest rates charged by the lender as compensation for bearing this risk.

Interest rates play a key role in the valuation of all kinds of financial instruments, specifically, interest rates are involved to a large extent in the pricing of all derivatives. For any given currency, there are many types of rates that are quoted and traded. Therefore, it is important to understand the differences between these rates and the implications of each on the valuation of financial instruments.

1.2.1 LIBOR vs Treasury Rates

Among the more popular rates, we find Treasury rates and LIBOR rates. Treasury rates are the rates earned from bills or bonds issued by governments. Depending on the issuing sovereign body, these can be considered as risk-free rates since it is assumed that certain governments will not default on their obligations. However, derivatives traders may use LIBOR rates as short-term risk-free rates instead of Treasury rates.

The London Interbank Offered Rate (LIBOR) is the interest rate at which a bank offers to lend funds to other banks in the interbank market. LIBOR rates can have different maturities corresponding to the length of deposits and are associated with all major currencies. For instance, 3-month EURIBOR is the rate at which 3-month deposits in euros are offered; 12-month US LIBOR is the rate at which 12-month deposits in US dollars are offered; and so on. LIBOR will be slightly higher than the London Interbank Bid Rate (LIBID), which is the rate at which banks will accept deposits from other financial institutions.

Typically, a bank must have an AA credit rating (the best credit rating given by the rating agency Standard and Poor's being AAA) to be able to accept deposits at the LIBOR rate. A rating as such would imply that there is a small probability that the bank defaults. This is why LIBOR rates are considered to be risk free although they are not totally free of credit risk. Moreover, a number of regulatory issues can impact the value of Treasury rates and cause them to be consistently low. For this reason, LIBOR is considered by derivatives traders to be a better measurement of short-term risk-free rates than Treasury rates. In the world of derivatives, people think directly of LIBOR rates when talking about risk-free rates.

The difference between the interest rate of 3-month Treasury bills and the 3-month LIBOR is known as the TED spread, and can be used as a measure of liquidity in interbank lending. LIBOR, which corresponds to interbank lending, compared to the risk-free rates of Treasury bills is an indication of how willing banks are to lend money to each other. LIBOR rates involve credit risk, whereas Treasury rates do not, and thus the TED spread serves as a measure of credit risk in the interbank market. Higher TED spreads correspond to higher perceived risks in lending, and vice versa.

1.2.2 Yield Curves

For any major currency, the interest rates paid on bonds, swaps or futures are closely watched by traders and plotted on a graph against their maturities. These graphs are commonly called yield curves and they emphasize the relationship between interest rates and maturity for a specific debt in a given currency. The points on the curve are only known with certainty for specific maturity dates; the rest of the curve is built by interpolating these points.

For each currency, there are several types of yield curves describing the cost of money depending on the creditworthiness of debtors. The yield curves showing interest rates earned by the holders of bonds issued by governments are called government bond yield curves. Besides these curves, there are corporate curves that correspond to the yields of bonds issued by companies. Because of a higher credit risk, the yields plotted in corporate curves are usually higher and are often quoted in terms of a credit spread over the relevant LIBOR curve. For instance, the 10-year yield curve point for Renault might be quoted as LIBOR + 75 bp (a basis point or bp being equal to 0.01%), where 75 bp is the credit spread. In order to price a financial instrument, a trader will choose the yield curve that corresponds to the type of debt associated with this instrument. Despite there being different time-periods corresponding to the various rates, they are typically expressed as an annual rate. This allows interest rates to be compared easily.

Yield curves are typically upwards sloping, with longer term rates higher than shorter term rates. However, under different market scenarios the yield curve can take several different shapes, being humped or possibly downward sloping. We go into much further detail regarding the shapes of yield curves when we discuss interest rates in the context of hybrid derivatives in Chapter 17. Credit spreads are also discussed in more detail in Chapter 18 in the context of defaultable bonds and credit derivatives.

1.2.3   Time Value of Money

The concept of the *time value* of money is key to all of finance, and is directly related to interest rates. Simply put, an investor would rather take possession of an amount of money today, for example $1,000, than take hold of the $1,000 in a year, 10 years, or even one week. In fact, the concept of interest over an infinitesimally small period arises, and the preference is that an investor would rather have the money now than at any point in the future. The reason is that interest can be earned on this money, and receiving the exact same amount of money at a time in the future is a forfeited gain.

One hundred dollars to be paid one year from now (a future value), at an expected rate of return of $i = 5\%$ per year, for example, is worth in today's money, i.e. the *present value*:

$$PV = FV \times \frac{1}{(1+i)^n} = \frac{100}{1.05} = 95.24$$

So the present value of 100 dollars one year from now at 5% is $95.24. In the above equation $n = 1$ is the number of periods over which we are compounding the interest. An important note is that the rate i is the interest rate for the relevant period. In this example we have an annual rate applied over a 1-year period. Compounding can be thought of as applying the interest rate to one period and reinvesting the result for another period, and so on.

To correctly use interest rates we must convert a rate to apply to the period over which we want to compute the present value of money. Interest rates can be converted to an equivalent continuous compounded interest rate because it is computationally easier to use. We can think of this as compounding interest over an infinitesimally small period. The present value, PV, at time 0 of a payment at time t in the future, is given in terms of the future value, FV, and the continuously compounded interest rate r by

$$PV = FVe^{-rt}$$

Exercise

Consider you make a deposit of $100 today. Let's assume that interest rates are constant and equal to 10%. In the case of annual compounding, how many years are needed for the value of the deposit to double to $200?

Discussion

Let y denote the number of years needed to double the initial investment. Then: $FV = PV \times (1 + i)^y$. The present value formula can be rearranged such that

$$y = \frac{\ln(FV/PV)}{\ln(1 + i)} = \frac{\ln(200/100)}{\ln(1.10)} = \frac{0.693}{0.0953} = 7.27$$

years[1].

This same method can be used to determine the length of time needed to increase a deposit to any particular sum, as long as the interest rate is known.

1.2.4 Bonds

A bond is a debt security used by governments and companies to raise capital. In exchange for lending funds, the holder of the bond (the buyer) is entitled to receive coupons paid periodically as well as the return of the initial investment (the principal) at the maturity date of the bond. The coupons represent the interest rate that the issuer pays to the bondholders in exchange for holding their debt. Usually, this rate is constant throughout the life of the bond; this is the case of fixed rate bonds. The coupons can also be linked to an index; we then talk about floating rate notes. Common indices include money market indices, such as LIBOR or EURIBOR, or CPI (the Consumer Price Index) inflation rate linked bonds. Bonds can have a range of maturities classified as: short (less than 1 year), medium (1 to 10 years) and long term (greater than 10 years). In this section we now focus on fixed rate bonds.

The market price of a bond is then equal to the sum of the present values of the expected cashflows. Let t denote the valuation date and C_i the value of the coupons that are still to be paid at coupon dates t_i, where $t \leq t_i \leq t_n = T$. The value of a bond is then given by the following formula:

$$\text{Bond}(t, T) = \sum_{i=1}^{n} C_i B(t, t_i)$$

which results in

$$\text{Bond}(t, T) = \sum_{i=1}^{n} C_i e^{-r(t, t_i) \times (t_i - t)}$$

The price of a bond can be quoted in terms of a normal price as shown above or in terms of yield to maturity y, which represents the current market rate for bonds with similar features.

---

[1] This is often referred to as *The Rule of 72*.

Yield to maturity is defined as follows:

$$\text{Bond}(t, T) = \sum_{i=1}^{n} C_i e^{-y \times (t_i - t)}$$

The market price of a bond may include the interest that has accrued since the last coupon date. The price, including accrued interest, is known as the dirty price and corresponds to the fair value of a bond, as shown in the above formula. It is important to note that the dirty price is the price effectively paid for the bond. However, many bond markets add accrued interest on explicitly after trading. Quoted bonds, such as those whose prices appear in the *Financial Times* are the clean prices of these bonds.

$$\text{Clean Price} = \text{Dirty Price} - \text{Accrued Interest}$$

Bonds are commonly issued in the primary market through underwriting. Once issued, they can then be traded in the secondary market. Bonds are generally considered to be a safer investment than stocks due to many reasons, one being that bonds are senior to stocks in the capital structure of corporations, and in the event of default bondholders receive money first. Bonds can pay a higher interest compared to stocks' dividends. Also, bonds generally suffer from less liquidity issues than stocks. In times of high volatility in the stock market, the bond can serve as a diversification instrument to lower volatility.

Nonetheless, bonds are not free of risk, because bond prices are a direct function of interest rates. In fact, fixed rate bonds are attractive as long as the coupons paid are high compared to the market rates, which vary during the life of the product. Consequently, bonds are subject to interest rate risk, since a rise in the market's interest rates decreases the value of bonds and vice versa. We can also understand this effect by looking at the bond price formula: if the interest rate used to discount the coupons goes up, their present value goes down and the price of the bond decreases. Alternatively, if interest rates go down, bond prices increase.

Moreover, bond prices depend on the credit rating of the issuer. If credit rating agencies decide to downgrade the credit rating of an issuer, this causes the relevant bonds to be considered a riskier investment, therefore a bondholder would require a higher interest for bearing greater credit risk. Since the coupons are constant, the price of the bond decreases. Therefore, credit risk increases the volatility of bond prices. When turning to some government bonds (for example, US Treasuries), one considers these to be risk free, but any deviation from these in terms of creditworthiness will be reflected in the price as an added risk.

In the case of callable bonds, the bond can be *called*, i.e. bought back, by the issuer at a pre-specified price during some fixed periods laid out in the contract. The bondholder is subject to reinvestment risk. Buying a callable bond is equivalent to buying a bond and selling an American call option on this bond. When interest rates go down, the bond's price goes up and the issuer is more likely to exercise his call option and buy back his bond. The bondholder would then have to reinvest the money received earlier; but in such a scenario, with lower interest rates, it would be hard to enter into a better deal.

1.2.5 Zero Coupon Bonds

Zero coupon bonds are debt instruments where the lender receives back a principal amount (also called face value, notional or par value) plus interest, only at maturity. No coupons are paid during the life of the product, thus the name. In fact the interest is deducted up front and is reflected in the price of the zero coupon bond since it is sold at a discount, which means that its price is lower than 100% of the notional. Issuing zero coupon bonds is advantageous from a medium-term liquidity perspective, compared to issuing coupon-bearing bonds in which payments will have to be made at various points in the life of the bond. A US Treasury Bill is an example of a zero coupon bond.

The price of a zero coupon is equal to the present value of the par value, which is the only cashflow of this instrument and paid at maturity T. Zero coupon bonds are tradeable securities that can be exchanged in the secondary market. Let $B(t, T)$ denote the price in percentage of notional of a zero coupon bond at time t. Depending on the discounting method used by a trader to compute the interest amount, $B(t, T)$ is directly related to interest rates by the following formulas:

Linear: Interest is proportional to the length of the loan

$$B(t, T) = \frac{1}{1 + r(t, T) \times (T - t)}$$

Actuarial: Interest is compounded periodically

$$B(t, T) = \frac{1}{(1 + r(t, T))^{T-t}}$$

Continuous: Interest is compounded continuously

$$B(t, T) = e^{-r(t,T) \times (T-t)}$$

Here $r(t, T)$ stands for the appropriate interest rate at time t and maturity $(T - t)$, which is the time to maturity of the loan expressed in years.

Also note that in order to compute, at time t, the present value of any cashflow that occurs at time T, one must multiply it by $B(t, T)$. From now on, we are going to use continuous compounding to discount cashflows for the valuation of derivatives.

1.3 EQUITIES AND CURRENCIES

1.3.1 Stocks

Companies need cash to operate or finance new projects. It is often the case that their cash income does not always cover their cash expenditures, and they can choose to raise capital by issuing equity. A share (also referred to as an equity share) of stock entitles the holder to a part of ownership in a corporation. To compensate stockholders for not receiving interest that they might have received with other investments, companies usually pay them dividends. Dividends can vary over time depending on the company's performance and can also be viewed as a part of the company's profit redistributed to its owners. Therefore, the price of a stock normally drops by approximately the value of the dividend at the ex-div date, which is the last date after which the buyer of a stock is not entitled to receive the next dividend payment. Note that dividends can be expressed as discrete dividends or as a continuous equivalent dividend yield q.

When buying stocks, investors typically expect the stock price to increase in order to make profit from their investment. On the other hand, consider an investor who believes a stock price is going to decrease over time. She is then interested in having a short position in this stock. If her portfolio doesn't contain it, she can enter into a repurchase agreement or *repo*. This is a transaction in which the investor borrows the stock from a counterparty that holds the stock and agrees to give it back at a specific date in the future. Repos allow the investor to hold the stock and sell it short immediately in the belief that she can buy it back later in the market at a cheaper price and return it to the lending counterparty. Repos play a large role as speculative instruments. It is interesting to note that stock lenders are, for the most part, people who are just not planning to trade in it. They could be investors that own the stock in order to take control of the company, and repos offer them the advantage to earn an added income paid by the borrowers. The rate of interest used is called the *repo rate* or *borrowing cost*.

The stock price's behaviour is not the only important parameter that should be taken into account when trading stocks. An investor should be cautious with liquidity that can be quantified by looking at the average daily traded volume. A stock is said to have liquidity if there are many active participants buying and selling it, and that one can trade the stock at a relatively small bid–ask spread. For a stock to be considered liquid, one should be able to buy or sell it without moving its price in the market. Take the scenario where an investor wants to sell a large position in stocks. If the stock is not liquid enough, it is likely that the investor wouldn't find a buyer at the right time and would not be able to make a profit from his investment. At least, it is possible that the seller might not find a buyer who is willing to buy the stock at its fair price, and would have to sell at a price below the actual price just to conduct the transaction. Note that liquidity is correlated to the stock price. If the latter is too high or too low, the liquidity of the stock suffers. Expensive stocks are not affordable to all investors, causing the traded volume to be low. Alternatively, very cheap stocks may be de-listed.

Another parameter that has to be taken into account is corporate actions. These constitute an event initiated by a public company, and that may have a direct or indirect financial impact on the security. Companies can choose to use corporate actions to return profits to shareholders (through dividends for example), to influence the share price or for corporate restructuring purposes. Stock splits and reverse stock splits are respectively used to increase and decrease the number of outstanding shares. The share price is then adjusted so that market capitalization (the share price times the number of shares outstanding) remains the same. These events can be an interesting solution to increase the liquidity of a stock. Finally, mergers are an example of corporate actions where two companies come together to increase their profitability. From a trading perspective, one should be cautious with corporate actions since they can have a great impact on the price or the liquidity of a stock.

Let us now analyse the *forward* price of a stock, which is defined as the fair value of the stock at a specific point of time in the future. The forward price of a stock can be viewed as equal to the spot price plus the cost of carrying it. Consider a share that pays no dividends and is worth \$50. Assume that the 6-month interest rates are equal to 6%. Here, the cost of carry is equal to the interest that might be received by the stockholder if he had immediately sold his shares and invested his money in a risk-free investment. This represents a cost for the stockholder that will be reflected in a higher forward price. Therefore, the 6-month forward price of the stock would be equal to $50e^{6\% \times 6/12} = \$51.52$.

If a stock provides an additional income to the stockholder, this causes the cost of carry to decrease, since the stock also becomes a source of profit. Dividends and stock loans constitute a source of income when carrying a stock. Therefore, those parameters decrease the forward price whereas interest rates increase it. Let r, q and b respectively denote the risk-free rate, the dividend yield and the repo rate for a period T. Then the forward price $F_0(T)$ for a specific stock S is given as follows: $F_0(T) = S_0 \times e^{(r-q-b) \times T}$. From this relationship we can see that an increase of 1% in the stock price will result in a 1% increase in the forward price, all else being equal.

1.3.2 Foreign Exchange

A currency is a financial instrument that can be traded in terms of spot or forward contracts in foreign exchange markets. Most of the major currencies are very liquid and can involve large transactions. However, one should be cautious with exchange rate quotes and be clear on the foreign exchange (FX) market's conventions. FX futures are always quoted in number of US dollars (USD) per one unit of foreign currency. Spots and forward prices are quoted in the same way; for the British pound GBP, the euro EUR, the Australian dollar AUD and the New Zealand dollar NZD, the spot and forward quotes show the number of USD per one unit of foreign currency. These quotes can be directly compared to futures quotes. For all other major currencies, forward and spot prices are quoted in number of units of foreign currency per one USD. For instance, if the spot exchange rate between GBP and USD is equal to 2, this means 1 GBP = 2 USD.

A foreign currency entitles the holder to invest it at the foreign risk-free interest rate r_f. If an investor converts the FX into domestic currency, he can make a deposit at the domestic risk-free rate r_d. A currency can then be viewed as a stock with a dividend yield equal to r_f. Let S_0 denote the current spot price expressed in dollars of one unit of a foreign currency and $F_0(T)$ denote the fair value of the forward price at time T expressed in dollars of one unit of a foreign currency:

$$F_0(T) = S_0 \times e^{(r_d - r_f) \times T}$$

The market forward price can be different from the fair value of the forward price expressed above. This event leads to an *arbitrage* opportunity, which is an opportunity to make a profit without bearing risks.

Finally, if a trader wants to exchange a currency A for a currency B but cannot find a quoted price for the exchange rate, he can use the available exchange rates of these currencies with respect to a reference currency C. He would then compute the cross rate A/B as follows:

$$A/B = A/C \times C/B$$

Foreign exchange is discussed in more detail in the pre-hybrid derivative asset class analysis of Chapter 18.

1.3.3 Indices

A stock market index is composed of a basket of stocks and provides a way to measure a specific sector's performance. Stock market indices can give an overall idea about the state of an economy, as is the case for broad-base indices that include a broad set of equities that represent the performance of a whole stock market. These indices are the most regularly quoted and are composed of large-cap stocks of a specific stock exchange, such as the American S&P 500, the Japanese Nikkei, the German DAX, the British FTSE 100, the Hong Kong Hang Seng Index and the EuroStoxx 50. A stock market index can also be thematic or can cover a specific sector such as the technology or banking sectors.

An index value can be computed in two ways. For price-weighted indices, such as the Dow Jones Industrial Average in the US, each component's weight depends only on the price of the stocks and does not take into account the size of the companies. Therefore, a price-weighted index value is sensitive to price movements even if it only affects one of its constituent stocks. Another way to compute an index is based on the market capitalization of stocks. This is the case of market-value-weighted indices, also called capitalization-weighted indices, where the largest companies have the greatest influence on their price. The Eurostoxx 50 index and the Hang Seng are good examples of capitalization-weighted indices.

1.3.4 Exchange-traded Funds

Much like stocks, an *exchange-traded fund* (or ETF) is an investment vehicle that is traded on stock exchanges. An ETF holds assets such as stocks or bonds and is supposed to trade at (at least approximately) the same price as the net asset value of its assets – throughout the course of the trading day. Since diversification reduces risk, many investors are interested in indices or baskets of assets, however, it is impractical to buy indices because of the large numbers of constituent stocks and the need to rebalance with the index. Therefore, ETFs can be a great solution since one can often find ETFs that track a specific index, such as the Dow Jones Industrial Average or the S&P 500. In one transaction the investor gains exposure to the whole index without having to buy all the stocks composing the index and adjust their weights as the index's weights are changed.

ETFs generally provide transparency as well as the easy diversification across an entire index. They can have low costs and expense ratios when they are not actively managed and typically have lower marketing, distribution and accounting expenses. Another advantage of ETFs is the tax efficiency of index funds, while still maintaining all the features of ordinary stocks, such as limit orders, short selling and options. For an investor, one disadvantage can be that in some cases, and depending on the nature of the ETF and the complexities involved in its management, relatively significant fees may be charged. Because ETFs can be traded like stocks, some investors buy ETF shares as a long-term investment for asset allocation purposes, while other investors trade ETF shares frequently to implement investment strategies. ETFs and options on ETFs can also serve as hedging vehicles for some derivatives.

1.3.5 Forward Contracts

A forward contract is an agreement between two parties to buy or sell an asset at a specified point of time in the future. This is a pure over-the-counter (OTC) contract since its details are settled privately between the two counterparties. When issuing a forward contract, the price agreed to buy the asset at maturity is called the strike price. Trading in forwards can be for speculative purposes: (1) the buyer believes the price of the asset will increase from the trade date until the maturity date; (2) the seller thinks the value of the asset will appreciate and enters into a forward agreement to avoid this scenario. Additionally, forward contracts can serve as hedging instruments.

Generally, the strike price is equal to the fair value of the forward price at the issue date. This implies that forward contracts are usually arranged to have zero mark-to-market value at inception, although they may be off-market. Examples include forward foreign exchange contracts in which one party is obligated to buy foreign exchange from another party at a fixed rate for delivery on a preset date. In order to price a forward contract on a single asset, one should discount the difference between the forward price and the strike price. Assuming that $F_t(T)$ is the theoretical forward price of the asset, the value at time t of the forward contract

Forward$_t(T)$ is computed as follows:

$$\text{Forward}_t(T) = (F_t(T) - K) \times e^{-r \times (T-t)}$$

The main advantage of forwards is that they offer a high degree of flexibility to both parties involved, allowing them to set any contract specifications as long as they are mutually accepted. This is due to the fact that forward contracts trade in OTC markets and are not standardized contracts. Besides, it is important to note that a forward contract is an obligation and not an option to buy/sell the asset at maturity. However, the risk remains that one party does not meet its obligations and can default. This risk, called the counterparty risk, is the main disadvantage encountered in trading forwards.

Exercise

Suppose that John believes the stock price of Vodafone will appreciate consistently over the course of a year. Assume that Vodafone is worth £80 and the 1-year LIBOR rate r is equal to 6%. Also, the dividend yield q is equal to 2% and the borrowing costs are null. John decides to enter into a 1-year forward contract allowing him to buy 1,000 shares of Vodafone in one year at a strike price of £82. After one year, Vodafone's spot price is equal to £86. Did John realize a profit from this transaction?

Discussion

First of all it is interesting to compute the theoretical value of the 1-year forward price F_0 of Vodafone that is given by $F_0 = 80 \times e^{(6\% - 2\%) \times 1} = £83.30$. As the theoretical forward price is higher than the strike price K, John has to pay a premium Forward$_{\text{price}}$ for the forward contract that is equal to the number of shares times the present value of the difference between the forward price and the strike price, as follows:

$$\begin{aligned}\text{Forward}_{\text{price}} &= 1,000 \times (F_0 - K) \times e^{-rT} \\ &= 1,000 \times (83.30 - 82) \times e^{-5\% \times 1} = £1,224\end{aligned}$$

At the end of the year, the forward contract entitles John to receive 1,000 shares of Vodafone at £82 with a market value equal to £86. Therefore, John makes a profit equal to $1,000 \times (86 - 82) = £4,000$ knowing that he paid £1,224 as a forward contract premium.

1.3.6   Futures

A futures contract is an exchange-traded contract in which the holder has the obligation to buy an asset on a future date, referred to as the final settlement date, at a market-determined price called the futures price. The price of the asset on the final settlement date is called the settlement price. The contract specifications, including the quantity and quality of the asset as well as the time and place of delivery, are determined by the relevant exchange. The asset is most often a commodity, a stock or an index. Stock market index futures are popular because they can be used for hedging against an existing equity position, or speculating on future movements of the asset.

Futures constitute a safer investment since the counterparty risk is (almost) totally eliminated. Indeed, the clearing house acts as a central counterparty between the buyer and the seller and also provides a mechanism of settlement based on *margin calls*. Futures are marked-to-market (MTM) on a daily basis to the new futures price. This rebalancing mechanism forces the holders to update daily to an equivalent forward purchased that day. On the other hand, the benefits of having such standardized contracts are slightly offset by the lack of flexibility that one has when setting the terms of an OTC forward contract. The futures contract is marked-to-market on a daily basis, and if the margin paid to the exchange drops below the margin maintenance required by the exchange, then a margin call will be issued and a payment made to keep the account at the required level. Margin payments offset some of the exchange's risk to a customer's default.

The quoted price of a futures contract is the futures price itself. The fair value of a future is equal to the cash price of the asset (the spot value of the asset) plus the costs of carry (the cost of holding the asset until the delivery date minus any income). When computing the fair value of futures on commodity, one should take into account the interest rates as well as storage and insurance fees to estimate the costs of carry.

As long as the deliverable asset is not in short supply, one may apply arbitrage arguments to determine the price of a future. When a futures contract trades above its fair value, a cash and carry arbitrage opportunity arises. The arbitrageur would immediately buy the asset at the spot price to hold it until the settlement date, and at the same time sell the future at the market's futures price. At the delivery date, he would have made a profit equal to the difference between the market's futures price and the theoretical fair value. Alternatively, a reverse cash and carry arbitrage opportunity occurs when the future is trading below its fair value. In this case, the arbitrageur makes a risk-free profit by short-selling the asset at the spot price and taking at the same time a long position in a futures contract at the market's futures price. When the deliverable asset is not in plentiful supply, or has not yet been created (a corn harvest for example), the price of a future is determined by the instantaneous equilibrium between supply and demand for the asset in the future among the market participants who are buying and selling such contracts. The convenience yield is the adjustment to the cost of carry in the non-arbitrage pricing formula for a forward and it accounts for the fact that actually taking physical delivery of the asset is favourable for some investors. These concepts are discussed at length for the various asset classes in Chapters 17 and 18 where futures and forward curves are analysed.

1.4 SWAPS

1.4.1 Interest Rate Swaps

Interest rate swaps (IRSs) are OTC agreements between two counterparties to exchange or swap cashflows in the future. A specific example of an IRS is a plain vanilla swap, in which two parties swap a fixed rate of interest and a floating rate. Most of the time, LIBOR is the floating interest rate used in a swap agreement. In an IRS, the notional is the principal amount that is used to compute interest percentages, but this sum will not actually change hands. Payments are netted, because all cashflows are in the same currency; for instance payment of 5% fixed and receipt of 4% floating will result in a net 1% payment. Payments are based on the floating interest rate observed at the start of the period, but not paid until the end of the period. More exotic swaps exist where cashflows are in different currencies, examples of which can be found below.

The *payer* on the swap is the person who agrees to pay the fixed rate (and receive the floating rate) on a vanilla swap. The payer is concerned that interest rates will rise and would then be referred to as long the swap. The *receiver* is the person who agrees to receive the fixed rate (and pay the floating rate) on an IRS. The receiver expects interest rates to fall and would therefore be referred to as being short the swap. It is because of the different methods of borrowing that interest rate swaps are useful. A company may either borrow money at fixed or variable rates; it would borrow fixed if it thought rates were going up and variable if it thought they were going to fall. An IRS will allow the company to change borrowing styles part way through the term of the original loan. These are OTC products and, as such, can be tailored to an investor's cashflow needs accordingly.

Consider for example a 5-year 3-month borrowing facility. The 5 years are split into 3-month periods; at the beginning of each period the 3-month LIBOR rate is set and applied to the loan. At the end of each period (the reset date), the interest is paid, and a new LIBOR rate is set for the next 3-month period. A company with such a facility may approach another institution and arrange an IRS. The institution would agree to pay LIBOR to the company at the end of each 3-month period in exchange for interest payments from the company at a fixed rate.

A basis swap is a particular type of IRS where a floating rate is swapped for a different floating rate. These transactions are used to change the floating rate basis from one index to another, e.g. exchanging 3-month LIBOR for 6-month LIBOR, or 3-month T-bill rate for 6-month Fed Funds. The floating indices used in these swaps range from LIBOR rates of different tenors or possibly different currencies, to other floating rates.

To compute the value of a swap, one should calculate the net present value (NPV) of all future cashflows, which is equal to the present value from the receiving leg minus the present value from the paying leg. Initially, the terms of a swap contract are defined in such a way that its value is null, meaning that one can enter into the swap at zero cost. In the case of an IRS, the fixed rate is agreed such that the present value of the expected future floating rate payments is equal to the present value of future fixed rate payments.

Exercise

Let E denote the 3-month EURIBOR rate. Consider an interest rate swap contract where Party A pays E to Party B, and Party B pays $24\% - 3 \times E$ to Party A. Let N denote the notional of this swap. Can you express this deal in simpler terms?

Discussion

Party A pays E and receives $24\% - 3 \times E$. This means that Party A receives $24\% - 4 \times E = 4 \times (8\% - E)$. This contract is then equivalent to an interest rate swap arrangement where Party A (the receiver) receives 8% from Party B (the payer), and pays E to Party B. The notional of the equivalent contract is equal to $4 \times N$.

1.4.2 Cross-currency Swaps

A currency swap is another popular type of swap in which cashflows are based on different currencies. Unlike an IRS, in a currency swap the notional principal should be specified in both currencies involved in the agreement. Here, a notional actually changes hands at

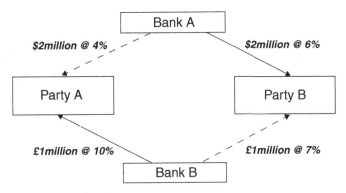

Figure 1.1 Borrowing rates.

the beginning and at the termination of the swap. Interest payments are also made without netting. It is important to note that principal payments are usually initially exchanged using the exchange rate at the start of the swap. Therefore, notional values exchanged at maturity can be quite different. Let's consider an example of a fixed-for-fixed currency swap, where interest payments in both currencies are fixed, to clarify the payoff mechanism and the cross-currency swap's use in transforming loans and assets.

Figure 1.1 shows the case of an American company (Party A) that wants to raise £1m from a British bank (Bank B) and a British company (Party B) that needs to borrow $2m from an American bank (Bank A). In this example, we assume that 1 GBP = 2 USD. Let's keep in mind that interest rate values depend on the creditworthiness of the borrower. In this example, both companies have similar credit ratings but banks tend to feel more confident when lending to a local company. Bank B is then ready to lend £1m to Party A at a fixed rate of 10% per annum over a 3-year period, whereas the interest rate is fixed at 7% for Party B. For the same reasons, Bank A accepts to lend its funds at a fixed rate of 4% for Party A, whereas the interest rate would be equal to 6% for Party B.

Both companies decide to enter into a currency swap agreement, described in Figure 1.2, to benefit from the difference of loan rates. Party A borrows $2m from Bank A at 4% annual fixed rate and Party B borrows £1m from Bank B at a 7% annual rate. At the start date of the swap, both principals are exchanged, which means that Party A gives $2m to Party B and

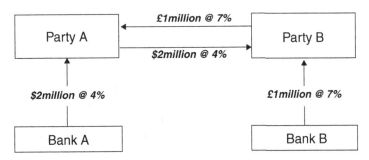

Figure 1.2 Currency swap (fixed for fixed).

receives £1m. At the end of each year, Party A receives $80,000 from Party B (used to pay the 4% interest to Bank A) and pays £70,000 to Party B (used to pay the 7% interest to Bank B). At the outset of the swap, the notional amounts are exchanged again to reimburse the banks. The overall effect of this transaction is that both companies raised funds at lower interest rates. Party A has borrowed £1m at a rate of 7% instead of 10%. Party B has also made a profit from this currency swap since it has paid 4% interest rate instead of 6%. Note that this is a fixed-for-fixed currency swap. It is also possible to swap fixed-for-floating.

1.4.3   Total Return Swaps

A total return swap is a swap agreement in which a party pays fixed or floating interest and receives the *total return* of an asset. The total return is defined as the capital gain or loss from the asset in addition to any interest or dividends received during the life of the swap. Note that the party that pays fixed or floating rates believes the asset's value will appreciate. This party receives the positive performance of the asset and pays its negative performance. A total return swap enables both parties to gain exposure to a specific asset without having to pay additional costs for holding it.

An equity swap is a particular type of total return swap where the asset can be an individual stock, a stock index or a basket of stocks. The swap would work as follows: if an investor believes a specific share will increase over a certain period of time, she can enter into an equity swap agreement. Obviously, this is a purely speculative financial instrument since the investor does not have voting or any other stockholder rights. Compared to holding the stock, she does not have to pay anything up front. Instead, she would deposit an amount of money, equal to the spot price of the stock (a different amount in the case of a margin), and would receive interest on it.

Thus, the investor creates a synthetic equity fund by making a deposit and being long the equity swap. Typically, equity swaps are entered into to gain exposure to an equity without paying additional transaction costs, locally based dividend taxes. It also enables investors to avoid limitations on leverage and to get around the restrictions concerning the types of investment an institution can hold.

1.4.4   Asset Swaps

An asset swap is an OTC agreement in which the payments of one of the legs are funded by a specified asset. This asset can be a bond, for example, where the coupons are used as payments on one leg of the swap, but the bond, and generally the asset underlying this swap, does not exchange hands. This allows for an investor to pay or receive tailored cashflows that would otherwise not be available in the market.

1.4.5   Dividend Swaps

Lastly, a dividend swap is an OTC derivative on an index or a stock and involves two counterparties who exchange cashflows based on the dividends paid by the index or the stock. In the first of the two legs a fixed payment is made (long the swap), and in the second leg the actual dividends of the index or the stock are paid (short the swap). The fixed leg payments involve a fixed amount that depends on the initial price of the index of the stock. The cashflows are exchanged at specified valuation periods and are based upon an agreed notional amount. In the case of an index dividend swap, or a dividend swap on a basket of stocks, the dividends of the constituents are weighted by the same weights of the index/basket constituents. The dividend swap is a simple and price effective tool for investors to speculate on future dividends directly, and it can also serve as a vehicle for traders holding portfolios of stocks to hedge dividend risk. The liquidity of such swaps has increased in recent years for both these reasons.

2
The World of Structured Products

I am long on ideas, but short on time. I only expect to live only about a hundred years.
Thomas A. Edison

The business of equity and hybrid structured products grew quickly over the last 20 years. This chapter describes how structured products came into existence and why they became so popular. Structured products can serve as diversification or yield enhancement vehicles, and also as specifically tailored hedging or speculative tools. We shall consider each of these roles and analyse the composition of structured products from a technical point of view. Investment banks typically sell structured products to retail clients and institutionals through issues that can be of small or large size. In a platform of structured products and exotic options, we can find distinct roles involved in the different stages of the life of a product. On the front office side, the sales people, the structurers and traders are all of central importance in the development of this business. We discuss their various tasks in the context of structured products. We then explain how financial institutions issue these sophisticated assets in the over-the-counter (OTC) markets and guarantee their valuation on secondary markets. The design and composition of a structured note is analysed as an example.

2.1 THE PRODUCTS

2.1.1 The Birth of Structured Products

In the early 1990s, many investment banks thought up new solutions to attract more investors to equity markets. The idea was to create innovative options with sophisticated payoffs that would be based on all types of assets such as stocks, indices, commodities, foreign exchange and all kinds of funds. Also, banks were looking for intelligent ways to provide investors with easy access to these innovations through issuing wrappers (medium-term notes, insurance life contracts, collective funds) in a tax efficient manner. Moreover, it was important to structure a business that was capable of following an issued financial asset throughout its life. Therefore, structuring roles were created to compose complex OTC products; while quantitative analysts developed pricing models to enable traders to hedge the products until maturity. Banks were also conscious about the importance of providing secondary markets that introduced the liquidity the business needed to expand.

Efforts were made to provide access and exposure to market configurations that previously presented entry barriers and were unattainable using standardized financial instruments. Structured products constitute a great solution to benefit from the dynamism of financial markets with risk/return profiles that can be tailored to any investor's appetite in a cost-effective manner. One example is placing part of an investment in non-risky assets in order to deliver a level of protected capital, while the remaining is invested in options that offer upside opportunities with no downside.

2.1.2 Structured Product Wrappers

A structured product can be launched in a specific wrapper, with a determined legal status, to meet the clients' requirements in terms of regulatory issues and investment preferences. The payoff of a structured product is important, although it is equally important to know about the regulations and laws surrounding a certain market in order to determine the appropriate wrapper.

Deposits are a form of wrapper where the bank accepts money from an investor and, at the end of an agreed fixed term, makes a payment back to the depositor. The bank can charge the depositor a penalty if they choose to end the deposit before its term is up. The interest paid on structured deposits is defined as a payoff formula linked to the performance of an asset. Certificates of Deposits (CDs) are deposits that are structured to be a tradeable certificate. CDs also have a fixed term and interest is determined on the basis of the performance of an asset. Indeed, in certain regulatory zones, investors can avoid some tax by buying certificates, instead of other available products, because the returns paid on such investments are taxed differently to others.

Notes and bonds are debt instruments issued by a financial institution or corporation. They are typically issued as senior unsecured debt (taking priority over other debt in the event of a default of the issuer) and can be listed or unlisted. It is important to point out that investing in a note does not mean that the capital invested is guaranteed. In fact, the investor could be selling an option inside a note (an embedded option) that causes the capital to be at risk. An example of this would be a reverse convertible, where the investor usually sells a put option at maturity of the note. Even if the note is structured with an option in a manner that capital is protected, there is still the risk that the issuer of the note defaults. Although it may have seemed unlikely, examples from the crash of 2008 were learned the hard way.

A structured product can be launched as a fund. A fund is an investment scheme that is set up to produce a certain return, typically a minimum return with the possibility of returns greater than this minimum amount depending on the performance of some assets. In the context of structured products, funds can be set up to enter into derivative transactions to provide a desired exposure, and the investor buys units in this fund. These are generally more expensive than notes and certificates, but can prove the optimal choice depending on tax and regulatory issues.

Structured products can also be launched in the form of over-the-counter options or warrants. The holder of the warrant is entitled to buy a specific amount of shares in a company at an agreed price – typically higher than the underlying stock's price at the time the warrant is issued.

2.1.3 The Structured Note

A structured note is composed of a non-risky asset providing a percentage of protected capital and a risky asset offering leverage potential. The non-risky part can be a zero coupon bond, paying a guaranteed amount at maturity, or a bond that pays fixed coupons throughout the life of the note; this is the case for income products. The bond is considered non-risky in the sense that if there is no default by the issuer, then it is guaranteed to return the principal at maturity plus whatever interest is agreed on. A zero coupon bond is always bought at discount; its price is lower than the principal redeemed at maturity. We can then consider that its value increases linearly (considering very low rate variations) through the life of the product to reach the level

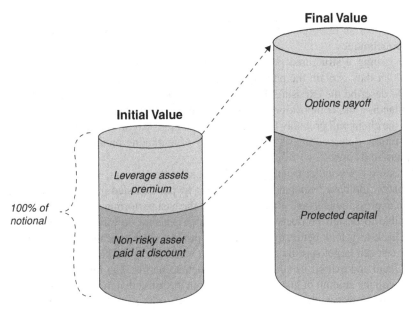

Figure 2.1   Breakdown of a typical note.

of protected capital at maturity. The principal is not necessarily guaranteed if the investor sells the product before maturity.

The risky part of a structured note can be composed of options on single or multiple assets. An option gives the right but not the obligation to buy or sell underlying assets; as such, its value is always positive. Options enable their holders to make additional profit with high leverage potential. These are risky investments since their value can vary greatly. They can provide option holders with high returns, but they can also lose all their value, expiring worthless, in the case of wrong market expectations. An options price is non-linear and is subject to many market parameters. The financial risks involved in options trading can be complex and vary significantly from one type of option to another. Pricing models are built and developed by quantitative analysts and then used for pricing and risk analysis by structurers and traders. Figure 2.1 shows the composition and the value of structured notes. These products enable investors to receive high leverage potential while simultaneously providing capital protection.

2.2   THE SELL SIDE

In this section we focus on the distinct and key aspects of the roles of people involved on the sell side of structured products. We note that at different institutions, roles and responsibilities vary, but most features of the roles discussed here are constant throughout.

2.2.1   Sales and Marketing

The salespeople are in charge of creating new markets and servicing existing clients. They typically sell structured products to existing or new clients but they could also be in charge of buying products from other counterparties. Salespeople get commission for the transactions they settle; this remuneration depends on the number, the size and the nature of the deals. Salespeople play an important role as they initiate the birth of a structured product through marketing techniques.

Before issuing a structured product, salespeople will spend time with potential buyers during which they explain the payoff through formulas and examples of possible scenarios in order to describe the exposure the product offers. The client is not necessarily interested in understanding the composition of the structured product from a technical point of view; however, the client will probably be keen to understand its payoff mechanism in addition to its potential return. Salespeople use the whole array of marketing methods to explain a product and emphasize its uses.

Back-testing is a popular technique used by a sales department. The idea is to present the returns that would have been paid to the client if he had invested in this product in the past. These can express the leverage potential through the past performance of structured products. It is possible to design products or change the parameters of various existing products to make the back-tests look better, thus making the product more appealing and easier to market. The back-test can target specific times or market scenarios in the past that are relevant to the payoff at hand and exhibit its strengths under such scenarios. The reliability of back-testing increases with the amount of historical data used, in the sense that more market scenarios have been covered. However, the famous line that appears with each back-test stating that 'past performance is not indicative of future performance' is true: we cannot know for sure what will happen in the market, and though a product may exhibit a stellar back-test, it may fail to hold up such returns in the future. Despite this, the back-test remains a powerful marketing tool.

Other marketing techniques include stress tests that consist of scenarios showing the behaviour of the marketed product in the hypothetical context of a difficult market. The aim here is to show that the structured product to be issued is strong enough to bear the financial risks that can appear in extreme market conditions. For instance, a stress test can be used to show that a growth and income product would still behave well in the context of a market crash. Stress tests can be presented to emphasize the safety behind investing in structured products, particularly if they are set up for a scenario for which no precedence exists, i.e. in this case the back-test would be impossible to conduct.

2.2.2 Traders and Structurers

The role of the structurer varies from one institution to the next, but generally involves creating new structures as well as pricing these structures. When creating new products, the structurer is involved in innovation, and to do this meaningfully there must be a clear interaction with sales teams because there must ultimately be an investor willing to buy such product for it to be traded. This role is of key importance in the business of derivatives since an investment bank can stand out with its capability of innovating in a competitive market. The role of the structurer in pricing structured products involves analysing their risks before the trade can be done. The structurer will work closely with traders to agree on the levels they charge for taking on certain risks, and reflect these when making prices and considering new payoff structures.

After a deal is sealed with the word "done", the structured product sold is booked in the portfolio of a trader who will be in charge of hedging its risks. Vanilla products are typically risk managed by volatility traders, whereas exotic traders are in charge of more complex products. Depending on the size of the trading desk in a bank, these will break down into further categories where single stock options, multiple stock options, index options are additionally broken down after separation of exotics from vanillas. Even further sector-wise or region-wise breakdowns are common. At investment banks, which in the context of structured products are structurally sell-side institutions, the role of exotic traders is that of a hedger primarily; not a speculator. Although various levels of speculation are necessary, the central role is to identify and hedge risk. The more complex the product the more elaborate the risks, with many of these risks impossible to hedge completely. As such it is the role of the exotics trader to manage these risks as best as possible to be within certain specified limits.

Sales are primarily interested in settling as many deals as possible to increase their commissions. Traders, on the other hand, want business, but unless forced to by management will not want to take on unhedgeable risks if they feel such positions will cost them money, resulting in a loss in their compensation. There are different balances of power at play, where sales can sometimes force a trade to happen even if the structurer and trader believe it is undervalued and is a losing deal. This can be the case when other players in the market are mispricing derivatives, and a misprice must be met if the bank wants to win an auction-based trade. Alternatively, a relatively powerful trading desk will not be forced to take on a position with which it is not comfortable. A large part of this boils down to the bank's business model that will govern how structurally conservative or aggressive the desk is.

2.3   THE BUY SIDE

To have meaning, an *exchange* of cashflows must involve more than one party. While the sell side is set up to offer structured products, there must be some form of client who will *buy* the said products. Without having two parties there can be no such business. It is important to differentiate between the various clients that form the buy side in the structured products business, specifically, their exposure requirements and risk appetites. Buy side clients can be classified into two categories: retail and institutionals.

2.3.1   Retail Investors

Retail investors are usually asset management institutions that buy structured products from investment banks and redistribute them to individuals. For example, customers of high street banks can get relatively easy access to some structured products that their bank is distributing. Naturally, the payoff is simplified and marketed; individuals then have access to attractive payoffs and can spend small or large amounts of money in such investments. Obviously, individuals do not need to know about the composition of the product or the technical details behind its structure, but they should be aware of the risks involved.

Retail investors are prepared to market many structured products, especially if they believe they can find enough demand among their client base. Selling a financial derivative implies bearing the risks associated with it, and retail investors are usually not willing or not able to take those risks – it is not their job. Instead, they prefer to pay commissions to an investment bank that has its own trading teams to hedge the marketed structured products. Structured products transfer risk over to those who are willing to bear it, typically based on their ability to hedge these risks. For instance, consider a retail investor who buys a note at 98% of the notional and sells it to individuals at a price of 100% of the notional, realizing a profit of 2% on whatever notional amount they are able to sell. The transaction is not really free of risk since a retail investor is still exposed to credit risk.

Depending on the retail investor's relationship with the investment banks it trades with, it may request prices from multiple banks. Before doing a trade, the investor will have seen *indicative* prices from all the counterparties and will move to a *live* auction once their requirements are fulfilled. One reason for this could be to obtain the best price possible by trading with the bank offering the most competitive live price for the same product. The investor may also spread a large notional over several of the banks with the best prices. The categories of yield enhancement products and diversification instruments are popular among retail investors.

2.3.2   Institutional Investors

Institutional investors represent a different category of structured product clients of investment banks. They are more financially sophisticated than a retail investor, and these include institutions such as hedge funds and mutual funds. Such clients often hold large portfolios and the notional sizes of their transactions can be quite significant in both size and complexity. The complexity comes from both the sophistication of some of their investment strategies, and also from their standing with respect to securities laws or the inapplicability thereof. Other institutional investors include central banks, sovereign wealth funds, state or corporate pension funds, social security organizations, insurance companies, proprietary desks at banks, endowments, charities and foundations. All are examples of possible institutional investors emphasizing the great scope of clients interested in structured products.

Institutional investors typically have cash to invest and subsequently search for attractive and interesting products that match their target of risk and returns. Investment banks will produce the business-tailored solution that will best suit the needs of institutionals. In many cases, this is less competitive than the retail business but more difficult in the sense that the development of the solution is a much larger part of the job. Owing to their sophistication over end retail investors, the scope of products that can be marketed to them is larger and room for innovation is thus greater.

Examples of these can be tailored derivatives that encapsulate the views a hedge fund wishes to express, and can reach any level of complexity. These can be complex equity exotics and possibly hybrid derivatives. Structuring specific portfolio hedges for such clients is another example, and again, the complexities of these investors' strategies can require complex exotic products. Others include the structuring of vanilla options based on complex underlyings instead of complex options on common underlying assets. The underlyings designed can be thematic indices or dynamic strategies (discussed in Chapter 21) that can be designed to meet the investors' required market exposures, and also their risk–return appetites.

2.3.3   Bullish vs Bearish, the Economic Cycle

A bullish investor believes a market, sector or specific asset will appreciate in value whereas a bearish client expects its value to go down. We can see different amounts of demand for the types of structured products, given the economic outlook and the views these products express. During wealth and economical growth periods, investors are usually bullish whereas they tend to be bearish during recession periods. Greed and fear are two distinct emotions that manifest themselves at different speeds and for different amounts of time during economic cycles.

An individual buying a specific asset wants its value to appreciate over time. He is then said to be long this asset. Alternatively, somebody selling a financial asset wants its value to decrease and is said to be short this asset. Using the terms *long* and *short* more generally, one being long or short any parameter impacting an asset would like its value to go up or down depending on it having a positive or negative impact on the asset respectively. For example, the holder of a floating bond is long the bond but is also short interest rates since the bond's value increases explicitly when the interest rate on which it is based decreases.

Structured products offer a great range of bearish financial products, bullish products and also mixtures, thus supplying the demand side with a variety of choices for their various outlooks. Depending on their levels of risk aversion, investors will choose among the different types of structured products offered by investment banks. Capital protected structures are popular since they provide investors with a guaranteed minimum return at maturity at least equal to the original investment, while offering leverage potential. Yield enhancement products, on the other hand, offer above market returns as long as an event does not occur – typically a large equity downside move – in which case capital is at risk.

There are several types of products providing different streams of payments, again depending on the way a client wants to be paid. *Income* structured products are financial structures that offer periodic coupon payments, i.e. a stream of income. The coupons are, most of the time, higher than the rate of interest available on fixed rate bank deposits. Here, it is easy to figure out that in the case of a capital guaranteed income product, the non-risky part paying fixed coupons is composed of a bond paying periodic fixed coupons and 100% of the notional at maturity.

A *growth* product produces a return at maturity based on the performance of an underlying asset or the basket of underlying assets, with no coupon payments during the product life. A growth product can be either principal guaranteed or non-guaranteed, although the former is common. Here the non-risky part of the structured note is composed of a zero coupon bond since no intermediate payments are made during the life of the product. *Growth and Income* describes a structure that produces fixed returns at specified periods during the life of the product and a return at maturity based on the performance of one or more underlying assets.

After choosing the type of payoff that will meet the investor's view on the market, the maturity of the structured product has to be specified; and this can be done according to the period of time during which the investor believes his expectations will be realized. Maturities vary from 3 months (short-term investment periods) to 10 years (long-term investment periods). Most of the time, maturities are around 2–5 years, which corresponds to medium-term investments.

Short-term investments can be structured that involve high risk and offer enhanced yields. In these cases investors hope to obtain the above market coupon and get their money back quickly. The appetite for perceived high risks reduces as maturities grow longer. As such, longer-dated structures tend to have different features to short-dated ones. Some structures with a fixed maturity can be *callable* prior to this date, i.e. redeemable by the issuer prior to the product's maturity. This is the case of autocallable products (which will be analysed in detail in Chapter 12) that mature early once a predetermined target coupon level is reached.

2.3.4   Credit Risk and Collateralized Lines

The buyer of a financial product from an investment bank must pay careful attention to the seller's credit rating. It gives valuable information regarding the creditworthiness of an issuing financial institution. An investor can decide to trade in a product with a top credit-rated company even if he finds a more attractive and cheaper one issued by a financial institution with a lower credit rating. Before the subprime crisis, investors were confident in the financial system and were paying less attention to credit risk. In 2008, banking firms were battered during the crisis and many banks collapsed because of the lack of liquidity. Everybody will remember the collapse of Lehman Brothers Holdings Inc. as well as the cases of Bear Stearns Cos, Inc. and Merrill Lynch & Co., Inc. that had to be taken over. These events shed light on the seriousness of credit risk in the trade process. Credit risk resulting from a financial firm's issuance of bonds, which are often used as the non-risky part of a structured product, can be hedged using credit default swaps (CDSs). These are looked at in more detail when discussing credit as an asset class in Chapter 18.

Collateralized line investments are those that do not involve counterparty risk. When we consider swaps, the way to avoid problems with default events is to structure the swap along collateralized lines. This involves computing the value of the swap and setting aside the equivalent amount of collateral, typically with a third party. In a swap this would typically be done on (or at least around) the dates where cashflows are computed. This can also be applied to OTC derivatives, and be used to protect the investors buying these derivatives. Naturally this requirement comes at a cost to the investor, but, nonetheless, with the collapses witnessed in 2008 collateralized products have gained further popularity. The seller of the OTC product would essentially need to set aside cash in order to safeguard any returns earned on the derivative prior to maturity. It is expected that a larger portion of structured products in the future will be structured with some method of mitigating counterparty risk.

The rate used when pricing the zero coupon bond part of the note is essentially a reference rate, for example LIBOR, plus some spread. This spread, which is the rate that the treasury of the bank offers on deposits, reflects the credit rating of the bank, yet the implied offered rate is typically less than the spread implied from credit default swaps on the same bank. The funding rate for AAA-rated companies can be around 20 bp per annum, whereas it can reach levels of 600 bp (6%) and above for riskier companies of lower credit ratings.

When building a structured note, the bonds of the bank with the lower credit rating cost less, and thus there is more money remaining to put into the risky part of the note. This means that the riskier bank can potentially offer a higher participation rate on a structure than the less risky bank can. Investors know the implications of lower credit ratings on their structured note investments, and understand why a lower-rated bank may be offering better prices on the same structure. In times of distress there is what is known as a *flight to quality*, where investors seek to hold the notes of the highest credit-rated firms to lower their risk as much as possible.

2.4 THE MARKET

2.4.1 Issuing a Structured Product

Investment banks can raise capital through issuing structured products at a specific price expressed in percentage of the notional size. The size of transactions depends on the type of business involved. Concerning retail investors' business, a typical notional of transactions would be around $5–20 million. Transactions can be bigger and deals can have notionals around $100 million or more, especially in the case of large retail distributors. In this case, investors may prefer to cut the notional into separate tranches. For instance, an investor who wants to have $100 million exposure to a financial asset can buy for $50 million notional from the bank that offers the cheapest price, $30 million notional from the bank that offers the second cheapest price and $20 million notional from the bank that offers the third cheapest price. This enables the investor not to be fully dependent on the bid–ask quotes of a unique bank if he wants to close or decrease his exposure, and this method can also help to spread some of the risk of having just one counterparty.

The size of transactions is important in the valuation of the options composing the structured product. In some cases where the notional of a transaction is large and the product carries a large amount of unhedgeable risk, one will see a substantial dispersion in the prices offered by different banks. Assuming that all the banks involved are correctly aware of all the risks, then the differences in prices are a reflection of how aggressive or conservative the banks are. From the banks' perspective, the advantage of having one big size transaction, compared to many smaller ones – besides continuing business with a client and gaining new business – is two-fold. First, from the structural point of view of the firm, and considering the number of people involved in such a deal from start to finish, there is cost involved in terms of hours spent. Depending on the setup of the bank, this can be cheaper than several smaller products. Secondly, the profit is a percentage of the transaction's notional; then a big size issue can imply a large dollar amount of P&L. In competitive auctions, sellers cannot charge high levels of P&L, but do typically have priority should the investor wish to unwind the product; if the seller is offering a two-way market, they can potentially charge if the trade is unwound. For relatively simple trades in auction sales, margins are typically of the order of 50 bp to 1%. For solution-driven products, especially where the bank is offering a proprietary solution, margins can go as high as several percent.

The contractual agreement explaining the features of the issue of a specific structured product is referred to as a *term sheet*. It includes such information as: the issuer, its credit rating, the notional size and price of the product; and the denomination of its currency. Also, term sheets contain formulas explaining the payoff in detail and specify with complete clarity the underlying assets involved in the product. The observation and payment dates are also precisely specified in the term sheet. As structured products are sold over the counter, the term sheet must be a sound legal contract.

2.4.2 Liquidity and a Two-way Market

Structured products became popular because they can provide good returns in a cost-effective manner. An important factor that allowed these attractive OTC products to be sold is the two-way market the sell side offers, thus providing the investor with liquidity. Investment banks and other financial institutions issuing structured products are aware that the banking system is based on confidence and are willing to gain more clients by offering them enough liquidity, enabling them to close their investment positions or unwind partial notionals if they wish. The introduction of this feature has helped the business to grow, and there is a secondary market for structured products. The mess of 2008–2009 in the financial world has, however, proved that, when dealing with secondary market valuations there is a greater need for transparency, to help to address the issue of liquidity.

Traders estimate the market value of structured products and make bid and ask quotes that are often available for investors. The *bid* price is equal to the fair price minus a spread, whereas the *ask* price (also called the *offer* price) is equal to the fair value plus a spread. In normal market conditions, bid–ask spreads are equal around the mid-price and decrease with increased liquidity. If investment banks issuing structured products face problems in risk-managing a specific product, they will increase the bid–ask spreads. In order to produce a consistent valuation for an OTC structured product, the trader must *mark to market* so that the valuation reflects current market data.

Valuation teams, responsible for reporting valuations, help the salespeople to provide the investors with quotes. This is again important since the clients may want to decrease their exposure to the structure by selling a part of their notional at the bank's bid price, or may want to increase their exposure by buying more notional at the bank's offer price. The roles of valuation teams will prove more important as we move forward in the financial world. Additionally, other than marking to market based on liquid data, illiquid parameters that cannot be implied easily, such as correlation, will need to be monitored more closely. These can greatly impact valuations and the whole value of the trading books that are exposed to them. Market consensus data providing firms can be utilized so that illiquid parameters impacting the value of trading books are at least marked at some market consensus between participating firms.

2.5   EXAMPLE OF AN EQUITY LINKED NOTE

The equity linked note (ELN) is a simple structured product that makes a single payment to the investor at maturity, of a percentage of capital plus participation on the positive performance of a specific underlying equity asset (stock, index, basket of stocks). It is composed of a zero coupon bond delivering a guaranteed notional amount at maturity, and a European call option on the underlying asset. Figure 2.2 describes how a bank creates a structure (in this

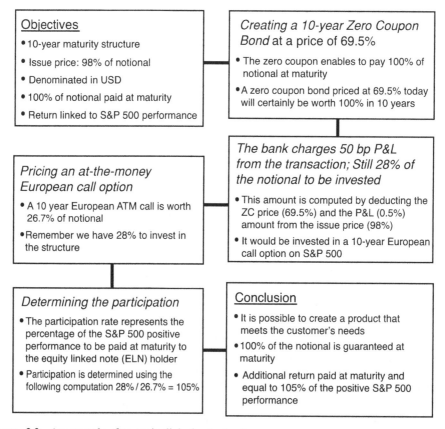

Figure 2.2   An example of an equity linked note structure.

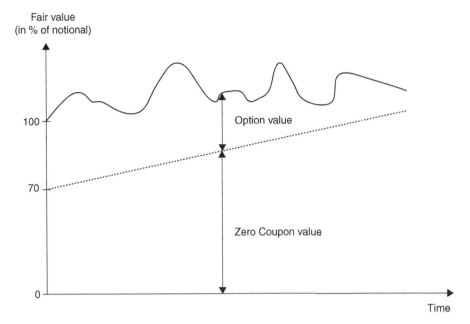

Figure 2.3   Valuation in secondary market.

case an ELN) in order to meet some predetermined targets depending on client requirements.

$$ELN_{value} = ZC_{price} + Call_{price} + P\&L \text{ @ origination}$$

Figure 2.3 emphasizes the fair value of the product quoted in secondary markets after the issue has been done. The non-risky part has an initial price linked to interest rates. High interest rates decrease the initial value of the zero coupon bond, enabling the structurer to create an attractive payoff through issuing increased upside in the equity. During the life of the structured note, the value of the non-risky part increases when interest rates decrease. At maturity, the value of this zero coupon bond is equal to 100% of the notional. On the other hand, the value of the risky part is non-linear and fluctuates depending on many market parameters such as the underlying's spot, interest rates, borrowing costs, dividend yield or volatility. All these sensitivities will be covered in the following chapters.

3

Vanilla Options

If your knowledge teaches you not the value of things, and frees you not from the bondage to matter, you shall never come near the throne of Truth.

Kahlil Gibran

An option is a contract between two parties that gives the buyer some form of rights, but not obligation, to buy or sell a particular asset in the future at a certain price. The term *vanilla* is used to describe an option that doesn't have a complicated structure. These are typically European call or put options that have quite simple payoffs, though other slightly more complicated structures can also be considered vanillas. It is important to fully understand the payoff mechanism as well as the risks associated with trading in vanilla options before discussing exotic structures. The term *exotic* is used to describe derivatives that are more complex in nature.

In this chapter, we first present the general features of European option contracts, and discuss their nature as leverage instruments; indeed calls and puts constitute low-cost investments to get upside or downside exposure to an underlying asset. We also see European options in their role as hedging instruments. The concepts behind the Black–Scholes theory of option pricing are discussed, and we give the Black–Scholes formulas for calls and puts on a stock. These closed formulas can be extended to FX rates since a currency can be viewed as a stock, as shown in Chapter 1. Note that the underlying asset can also be a commodity or an interest rate (these cases are covered in Chapter 17 in discussions of separate asset classes). This leads to the discussion of American and Asian options, which can also be considered as relatively vanilla. The chapter ends with a section dedicated to presenting examples of the structuring process, using what we have learned so far.

3.1 GENERAL FEATURES OF OPTIONS

A European call/put option is a contract that gives the holder the right, but not the obligation, to buy/sell an agreed quantity n of a predetermined underlying asset S, at a specific price K referred to as the strike, at maturity T. At maturity, the buyer of a European call option would *exercise* this right as the holder of the option, if the underlying asset's spot price is higher than the strike price of the option. Conversely, a put option would be exercised if S_T, the value of the underlying asset at time T, is lower than K. An option is said to be European if it pays at maturity and is only based on S_T. In the case of American options, the holder has the right to exercise his option at any time before the expiry date. Bermudan options, which are in a sense in between European and American options, give the holder the right to exercise during some specified set of dates between the initial and expiry dates.

Some option contracts contain a physical delivery feature. This means that the call option seller or the put option buyer will deliver the stocks at maturity when the option is exercised. Indeed, the holder of a call would buy the underlying stock at the strike price K by exercising the option, take hold of the stock, and immediately sell it at the higher market price S_T in the market. On the other hand, the put option seller would sell the stocks at K and immediately buy it back from the market at a lower price S_T. Other specifications of the option can be to cash settle the option. In this case, the call option seller makes a cash payment at maturity equal to the positive difference between the final spot and strike prices; and the put buyer would receive the positive difference between K and S_T. Cash delivery is often preferred when the underlying stock has poor liquidity.

An option is said to be *at-the-money* (ATM) if the strike price is the same as the current price of the underlying asset when the option is written; i.e. the strike is at 100% of the current value of the underlying asset. A call option is said to be *in-the-money* (ITM) when the strike price is below the current trading price. A put option is in-the-money when the strike price is above the spot price. Another characteristic of in-the-money options, as we shall see, is when the current price is much higher than the strike price; for a call option, this option behaves like the underlying security. Following the definition of call and put options, at the maturity date, only in-the-money options are exercised. The third state of a call option is *out-of-the-money* (OTM), and this is when the strike price is above the current trading price of the underlying security. A put option is out-of-the-money when the strike price is below the current trading price of the underlying security.

Recall that assets have a spot price and a forward price (the price for delivery in future). One can talk about moneyness with respect to either the spot price or the forward price (at expiry): thus one talks about ATMS = ATM Spot (also referred to as just at-the-money) versus ATMF = ATM Forward, and so forth.

3.2   CALL AND PUT OPTION PAYOFFS

Call options correspond to a bullish view on the market; a client would buy a European call when he believes the underlying stock price will be above the strike at expiry date. The European call payoff at T is as follows:

$$\text{Call}_{\text{payoff}} = n \times \max[0, S_T - K]$$

where S_T is the price of the underlying stock at maturity. In the example shown in Figure 3.1, we are dealing with a 1-year European call on Total struck at 52 EUR. The holder of this call has paid an initial premium equal to 450,000 EUR to get the right to buy 100,000 shares of

Underlying Asset	Total
Exercise Style	European
Number of Shares	100,000
Currency	EUR
Initial Spot Price	50.00
Strike Price	52.00
Initial Date	14/11/2008
Maturity Date	14/11/2009
Delivery Method	Physical
Option Price	450,000 EUR (i.e. 4.5 EUR per share)

Figure 3.1   Terms of a 1-year European call option.

Total at the strike price on 14/11/09. This means the investor has a bullish view on Total and believes its stock price will be above 52 EUR after one year. At maturity date, if the closing price of Total shares is equal to 51 EUR, the call option will not be exercised since the final spot price of Total is below the strike. The payoff being null, the call option buyer would have lost the premium paid to this contract seller. Now, what if the spot price is equal to 62 EUR on 14/11/09? The investor exercises his option and buys 100,000 Total shares from the call seller at a price of 52 EUR per share. He can then immediately sell these shares at the market price (62 EUR), realizing a profit of $[100,000 \times (62 - 52)] - 450,000 = 550,000$ EUR. Note that the profit and loss is computed by subtracting the premium initially paid from the payoff of the call. Here, the option buyer is bullish on the underlying stock; he could instead have chosen to go long the share itself. He would have paid $100,000 \times 50 = 5,000,000$ EUR to buy 100,000 shares of Total. Then he would have realized a potential gain of 1,200,000 EUR at maturity date, which is equivalent to 1,200,000/5,000,000 = 24% of the capital invested. Note that the return realized from buying the call is equal to 550,000 / 450,000 = 122%. This is the reason why call options are said to be leverage instruments; one gets a high potential payoff compared to the invested capital.

On the other hand, put options correspond to a bearish view on the market; a client would buy a European put when he believes that the underlying stock price will be below the strike at expiry date. The European put payoff at T is as follows:

$$\text{Put}_{\text{payoff}} = n \times \max[0, K - S_T]$$

Figure 3.2 shows the terms of a 2-year put option contract on Vodafone. The initial spot price of Vodafone is equal to £1.50. In this example, a strike of 100% means that the strike price is equal to 100% of the Vodafone initial spot price. Also, one can notice that the option notional is specified instead of the number of shares, because an option can be defined in terms of stock returns:

$$\text{Put}_{\text{payoff}} = \text{Put}_{\text{Notional}} \times \max[0, K - \text{Perf}(T)]$$

where K is expressed as a percentage of the initial spot, $\text{Perf}(T) = S_T/S_0$ is the performance since inception of Vodafone at time T. Also, note that $\text{Put}_{\text{Notional}}$ is given by

$$\text{Put}_{\text{Notional}} = n \times S_0$$

The buyer of this put pays a premium at the initial date equal to £2,584,500, which represents 17.23% of the contract notional. At the end of the second year, if the spot of Vodafone is equal to 102% of its initial spot, then Vodafone performance is above the strike and the payoff is

Underlying Asset	Vodafone
Exercise Style	European
Notional	£15 million
Currency	GBP
Maturity	2 years
Strike	100%
Delivery Method	Cash
Option Price	17.23% (£2,584,500)

Figure 3.2   Terms of a 2-year European put option.

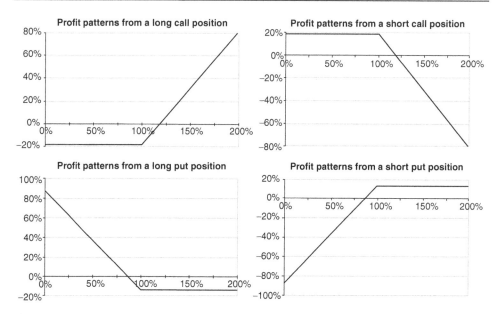

Figure 3.3   Profit patterns from trading in European call and put options.

null; the put buyer would have lost all his invested capital. Now, let's imagine Perf$(T) = 80\%$ (i.e. Vodafone stock price at maturity is equal to £1.50 × 80% = (£1.20), then the put pays the holder an amount equal to £15, 000, 000 × (100% − 80%) = £3, 000, 000.

Figure 3.3 shows the profit that can be made by buying/selling calls and puts struck at 100%. Note that these graphs represent the profit and not the payoff. For an option buyer, the profit is computed as the difference between the payoff and the premium, whereas it is equal to the opposite for an option seller.

The buyer of a call can get an unlimited profit, whereas the maximum loss incurred is the premium paid for the option at initial date. Alternatively, selling a *naked* call option, where Delta (see section 3.5) is not hedged, is a risky position since the seller could end up paying an unlimited amount. The maximum profit for bearing this risk is equal to the price of the call received at inception. On the other hand, the maximum loss and the maximum profit from buying or selling a put are bounded. Indeed, in the worst case scenario, a put option buyer can lose the premium he initially paid to get a maximum potential gain equal to $K - \text{Put}_{\text{price}}$, which is lower than 100% of the underlying stock initial spot price. Conversely, the put seller could earn a maximum profit equal to the option premium received and could lose a maximum amount equal to $K - \text{Put}_{\text{price}}$.

3.3   PUT–CALL PARITY AND SYNTHETIC OPTIONS

Put–call parity specifies a relationship between the prices of call and put options with the identical strike price K and expiry T. In order to derive the put–call parity relationship, we must assume that the call and put options involved are only exercised at maturity. This is, of course, a feature of European options. Perhaps the most important feature of put–call parity is that it is derived, and must be satisfied at all times, in a model independent manner. The implication of this is that irrespective of how one is pricing options, put–call parity must be conserved. A violation of this leads to arbitrage opportunities as we see below. The put–call parity relationship is given by:

$$\text{Call}(K, T) + K\text{e}^{-rT} = \text{Put}(K, T) + S_0\,\text{e}^{-qT}$$

where r and q are, respectively, the risk-free rate and the dividend yield.

Now, let's consider the following two portfolios to prove this result:

- *Portfolio A.* Purchase one call option on an underlying asset S, struck at K and expiring at T. Sell a put option on the same underlying, with the same strike price and maturity.
- *Portfolio B.* Purchase a forward contract that gives the obligation to buy S at a price K at maturity date T.

At maturity date, if S_T is above K, then the call option in Portfolio A is in-the-money, whereas the put ends out-of-the-money. Portfolio A pays an amount equal to $S_T - K$. Portfolio B pays the strategy holder $S_T - K$ no matter how the underlying stock price behaves. Moreover, if $S_T \leq K$, then the call payoff is null, whereas the put payoff is equal to $K - S_T$. Now, the holder of Portfolio A is selling the put; therefore he loses this amount. For the holder of Portfolio B, the scenario is the same since he loses $K - S_T$ as the buyer of a forward contract.

It follows that, in all states, Portfolio A has the same payoff at maturity as Portfolio B. For European options, early exercise is not possible. If the values of these two portfolios are the same at the expiry of the options, then the present values of these portfolios must also be the same, otherwise, an investor can arbitrage and make a risk-free profit by purchasing the less expensive portfolio, selling the more expensive one and holding the long-short position to maturity. Accordingly, we have the price equality:

$$\text{Call}(K, T) - \text{Put}(K, T) = \text{Forward}(K, T)$$

and since we know from section 1.3.5 that

$$\text{Forward}(K, T) = S_0\text{e}^{-qT} - K\text{e}^{-rT}$$

through the put–call parity relationship, we can see that one can be long a call and short a put, with the same underlying asset, strike price and maturity, and replicate the payoff of a forward contract with the same characteristics. The position taken in Portfolio A is called a *synthetic* underlying position. Generally, a synthetic option is a synthetic position that is constructed without actually buying or selling the option. By playing a bit more with the put–call parity, one would notice that a synthetic long call position is replicated by buying a put as well as the underlying forward. Also, a synthetic long put can be created by being long the call and short the forward.

3.4   BLACK–SCHOLES MODEL ASSUMPTIONS

In 1973, Fischer Black and Myron Scholes published their ground-breaking paper "The pricing of options and corporate liabilities" (Black and Scholes, 1973). This article contained the closed-form pricing formula for European options, now known as the Black–Scholes formula, but more importantly it described a pioneering general framework for the replication of European options. However, this relied on several simplifying assumptions that in practice must be given serious consideration. The initial closed form formula was only adapted to

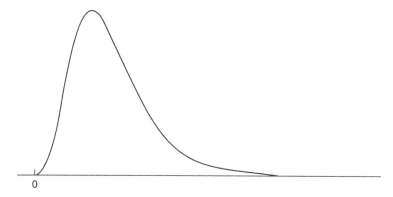

Figure 3.4   A log-normal distribution.

stocks paying zero dividends. Merton (1973) adjusted the Black–Scholes formula to enable it to price European options on stocks or stock indices paying a known dividend yield.

The market assumptions behind the adjusted Black–Scholes formula for pricing European options on equity are as follows:

- The volatility of the underlying asset is constant over time.
- The underlying asset can be traded continuously, and its price S_t is log-normally distributed. This means that the log-returns of S are normally distributed (Figure 3.4).
- One can always short sell the underlying stock.
- One does not incur transaction costs or taxes.
- All securities are perfectly divisible, meaning that it is possible to buy any fraction of a share.
- One can always borrow and lend cash at the known risk-free interest rate r, which is assumed to be constant.
- The stock pays a constant dividend yield q.

3.4.1   Risk-neutral Pricing

The concept of risk neutrality comes from economics, and it is the middle point between being risk seeking and risk averse. Consider a scenario where one has the choice between receiving 1 dollar, or receiving 2 dollars at 50% probability (meaning that there is an equal chance of getting 2 dollars or receiving nothing). The risk-averse investor will choose to take the 1 dollar, whereas the risk-seeking investor will take the 2 dollars with the 50% chance. To the risk-neutral investor these two choices are equivalent, and the investor has no preference between the two.

In finance, when pricing an asset, a common technique is to figure out the probability of a future cashflow, then discount that cashflow at the risk-free rate. For example, if the probability of receiving 2 dollars one instant from now is 50%, the value is 1 dollar. This is called the *expected value*, using real-world probabilities. In the theory of risk-neutral pricing, the real-world probabilities assigned to future cashflows are irrelevant, and we must obtain what are known as risk-neutral probabilities.

The fundamental assumption behind risk-neutral valuation is to use a replicating portfolio of assets with known prices to remove any risk. The amounts of assets needed to hedge determine the risk-neutral probabilities. Under the aforementioned assumptions, the Black–Scholes theory considers options to be redundant in the sense that one can replicate the payoff of a European option on a stock using the stock itself and risk-free bonds. As such, the key feature of the Black–Scholes framework is that it is preference-free: since options can be replicated, their theoretical values do not depend upon investors' risk preferences. Therefore, an option can be valued as though the return on the underlying is riskless.

The risk-neutral assumption behind the Black–Scholes model constitutes a great advantage in a trading environment. Even though one can debate whether options really are redundant, given the nature of some market inefficiencies, the Black–Scholes theory of option pricing still remains the only consistent one for pricing and hedging options.

3.5 PRICING A EUROPEAN CALL OPTION

The price of a call option C depends on the following parameters:

- The underlying spot price S at valuation date.
- The volatility σ of the underlying's returns.
- The interest rate r and the dividend yield q.
- The strike price K and the time to maturity T.

The Black–Scholes formula for a European call option is then given by

$$C = Se^{-qt}\mathcal{N}(d_1) - Ke^{-rt}\mathcal{N}(d_2)$$

where

$$d_1 = \frac{\ln(S/K) + (r - q + \sigma^2/2)T}{\sigma\sqrt{T}}, \qquad d_2 = d_1 - \sigma\sqrt{T}$$

and $\mathcal{N}$ is the standard normal cumulative distribution function

$$\mathcal{N}(x) = \frac{1}{\sqrt{2\pi}} \int_{-\infty}^{x} e^{-u^2/2}\,du$$

The first thing to note is that the expected rate of the return of the underlying S does not enter into this equation. In fact the relevant parameter is the interest rate r, which is taken to be the risk-free rate of interest.

If we write the forward F as

$$F = Se^{(r-q)T}$$

then in the Black–Scholes formula d_1 is given by

$$d_1 = \frac{\ln(F/K) + \sigma^2 T/2}{\sigma\sqrt{T}}$$

and the formula becomes

$$C = e^{-rt}[F\mathcal{N}(d_1) - K\mathcal{N}(d_2)].$$

In Figure 3.5, the solid line shows the price of a 1-year European call option with respect to the spot price. It is interesting to note that the curve is ascending, which makes its first

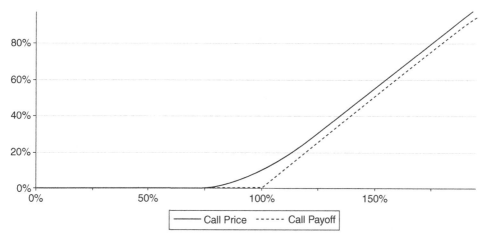

Figure 3.5   Price of a 1-year European call struck at 100%.

derivative with respect to the spot (the Delta) positive. Also, we can see that this curve is convex, which implies the second derivative of the call price with respect to the spot (the Gamma) is positive. The dashed line illustrates the payoff of the European call at maturity.

The payoff formula of an option is also known as its *intrinsic value*. In other words, it represents the value of exercising it now. An ITM option has positive intrinsic value – the deeper the option is in-the-money, the greater its intrinsic value – whereas an OTM option has zero intrinsic value. Figure 3.5 shows that the solid line is always above the dashed line. This positive difference between the call price and the intrinsic value is called the *time value* of the option, which measures the uncertainty of the option ending in-the-money. It is also interesting to note that the time value for a call is always positive and reaches a maximum value when the spot is equal to the strike price. As time to maturity decreases, the time value decreases to be equal to zero at expiry date. A call option usually loses two-thirds of its time value during the last third of its life. We can see these points in more detail when we discuss option risks in Chapter 5.

3.6   PRICING A EUROPEAN PUT OPTION

The Black–Scholes formula for a European put option price P is given by

$$P = Ke^{-rt}\mathcal{N}(-d_2) - Se^{-qt}\mathcal{N}(-d_1)$$

where d_2 and d_1 are as previously defined. Since $\mathcal{N}(x) + \mathcal{N}(-x) = 1$ for any real number x (a property of the normal CDF, illustrated in Figure 3.6), the price of a European put can also be written as follows:

$$P = Se^{-qt}[\mathcal{N}(d_1) - 1] - Ke^{-rt}[\mathcal{N}(d_2) - 1]$$

In Figure 3.7, the solid line shows the price of a 1-year European put option plotted against the underlying spot price. The curve decreases when the spot goes up, which makes its first derivative with respect to the spot (the Delta) always negative. Also, we can see that this curve is convex, which implies that the second derivative of the put price with respect to the spot (the Gamma) is positive. The dashed line on Figure 3.7 illustrates the payoff of the European

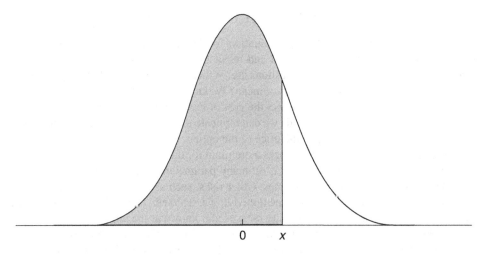

Figure 3.6 The cumulative probability distribution function for a standardized Normal distribution. Note that the shaded area represents $\mathcal{N}(x)$ which is the probability that a normally distributed variable with mean 0 and variance 1 will be lower than the value x. Because of the symmetry of the standard Normal distribution, one can easily figure out that $\mathcal{N}(-x)$ is represented by the non-graded area. Note that the area under the bell curve is equal to 1.

put at maturity, or its intrinsic value. When the spot is below the strike, the put is in-the-money and the intrinsic value is positive. Otherwise, it has no value.

Moreover, we can see through Figure 3.7 that the time value (the difference between the put price and its intrinsic value) is not always positive. Indeed, for ITM put options, the dashed line tends to be above the solid line, which implies that puts can have a negative time value. This result will also be shown when analysing the Theta of a put option in Chapter 5 on the Greeks.

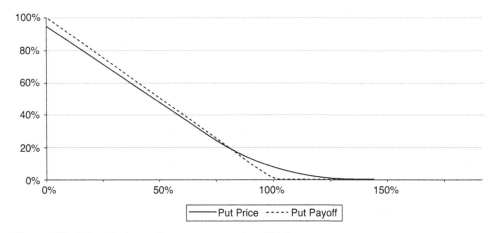

Figure 3.7 Price of a 1-year European put struck at 100%.

3.7   THE COST OF HEDGING

When we discussed the Black–Scholes valuation for European options, we saw the closed formulas that can be easily implemented and result in a price according to the parameters plugged into the pricer. But the real questions are: Which parameters should be used to get a correct price? And what does a correct price mean? We know that this formula is derived so that the prices it generates for an option reflect the cost of hedging the option. If we dynamically trade the underlying and risk-free bonds we can replicate the payoff of the option. The cost of performing this hedging must equal the price of the option.

When a trader sells an option, he charges a premium for the risks he is bearing. Even in the case of vanilla options, the price depends on many parameters. Some of them are linked to the market; this is the case of interest rates. Other risks, such as the spot price, dividends or borrowing costs, are directly related to the underlying asset itself. The strike and maturity are specific to the option's terms. The volatility to be used is known as the implied volatility of the asset, and in the case of vanilla options is known in the market; this is the subject of discussion of Chapter 4. These parameters can be used in the Black–Scholes formula to obtain the prices of vanilla options, but for more complicated payoffs we may not have closed formulas that directly reflect the cost of hedging. As we move to more complicated options we must keep in mind that the cost of an option should reflect the cost of hedging the risks it entails.

We understand that, unlike many other commercial products, financial instruments are essentially produced after they are sold. They are not necessarily hedged to replication as this is typically not possible, but they are hedged to risk exposures that are tolerable. There are many risks to be understood, managed and priced into the ask and bid prices of structured products. Exact replication is, however, unlikely and we need to determine how one may make the holding of the residual an acceptable risk. Traders quote bid and ask prices that correspond respectively to the price they are willing to pay/receive for buying/selling a financial product.

Of course, the fewer the set of risks that are acceptable, the wider is the bid–ask spread and the less likely that there is a trading counterparty for any particular product. In other words, the traders charge a lower premium as well as a small bid–ask spread if they feel comfortable hedging the risks associated with trading in a specific option. Hence a proposed product coming from a tailored customer request must be analysed for the risks associated with its issue. One may then determine strategies to control the risk exposure and the likely costs of doing so. The latter can then be built into the price. We will also see in Chapter 5 the interplay between the option risks and how a trader can make money through hedging.

Exercise

Consider a stock Alpha that can take two specific values 70 and 120 after 5 years. Alpha's initial spot is equal to 100. The equity analysts covering this stock and working for a major financial institution state that there is a 60% probability that the final spot price will be 120 and a 40% probability that the final spot ends at 70. Then, what would be the fair price of a 5-year European at-the-money call option on Alpha? To keep things simple, let's assume that interest rates and dividends are both zero.

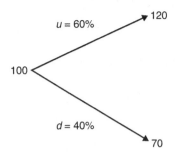

Discussion

Since interest rates and dividends are assumed to be null, the price of the call is equal to the expected value of the stock minus the strike (that is equal to 100). If one thinks that the expected value of the stock at maturity is equal to $120 \times 60\% + 70 \times 40\% = 100$, then he is definitely lost. The price of the call would have been equal to $100 - 100 = 0$. One could use probabilities if we are working in a risk-neutral environment, which is not the case of the real world. Therefore, these probabilities are useless in our pricing.

Firstly, the price of an option represents the cost of the hedge. Let's assume that you are short the call, then you have to be long a number Δ of stocks in order not to be sensitive to the spot price (options sensitivities are fully covered in Chapter 5 on Greeks). In this case, your P&L is always equal to zero no matter what happens to the stock price.

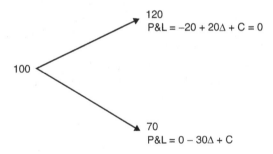

Let C denote the call premium that you received at start date. If the stock price finishes at 120, then the call is exercised and you have to pay 20 to the option's holder. On the other hand, you realized a profit of 20Δ from your stock position. Alternatively, if the final stock price is equal to 70, then the call is not exercised but you lose 30Δ on your stock position.

Since the P&L is null in all cases, we have to solve the following system:

$$\begin{cases} -20 + 20\Delta + C = 0 \\ 0 - 30\Delta + C = 0 \end{cases}$$

This gives us $\Delta = 40\%$ and $C = 12$, which answers our question.

3.8 AMERICAN OPTIONS

American options can be exercised at any time during their life. Since investors have the freedom to exercise their American options at any point during the life of the contract, they are more valuable than European options which can only be exercised at maturity. This extra feature implies:

$$C_A(t, K, T) \geq C_E(t, K, T)$$

where $C_A(t, K, T)$ and $C_E(t, K, T)$ are respectively the prices at time t of an American and European call with strike K and maturity T. And

$$P_A(t, K, T) \geq P_E(t, K, T)$$

where $P_A(t, K, T)$ and $P_E(t, K, T)$ are, respectively, the prices at time t of an American and a European put with strike K and maturity T.

Now, is there an optimal timing to exercise American options? And, if so, what does it depend on? To answer these crucial questions linked to trading in American options, we first have to establish some important formulas. To do so, let's consider the following two portfolios:

- *Portfolio A.* Purchase an underlying asset S. Let D denote the future value at time T of its dividend payments.
- *Portfolio B.* Purchase one European call option on the underlying asset S, struck at K and expiring at T. Make a bank deposit equal to $[D + K]e^{-rT}$ invested at the risk-free rate r.

At date T, the holder of Portfolio A would have received a total amount equal to $S_T + D$. If S_T is above K, then the call option in Portfolio B is in-the-money and pays $S_T - K$. And since the deposit amount $(D + K)e^{-rT}$ redeems at $D + K$, then Portfolio B pays an amount equal to $S_T - K + D + K = S_T + D$. Moreover, if $S_T \leq K$, then the call payoff is null and Portfolio B pays $D + K$, whereas Portfolio A pays $D + S_T$ (lower than $D + K$). It follows that, in all states, Portfolio A has a payoff at maturity lower than or equal to the payoff of Portfolio B. Therefore, holding Portfolio A is cheaper than holding Portfolio B. In the absence of an arbitrage opportunity, we get the following result:

$$C_E + [D + K]e^{-rT} \geq S_0$$

and since an American call is more expensive than a European call with the same strike and maturity, this implies that

$$C_A(t, K, T) \geq S_t - De^{-r(T-t)} - Ke^{-r(T-t)}$$

At any time t during the life of the American option, one would exercise his option if its value is lower than the payoff he would receive, i.e. if

$$S_t - K > C_A(t, K, T)$$

which leads to

$$S_t - K > S_t - De^{-r(T-t)} - Ke^{-r(T-t)}$$

or, equivalently,

$$D > K \times (1 - e^{-r(T-t)})$$

And since $(1 - e^{-r(T-t)})$ can be approximated by $r(T - t)$ to first order, this implies that

$$\frac{D}{K} > r(T - t)$$

Therefore, if the formula above is verified at any time t, this means that it is optimal to exercise the American call. Intuitively now, if one exercises the American call, he pays a specific amount of money to buy the underlying shares. On the one hand, he doesn't receive interest on this cash amount; and, on the other, he would receive future dividends for holding the stocks. In other words, if the dividend yield is higher than the interest rate until maturity, it is optimal to exercise the American call; and this is what the formula above emphasizes. Also note that for stocks not paying dividends, it is never optimal to exercise the American call.

Ultimately, it can be optimal for the holder of an American put option to choose to exercise if the interest rate that would be received on a cash deposit equal to K is higher than the dividend payments until maturity. In particular, for non-dividend-paying stocks, an American put should always be exercised when it is sufficiently deep in-the-money. This result can be illustrated in the same way as we did for American call options.

3.9   ASIAN OPTIONS

An Asian option is a derivative with a payoff at maturity date T based on the average performance $S_{average}$ of the underlying recorded at different dates against the initial date during the product life. An Asian call option is a European style call (bullish view) that has the following payoff at maturity T, based on the average $S_{average}$ given by

$$\text{Asian Call}_{payoff} = \max[0, S_{average} - K]$$

where K is the strike price. Conversely, an Asian put is a European style put option (bearish view) that gives the holder the following payoff at maturity T:

$$\text{Asian Put}_{payoff} = \max[0, K - S_{average}]$$

Since the payoff of Asian options is based on the average of the underlying asset prices during the term of the product, the uncertainty concerning the fluctuations of the underlying price at maturity decreases. Therefore, the risk exposure to the spot price and volatility is lower for an Asian option compared to a regular European option. Also, the higher the number of observations, the lower the price of the option.

The averaging periods can be uniform during the life of the option, i.e. the structure can take many forms including weekly, monthly, quarterly or annual averagings from inception to maturity date. These Asian options are said to be *averaging-in* style. For instance, a 2-year at-the-money Asian call averaging-in quarterly is a call paying the positive average of the eight underlying returns observed at the end of each quarter throughout the term of the product. Asian options can also be *averaging-out* style, which means that the average is computed during a specific period near the maturity date. A 2-year 90% Asian call averaging-out monthly during the last year is an out-of-the-money put struck at 90% and for which the average price of the spot is based on the underlying spot closing prices observed during the last 12 months of the product's life.

In the general case, averaging-in style options are less risky than averaging-out Asian options. Indeed, the uncertainty about future spot prices is lower when the average is computed periodically since inception date. In the case of averaging-out style Asian options, the future spot prices would have a higher impact on the option's value, thus increasing the risk exposure to spot price and volatility.

Moreover, there are many ways to compute the average of the stock returns. Indeed, S_{average} can be a geometric or arithmetic average. In the case of a geometric average, it is possible to find analytical formulas for pricing Asian call and put options. This is due to the fact that the geometric average of log-normal variables is log-normally distributed in the risk-neutral world. A good approximation for the price of an average option is given in Kemna and Vorst (1990) where the geometric average option is priced using Black–Scholes closed formulas, with the growth rate $(r - q)$ set to $(r - q - \sigma^2/6)/2$, and the volatility set to $\sigma/\sqrt{3}$.

However, in most of the cases, the average of the underlying asset prices is arithmetic, and there are no closed formulas for pricing arithmetic average options since the arithmetic average of log-normal variables is not log-normal. Bearing in mind that the distribution of this arithmetic average is nearly log-normal, good approximations of the Asian option prices are available in the literature. (e.g. Kemna and Vorst, 1990). In general, one will simply obtain the implied volatility of the option implied from vanilla derivatives, and perform a Monte Carlo simulation of a log-normal process using this volatility, where the paths are simulated to reflect the period over which the averaging is taking place.

3.10   AN EXAMPLE OF THE STRUCTURING PROCESS

In this section we apply what we have learned so far regarding structures in Chapter 2, making use of section 2.5 regarding the equity linked note, with what we have seen in this chapter on vanilla options.

3.10.1   Capital Protection and Equity Participation

Assume that an investor is interested in gaining equity exposure, but does not want to risk capital. A simple note structure as described in Figure 2.1 (page 21) is a good starting point. If we assume that we are looking at a 4-year maturity, then to guarantee that the capital is returned at 100% we set aside a percentage of capital to put into a zero coupon bond that will pay 100% of the notional at maturity. Taking interest rates to be 3%, plus a funding spread of 35 bp per annum, we have a bond price of 87.46%, leaving us with $100\% - 87.46\% = 12.54\%$ of the notional to spend on the option. Let's take 54 bp of P&L, then we are left with 12.00% to put into an option that offers equity exposure.

Starting with the vanilla options we have seen here, the easiest choice is to spend this on a call option. Depending on the investor's preference, let's take one of the global indices, for example the EuroStoxx50, and try to use an ATM call option. Pricing a 4-year ATM call option on EuroStoxx50 gives us an option price of 15%, and we run into our first problem. We only have 12.00% to spend on the equity part of the note, and an ATM call option is too expensive.

The first possibility is to offer a participation rate of less than 100%. A *participation rate* of 100% would mean that the investor will receive, on the equity part of the note, a return exactly equal to any increase in the price of the index from the start date to the expiry of the option. For example, if the index rose by 27%, the return will also be 27%. Obviously there is no downside risk here as the call option has a minimum payoff of 0%, because if the index has a negative return during the period under consideration, the call option is not exercised and the payoff is zero. The bond still pays 100% and the investor's money is secure. To write this in the form of a payoff we have

$$\text{Note}_{\text{payoff}} = 100\% + \max\left[0\%, \frac{\text{Index}(T) - \text{Index}(0)}{\text{Index}(0)}\right]$$

In our present case, since we have only 12% to spend, but the ATM call option costs 15%, we could offer a lowered participation rate, also known as *gearing*, of 80%. This means that the upside is now 80% of any increase in the index, and this will cost the structurer 80% × Price of ATM call = 80% × 15% = 12%. Solving for the gearing in a case like this, one can simply divide the amount available to spend on the option by the option price. So, 12%/15% = 80% is where we get the 80% participation. In this case, the participation in the index return of 27% would in fact be

$$27\% \times \text{Participation} = 27\% \times 80\% = 21.60\%$$

and the payoff would be

$$\text{Note}_{\text{payoff}} = 100\% + 80\% \times \max\left[0\%, \frac{\text{Index}(T) - \text{Index}(0)}{\text{Index}(0)}\right]$$

Now as such, the investor may find that taking a participation rate of less than 100% is not appealing. Keep in mind that the investor has the option to simply place his money into the same bond with no equity exposure and, assuming the same interest rates used to compute the bond price above, has the potential to earn 3.35% annually. In this case we turn to our second possibility, which is to introduce some form of averaging. Starting at the end and working backwards, we can try taking the call option on the average of the index price over the last 3 months of the maturity. This will reduce the price as discussed above in the context of Asian or average options. If this is not enough to bring the price down to the amount available for the equity part of the note, then the structurer can try further averaging (last 6 months, last 9 months, last 12 months) to get the prices to fit. Again, too much averaging may not appeal to the investor; although a 4-year maturity with the last 12 months averaged out is not too outrageous.

On the other hand, if interest rates were higher and we had more to put into the equity part of the note than the cost of the ATM call, we can increase the participation and have a gearing greater than 100%. This would also fit into the scenario where rates are relatively high and the investor, although bullish on an equity index, may want to receive a minimum guaranteed coupon. Taking the same 4-year maturity, assume that the investor is willing to forgo putting all the money into a bond, in exchange for some equity participation, but wants to earn at least 5% at maturity in addition to the 100% guaranteed capital. This means that redemption at maturity is given by the payoff

$$\text{Note}_{\text{payoff}} = 100\% + \max\left[5\%, \frac{\text{Index}(T) - \text{Index}(0)}{\text{Index}(0)}\right]$$

and, as such, will receive back at least 105% of the notional. To see the breakdown of the payoff on the right-hand side, we subtract the 5% to get

$$\text{Note}_{\text{payoff}} = 105\% + \max\left[0\%, \frac{\text{Index}(T) - \text{Index}(0)}{\text{Index}(0)} - 5\%\right]$$

and we notice that the right-hand side is an OTM call option, at the OTM strike of 5%. The OTM call option will need to be correctly priced and the structure as such now includes a minimum guarantee of 5%.

Yet another way to cheapen the equity part to fit into a note is to introduce a cap into the payoff.

$$\text{Note}_{\text{payoff}} = 100\% + \max\left[0\%, \min\left(\frac{\text{Index}(T) - \text{Index}(0)}{\text{Index}(0)}, \text{Cap}\right)\right]$$

where the payoff is computed on the basis of a prespecified cap that essentially *caps* the unlimited upside in the call option thus making the structure cheaper. As such, this structure breaks down into what is known as a call spread, which is discussed in detail in later chapters.

3.10.2   Capital at Risk and Higher Participation

Let's now consider the case where the investor is willing to take on some downside risk in exchange for enhanced participation in the upside. Following the note construction as before, assume now that the investor is willing to put 3% of his capital at risk. In this case the investor has $100\% - 3\% = 97\%$ guaranteed capital, and we then put part of the notional into a bond that pays 97% at maturity instead of the 100% above. If we have the same parameters as in the first example in this section, the bond is only worth 84.83%, which leaves $100\% - 84.83\% = 15.17\%$ for the structurer to spend on the option. As this covers the cost of the ATM call option of 15%, no additional gearing or averaging is needed.

Another example, and one which combines put options as well as call options, can be structured by offering the investor participation in the upside through a call option, and some participation in the downside through a put option. In all the above examples the bank sells the investor one of the call options of the above forms; consider the case where the seller adds a put option such that the investor is short the put option. Recall that the put option pays when the underlying ends below the strike, so if the investor is short the put option then she has capital at risk in the event the index ends below its starting level (assuming the put is struck ATM).

As such, in addition to the 12.00% to spend on the equity part of the note (following the same numbers as the start of the section) then, in addition, we have the premium from the put option. Let's assume that the ATM put option costs 17% and the investor is willing to take 50% participation in the downside in exchange for increased participation in the upside. Then the seller of the structure has $50\% \times 17\% = 8.5\%$ excess to offer upside in the equity. In total this gives $12\% + 8.5\% = 20.5\%$, and since the ATM call is worth 15% then the participation in the upside can now be increased to $20.5\%/15\% = 170.83\%$. So, in exchange for accepting a potential downside risk at 50% of any downturn in the index value, the investor now gets a far greater participation than 100% in the upside.

Adding different types of put options to enhance the payouts of various structures is a common technique. A key point is that although this can significantly enhance the upside potential in even a simple structure such as this, in the event of a market crash the investor's capital is not protected. The payoff at maturity of the combined long position in the geared call option and short position in the geared put option is depicted in Figure 3.8.

An important point here is that although this section describes the process of combining the concepts we have seen so far, one must keep in mind that when a bank sells a call option it is in fact selling volatility. If a bank sells a call option and volatility goes up, then the value

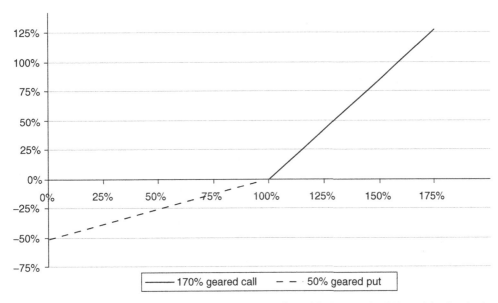

Figure 3.8 A combination of 50% participation in the downside (put) and 170% participation in the upside (call).

of the call option goes up, and thus the seller of the call option is short volatility. So, in an environment where volatility is high, the value of a call option will also be high in comparison with a lower volatility environment, and the prices offered on such a structure will not be appealing. In cases such as these, there are more suitably fitted structures one can use to obtain equity exposure, but where the seller of the instrument is able to buy volatility. As we go along, observing the volatility position of each product is key in understanding the environment for which it is best suited, and in doing so one can know which structures would offer the most appealing deals to investors. The last example, involving the addition of the put option, is one such case, because the put option's price also increases with volatility and since the seller of the structure is buying the put, he is buying volatility through the put. More complex structures than those described here will be seen throughout the book. The process described serves as a good example of combining an investor's requirements with price constraints, and that the only real limit is the structurer's imagination.

4

Volatility, Skew and Term Structure

Human behavior flows from three main sources: desire, emotion, and knowledge.

Plato

In this chapter we study the concept of volatility; specifically we discuss realized and implied volatility, their meanings, measurements, uses and limitations. This leads us to the discussion of the implied volatility skew and the term structure of implied volatility. We end the chapter with a non-technical treatment of various models that capture the different forms of volatility and skew and, accordingly, understand the models' uses. Interesting discussions regarding the implied volatility surface appear in the literature, including Derman (1999), Derman and Kani (2004), Dupire (1994) and Gatheral (2006).

4.1 VOLATILITY

One must distinguish between realized volatility and implied volatility of an asset. Both give us information about the asset, and although they are related, they are different concepts. The realized volatility of an asset is the statistical measure we know as the standard deviation. The implied volatility of the same asset, on the other hand, is the volatility parameter that one can infer from the prices of traded options written on this asset.

4.1.1 Realized Volatility

Realized volatility, also known as statistical volatility or historical volatility, is a measurement of how much the price of the asset has changed during a period of time. Often, volatility is taken to be the standard deviation of the movements in the price. Given a set of N price observations $S(t_1), S(t_2), \ldots, S(t_N)$, one would define the continuously compounded return r_i between time t_{i-1} and t_i as

$$r_i = \ln\left(\frac{S(t_i)}{S(t_{i-1})}\right)$$

then an unbiased estimate of the variance of the price returns on day t_N is

$$\sigma_{t_N}^2 = \frac{1}{N-1}\sum_{i=1}^{N}(r_{N-i} - \bar{r})^2$$

where $\bar{r}$ is the mean of the returns r_i given by

$$\bar{r} = \frac{1}{N}\sum_{i=1}^{N}r_{N-i}$$

This can be modified in several ways: firstly, the returns can be computed as a percentage return

$$r_i = \frac{S(t_i) - S(t_{i-1})}{S(t_{i-1})}$$

the mean return $\bar{r}$ is assumed to be zero, and $N - 1$ is replaced by N. As pointed out by Hull (2003), these three changes make little difference to the variance estimates, yet simplify the variance formula to

$$\sigma_{t_N}^2 = \frac{1}{N} \sum_{i=1}^{N} r_{N-i}^2$$

The standard deviation σ_{t_N} is the square root of the variance. The volatility of the process at time $t - 1$ is defined as the standard deviation of the time t return. Clients can freely specify the period over which they want to look at the realized volatility, and the frequency of price observations (provided price data for such observations exist), although often volatility is computed using the daily closing prices of the asset over a year, which is referred to as the annualized standard deviation.[1] The results from computing realized volatility with different units of time must be interpreted correctly. Over one day, the standard deviation in the price of an asset may be 1.5%, and over a year it may be 24%, so there is therefore a need to specify the volatility that is being selected. When no time frame is explicitly specified, the phrase "stock A has a volatility of 24%" generally means that stock A has an annual standard deviation of 24%.

Both volatility and variance are useful measurements with each having its own advantages. For example, volatility as a standard deviation is a good measurement of the price variability of an asset because it is expressed in the same units as the price data, thus making it easier to interpret. Along the lines of standard convention, volatility is defined as above and in cases when variance is used this will be specified.

When one thinks of volatility, i.e. realized volatility, the higher this is the riskier the asset since a high volatility means that the asset has had greater price fluctuations in the recent past. A higher volatility means more uncertainty about the size of an asset's fluctuations and, as such, it can be considered a measurement of uncertainty.

Volatility is dynamic and changes a great deal over time for numerous reasons. A property that is observed in a time series of realized volatility is that it experiences high and low regimes, but that it also has a long-term mean to which it reverts. Another characteristic is that, as a stock market witnesses a large decline, volatility shoots up: we therefore generally see a negative correlation between such assets and their volatilities.

Caution must be taken when interpreting the meaning of a certain volatility. Since realized volatility is obtained from a set of price data one must be sure that the period over which volatility is computed is not biased towards one regime or another. Also, although looking at past data can give an idea of how the price of an asset has behaved, many factors are always at play and the results from past data as such are not necessarily an accurate indication of future price fluctuations.

---

[1] Daily volatilities are annualized by using the square root of time rule. Be careful, an annual volatility is different to an annualized volatility.

In Chapter 16, on volatility derivatives, we see derivatives such as volatility and variance swaps with payoffs that are explicitly dependent on the volatility realized by an asset.

4.1.2 Implied Volatility

The realized volatility of an asset, as just seen, is a measure of how the asset's price fluctuated over a specific period of time. It is also called *historical* volatility because it reflects the past; however, it does not necessarily contain information about the current market sentiment. The implied volatility of an asset on the other hand, as the name suggests, is a representative of what the market is implying in terms of volatility.

If one looks at the prices of liquidly traded instruments, such as vanilla options, one can extract an implied volatility – a volatility that corresponds to these prices. Using the Black–Scholes formula, any given price corresponds to one and only one volatility parameter. In fact vanilla options are quoted in terms of their implied volatilities since this, or a given price, essentially amounts to the same information. Take an asset and look at the market's prices of calls and puts written on this asset: for each asset one can know the volatility that corresponds to the price of each option – the implied volatility.

An asset may have a realized volatility, based on its past performance given by $\sigma_{realized}$, computed today, as described above, and this gives us information about the fluctuations of the underlying during the past period over which this volatility is computed. But, one may take a look, today, at the prices of liquidly traded options on the same asset, with maturities in the future, and infer an implied volatility. Since these instruments are based on the market's perception of their true value, one can see the volatility of the asset that the market is inferring. The two volatilities do not necessarily coincide, and although they may be close, they are typically not equal.

The liquidity of such options means that supply and demand indicate that their prices are the market's consensus of the correct price. This means that the volatilities extracted from these option prices are in fact the market's consensus on the forward looking volatility of the asset. This implied volatility incorporates the forward views on all market participants on the asset's volatility.

Using the correct implied volatility of an asset allows one to price other derivatives on the asset, in particular those that are not liquidly traded. To price an exotic derivative, the volatilities used must be those that reflect the market's current view on the volatility of the asset. In particular, when a European option serves as a hedging instrument for a more exotic option, its associated implied volatility is of relevance to the pricing and hedging of the exotic option. We go into more depth below to study the properties of implied volatility, and the last section of the chapter discusses (a) the different models that capture the various characteristics of implied volatility and (b) when we need each of these models.

Where the implied volatility of an asset cannot be implied from traded instruments, one may resort to using the realized volatility as a proxy for implied volatility to get an idea of what volatility would be correct to use. This is discussed in the context of volatility sensitivities and hedging in Chapter 5. In contrast, the realized volatility of an asset can be used as a sanity check to ensure that the implied volatilities being used make sense. The two are different, with implied volatility generally being higher than realized volatility, but too far a spread could imply a mistake, or if correct, an arbitrage opportunity. Trading the spread between these two is discussed as a strategy in Chapter 16 on volatility derivatives.

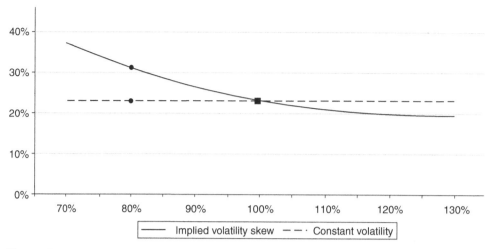

Figure 4.1 An implied volatility skew across strikes versus a flat volatility which is constant across strikes.

4.2 THE VOLATILITY SURFACE

The volatility surface, which, to be precise, is really the implied volatility surface, is the three-dimensional surface obtained when one plots the market implied volatilities of European options with different strikes and different maturities. By fixing a maturity and looking at the implied volatilities of European options on the same underlying but different strikes, we obtain what is known as the implied volatility skew or smile, depending on its shape, typically specific to the asset class. Fixing a strike, usually the ATM strike, of options on the same underlying and looking at their implied volatilities, we see what is known as the *term structure* of volatilities.

4.2.1 The Implied Volatility Skew

European options of the same maturity on the same underlying have implied volatilities that vary with strike, for example, the 80% OTM put has a different implied volatility to the ATM put. Plotting these implied volatilities across strikes gives us the implied volatility skew, also referred to as volatility skew, or even just skew. Although the volatility skew is dynamic, in equity markets it is almost always a decreasing function of strike. Other asset classes such as FX and commodities have differently shaped skews and we will see these in detail in Chapters 17 and 18 when we discuss these asset classes separately. To say there is a skew means that European options with low strikes have higher implied volatilities than those with higher strikes. Figure 4.1 gives an example of an implied volatility skew across strikes and a flat, i.e. constant, volatility also for comparison.

In Figure 4.1 the ATM volatility is the same in both, given by the square above the 100% strike (ATM). The implied volatility of OTM puts, whose strikes are below the ATM level, have higher implied volatilities in the presence of skew. The two dots on the graph are the implied volatilities of the 80% strike puts under flat volatility and skew; notice the difference between them. Also notice that OTM call options, i.e. call options whose strikes are above the

ATM level, have lower implied volatilities in the presence of skew compared to a flat volatility assumption.

There are several reasons for the existence of this implied volatility skew. Implied volatility is the market's consensus on the volatility of the asset between now and the maturity of the option. Put options pay on the downside and are thus good hedging instruments against market crashes. If an asset drops in price, this is generally accompanied by an increase in its volatility. In this case fear manifests itself because of the increased uncertainty and risk involved in such a drop. This is reflected in the implied volatilities of the OTM puts being higher than the OTM calls because puts pay on the downside. The market tends to consider a large downward move in an asset to be more probable than a large upward move, and so options with strikes below current levels will hold a higher implied volatility. A downward jump also increases the possibility of another such move, again reflected by higher volatilities. Additionally, one can discuss the leverage effect: a leverage increase given by a decline in the firm's stock price, with debt levels unchanged, generally results in higher levels of equity volatility.

As we will see in Chapter 5 on option sensitivities (the Greeks), call and put options have a positive sensitivity to volatility. This means that as their implied volatility goes up, their price goes up, and vice versa. This also means that the seller of a call or put is essentially selling volatility (and conversely for the buyer of a call or put). Since the values of these vanillas come from the implied volatility, the higher premium imposed upon the OTM puts over the OTM calls is reflected in the skew.

Also, as we will see in the chapter on Greeks, large costs can be involved in hedging OTM puts when the market is in decline. Higher hedging costs are reflected in increased premiums for downside options, and this is reflected in the skew where such puts are priced with a higher implied volatility.

Measuring and Trading the Implied Skew

The first thing in measuring the skew is to note its level, which is given by the ATM implied volatility. The skew can vary in shape, but the ATM volatility tells us where it is located, i.e. how high it is. The word *skew* is also used to refer to the slope of the implied volatility skew. Although the curve is not a straight line, the concept of being more skewed means that it is generally steeper (see Figure 4.2). This slope is negative since the implied volatilities are a decreasing function of strike and thus equity markets are often said to have a negative skew.

How much skew there is – generally as a measure of how steep the curve is – can be seen by computing the slope of the implied volatilities with respect to the strike. Assuming we had the set of implied volatilities as a function of strike $\sigma_{\text{Implied}}(K)$, then the slope is given by the first derivative, at a specific point, possibly the ATM point

$$\text{Slope} = \frac{\mathrm{d}\sigma_{\text{Implied}}(K)}{\mathrm{d}K} \tag{4.1}$$

In reality, however, we only have implied volatilities for a discrete set of strikes. One can use some form of interpolation to obtain the function $\sigma_{\text{Implied}}(K)$ in order to have a parametric form, but in practice, and to have a standard method of measuring skew, we take the difference between the implied volatilities of the 90% and 100% strike vanillas. These two points form a straight line and its slope with respect to the strike axis (the x-axis) tells us how negatively skewed the implied volatilities are. To actually get the value of the slope we would need to divide by the difference of the strikes, $100\% - 90\% = 10\%$, as this is the first-order finite

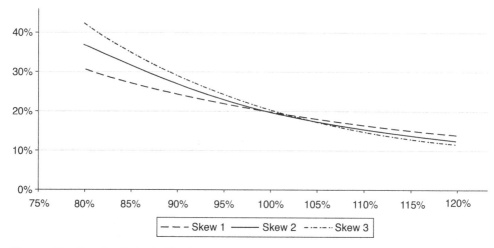

Figure 4.2 Three implied volatility skews. The ATM volatilities are the same in all the volatility skews. The 90% − 100% skew (slope) of implied skew 3 is twice as steep as implied skew 1.

difference approximation to the derivative in equation (4.1).[2] In Figure 4.2 note the three cases: the ATM volatility is the same, but they all have different skews. The 90%−100% skews are given by 0.4574, 0.7032 and 0.9148 respectively, here quoted as positive numbers (the absolute values) which is often done when it is assumed that the equity skew is always negative.

The reason for comparing the 90% strike (and not the 110% strike) with the 100% strike to quantify the skew, is because the downside skew (put skew) is more severe, and it also has implications that we will discuss later in Chapter 16 on volatility derivatives. Another possibility is to parameterize using the 90% and the 110% strikes, instead of the 90% and ATM points.

If one believes the skew to be steeper (or flatter) than it should be, one way to take this view is to sell (or buy) a put spread (this is the combination of two puts with different strikes). Since the put option has a positive sensitivity to volatility (that is, as volatility increases, its price increases) the buyer of the put is therefore buying volatility, and the seller of the put is selling volatility. This sensitivity to volatility is referred to as Vega and is discussed in Chapter 5. The level of volatility at which the buyer (or seller) of the put is buying (selling) is the correct implied volatility at the relevant strike. So, by selling a 90% strike put, and buying the ATM put, giving the long position in the 90–100% put spread, the investor has sold the 90% strike implied volatility and bought the ATM volatility. If in fact the skew was steeper than it should have been and the market begins to imply a flatter skew, the volatility of the 90% strike put will be lower and thus its price is lower, making the price of the put spread higher. The holder of the put spread is said to be short skew, in the sense that if skew increases, the put spread's value decreases. Alternatively, the seller of the put spread is long skew. In Figure 4.2 notice that the less steep skew carries lower OTM put volatilities. More details on call spreads and put spreads are discussed in Chapter 6 on options strategies.

---

[2] A first order approximation to the derivative of a function f at the point x is given by $\frac{f(x)-f(x-h)}{h}$

If we compare the implied volatility skews of an index and that of a stock we find that index volatilities are more skewed than those of a single stock. The reason for this is that if stocks are all dropping during a market decline, the realized correlation between them rises, and an equity index is a weighted average of different stocks. We see this further when discussing realized correlation in Chapter 7.

This is a useful property as one can use the skew of an index as a proxy for pricing skew-dependent payoffs on stocks whose implied skews are not as liquid as those of the index. For an index we are often able to find liquid quotes for options of different strikes, but for single stocks we typically find less liquidity in the options market on these stocks. Knowing that the index's implied volatilities are more skewed than those of the single stock, it is possible to take a percentage of the index skew and use this in the pricing. This is especially relevant if options on the index will be used in the volatility hedging of another option. Consider an asset for which we have ATM implied volatilities from the market but few OTM quotes: we can use the ATM volatility to specify the correct level of the implied volatility skew and then use a percentage (for example, 80%) of the index's skew as a proxy for the stock's skew. What percentage to use is primarily a function of whether the structure in question sets the seller short skew or long skew, and from there it is a function of how aggressive or conservative the trader wants to be on the skew position. For example, one may use a banking stock index's skew as the skew proxy for a basket option on banking stocks. This can prove handy when we introduce multi-asset options where, for example, we may have a skew-dependent payoff on a basket of stocks which we will see in detail in Chapters 7, 8 and 9 on correlation and dispersion, and also in Chapter 21 when constructing indices.

Measuring and Trading the Implied Skew's Convexity

Another measure that gives us information about the skew is its convexity. This is also known as the curvature of the implied volatility skew. To quantify this, one can consider a combination of the implied volatilities of vanillas with strikes at 90%, 100% and 110%. The sum of the 90% and the 110% implied volatilities minus twice the 100% strike volatility and dividing by the difference in strikes squared (that is, $(110\% - 100\%)^2 = (10\%)^2$), gives us the measure of the implied skew's convexity.[3,4] We need two points to measure the skew and three points to measure convexity. The more convex the implied volatility skew is, the more rapidly the volatilities grow as the strikes decrease (see Figure 4.3). In fact the combination of vanillas with the above strikes is known as a *butterfly spread*, discussed in Chapter 6 on option strategies.

The reason such a trade allows for one to take a view on convexity is similar to the analysis of skew in the case of the put spread above. If we go long a butterfly spread, then we are long a 90% and a 110% strike call option, meaning that we are long the implied volatilities at these two strikes. If the implied skew then becomes more convex, it means that these two implied volatilities have increased, making the butterfly spread more valuable. The holder of a butterfly spread is, therefore, long implied skew convexity.

---

[3] This follows similar reasoning to the case of skew. Convexity, or curvature, of the skew is the second-order derivative $d^2\sigma_{\text{Implied}}(K) / dK^2$.

[4] An approximation of the second derivative of a function f at the point x is given by $\frac{f(x+h)+f(x-h)-2f(x)}{h^2}$

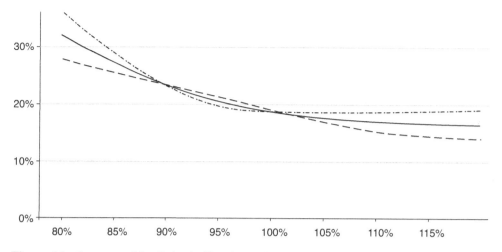

Figure 4.3 Curvature of implied volatility skew. All three implied volatility skews have the same 90–100% skew measurement, but different 90–100–110% convexity (or curvature).

The implied volatilities of a single stock generally have more curvature, i.e. they are more convex than those of an index. The reason for this is that jumps (downward jumps to be precise) have a larger impact on single stocks than they do on an index, and the risk of a single stock crashing completely is greater than that of a whole index doing so. So, although a stock may have less negatively skewed implied volatilities than an index, the former's implied volatilities are more convex in strike than those of the index.

4.2.2 Term Structure of Volatilities

When we plot the volatility skews over different maturities we obtain a volatility surface; and for the moment we will focus on the *term structure of volatilities* (Figure 4.4). For a given strike, ATM or otherwise, implied volatilities vary depending on the maturity of the option. Firstly, let us look at the ATM volatilities and consider the term structure of ATM implied volatilities, which is the set of implied volatilities of ATM vanilla options on the same underlying plotted against different maturities. In most cases, the term structure is an increasing function of maturity, that is, longer maturities tend to have higher implied volatilities than shorter maturities. This is generally the case in calm periods where short-term volatilities are relatively low. This curve could be decreasing if the market is volatile and short-term volatility is exceptionally high. This term structure can also reflect the market's expectations of an anticipated near term event in terms of the volatility that such an event would imply. The term structure also reflects the mean-reversion characteristic of volatility.

Depending on the investor's risk preference, increased demand for different maturities can be seen depending on the shape of the term structure. Those seeking high volatility will prefer longer maturities when the curve is pointing upwards, and shorter maturities when the curve is a decreasing function. One can also take a view on the term structure's shape, and a simple trade to provide this is the calendar spread, which is the difference of two call options of the same characteristics but different maturities.[5]

---

[5] See the section on calendar spreads in Chapter 6.

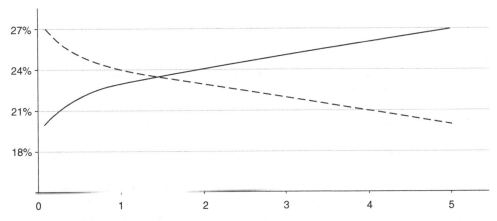

Figure 4.4 Term structure of implied volatilities: implied volatilities plotted against maturities in years. Note the two distinct shapes.

Skews through Maturities

If we look at the implied volatility skew for various maturities we notice that the short-term skew is much steeper than the long-term skew, and generally flattens out as maturities increase. The level each skew is at is given by the ATM volatility term structure, whereby a long maturity could have a skew at a level higher than the short-term maturity, but the short-term skew will be more pronounced. Again this has to do with supply and demand, since, in the short term, people may be less keen to sell OTM puts (and thus the OTM put volatility). A jump in the underlying's price in the immediate future would have a large impact on the price of the put; for the short term this is more severe as the market may not have time to recover. There is also an increase in the OTM call implied volatility compared to the longer maturities, again for similar reasons.

4.3   VOLATILITY MODELS

We now discuss various models in the light of what we now know about term structure and skew. As this book is not about how to build or implement models, we keep the discussion to an intuitive level and do not go into too many mathematical details.[6] Our goal is to explain what to do with the many models that already exist. Ultimately, a model is still just a model, and our goal is to find – given a specific derivative or set of derivatives – the model that is best suited. Models can be useful only if properly understood, in both their limits and their strengths. Here we discuss these with respect to which forms of volatility each of the different models captures.

4.3.1   Model Choice and Model Risk

Essentially, the choice of which model to use depends on the different risks involved in the option. As discussed earlier, the word option comes from the fact that such contracts offer

---

[6] See Appendix A, sections A.1, A.2 and A.3 for more technical details.

some form of optionality. Starting with the example of a call option, recall the present value of a call option as in Figure 3.5 on page 38, and how this value is a convex function of the underlying price. This convexity, or second-order effect (non-linearity), in the underlying's price is what gives the option value, and we must assume that the underlying's price has some randomness in order to see this effect in whatever model we choose. In all our options, and in all the models used, we will see that the price of the underlying on which the option is written is modelled as a random variable.

When specifying any model, we are faced with what is known as model risk: the risk that a derivative is modelled incorrectly. This is divided into three forms, the first of which is that the model being used has been incorrectly implemented. The focus of this book is not on this point, however, and we will assume that the models are readily available and correctly implemented, in order to answer the question of what to do with these models. Our focus is on the next two forms: (1) that the correct inputs are used in such models, and (2) that the correct model is chosen for the correct derivative. Since many of the more exotic structures to come are illiquid, it is imperative that we reduce these two forms of model risk as much as possible.

To give an example regarding correct model inputs, one must take account of the liquidity of the underlying and one's ability to trade it in order to know the hedging costs accurately. An example of the right choice of model can be related to the volatility skew: what if the option had skew dependence, that is, its price is sensitive not just to one implied volatility but to more than one. We call this a skew-sensitive product, and we need to use models that capture this effect. With regards to hedging, if one plans to trade European options in order to hedge the Vega or Gamma risk of an exotic structure, then all such hedging instruments must be correctly priced in the calibration. The model as such will show risk against these instruments. In fact, we specify a calibration according to which instruments we want to see risk against. We discuss these issues from the point of volatility to understand how to capture the different characteristics of volatility when necessary. Other risks will become apparent as we move along (e.g. correlation risk in multi-asset options) and at each stage, when we meet them, we will explain the models that can capture these risks.

4.3.2   Black–Scholes or Flat Volatility

The Black–Scholes model has become a market standard in the sense that the prices of vanilla options are quoted in terms of their implied volatilities rather than in dollar values. As we already saw, since we know the implied volatilities of call options from the market, we simply need to feed them into the Black–Scholes formula to get a price. There is a one-to-one relationship between the price of a vanilla option and its implied volatility in the Black–Scholes formula, i.e. there exists a unique implied volatility that when put into the Black–Scholes formula returns this price.

We will refer to this as the case of flat volatility, since the Black–Scholes model assumes that volatility, defined as the annual standard deviation of the asset price, is constant across strikes. This means that the model does not know about the implied volatility skew, nor does it know about the term structure of implied volatilities. However, the implied volatilities that one obtains for vanilla options in the market across strikes and maturities are those that should be fed into the Black–Scholes formula to obtain the correct values. As we saw, options with different maturities and/or different strikes will have different implied volatilities, but using the correct implied volatility in Black–Scholes gives the correct price. The model's other required inputs are the current level of the underlying, the strike price, the maturity, the dividend yields,[7] the repos and the interest rates that are all known to us. To obtain the price of a vanilla we only need the correct implied volatility based on the strike and the maturity of the vanilla.

Calls and puts are liquidly traded instruments, and there is no real pricing to be done there. So the question arises: What other derivatives can we price correctly using flat volatility? For example, the Asian (or average) options we saw in the previous chapter can be priced using the flat volatility Black–Scholes model. As long as we use the correct implied volatility we can apply the model, either using a closed formula for Asian options or by simulating the asset price, to obtain the price of the Asian option. The reason why we can apply such a model in this case is that the Asian option does not have skew sensitivity[8] or any hidden convexities other than that to the underlying's price. It is safe to assume that while the underlying's price is random, it has a constant volatility rendering the Black–Scholes model the appropriate one.

A second example, which involves skew, is the call spread. The call spread is a combination of a long call option (usually, but not necessarily, ATM) and a short call option of a strike greater than the first call with all else remaining the same (i.e. the underlying and maturity). In this case we can apply the Black–Scholes model on the condition that we use the correct implied volatilities. The reason is that although the call spread is sensitive to skew, it is only sensitive to two specific points on the skew: the volatilities at the correct strikes. This payoff can be broken down into two call options that can be correctly priced if we have the right implied volatilities for each. If the first call has strike K_1 and the second call has a strike K_2, we cannot directly apply the Black–Scholes model and price the call spread as the difference in price between the prices of the two calls. We need to use a different Black–Scholes model on each: for the first we use the usual inputs specifically using the implied volatility of the underlying for that particular strike K_1, plug into Black–Scholes and obtain the first price. Similarly, for the second all inputs are the same except the strike and the implied volatility of the K_2 strike call option. The difference between these two prices is the price of the call spread.

Essentially this is saying that even in the case of some skew dependence it may still be possible to apply the Black–Scholes model as long as we are cautious about the various effects, while keeping an eye on how the skew affects the price. In the call spread example, had we assumed a flat volatility (i.e. the same volatility for both call options) we would have drastically mispriced the call spread. The reason we were able to do this is because the payoff of the call spread is a linear combination of two vanillas.

It is possible to extend the case of a constant volatility across maturities to having a time-dependent but deterministic volatility, thus allowing for a term structure of volatilities.[9] It is also possible to allow for a term structure of interest rates which also makes this input more realistic compared to just a constant interest rate curve across maturities.[10] The extensions that allow for an implied volatility that is not constant across strikes are slightly more complex and

---

[7] Note that in some cases, it is difficult to estimate future dividend yields, particularly for long-dated options owing to the uncertainty in future dividends. As such, one typically takes a model reserve to compensate for this risk. How much is a function of the maturity of the option and a view regarding the dividends of the specific asset in consideration. Alternatively, dividend swaps can be used to hedge this dividend risk.

[8] The Asian option does have a slight skew sensitivity, but it is quite small and not something the market includes in prices.

[9] First appearance was in Merton (1973).

[10] In reference to the various yield curve points that exist as we go along maturities: a term structure of rates.

we now discuss models that capture some of the effects that Black–Scholes does not, pointing out where such models are necessary.

4.3.3   Local Volatility

Local volatility models offer a way of capturing the implied skew without introducing additional sources of randomness; the only source of which is the underlying asset's price that is modelled as a random variable. In the Black–Scholes model, the asset's price is modelled as a log-normal random variable, which means that the asset's log-returns are normally distributed. However, assuming that such a distribution allows for the simple formulas we see in the Black–Scholes system, it is obviously not a realistic representation of the market. The fact that we have a skew (i.e. that volatility is not constant across strikes) is the market telling us that the asset's log-returns have an implied distribution that is not Normal – a violation of Black–Scholes assumptions.

One way around this is to accept the additional source of randomness by letting the volatility itself be random. Although we need this, and discuss it below under stochastic volatility, the introduction of the additional random factor (the volatility) increases the complexity of the problem. Local volatility is still a one-factor model and it also allows for risk-neutral dynamics, which means that, like Black–Scholes, the model is preference free from the financial point (recall section 3.4.1 on risk-neutrality). This is not to say that other models cannot also be risk-neutral, but the local volatility model is the simplest one to account for skew and offers a consistent structure for pricing options.

How, therefore, does local volatility work? We can agree that the market is telling us that log-returns are not normally distributed, in fact, the market is implying some distribution. If we are given a set of prices of vanilla options for a fixed maturity across strikes, or equivalently, their implied volatilities, can we find a distribution that corresponds to these prices? This is to say, can we find a distribution for the asset price so that if we used this distribution to price vanilla options on this asset, it would give the same prices as the vanillas on this asset seen in the market? The answer was given to us by Dupire (1994) and also by Derman and Kani (1994) that, yes, theoretically, there is a way to find the distribution (local volatility model) which corresponds exactly to all vanilla prices taken from the skew. In fact, local volatility extends beyond skew and can also capture term structure. It can therefore theoretically supply us with a model that gives the exact same prices for vanillas taken from a whole implied volatility surface.

In a local volatility model, the volatility of the underlying asset's price is a deterministic function of the asset's price. It is not just a constant $\sigma = \sigma_{\text{implied}}$ (a constant) as in the case of Black–Scholes, or a random variable itself as in stochastic volatility $\sigma = \sigma(t)$ (randomly changing through time), but in a local volatility model it is a function $\sigma = \sigma(S(t), t)$ of the asset price and possibly also time in a deterministic non-random manner. This is to say that the future evolution of the asset price at any point t in time is a function of the asset price $S(t)$ at that time and also a function of time itself.

Local Volatility Models and Calibration

Finding this function $\sigma(S(t), t)$ is a process known as *calibration*. The inputs for these models are not only the current level of the asset, the curve of riskless interest rates, and the size and timing of known dividends to come, but also the implied volatility skew (possibly a whole surface). Given the set of implied volatilities of vanilla options, calibration is the process where we search for these volatilities $\sigma(S(t), t)$ so that the model matches these prices. Assuming that the implementation is sound, once calibrated, these models can now be used to price more exotic payouts, knowing that the model correctly prices the liquid vanillas.

There are computational difficulties in finding this function that will exactly fit all market prices, which is why Dupire's formula, though theoretically correct, has some practical drawbacks. These are discussed in more detail in Appendix A, section A.2 on local volatility. In particular, fitting all points may lead to unrealistic model dynamics – the local volatility model – although fitting the vanillas is actually not a good representation of how the asset really evolves. In practice, there may be more than one (often unlimited) local volatility model that fits a set of vanillas, so one must lay down a set of criteria to follow when choosing the model to use. Here we distinguish two types of local volatility from the calibration point of view. Recall that the surface is two-dimensional, one in time and one in strike, and the focus on one or both must be determined in order to correctly capture the effect of the volatility surface on certain payoffs.

Depending on the payoff of the option, we may want to favour one calibration, or equivalently one set of functions $\sigma(S(t), t)$, over another. If the payoff involves only one date – for example a payoff on an asset S that depends only on the value $S(T)$ at maturity but not before – this is equivalent to saying that there is no path dependency in the payoff. In this case, we only need to fit the distribution to that maturity by taking the vanilla skew at that date only, and the focus is on getting the calibration done correctly for the strike regions in which the payoff is sensitive.

As an example, consider a call option that has the usual payoff while additionally paying nothing if the underlying goes above a certain level: these are known as *barrier options*. As we will see in detail in barrier options, we must capture the skew if they are to be correctly priced; if this barrier is only monitored at maturity, this has no path dependency and we require only that the model fits as best as possible the vanillas maturing on the same date as this option.

Assuming that the call option is ATM (strike is at 100%), and the barrier is at 150% for example, we must make sure that the model correctly fits the skew up to the point 150%. The focus here is on getting the calibration to correctly fit the places where the derivative has skew sensitivity. European options with these strikes can serve as hedging instruments and the model must be calibrated to them to show risk against them. In the described example, the option is sensitive to skew, however its sensitivity to the volatilities in the 70% strike region for example is minimal. Getting the calibration right in that region should not be done at the expense of less accuracy in the skew-sensitive region. We will refer to this case as *exact date fitting*.

Take, on the other hand, a derivative that has a huge amount of path dependency and again look at the above example of a knock-out call option that pays like a call option unless the asset goes above the barrier, in which case it pays nothing. Now allow the barrier to be monitored on a daily basis. At the close each day we see if the underlying went above this barrier level, and, if so, the option is then immediately rendered worthless.

Our focus on the local volatility calibration in this case is different from the example above. We cannot in fact find liquid vanillas for all dates, and therefore we have to work with a finite set of maturities to which we can calibrate. In this instance we will only need vanillas of maturities up to the maturity of the knock-out call we are pricing, specifically because these can serve as hedging instruments for Vega or Gamma risk and must therefore be correctly priced in the model. What we do need to know is that the local volatility model does imply a reasonable volatility for those dates in between the dates where we have vanilla data; that is, we want to know that, through time, the calibration is smooth, so that we know that the model is implying reasonable dynamics throughout. We also want to make sure that the strikes are calibrated as best as possible, but must balance between these and a smooth calibration through time. This case we refer to as *smooth surface calibration*.

When implied volatility data is not available, one must resort to interpolation or extrapolation of the surface. Doing this in an arbitrage-free manner is discussed in Chapter 6, section 6.5. If we have implied volatilities for two strikes and need an implied volatility at a strike in between, we must interpolate in an arbitrage-free manner. In the case where, for example, we need data that is at extreme strikes (or maturities), we will have to extrapolate these from the data we already have. This may arise for long maturities for which we cannot find liquid instruments, and also for extreme OTM strikes. Again, the need to calibrate to such points is a function of the type of payoff and its relevant skew sensitivities. As we go through each new payoff we will specify if such problems arise through the discussions on the sensitivities of each.

Calibration errors are quantified by the *root mean square error* (RMSE), which measures the differences between the market data and those generated by the model. These are summed to give

$$\text{RMSE (market, model)} = \sqrt{\frac{\sum_{i=1}^{n}(\text{market}_i - \text{model}_i)^2}{n}}$$

where n instruments are involved in the calibration. The calibration aims to minimize the RMSE. If we wanted to place more emphasis on specific points of the market data, the formula can be modified to

$$\text{RMSE (market, model)} = \sqrt{\sum_{i=1}^{n} w_i(\text{market}_i - \text{model}_i)^2}$$

where $\sum_{i=1}^{n} w_i = 1$. In the case of equal weights this reduces to the above formula.

4.3.4 Stochastic Volatility

In stochastic volatility models, the asset price and its volatility are both assumed to be random processes. Recall, in Black–Scholes, that volatility is assumed to be constant, and in local volatility models the volatility is a deterministic function of the asset's level. Here in stochastic volatility models the volatility itself is assumed to be random. A quick observation of market data will show that the assumption that volatilities are constant is wrong, and that it would make sense to model volatility as a random variable as well as the underlying's price.

In allowing the volatility to be random, stochastic volatility models give rise to implied volatility skews and term structures. By this we mean that if one values European options using a stochastic volatility model, then the volatilities implied by the model's prices will exhibit skew and term structure. Stochastic volatility models can explain in a self-consistent manner the actual features we see in the empirical data from the market. Once such a model is specified, the skews generated by the model are a function of its parameters, and finding the parameters that fit a certain skew (or a surface) is again the act of calibration.

The question then arises: do we need such models? Do we need to always model volatility as a random variable, or can we still use constant or local volatility? The answer is that it depends on the derivative. As we saw in the example of the call and put spreads, options that can be broken down into vanillas can be priced using Black–Scholes as long as one uses the right implied volatility for each option. Now consider options such as the aforementioned barrier option. These have skew dependency yet such payoffs cannot be broken down into vanillas. In such cases, we can use local volatility assuming it is correctly calibrated to the skew (or surface) in a manner consistent with the skew sensitivity of the option. Stochastic volatility, on the other hand, goes beyond just skew and term structure allowing for Vega convexity and forward skew.

A derivative exhibits *Vega convexity* when its sensitivity to volatility is non-linear: there is a non zero second order price sensitivity (or convexity) to a change in volatility. The assumption that volatility is random in stochastic volatility models captures the Vega convexity, in much the same way that the assumption that the underlying's price is random in all models allows for convex payoffs in the underlying's price. We have seen that vanilla options are convex in the underlying's price, but are they also convex in volatility? The answer is that ATM vanillas are not, but OTM vanillas do have Vega convexity. However, these options are liquidly traded and their prices are obtained by using their implied volatilities in Black–Scholes. These implied volatilities (from the implied surface) give the market's consensus of the right price; therefore the cost of Vega convexity of OTM vanillas is included in the skew.

In more complex payoffs, as we will see as we progress, almost all the payoffs will exhibit some form of Vega convexity, although in many cases this is captured in the skew and can be correctly priced by getting the skew right (for example, with a local volatility model). Other payoffs exhibit such convexities that are not captured in the skew and we must in these cases use stochastic volatility. Since volatility is taken to be random, it must also have its own volatility, and this is known as the volatility of volatility, or vol-of-vol. This parameter corresponds to the Vega convexity term, and when the holder of an option is long Vega convexity, we say she is long vol-of-vol.[11] Since local volatility does not consider volatility to be random it does not know about Vega convexity. The second-order sensitivity to volatility is known as Volga (see section 5.7.1 in Chapter 5 on Greeks).

The second feature of stochastic volatility models is that they can generate forward skews. Take a call option that matures in 3 years from today but starts 1 year from today. This is known as a forward starting option and is discussed at length in Chapter 13 on cliquet structures. In this case, the correct volatility skew to use to price such an option is known as the *forward skew*; here in particular it is the 1- to 3-year forward skew. The T_1 to T_2 forward skew is different from the regular 0 to T_1 and 0 to T_2 skews, and if a derivative has exposure to forward skew, one must use a model that knows about forward skews in order to get a correct price.

Although local volatility models can capture the market's consensus on the prices of vanilla options by matching the volatility surface, the evolution of future volatility implied by these models is not realistic. In the case of forward skews we are faced with the problem that the forward skews generated by local volatility models flatten out as we go forward in time, even though, in reality, forward skews have no reason to do so. The local volatility model, therefore, does not provide the correct dynamics for products with sensitivities such as these. Stochastic

---

[11] Section A.3 of Appendix A discusses stochastic volatility and gives more technical details regarding Vega convexity.

volatility models, on the other hand – owing to the randomness of volatility – generate forward skews that do not fade. In the chapter on cliquets, we deal with these issues in depth since many cliquet structures are both convex in Vega and have exposure to forward skew. In Appendix A, section A.3.1, we discuss Heston's stochastic volatility model (Heston, 1993) as an example of a stochastic volatility model through which we elaborate on many of these issues.

This issue is related to the question of smile dynamics. By smile dynamics we refer to the phenomena of how the skew moves as the underlying moves: if the underlying moves in one direction, how should the skew move? The answer is that local volatility models can provide inaccurate smile dynamics, while the dynamics of stochastic volatility models are, in fact, more consistent with the dynamics observed in the market. If an option is sensitive to smile dynamics, then getting the smile dynamics wrong will have a large impact on both the price and the computation of the subsequent hedge ratios. We will see this concept in the context of option sensitivities as we move along.

On the calibration side, stochastic volatility models have difficulty fitting both ends of the surface, that is, fitting the skew for both short and long maturities at the same time. One remedy for this is to add jumps to a stochastic volatility model. Jumps are able to explain the short-term skew quite well, and we recall that the reason for the existence of the steep short-term skew has to do with jumps. Adding jumps to such a model does not generally affect the long-term skews which remain relatively flatter; the long-term implied skew is not driven by jumps in the underlying. In Appendix A, section A.4, we discuss combining models and see jumps in more detail.

5
Option Sensitivities: Greeks

Sometimes you have to risk what you want in order to get what you want.

The buying or selling of a derivative creates a position with various sources of risk, some of which may be unwanted risk. Hedging in this case is the act of reducing these risks by engaging in financial transactions that counterbalance these risks. If the seller of an option decides not to hedge, then this is referred to as a naked position and can be very risky. When a bank sells a derivative to a client, it should understand all the risks associated with the product and hedge its position accordingly. Once a sale is done, the product is added to an existing book of options, and it is the book that must be risk managed. In order to see where the risks lie, the trader hedging a derivative will need to know the sensitivity of the derivative's price to the various parameters that impact its value. The sensitivities of an option's price, also known as hedge ratios, are commonly referred to as the Greeks since many of them are labelled and referred to by Greek letters. Many articles and books in the literature discuss hedging, and Taleb (1997) is a very practical example.

In this chapter we will discuss the various Greeks, their meanings and their implications on the pricing and hedging of derivatives. Firstly, we cover the Greeks of derivatives involving only one underlying asset, then look at the cases of derivatives with multiple underlying assets. We end with a section presenting some useful formulas that give the approximations based on the Greeks as these can serve as quick mental checks.

To obtain the price of an exotic derivative, one is more often than not forced to use some model. As we discussed in Chapter 4, it is imperative that one uses the correct model to price, but since the sensitivities of the price are also computed using a model, we discuss the implications of various models on the option price's sensitivity. Most of the analysis is done under the Black–Scholes model seen in Chapter 3, but details are given for the cases where assumptions such as those of Black–Scholes can lead to false hedge ratios. One must understand the implications of any model, Black–Scholes or otherwise, and the impact of the model's assumptions on the hedge ratios it generates; if the model is wrong, then the hedge ratios computed using this model will typically also be wrong.

In some cases, although uncommon, an exotic product may have all its cashflows aligned with those of derivatives that can be traded liquidly in the market and can thus be hedged by taking the opposite position in such derivatives at the onset of the contract. This is known as a *static hedge* because once this hedge is put into place, as an initial hedge, there is no need for further hedging irrespective of how the market moves. If liquidly traded instruments allow for such a hedge, then the hedge is model independent: as discussed in Chapter 3, the cost of the derivative is the cost of its hedge, and in this case we know the cost of setting up such a hedge without resorting to any models. A static hedge can of course involve the underlying itself in addition to options. From a pricing perspective, the cost of setting up this hedge is the price of the derivative, and we do not need a model, just market prices. The existence of a static hedge can thus provide us with both a price and a hedge.

In the general case of exotic structures, such a hedge is not possible and what is known as a *dynamic hedge* must be put in use. To dynamically hedge means that from the day the trade is active[1] an initial hedge put into place will need to be readjusted at future dates. The reason for this is that once such a hedge is in place, it is sensitive to movements in the market and must be modified to still be a hedge. How often hedges should be adjusted is dependent on the nature of the sensitivity and its impact on the price. The day 1 hedge may consist of a static part that needs no further adjustment, and a dynamic part that will need adjustment through the life of the product. We see the risks introduced by single options and how these then contribute on a book level. Throughout this work we go through each new structure in detail, analysing the risks, on a product by product basis. Where notable we discuss, in the text, book level hedging. For example, the sale of many of the common multi-asset options results in large short correlation positions, on a book level.

Rebalancing dynamic hedges is a trading decision that depends on many factors, including market movements that result in the sizes of certain risks increasing, decreasing, or even changing sign. The frequency of the readjusting hedges must also take into account the transaction costs involved in buying and selling in the market. On an individual option basis one takes into account the notional size of the option, because this determines the *size* of the risks. On a book level, one thinks about aggregated risks because individual risks from different options may offset each other, and hedging can be done by buying or selling further options to explicitly eliminate existing risks.

5.1 DELTA

We begin the discussion of the Greeks with Delta, the most fundamental of all Greeks. A derivative is named as such because it *derives* its value from an underlying asset. Delta is the sensitivity of an option to the price of this underlying asset on which the derivative is written. To understand the concept of sensitivity we must first mention the Taylor series. There is no need to be alarmed mathematically, as this simply gives us the various orders of sensitivities. We were all taught how to compute the derivative of a function at some point, but what does this derivative mean? If we compute the derivative of a function $f(x)$ at a point, what information does this give us? If we consider the price of an option as a function of the underlying's price S, written Price(S), and ask how much is the rate of change of this price if the underlying moves by an amount x (that is, if the underlying's price moves from S to $S + x$, by how much does the price of the derivative change), the answer is given by the Taylor series

$$\text{Price}(S + x) = \text{Price}(S) + \frac{d\,\text{Price}(S)}{dS}x + \frac{1}{2}\frac{d^2\,\text{Price}(S)}{dS^2}x^2 + \cdots$$

So the change in price is given by

$$\text{Price}(S + x) - \text{Price}(S) = \frac{d\,\text{Price}(S)}{dS}x + \frac{1}{2}\frac{d^2\,\text{Price}(S)}{dS^2}x^2 + \cdots \qquad (5.1)$$

The first derivative w.r.t. S on the right-hand side of this equality is the first-order sensitivity of the price to a movement in S, and is known as the Delta. If x is small, meaning there is only a small movement in S, then the price of the derivative will move by Delta times x (the

---

[1] *Active* meaning it has sensitivities, often the start date of the option, but in some cases earlier if it is forward starting. Such cases are discussed under forward starting options in Chapter 13 on cliquet structures.

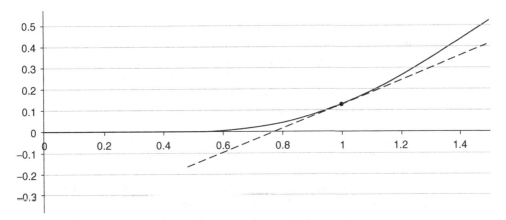

Figure 5.1 The present value of a call option across spot prices with the ATM Delta tangent.

rate of change in the price w.r.t. to S times the amount by which S moved). In Figure 5.1 the curved line is the price of a call option plotted against the underlying's price. The ATM Delta is 0.5635 and the dotted straight line has a slope of 0.5635, tangent to the curve of the price at the ATM point. A Delta of 0.5635 means that if the underlying moves by an amount, say 1%, then the value of the derivative will move by 0.5635 × 1%.

To hedge against movements in the underlying, a seller of a call option must buy Delta units of the underlying. Assume the call option is written on an underlying S whose price at the time of sale is $24.5, Delta is 0.5635 and that the notional of the call option is $1million, then the seller needs to buy $1,000,000 × 0.5635 = $563,500$ in the underlying stock.[2] This equates to $563,500/$24.5 = 23,000 shares. The portfolio consisting of the option (short) and Delta of stock (long), is Delta neutral. As Delta changes with movements in the underlying, the amount of the underlying that needs to be held to remain Delta neutral will need to be adjusted, thus this is a dynamic hedge. As the underlying moves, the seller will have to readjust this Delta hedge by buying more units of the underlying, or selling some units, depending on whether the underlying goes up or down. The Delta of a call option on a stock is non-negative and it can take any value in the range [0, 1]. As the option goes deep into the money, Delta approaches its maximum value of 1, and if the option is deep out-of-the-money, Delta will be close to zero. In the deep ITM case, a Delta of 1 reflects the high probability that the option will be exercised, and in the deep OTM case, the option will most likely not be exercised.

In a book consisting of many options, some of the Deltas of the various options may cancel each other. The linearity of addition of the Deltas within a portfolio follows from the fact that each Delta is essentially a mathematical derivative and the derivative is linear. Consider a portfolio P consisting of n options: $O_1, O_2, ..., O_n$ all written on the same underlying asset whose price we denote as S, then the sensitivity of the price of the portfolio P to a movement in the price of S is given by the sum of the individual Deltas of the n options:

$$\Delta_P = \Delta_{O_1} + \Delta_{O_2} + \cdots + \Delta_{O_n}$$

---

[2] Recall the discussion in Chapter 3 regarding the relationship between a call option with fixed notional, paying the positive returns of the underlying, and a call option to buy a specific number of shares.

Other than trading the underlying itself to Delta hedge, it is also possible to use forwards or futures. Recall that in the case of liquidly traded futures – for example, futures on major equity indices – the value of the futures/forward contract at time t (assuming, for simplicity, no dividends) with maturity T is given by $F(t) = S(t) e^{r(T-t)}$. So if the price of the underlying changes by δS, the futures price changes by $\delta S e^{r(T-t)}$, that is, the Delta of the futures contract is given by $e^{r(T-t)}$. Matching a required Delta hedge in the underlying asset, Δ_S, with a position in a futures contract on this underlying we simply require a position of $e^{-r(T-t)}\Delta_S$ in the futures contract.

One can further exploit correlations between assets to Delta hedge. Specifically, if an option is written on an asset with price S_1, then it is possible to use a second asset S_2 to Delta hedge, i.e. one can trade in the asset S_2 to offset the first-order sensitivity of the option to movements in S_1. Denoting the price of the option by P, where we know that $\Delta = \partial P / \partial S_1$ is the required amount of S_1 to buy or sell for Delta hedging, we want to find Δ_2, which is the amount of S_2 to buy or sell for Delta hedging. To do this we need to measure the expected movement in S_2 when S_1 moves, simply because of the chain rule:

$$\Delta = \frac{\partial P}{\partial S_1} = \frac{\partial P}{\partial S_2} \frac{\partial S_2}{\partial S_1} = \Delta_2 \frac{\partial S_2}{\partial S_1} \tag{5.2}$$

If we use Black–Scholes assumptions, specifically the log-normality of the asset prices, and denote $\rho_{1,2}$ to be the correlation between S_1 and S_2 – i.e specifically the instantaneous correlation between the returns – then we can measure the change in S_2 for a change in S_1 by

$$\frac{\partial S_2}{\partial S_1} = \rho_{1,2} \frac{\sigma_2 S_2}{\sigma_1 S_1} \tag{5.3}$$

and accordingly we know the value of Δ_2 in equation (5.2). The ability to do this can be extremely useful when Delta hedging in practice, and we will see examples of this use as we proceed.

Under Black–Scholes assumptions, the Deltas for call and put options are given by

$$\Delta_{\text{Call}} = e^{-qT} \mathcal{N}(d_1) \qquad \Delta_{\text{Put}} = e^{-qT} [\mathcal{N}(d_1) - 1]$$

where d_1 is defined as usual in Black–Scholes following Chapter 3, and q is the dividend yield. In Figure 5.2, the Deltas of three different options are plotted against the price (in percentages) of the underlying: the ATM call option, the 80% strike ITM and 120% OTM calls. Notice that, although we are on the extreme cases of very low and very high levels of the underlying, Delta approaches the limits of its range. This is because a very high level of the underlying would imply that the call option will most probably be exercised, and if it is exercised, recall from the definition of the call option that the holder of the call has the right to buy the underlying asset at the agreed strike price. On the other hand, if the underlying's level is low and the option deep OTM, then the Delta will be close to zero because this option will have very low intrinsic value.

The Delta of a European option is sensitive to the time to expiry, the volatility of the underlying asset, and the difference between the strike and spot prices. In Figure 5.3 we can see the effects of time and volatility on the Delta of the call option.

Figures 5.4 and 5.5 illustrate how Delta changes with movements in the underlying. They also illustrate the effects of moneyness and time to expiry. The expiry of the option corresponds to where the series for the underlying's price ends, one year. Figure 5.4 has three different scenarios for the path of the underlying, expressed in terms of percentages, and Figure 5.5

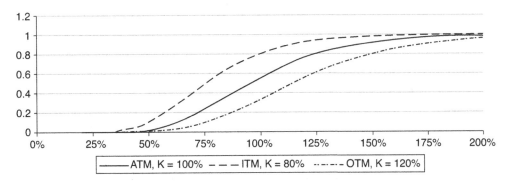

Figure 5.2 The Delta sensitivities of call options with different strikes.

gives the values of the Deltas of an ATM option assuming each of the scenarios in Figure 5.4. We assume that we are long the ATM call option and will thus go short Delta of the underlying asset to remain Delta neutral. The Delta in Figure 5.3 is positive owing to the fact that we are long the option, but to become Delta neutral we will need to take the opposite position and short Delta of stock.

The volatility of the underlying is assumed constant throughout when computing these Deltas, which may not be a realistic assumption but illustrates the point. In fact, ideally we would use the realized volatility of the underlying to compute Delta, but the problem is that we cannot know in advance what the realized volatility of the underlying's price will be. The hedging errors resulting from the wrong volatility are discussed in Chapter 6, on option strategies.

In Figures 5.4 and 5.5, both the series for the underlying and the Deltas are computed using daily observations. There are a few interesting points to be made regarding these figures: firstly, note that all three Deltas start at the same point, but as time moves on and the underlying moves, each of the Deltas goes up or down depending on whether the underlying went up or down. In series 1, notice that the underlying actually reached a level around half-way through the year that was actually lower than the point at which it ended; however, the Deltas at these

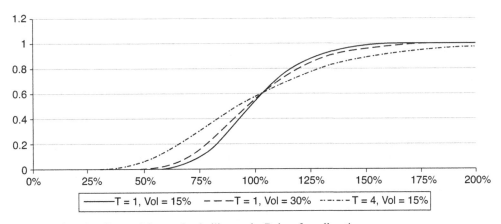

Figure 5.3 The effects of time and volatility on the Delta of a call option.

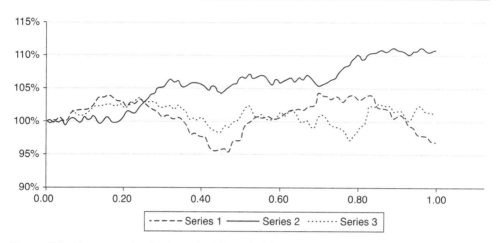

Figure 5.4   Three scenarios for the path of the underlying asset.

two points are different. This is due to the effect of time to expiry since, when it reached its low, there was still half a year to go, but as it dipped lower than the strike in the last month, Delta dropped substantially and ended up at zero, close to expiry.

In series 2 the underlying, apart from the first period, generally kept increasing further and further into the money, and Delta also gradually increased to reach the value of 1 before maturity. It remained close to 1 until maturity even though the underlying moved slightly because the option was deep in-the-money and approaching maturity, meaning it was likely to be exercised. In series 3, Delta moved around but shot up in the last few days as the underlying was still close to the strike, but stayed above it approaching maturity.

Note that in all the scenarios, from the start to expiry, as Delta increases we need to sell more stock to remain Delta hedged since we are long the option and thus short Delta of the

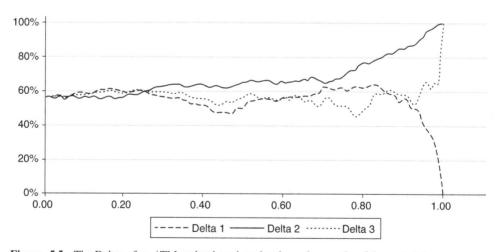

Figure 5.5   The Deltas of an ATM option based on the above three paths of the underlying.

underlying. Vice versa, as the underlying decreases and Delta decreases, we need to buy back stock in order to remain Delta neutral.

Owing to the uncertainty involved in Delta hedging, and the costs involved in buying and selling the underlying asset, one would want to keep Delta hedging to a minimum; traditionally Delta hedges are rebalanced on a daily basis. One should adjust the effect of time on Delta for holidays and weekends, because even if the underlying does not move, time will have elapsed and this has an impact on Delta, especially in the cases where there is little time left to expiry and the underlying is still close to the strike. The effect of time elapsing on the price of the option is the Greek known as Theta, discussed below, and the effect of time on Delta is known as Charm.

Liquidity is also a concern, and must be taken into account. The bottom line is that to be hedged one will need to buy or sell a certain amount of stock on day 1 and adjust this hedge as time goes by. If the stock is illiquid and hard to trade, one must make adjustments. In some cases it is difficult to short stocks, which may be necessary to Delta hedge, and borrow costs (repos) will need to be factored into the price.

Other parameters impacting Delta hedging are dividends and interest rates. Although the Deltas of an exotic derivative can be quite different to those of vanillas, a desk selling exotic products will typically be structurally long the underlying assets from having to buy Delta in these assets. When long Delta in an underlying, the trader will be long the dividends paid by the underlying, and dividends are a necessary input to obtain a correct price and hedge, but they are uncertain in the sense that a company's dividends may change owing to various factors. Expectations regarding dividends can be factored into the price in the form of a term structure of dividend yields, or priced at current levels and hedged using a dividend swap. On a book level, large exposures to dividend fluctuations will need to be hedged.

Regarding interest rates, we note that when a trader needs to buy Delta of stock, the trader will have to borrow money in order to buy whatever units of stock are needed. If rates go up, then it costs more to borrow money thus making the hedging process more expensive. This is discussed in the section below under the interest rate sensitivity of options, referred to by the Greek letter Rho.

Exercise

Imagine you are in charge of Delta hedging a portfolio of options. And let's assume that you are short skew and volatility goes down. Would you end up buying or selling underlying shares?

Discussion

As discussed in Chapter 4, the skew increases the price of OTM puts and ITM calls; and decreases the price of OTM calls and ITM puts. Being short the skew can mean being short OTM puts, short ITM calls, long OTM calls or long ITM puts. Let's consider the case where you are long OTM call options. If volatility goes down, the Delta of OTM calls goes down, as shown in Figure 5.3. Since you are long the options, the portfolio overall Delta is then negative. Therefore, you have to buy shares to maintain zero sensitivity to the spot price of underlying shares.

5.2 GAMMA

Gamma represents the second-order sensitivity of the option to a movement in the underlying asset's price. In the Taylor series of equation (5.1) this is given by the second term on the right-hand side involving the second derivative of the price w.r.t. the asset price

$$\Gamma = \frac{\partial^2 \text{Price}(S)}{\partial S^2}$$

As is clear from Figure 5.1 above, the price of a call option as a function of the underlying price is non-linear. Gamma allows for a second-order correction to Delta to account for this convexity. For a non-small move x as in equation (5.1), i.e. the corresponding movement in the option price, the second-order effect is not negligible. This convexity in the underlying price is what gives the call option value, and in order to see the second-order effect in pricing we will always use models that assume some form of randomness in the asset's price.

The Black–Scholes Gamma for both calls and puts is given by

$$\Gamma = \frac{\mathcal{N}'(d_1)\,e^{-qT}}{S\sigma\sqrt{T}}$$

The dollar or cash Gamma is given by Gamma times S^2:

$$\Gamma^{\$} = \frac{\partial^2 \text{Price}(S)}{\partial S^2} \cdot S^2$$

and, as the name implies, once we multiply by the asset price squared, the unit of the cash Gamma is the dollar (or whatever currency we are working with) value of Gamma.

In Figure 5.6 notice the effect of volatility on Gamma: a higher volatility lowers the Gamma of the call option when the underlying is near the strike, but raises it when the underlying moves away from the strike. We can think of this effect in terms of the time value of European options. For low levels of volatility, the Gamma is low for deep ITM and OTM options because, for low levels of volatility, these options have little time value and can only gain time value if the underlying moves closer to the strike. On the other hand, a high volatility means that both

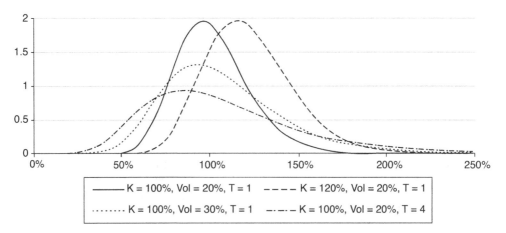

Figure 5.6 The effects of strike price, time and volatility on the Gamma of a call option. Here interest rates are set to 4% and dividend yield at 2%.

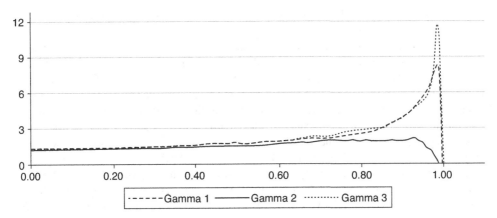

Figure 5.7 Scenarios for Gamma. These series correspond to the series of the underlying in Figure 5.4.

ITM and OTM options have time value and so the Gamma sensitivity near the strike should not be too different from the Gamma away from the strike.

Gamma, being the second derivative, is the first-order sensitivity of Delta to a movement in the underlying. Gamma tells us how much Delta will move if the underlying moves. Recall that the corresponding graphs of Figures 5.4 and 5.5 show how Delta changes as the underlying moves. The magnitude of these changes is given by Gamma. In Figure 5.7 we see the Gamma of an ATM call option making the same assumptions as the discussion of Figures 5.4 and 5.5. The Gammas in series 1 and 3 grow quite large close to maturity, because the underlying in both these series was close to the strike and a small movement could have sent the option in or out of the money. This, in turn, means that Delta can change substantially if the underlying moved even slightly and thus the Delta's sensitivity to the underlying's price, given by Gamma, is quite large.

Although all three series followed different paths, their Gammas in Figure 5.7 during the first half of the life of the option are quite similar. This shows the impact of time to expiry on Gamma when the underlying is trading near the strike. For example, at the points 0.33 and 0.89 of the year the asset prices in series 3 were the same, but since the latter case was much closer to maturity, the corresponding Gamma was much larger. In series 2 the option became deep in-the-money, and as maturity approached a small change in the underlying was not going to affect the fact that it was probably going to stay in-the-money and be exercised. Thus the Gamma fades away as we approach maturity because Delta is close to 1 and small movements do not have a large effect on our need to have one unit of the underlying in order to pay out once the call is exercised.

The Gamma of a European option is high when the underlying trades near the strike. Notice the ATM call option's Gamma in Figure 5.6 and also the scenarios of Figure 5.7. Near these points, there will be the need for more frequent Delta hedging and thus inflict more hedging costs upon the trader. In the example of an OTM put that pays when the market declines, its Gamma will be lower on day 1 than it will if the market declines. The Gamma of the put increases as the market declines and the option becomes closer to the money, with Gamma being highest when the underlying is at the strike. In addition, the scenario of a market decline is generally accompanied by an increase in volatility (recall the discussion in

Chapter 4 on volatility and skew), and more movements in the underlying means more need for readjustments in Delta.

The concept of a Delta-hedged portfolio of options means that the portfolio has been hedged by trading in the underlying assets against small movements in these assets. Gamma represents the sensitivity of Delta to a movement in the underlying asset's price, and Gamma hedging can lower the sensitivity of Delta on a movement in price. As a second-order effect, Gamma becomes increasingly significant when a large move in the underlying's price occurs and the Delta moves with according significance. To hedge this Gamma one will need to trade other European options in a manner that the Gammas cancel out and yield a lower overall Gamma. We note that the need for trading options to Gamma hedge instead of again using the underlying asset, a forward or a futures contract, is that these three tradeable instruments are all linear in the underlying price, and thus add no convexity. Gamma represents the convexity (non-linear) of the option price, and to remove (some of) this convexity one must use another convex instrument, i.e. another option. By lowering Gamma (i.e. lowering the overall convexity of the position) we lower the need for the large and frequent rebalancing of Delta.

Like Delta, the Gamma of a portfolio is the sum of the individual Gammas of the options in the portfolio. Take a portfolio that has a Gamma Γ_P and an option O with Gamma Γ_O, then, depending on the sign of the portfolio's Gamma, we either buy (when Γ_P is negative) or sell (when Γ_P is positive) a number of units n of the option, so that the absolute value of the new portfolio $P' = P \pm n \cdot O$, given by $\Gamma_{P'} = \Gamma_P \pm n\Gamma_O$ is as close to zero as desired.

As we move into exotic structures, we find that these may have quite different Gamma profiles to the European options seen here. For example, in the cliquet structures seen in Chapter 13, Gamma can change sign. In the case of barriers and digitals (Chapters 10 and 11), the Greeks near the barriers can become extremely large and unstable, and we will discuss further methods of handling such Greeks.

5.3 VEGA

Vega isn't actually a Greek letter, but it now represents an important Greek. Vega is the sensitivity of the option price to a movement in the volatility of the underlying asset. Since European options are priced using their implied volatilities, the Vega is the sensitivity to a movement in the implied volatility of the underlying asset. We note that this contradicts the Black–Scholes theory in which volatility is assumed to be constant through time; however, it is important to see how an option's price, or the value of a book of options, changes as the result of a change in this parameter. Differentiating the price w.r.t this volatility gives us Vega, the first-order sensitivity.

Under Black–Scholes the Vega of both calls and puts is given by

$$\mathcal{V} = Se^{-qT}\mathcal{N}'(d_1)\sqrt{T} \tag{5.4}$$

where

$$\mathcal{N}'(x) = \frac{1}{\sqrt{2\pi}}e^{-x^2/2}$$

A drawing of this formula is shown in Figure 5.8. In formula (5.4) for Vega, the moneyness term $(\ln S/K)$ appears in (and only in) the term $\mathcal{N}'(d_1) = \frac{1}{\sqrt{2\pi}}e^{-d_1^2/2}$, so with respect to moneyness, Vega is greatest when moneyness is zero (ATM, that is) and decays exponentially on both sides thus giving the bell-shaped curve we see in Figure 5.9. This makes sense intuitively because if

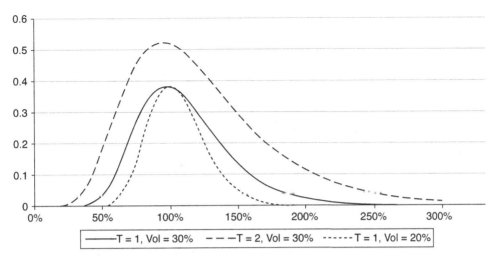

Figure 5.8   Effects of different volatilities and maturities on a European's Vega.

we are at the money then a change in the volatility of the underlying asset can send the option either in-the-money or out-of-the-money, thus the large effect on the price. Should we be quite in-the-money (or relatively out-of-the-money), then although a change in volatility will have an impact on the price, its impact is not as much as a change in volatility is if we are at the money.

For European options the Vega position is simple. Both calls and puts have positive Vega, which means that if we sell a European option, then we are short the volatility of the underlying asset. If we buy a European option, then we are long this volatility. For more exotic structures, the Vega profile, like the Gamma profile, can change sign, and whether we are short or long volatility depends on the underlying's price. An example of this is the call spread discussed in Chapter 6 on options strategies.

The overall sensitivity of a portfolio to volatility can be hedged by adding more positions in options (specifically liquid ones), so that the added (or subtracted) Vegas lower the absolute value of the portfolio's Vega. A book of exotics, or even a single exotic product, can have different sensitivities to the various implied volatilities along the term structure, and these

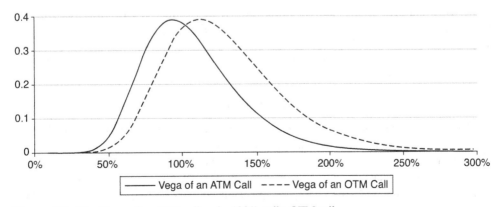

Figure 5.9   The Vegas of an ATM call and a 120% strike OTM call.

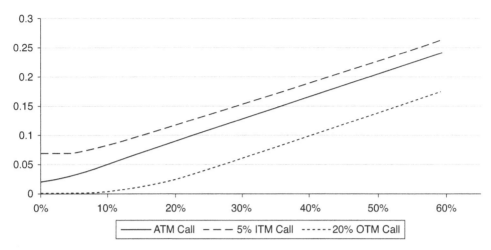

Figure 5.10   The prices of three different 1-year call options plotted against volatility.

are referred to as *Vega buckets*, each corresponding to the volatility sensitivity of a particular maturity on the term structure of implied volatilities. Depending on the product, movement in the underlying assets can trigger barriers or replacement events, for example, which then greatly vary the Vega to the relevant implied volatilities requiring rebalances in the Vega hedges. We discuss these effects on a product by product basis, but note again that the cost of an option should reflect the cost of hedging it, and it is imperative that one understands the risks entailed in hedging an option. As discussed in the context of models in Chapter 4, all such hedging instruments must be correctly priced in the calibration, so that the model as such will show risk against these instruments – specifically, those instruments with maturities that correspond to the Vega buckets in which the option has Vega risk.

In Figure 5.10 the prices of three call options are plotted against volatility. Rates are set at 2% and dividends are assumed to be zero. The ATM option is almost linear in volatility. The prices of the ITM and OTM options are convex in volatility up to a certain level then become linear for large volatilities. This non-linearity is called Vega convexity and is discussed below as Vega–Gamma, also known as *Volga*.

The ATM and ITM options are not worth zero when volatility is zero. In the case of the ATM, even if volatility were zero, the forward is not null and the call option still has a value of approximately $r \times T = 2\% \times 1 = 2\%$. This also applies to the ITM call, but – and only in this case – the option additionally already has 5% in intrinsic value.

5.4   THETA

The Theta of an option is the rate at which the option price varies over time (Figure 5.11). The previous Greeks measured the change to the option price if one of the discussed factors changed, but time is always moving forward and so even if all else remained the same, the option's value will change as time goes by. The rate at which it changes is usually expressed in days, meaning how much does the option price change after one day, all else being equal?

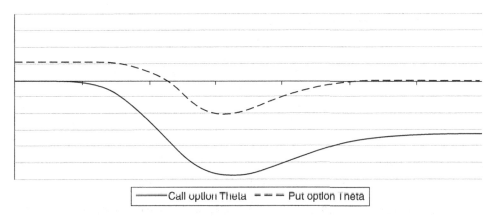

Figure 5.11 Theta of a call and put with respect to the spot price.

An option that loses 0.05% per day is said to have a Theta of -0.05%. If we buy a call option (or a put) we will have a negative Theta, and vice versa.

Assume, for example, that we buy an OTM call option and the underlying does not move at all. Then as time passes, the value of this call option decreases because the option simply has less time to expiry. If the Theta of an option is negative, then the passing of time will lower the value of the option, and vice versa.

Under Black–Scholes, the Theta of a call option is given by

$$\Theta_{\text{call}} = -\frac{S\sigma e^{-qT}\mathcal{N}'(d_1)}{2\sqrt{T}} - rKe^{-rT}\mathcal{N}(d_2) + qSe^{-qT}\mathcal{N}(d_1)$$

and for put options, Theta is

$$\Theta_{\text{put}} = -\frac{S\sigma e^{-qT}\mathcal{N}'(d_1)}{2\sqrt{T}} + rKe^{-rT}\mathcal{N}(-d_2) - qSe^{-qT}\mathcal{N}(-d_1)$$

Following the same series as in Figure 5.4, in Figure 5.12 we plot the Theta of the ATM call option based on the three different series. The first thing to note is that the Theta of the call option is always non-positive. As we can see, the options that are close to the money near maturity will exhibit the most time decay.

5.5 RHO

Rho is the Greek letter used to represent the sensitivity of an option's price to a movement in interest rates. In the Black–Scholes model, the Rho of a call option is given by

$$\text{Rho}_{\text{call}} = KT e^{-rT}\mathcal{N}(d_2)$$

and the Rho of a put option is the negative of this. The prices of call and put options are almost perfectly linear in interest rates; the reason for this is that a change in rates only has a first-order effect on the price of the option. This effect comes from the impact of an increase in rates on the cost of Delta hedging and also from discounting the option price. For a small change in rates this combines for a linear effect on the price of the derivative. This is emphasized using a hedging argument to answer the questions posed in the exercise.

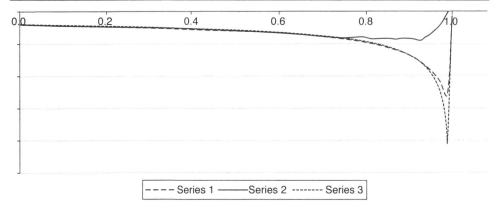

Figure 5.12 Scenarios for Theta. These series correspond to the series of the underlying in Figure 5.4.

Exercise

What impact will an increase in interest rates have on the price of a call option? How about a put option? There is also the question of the effect on dividends.

Discussion

Assume that we sell a call option, then we need to buy Δ of stock. To buy Δ we will need to borrow money, so if the rates go up, it costs us more to borrow money (sell bonds) in order to Delta hedge. Since the option price reflects the cost of hedging, the price of the call must go up if hedging costs go up.

For a put option it is the other way around. If we sell a put then we need to sell Δ of stock. We sell Δ of stock and lend this money (buy bonds), so if rates go up we will make more money from our hedging strategy and thus the price of the put should be lower if rates go up.

We can add the effect of discounting. If rates go up, the discount factor goes down thus lowering the price of options. This is the case for both calls and puts, but in both this effect is generally smaller than the effect of rates on our Delta hedge. In the case of the call, the effect of discounting counters slightly the effect of the rise in the cost of borrowing money. In the case of the put, higher rates mean lower prices and the discount factor lowers them further.

Similar arguments can be made in regards to the price sensitivity to the dividend yield of the underlying asset. If we sell a call option, we need to buy Delta of the asset. If we hold the asset we are long the dividends paid by this asset. If dividends are higher, it means that we make more money on our Delta hedge and thus the cost of hedging is less and the option premium will be less.

5.6   RELATIONSHIPS BETWEEN THE GREEKS

Other than those already described where, for example, the Vega and Gamma of calls and puts are equal, and the relationship between the Delta of a call and that of a put – all of which can be derived directly from the model-free put–call parity formula – there exist other relationships between the Greeks that we discuss here. Firstly, consider the equation, known as the Black–Scholes PDE, derived using the assumptions of the theory,

$$\Theta + rS\Delta + \frac{1}{2}\sigma^2 S^2 \Gamma = rV \tag{5.5}$$

This relationship shows the trade-off between movements in the underlying asset (Delta and Gamma) and the time decay (Theta) of a European option. Here V represents the value of the call or put.

Let's take the case of a trader Delta hedging a long position in a European call option, C. A long position in a call option will require a short position in the underlying stock: the initial Delta hedge involves selling Δ of the underlying S, and the global Delta of the position (long option, short Delta: $C - \Delta S$) is then zero. If the underlying spot price goes up, then the Delta of the call goes up. In order for the trader to keep his portfolio Delta neutral, he has to sell a quantity of stock equal to the increase of the global Delta. Alternatively, if the underlying stock price decreases, the Delta of the call decreases, which makes the global Delta negative; then the trader buys more stocks to maintain the Delta of the portfolio null. When one buys a call and eliminates dynamically the first-order spot risk (i.e. global Delta is equal to zero), he buys the stocks when the spot price decreases and sells it when the spot price increases, thus making profit from these variations. This is referred to as being long the Gamma. At the same time, the time value of the option decreases; this is due to the fact that Theta is negative. The holder of a call option is then long Gamma and short Theta. The opposite is true for a seller of a call option.

We get the same results for put options. Indeed, the holder of a European put, P, applies an initial Delta hedge by buying Δ of the underlying stocks. The position $P + \Delta S$ has zero Delta. If the stock price goes up, the Delta of the put goes up although it is still negative; this makes the global Delta positive, which means that stocks have to be sold to rebalance the global Delta to zero. If the underlying stock price goes down, the global Delta becomes negative since the put Delta decreases. Then one has to buy stocks to keep the portfolio Delta neutral. Here again, when Delta hedging a long position in a put, one buys when the stock price is cheap and sells when it is expensive. And since the time value of a put decreases, one buying a put is long Gamma and short Theta. This relationship is clear in formula (5.5), and is discussed in the following exercise.

Exercise

Ania Petrova is a Russian vanilla options trader. One of her Delta-neutral portfolios is composed of shares of Gazprom as well as options on this stock. The portfolio daily global $\Theta_{1d} = -1,000$ RUB. Assuming a realized volatility σ of 16%, what would the daily P&L of Ania be if the stock moves by $\pm 2\%$ during one trading day?

Discussion

Let δ_Π denote the change in the portfolio value. Then,

$$\delta_\Pi = \Theta \times \delta t + \Delta \times \delta S + \frac{1}{2}\Gamma \times \delta S^2$$

Here, Ania is managing a Delta-neutral portfolio, which means that $\Delta = 0$. Therefore

$$\delta_\Pi = \Theta \times \delta t + \frac{1}{2}\Gamma \times \delta S^2$$

This means that for a realized annual volatility of 16%, the loss due to Θ is equal in absolute terms to the gain due to the Γ. In other words, the daily P&L breakeven occurs when the spot moves by $\sigma_{1d} = \sigma/\sqrt{252} = 1\%$.

$$-1,000 \times 1 + \frac{1}{2} \times \Gamma_{1d} \times \sigma_{1d}^2 = 0$$

which implies

$$\frac{1}{2} \times \Gamma_{1d} \times \sigma_{1d}^2 = 1,000$$

Since $\sqrt{252}$ is approximately equal to 16, Ania loses money on a daily basis when $|\delta S| < 1\%$ and makes positive P&L when $|\delta S| > 1\%$. Note that the $\Gamma - $ P&L is only dependent on the absolute value of the spot's move and not on its direction.

In this case $|\delta S| = 2\%$, then the daily P&L is as follows:

$$\text{P\&L}_{1d} = -1,000 \times 1 + \frac{1}{2} \times \Gamma_{1d} \times \delta S^2$$

Then

$$\text{P\&L}_{1d} = -1,000 \times 1 + \frac{1}{2} \times \Gamma_{1d} \times (2 \times \sigma_{1d})^2$$

Or equivalently

$$\text{P\&L}_{1d} = -1,000 \times 1 + 4 \times \frac{1}{2} \times \Gamma_{1d} \times \sigma_{1d}^2$$

This implies that

$$\text{P\&L}_{1d} = -1,000 \times 1 + 4,000 = 3,000 \text{ RUB}$$

Ania makes an overall profit of 3,000 RUB due to the large move of the underlying spot compared to its realized volatility.

5.7 VOLGA AND VANNA

5.7.1 Vega–Gamma (Volga)

Vega–Gamma, or Volga, is the second-order sensitivity of the option price to a movement in the implied volatility of the underlying asset. When an option has such a second-order sensitivity we say it is convex in volatility, or has Vega convexity. ITM and OTM European options do exhibit Vega convexity, as seen in Figure 5.10 and discussed in Chapter 4 on volatility, but these can be captured in the skew.

Other structures we will see later, for example Napoleons that are discussed in Chapter 13, exhibit a lot of Vega convexity and will result in losses if we do not use a model that prices this correctly. The reason is that as volatility moves, a Vega convex payoff will have a Vega that now moves with the volatility and this must be firstly priced correctly and then hedged accordingly. We will see this in detail in our discussion of cliquets in Chapter 13 and also in volatility derivatives in Chapter 16.

5.7.2   Vanna

Vanna is also a second-order sensitivity. It measures the sensitivity of the option price to a movement in both the underlying asset's price and its volatility. We can thus think about Vanna as the sensitivity of the option's Vega to a movement in the underlying's price, also as the sensitivity of an option's Delta to a movement in the volatility of the underlying. As such, Vanna gives important information regarding a Delta hedge by telling us by how much this hedge will move if volatility changes. It also tells us how much Vega will change if the underlying moves and can thus be important for a trader who is Delta or Vega hedging. If Vanna is large, then the Delta hedge is very sensitive to a movement in volatility.

5.8   MULTI-ASSET SENSITIVITIES

In addition to all the Greeks mentioned above, we have others relating to the cross effects between the assets and the sensitivity to the correlation between the assets.

Cross Gamma

The cross Gamma is the sensitivity of a multi-asset option to a movement in two of the underlying assets. Let us assume that an option is written involving more than one underlying, $S_1, S_2, \ldots, S_N$, then the cross Gamma involving S_i and S_j (two of the underlyings) is given by

$$\Gamma_{S_i,S_j} = \frac{\partial^2 \text{Price}(S_i, S_j)}{\partial S_i \partial S_j}$$

This mixed term can be thought of as the effect of a movement in S_i on the Delta sensitivity of the option to S_j, meaning that, in multi-asset options, it is possible that the Delta w.r.t. one asset can be affected by a movement in another underlying asset even if the first asset has not moved. These are important in the context of basket options in Chapter 7 on correlation, and also dispersion in Chapters 8 and 9, and generally in the context of almost all multi-asset options.

Correlation Delta

The correlation Delta is the first-order sensitivity of the price of a multi-asset option to a move in the correlations between the underlyings. This must be looked at for every multi-asset derivative, if for no other reason than to see which position the derivative has w.r.t. the correlation (i.e. are we long or short the correlation between the assets?) and to assess the magnitude of this sensitivity (is it highly sensitive to correlation or not?). The correlation sensitivity in all the products we will see is discussed in detail on a product by product basis. This arises from the fact that correlations vary over time, and that a multi-asset product's sensitivity to the correlation between a pair of underlying assets can vary as the other parameters (for example, the underlying's prices) change.

While correlation is not as easily tradeable as underlying assets or even volatility, there are some methods of trading correlation that we will discuss in Chapter 7, and the correlation sensitivity of an option or a book of options is thus meaningful in the context of reducing this correlation exposure on either level. Many correlation risks we will see are not completely hedgeable, if at all, and in many cases traders must resort to maintaining dynamic margins for the unhedged correlation risk. Knowing the sign and magnitude of correlation sensitivity is again necessary in this case.

Some multi-asset derivatives are convex in correlation, meaning that the second-order effect on the price from a movement in the correlation is non-zero and needs to be taken into account.

5.9   APPROXIMATIONS TO BLACK–SCHOLES AND GREEKS

In this section we look at some simple approximation formulas for vanilla prices and some Greeks. The idea is to derive formulas that are simple enough to be quickly calculated mentally. We leave the derivations of these for Appendix B, section B.1. It is also a good opportunity to put together some of the issues we have covered so far in terms of what the Greeks mean in reality and their relationship to pricing. To begin, we look at the case of zero rates and dividends.

Vega and Price

Starting with an approximation of the BS Vega given by

$$\mathcal{V}_{\text{ATM}} \approx S \times \sqrt{\frac{T-t}{2\pi}}$$

this comes from approximating the distribution function $\mathcal{N}'(d_1)$ appearing in Vega $\mathcal{V} = S\mathcal{N}'(d_1)\sqrt{T}$. Now we make the claim that an ATM call option Vega does not depend on the level of volatility. This is because the second-order volatility sensitivity, Volga, is zero (or very close to it) in line with the almost linear graph seen in Figure 5.10. If the ATM call option is linear in volatility, then if we know Vega, its price is easily obtained as

$$\text{Price}_{\text{ATM call}} \approx \sigma \times \mathcal{V}_{\text{ATM}} = \sigma \times S \times \sqrt{\frac{T-t}{2\pi}}$$

One can understand this from the fact that Vega is the sensitivity of the price to a move in volatility, the ATM call's Vega does not depend on where the volatility is, so the above formula holds for all sigma, in particular it holds for $\sigma = 1\%$. If we were to write a Taylor series like the one for Delta in equation (5.1) but as a function of σ, then the second term will in this case be zero, and the price is just Vega times the level of volatility. The derivations appearing in this section are explained mathematically in section B.1 in Appendix B.

For the remainder of this section, we assume that $S = 100\%$. Next we add the useful and quite accurate approximation

$$\frac{1}{\sqrt{2\pi}} \approx 0.4$$

If we are using percentages, then we know that the first-order approximation for Vega of an ATM call is given by

$$\mathcal{V}_{\text{ATM call}} \approx 0.4\sqrt{T-t}$$

and the call price is approximated by

$$\text{Price}_{\text{ATM call}} \approx 0.4 \times \sigma \times \sqrt{T-t} \tag{5.6}$$

where, in both of these, the values obtained are percentage prices. Similar approximations exist in the literature, for example Brenner and Subrahmanyam (1988). As an example of this formula, let's ask the following question: What is the Vega of a 1-year ATM call option with an implied volatility of 32%?

The Vega of an ATM does not depend on the level of volatility, and we can approximate it with the formula above as Vega $= 0.4 \times \sqrt{1} = 0.40$ of 1% for a 1% movement in vol, in basis points Vega is 40 bp.

The price of the call is then approximately $\mathcal{V} \times \sigma = 0.4 \times 32\% = 12.8\%$. The accuracy of these approximations and those to come are shown in comparison to the real values in Table 5.1.

Exercise

Assuming a volatility of 20%, can you give a quick estimation for the price of a 1-year European at-the-money (ATM) call option? Also, what would you say concerning the cheapest between a basket composed of two 1-year ATM European calls and a single ATM call option expiring in 2 years?

Discussion

Concerning the pricing of European at-the-money calls, you should be able to give an accurate straightforward estimation using formula (5.6). Then, the price of a 1-year ATM European call is as follows:

$$C_{1y} = 0.4 \times \sigma \times \sqrt{1} = 0.4 \times 20\% \times 1 = 8\%$$

Now, still using the same approximation, we get the price C_{2y} of an ATM European call option with a maturity of 2 years:

$$C_{2y} = 0.4 \times \sigma \times \sqrt{2}$$

On the other hand, the price B_{1y} of a basket composed of two ATM European calls having a maturity of 1 year is equal to

$$B_{1y} = 2 \times C_{1y} = 2 \times 0.4 \times \sigma \times \sqrt{1} = \sqrt{2} \times C_{2y}$$

This implies that $B_{1y} > C_{2y}$. We can conclude that a 2-year ATM European call option is cheaper than two 1-year ATM European calls.

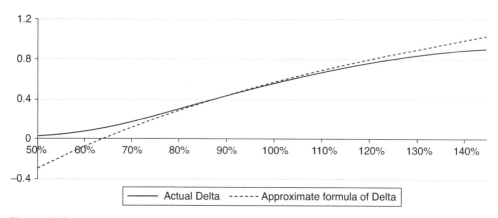

Figure 5.13 A plot of the actual Delta and that of its approximation given by the formulas present in this section. As is clear, around the ATM point the approximation is almost exact. The further we move away from the money the more it diverges from the actual Delta.

Delta

Now we look at an approximation of Delta.

$$\Delta_{\text{call}} = \mathcal{N}(d_1) \approx \frac{1}{2} + \frac{1}{\sqrt{2\pi}}d_1 \approx \frac{1}{2} + 0.4d_1$$

The call is ATM in the example above, and so $d_1 = \sigma\sqrt{T}/2 = 16\%$, then the approximation for the ATM Delta in this case is given by

$$\Delta_{\text{ATM call}} = \frac{1}{2} + 0.2\sigma\sqrt{T} = \frac{1}{2} + (0.2 \times 32\%) = 0.564$$

In the case of away-from-the-money calls, we have to include the term $\ln S/K$ in d_1. In this case, yet another useful approximation that would allow one to approximate this mentally is given by

$$\ln\left(\frac{S}{K}\right) \approx 1 - \frac{K}{S}$$

the accuracy of which depreciates quickly the further K is from S, as is clear in Figure 5.13. As an example, let's assume that the call is 5% OTM, that is, $S = 100\%$ and $K = 105\%$. Then $\ln(S/K) = -4.88\%$ and the approximation is $100\% - 105\% = -5\%$.

As another example, given the price of an ATM call option and its Delta, what is the first-order approximation for the price of a 2% OTM call?

Shifting strike is like shifting spot (the opposite way), so let $\delta S = -2\%$ and check

$$\text{OTM Price} \approx \underbrace{\text{ATM Price}}_{\text{zeroth order}} + \underbrace{\Delta \times \delta S}_{\text{first order}}$$

This comes from writing a Taylor series of the price of a call option of strike K around the point $K = S$

$$\underbrace{C(K)}_{\text{Call at strike } K} = \underbrace{C(S)}_{\text{ATM Call strike } S} + (K - S) \underbrace{\left. \frac{\partial C}{\partial S} \right|_{S=K}}_{\text{Delta at } S=K} + \cdots$$

Next we look at more sensitivities and make use of the above formulas for Delta along with some replication arguments to obtain some more approximations.

Dividend Sensitivity

These formulas assume zero dividends and zero interest rates, but what is the sensitivity of the price of the call to a 1% increase in dividends?

The answer is that if we are selling the call, then we will be long Δ of stock. If we hold the stock then we receive the dividends, and this makes our cost of hedging less; therefore the price of the call will be less. So we know that a 1% increase in dividends will lower the call price, but by how much? We hold Δ_{call} of stock, and therefore from our hedge, a 1% increase in dividends gives us

$$\Delta_{\text{call}} \times (\text{Dividend increase}) = 0.564 \times 1\% = 56.4 \text{ bp}$$

so the call price will go down by 56.4 basis points.

Rho

Now, what are the effects of interest rates on the price of a call option? Here we have a double effect: on the one hand, if rates go up by 1% then it will cost us, as we saw before, more money to borrow the amount we require to buy our Δ_{call} hedge. But, on the other hand, the option price must be discounted, bringing the price down as rates go up. So, from the first effect we will need to now borrow an additional

$$\Delta_{\text{call}} \times (\text{Rate increase}) = 0.564 \times 1\% = 56.4 \text{ bp}$$

bringing the price up by 56.4 bp, but a first-order discounting brings the price down by

$$\text{Rate increase} \times T \times \text{Price} = 1\% \times 1 \times 12.8\% = 12.8 \text{ bp}$$

Thus, overall a 1% increase in rates increases the price by $56.4 - 12.8 = 43.6$ bp. Given that, as we saw in the section on Rho (rate sensitivity), the call price is almost linearly increasing

Table 5.1 Actual values of price and Greeks under Black–Scholes and their approximations using the described formulas.

	Black–Scholes	Approximation	Approximation Error
Price	12.71%	12.8%	9bp
Vega	39.4 bp	40 bp	0.6bp
Delta	0.5635	0.564	5bp
Gamma	1.231%	1.25%	19bp
Rho	43.64 bp	43.6 bp	0.04bp

as rates go up, we can extend this to say that the approximate price of an ATM call with vol and maturity, as in the example, is given (when rates are now 4%) by

$$C = C(0) + 0.436\% \times 4 = 14.54\%$$

where $C(0)$ is the call price approximation above with zero rates assumed.

To this we have added the rate sensitivity for a 1% increase in rates times 4 to represent the fact that rates are now 4%, not zero. As the actual value is 14.51%, we are close and this should make the concept of a price being linear in a parameter clearer.

Gamma

A zeroth-order approximation of Gamma is given by

$$\Gamma_{\text{ATM call}} \approx \frac{1}{\sqrt{2\pi}} \frac{1}{\sigma\sqrt{T}} \approx \frac{0.4}{\sigma\sqrt{T}}$$

in our example our Gamma works out to be 1.25%, which means that if the spot goes up by 1% our Delta will increase by 1.25%, and the actual value of Gamma is 1.231%. Table 5.1 summarizes these results in comparison to their actual values.

6

Strategies Involving Options

The peak efficiency of knowledge and strategy is to make conflict unnecessary.

Sun Tzu

In this chapter, we examine the different portfolios, also called option strategies, that can be created by traders or investors using stocks and vanilla options on these stocks. In the first section, we will present two popular elementary hedging strategies using a stock and a single option on the same stock. Traders and fund managers holding stocks in their portfolios can use these strategies to get protection against their stock prices going down; we will see how they can do so by buying protective puts or writing covered calls. We then move on to option spreads and combinations, which are trading strategies combining different positions in call and put options; these strategies can be used for speculative purposes and enable investors to realize a profit that perfectly fits their market expectations, but can also be used for hedging purposes.

Options spreads are defined as positions in two or more options of the same type (two calls or two puts). A vertical spread is a strategy that consists of buying and selling two options of the same type with the same maturity date but having different strikes. Section 6.2 is dedicated to explaining and analysing the risks of vertical spreads, whereas the other types of spread trading strategies are presented in the following section. After doing so, we discuss how we can take speculative positions in the volatility of the underlying asset by adopting combinations. These strategies consist of buying (or selling) calls and puts with the same maturity date and on the same underlying stock. We finish this chapter with a discussion on volatility models to be applied to these trading strategies in order to fully understand their risks.

6.1   TRADITIONAL HEDGING STRATEGIES

6.1.1   Protective Puts

A protective put is a portfolio composed of a European put option and the underlying stock. Being long a protective put is equivalent to holding a share and a put option on the same share; this is one of the most popular trading strategies involving a single vanilla option on an underlying stock and the stock itself. In Figure 6.1 the solid line illustrates the profit from a long position in a protective put, whereas the dashed lines show the relationship between the profit and the stock price for the individual assets composing the portfolio. As the name suggests, the motivation for buying a protective put is mainly for hedging purposes. To enlighten the aim of this strategy, let's consider the case of a fund manager holding 10,000 stocks of Danone bought at an average price of 50 euros. He is worried about the market going down during the next 3 months but still does not want to sell his shares. The actual stock price of Danone is equal to 72 euros. The fund manager decides to buy 10,000 3-month European puts on Danone with a strike price of 68 euros. Each put premium is equal to 1.50 euros. Here, the trader is holding 10,000 protective puts on Danone that protect him from a big decrease in his shares' stock price. Indeed, the fund manager is assured to sell his shares for at least 66.5 euros (exercise price minus premium). In fact, buying protective puts

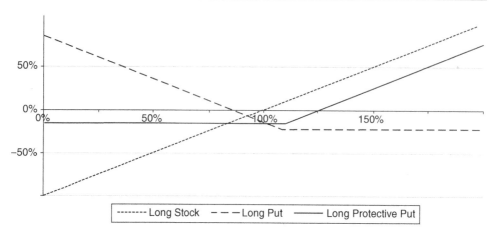

Figure 6.1 Profit patterns from holding a protective put.

enables an investor to fix the maximum loss he could potentially suffer if the market goes down. The maximum downside risk is then equal to $\text{Put}_{\text{premium}} + S_0 - K$, where K is the strike price.

On the other hand, an investor holding a large amount of stocks that have already increased can immediately sell his shares to realize the profit and be protected against future market risk. In this case, the transaction fees incurred for selling the whole portfolio can be high; the investor can then choose to buy an equivalent amount of puts (at a potentially lower fee) that enable him to lock a level of profit (protection against downside risk) and still have the possibility to realize additional return in the case of a favourable market. Buying protective puts serves as insurance against a market going down.

The payoff of a protective put is as follows:

$$\text{Protective Put}_{\text{payoff}}(K, T) = S(T) + \text{Put}_{\text{payoff}}(K, T)$$

and from this, we can easily compute the Greeks associated with protective puts and perfectly analyse the risks involved in trading such strategies. By taking derivatives both sides with respect to the stock price, we get the Delta of a protective put, which is equal to $1 + \Delta_{\text{Put}}(K, T)$. Therefore, one buying a protective put is long the stock price since the Delta of this strategy is always positive (its values fluctuate between 0 and 1). Also, the Vega and Gamma of a protective put are respectively equal to the Vega and Gamma of the put composing the strategy.

It is interesting to note that a protective put strategy is equivalent to buying a call option. Indeed, the profit patterns of a long position in a protective put emphasized in Figure 6.1 have the same general profit patterns as those discussed in Chapter 3 for a long call position. An easy way to understand where this result comes from is to look at the put–call parity explained in Chapter 3:

$$\text{Put}(K, T) + S(0) - D = \text{Call}(K, T) + K e^{-rT}$$

where $\text{Put}(K, T)$ and $\text{Call}(K, T)$ are, respectively, the premiums of a European put and call with strike K and maturity T, $S(0)$ is the stock price at time 0, r is the risk-free interest rate and D is the present value of the future expected dividends occurring during the life of the options. This equation shows that a long position in a protective put $(= \mathrm{Put}(K, T) + S(0))$ is equivalent to holding a call plus investing a cash amount of money $(= Ke^{-rT} + D)$ at the risk-free rate.

6.1.2 Covered Calls

A covered call is a portfolio that consists of holding a European call option and short selling the underlying stock. Its payoff is as follows:

$$\mathrm{Covered\,Call}_{\mathrm{payoff}}(K, T) = \mathrm{Call}_{\mathrm{payoff}}(K, T) - S(T)$$

Writing a covered call is another popular hedging strategy that is equivalent to holding a share and selling a European call option on the same share. This strategy is employed by fund managers because it enables them not only to get protection from a small decrease in the stock price, but also to increase their portfolio returns in the form of income from the option's premiums. In Figure 6.2 the solid line illustrates the profit from a short position in a covered call, whereas the dashed lines show the relationship between the profit and the stock price for the individual assets composing the portfolio. Selling covered calls is a strategy that can be used in many situations. First, consider a trader holding some shares of a specific company and who strongly believes that the stock price of this company will increase in the long term. She is not willing to sell those shares; however, she thinks that the stock price is going to decline in the short term. She decides to sell short maturity European calls on these underlyings and use their premium to compensate for the potential expected stock price decrease. In this case, if expectations are correct and the stock price slightly goes down in the short term, the sold calls are not exercised by the buyer and the negative stock performance is balanced by the premium of the calls. Alternatively, if the stock price goes up significantly enough to make the call finish in-the-money, she will have to deliver the stocks she is holding. She wants to hold the stocks in her portfolio; therefore, as soon as the stock price becomes higher than the strike, she rolls-over the position by buying an identical call and issuing another call on the same underlying with the same maturity date but with a higher strike.

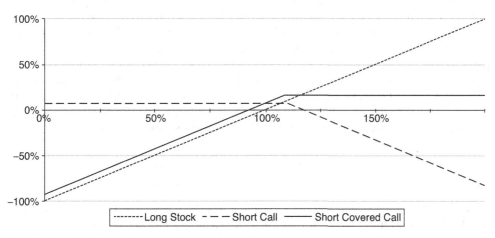

Figure 6.2 Profit patterns from writing a covered call.

Here, we can see that writing covered calls is not a pure hedging strategy since it only provides the investor with a small insurance against a stock price decline. Figure 6.2 shows that selling covered calls does not provide protection against a significant decrease in stock prices. The premium earned is then too small compared to the loss caused by a market crash. If one wants to generate significant income from selling options, he has to sell call options with lower strike. But in the case the market goes up, the investor's maximum profit is locked to $\text{Call}_{\text{premium}} + K - S_0$. This is why traders tend to roll-over their positions; but even rolling-over can be difficult to achieve for many reasons linked to transaction fees or the call option's liquidity. Many institutions manage their pension funds by taking short positions in covered calls to increase their return in stable markets where volatility is low. If the stock price fluctuates slightly, the out-of-the-money calls are not exercised and the calls' prices provide the fund managers holding shares with additional income. If we rearrange the put–call parity, we get the following result:

$$\text{Covered Call}(K, T) = \text{Put}(K, T) - [K e^{-rT} + D]$$

Here, we can see that writing a covered call with strike K and maturity T is equivalent to selling a European put option with the same strike and maturity, and investing an amount of cash ($= K e^{-rT} + D$) at the risk-free interest rate. This result can also be deducted from the profit patterns of a short position in a covered call, emphasized in Figure 6.2, which are similar to those discussed in Chapter 3 for a short put position. Therefore, a trader selling a covered call is then subject to the same risks involved in selling the equivalent put option. The seller of a covered call is then long the stock price since the Delta of a covered call is equal to the Delta of the equivalent put (its values vary between -1 and 0). Also, the Vega and Gamma of a covered call are respectively equal to the Vega and Gamma of the call composing the strategy. If volatility decreases, the price of the covered call decreases, and one writing covered calls is then short volatility.

6.2   VERTICAL SPREADS

6.2.1   Bull Spreads

Bull spreads are the most popular vertical spread strategies and correspond to a bullish view on the market. Investors use bull spreads when they believe an underlying asset value is going to increase above a specific level K_1 but will not be able to reach a level K_2 (with $K_2 > K_1$). In this case, investors are willing to capture the positive performance of the underlying asset and pay a smaller premium for this option; bull spread strategies answer this scenario perfectly.

A bull spread strategy can be constructed using call options (bullish call spread) or put options (bullish put spread). Let's first examine the case of bull call spreads that consist of buying a call with strike K_1 and selling a call on the same underlying with strike K_2 higher than K_1. Both options have the same maturity T. The bull call spread payoff is as follows:

$$\text{Bull Call Spread}_{\text{payoff}} = \begin{cases} 0 & \text{if } S_T \leq K_1 \\ S_T - K_1 & \text{if } K_1 < S_T < K_2 \\ K_2 - K_1 & \text{if } S_T \geq K_2 \end{cases}$$

Figure 6.3 shows the profit that can be made by holding a bull spread strategy using calls struck at 80% and 120%. The dashed lines indicate the profits from the positions in calls taken separately; the profit from the whole bull spread strategy (shown by the solid line) constitutes

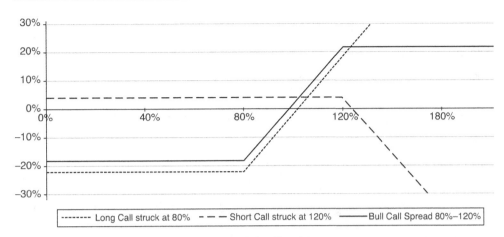

Figure 6.3 Profit patterns from a bull spread using call options.

the sum of the two profits (shown by the dashed lines). Note that holding a bullish call spread implies buying a call at a price higher than the premium of the sold call since both calls have the same maturity and K_1 is lower than K_2. Therefore, holding a bull call spread requires an initial investment equal to Call $(K_1, T)-$ Call (K_2, T). A bull spread strategy limits not only the downside risk but also the upside since the maximum payoff that can be received by the holder is equal to $K_2 - K_1$. The profit patterns shown in Figure 6.3 are obtained by deducting the price of the bull spread from the strategy payoff.

The bull call spread is considered to be a double-sided hedging strategy. The price received from selling the call with strike K_2 is used to partially finance the premium paid for the call struck at K_1. Consequently, the investor long the call with the lower strike price hedges the risk of losing the entire premium. On the other hand, the financial risk associated with the written call is reduced by the long call position. If the call with the higher strike price expires in-the-money, the loss incurred is offset through exercising the purchased call with the lower strike. However, it is important to note that the written call limits the maximum profit for the strategy to $K_2 - K_1$.

A bull spread strategy can also be realized by combining a short position in a put struck at K_2 and a long position in a put struck at K_1. Both puts are on the same underlying asset and have the same maturity date. The resulting portfolio is called a bull put spread. The strategy is said to be bullish since the idea is to gain profit from selling a first put struck at K_2 and expecting the stock price to increase. Then the seller limits the downside risk by buying a put with a lower strike. The payoff of a bull put spread is given by

$$\text{Bull Put Spread}_{\text{payoff}} = \begin{cases} K_1 - K_2 & \text{if } S_T \leq K_1 \\ S_T - K_2 & \text{if } K_1 < S_T < K_2 \\ 0 & \text{if } S_T \geq K_2 \end{cases}$$

The solid line in Figure 6.4 shows the profit from a bull spread strategy realized by combining a short position in a put struck at 120% and a long position in a put struck at 80%. The profit patterns given by this figure are similar to those shown in Figure 6.3. However, it is important to note that the payoff of a bull put spread is always negative, whereas the payoff of a bull call spread is always positive. This is due to the fact that an investor holding a bull put spread

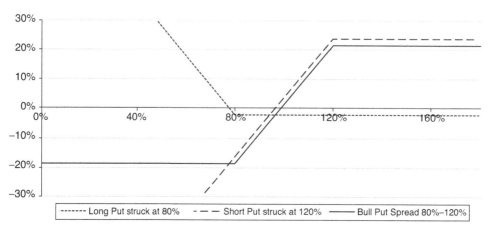

Figure 6.4 Profit patterns from a bull spread using put options.

strategy is in fact selling a product and receives a global premium equal to Put (K_2, T)− Put (K_1, T). This represents the maximum profit he could get and occurs if the underlying stock price ends above K_2. Otherwise, the investor holding a bullish put spread strategy starts losing money, which is why the payoff is negative. On the other hand, an investor performing a bull spread strategy using call options is buying a product at a price Call(K_1) − Call(K_2) and starts to get paid (positive payoff) when the price of the underlying stock increases. We can then conclude that a bull spread strategy can be achieved through buying bullish call spreads or selling bullish put spreads.

Concerning the risks involved in trading bull spreads, it is crucial to understand these strategies because they are used as components for more sophisticated structured products (described further in this book) such as capped cliquets or other payoffs involving digitals. To make it simple, we will base our risk analysis on the case of bullish call spreads. Indeed, a bull call spread and a bull put spread involve the same risks. Figure 6.5 shows the Delta of a call spread composed of a long position in a call struck at 80% and a short position in a call struck at 120%, with respect to the underlying stock price. The shape of the curve reminds us of the

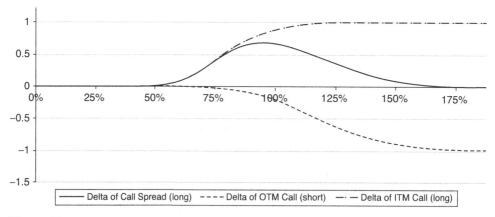

Figure 6.5 The Delta of an 80–120% call spread and Deltas of the two calls that form this call spread.

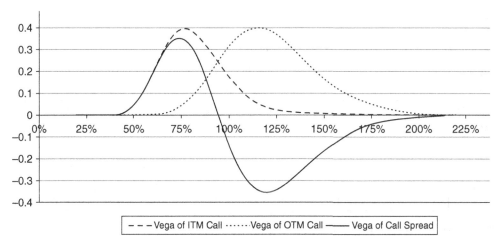

Figure 6.6 The Vegas of an 80–120% call spread and the two calls. Being long the 80–120% call spread means being long the 80% strike call and short the 120%. As is clear in the graph, the Vega of the call spread is the difference between the two Vegas as we are long the Vega of the 80% call and short volatility on the 120% call.

shape of the Gamma of vanilla options analysed in Chapter 5. Also note that the Delta of a bull call spread is always positive, which proves that the holder of the bull spread strategy is always long the stock price. The strategy is indeed bullish since a higher stock price increases the value of the bull spread.

The Gamma and Vega of bull call spreads are more difficult to manage since their sign changes on the basis of movement in the underlying's price. The point at which the Vega of a call spread changes sign is around $(K_1 + K_2)/2$. If the stock price is below this breakeven point, the Vega of a call spread is positive and it becomes negative for stock prices above this point. The Vega of a bull call spread 80–120% is illustrated against the spot in Figure 6.6.

As is clear in the graph, the Vega of the bull call spread is the difference between the two Vegas as one is long the Vega of the 80% call and short volatility on the 120% call. In the case of a flat forward, meaning the zero dividends and rates assumption, the Vega changes sign at the 100% point. In the general case, the Vega changes sign around the forward, which we note could be several percent away from the 100% ATM point. Traders have to be cautious when managing the Vega of call spreads, especially around the forward.

As for the skew effect on the bull spread strategy, buying a bull call spread implies buying a call with a lower strike K_1 and selling a call with a higher strike K_2. Because of the skew, the call struck at K_1 is priced with a volatility σ_1 that is higher than the volatility σ_2 linked to the call struck at K_2. Taking into account the skew effect means that the holder of a bull call spread buys a call with an expensive volatility and sells a call with a cheap volatility. Therefore, skew makes the bull spread more expensive; the buyer of the spread is long skew.

6.2.2 Bear Spreads

Bear spreads are vertical spread strategies that have a similar payoff mechanism compared to bull spreads but correspond to a bearish view on the market. Investors use bear spreads when they believe an underlying asset value is going to decrease below a specific level K_2 but will

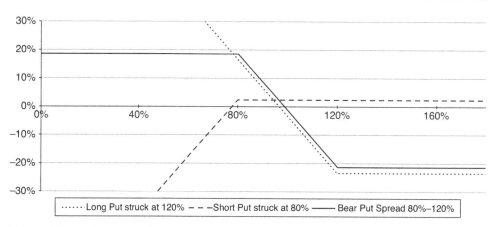

Figure 6.7   Profit patterns of a bear spread using put options.

not be lower than another level K_1 (with $K_2 > K_1$). Investors are then willing to capture the moderate negative performance of the underlying asset and pay a smaller premium for this option.

As is the case for bull spreads, a bear spread strategy can be constructed using call or put options. Let's first examine the case of bear put spreads which consist of buying a put with strike K_2 and selling a put on the same underlying with strike K_1 lower than K_2. Here, we are still dealing with vertical spreads, so both options have the same maturity T. The bear put spread payoff is as follows:

$$\text{Bear Put Spread}_{\text{payoff}} = \begin{cases} K_2 - K_1 & \text{if } S_T \leq K_1 \\ K_2 - S_T & \text{if } K_1 < S_T < K_2 \\ 0 & \text{if } S_T \geq K_2 \end{cases}$$

Figure 6.7 shows the profit that could be made by performing a bear spread strategy using puts struck at 80% and 120%. The dashed lines indicate the profits from the positions in calls taken separately; the profit from the whole bear spread strategy shown by the solid line constitutes the sum of the two profits given by the dashed lines. Note that holding a bearish put spread implies buying a put at a price higher than the premium of the sold put since both puts have the same maturity and K_1 is lower than K_2. Therefore, holding a bear put spread requires an initial investment equal to $\text{Put}(K_2, T) - \text{Put}(K_1, T)$.

A bear spread strategy limits not only the upside risk but also the downside since the maximum payoff that can be received by the holder is equal to $K_2 - K_1$. The profit patterns shown in Figure 6.7 are obtained by deducting the price of the bear spread from the strategy payoff. The premium received from selling the lower strike put offsets the premium paid for the put with the higher strike. Thus, the risk associated with losing the premium paid for the long put is (partially) reduced and the position hedged.

On the other hand, a bear spread strategy can also be realized by combining a long position in a call struck at K_2 and a short position in a call struck at K_1, both calls being on the same underlying asset and having the same maturity date. The resulting portfolio, called a bear call spread, is said to be bearish since it is based on the idea of making profit from selling a first call struck at K_2 and expecting the underlying stock to go down. Then the seller limits the upside risk by buying a call with a lower strike. The payoff of a bear call spread is given by

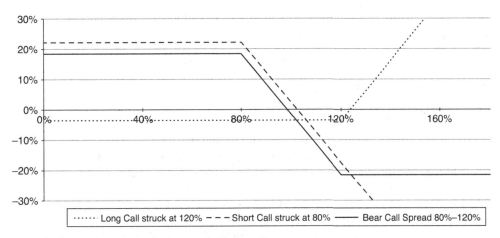

Figure 6.8 Profit patterns of a bear spread using call options.

the following formula:

$$\text{Bear Call Spread}_{\text{payoff}} = \begin{cases} 0 & \text{if } S_T \leq K_1 \\ K_1 - S_T & \text{if } K_1 < S_T < K_2 \\ K_1 - K_2 & \text{if } S_T \geq K_2 \end{cases}$$

The solid line in Figure 6.8 shows the profit from a bear spread strategy realized by combining a long position in a call struck at 120% and a short position in a call struck at 80%. The profit patterns given by this figure are similar to those shown in Figure 6.7. However, it is important to note that the payoff of a bear call spread is always negative whereas the payoff of a bear put spread is always positive. This is due to the fact that an investor implementing a bear call spread strategy is in fact selling a financial product and receives a global premium equal to $\text{Call}(K_1, T) - \text{Call}(K_2, T)$. This amount represents the maximum profit he could get and it occurs if the underlying stock price finishes below K_1. Otherwise, the investor holding a bearish call spread strategy starts losing money, which is why the payoff is negative. On the other hand, an investor performing a bear spread strategy using puts is buying a product at a price $\text{Put}(K_2) - \text{Put}(K_1)$ and starts to get paid (positive payoff) when the price of the underlying stock decreases. We can then conclude that a bear spread strategy can be achieved through buying bearish put spreads or selling bearish call spreads.

As for the risks involved in trading bear spreads, to keep it simple we will base our risk analysis on the case of bear put spreads. First, let's analyse the Delta of a bear put spread:

$$\text{Bear Put Spread} = \text{Put}(K_2, T) - \text{Put}(K_1, T)$$

So, taking the first derivative with respect to S, we get:

$$\Delta_{\text{Bear Put Spread}} = \Delta_{\text{Put}(K_2,T)} - \Delta_{\text{Put}(K_1,T)}$$

And since $\Delta_{\text{Put}(K,T)} = \Delta_{\text{Call}(K,T)} - 1$, then:

$$\Delta_{\text{Bear Put Spread}} = \Delta_{\text{Call}(K_2,T)} - \Delta_{\text{Call}(K_1,T)} = -\Delta_{\text{Bull Call Spread}}$$

Keeping in mind the Delta analysis of a bull call spread described in the previous section, we can see that the Delta of a bear put spread is always negative; which proves that one holding a bear spread strategy is always short the stock price. The strategy is indeed bearish since a lower stock price increases the value of the bear spread portfolio. Similarly, after deriving the bear put spread with respect to σ, we get:

$$\text{Vega}_{\text{Bear Put Spread}} = \text{Vega}_{\text{Put}(K_2,T)} - \text{Vega}_{\text{Put}(K_1,T)}$$

And since $\text{Vega}_{\text{Put}(K,T)} = \text{Vega}_{\text{Call}(K,T)}$ we have

$$\text{Vega}_{\text{Bear Put Spread}} = \text{Vega}_{\text{Call}(K_2,T)} - \text{Vega}_{\text{Call}(K_1,T)} = -\text{Vega}_{\text{Bull Call Spread}}$$

The values of Gamma and Vega of bear put spreads are the opposite values of Gamma and Vega of bull call spreads (with equivalent strikes) analysed in the previous section. Here again, traders have to be cautious when managing the Vega of call spreads because they can change sign as the underlying moves.

As for the skew effect, buying a bear put spread implies buying a put with a strike K_2 and selling a put with a lower strike K_1. In the presence of an implied volatility skew, the put struck at K_1 is priced with a volatility σ_1 that is higher than the volatility σ_2 linked to the put struck at K_2. Taking into account the skew effect means that the holder of a bear put spread buys a put with a cheap volatility and sells a put with an expensive volatility. Therefore, skew decreases the price of a bear spread.

6.3 OTHER SPREADS

6.3.1 Butterfly Spreads

The butterfly spread is considered to be a neutral vanilla option-trading strategy. It is a combination of a bull spread and a bear spread with the same maturity. The butterfly spread offers a limited profit at a limited amount of risk. There are three strike prices specifying the butterfly spread and it can be constructed using calls or puts. A butterfly spread can be bought by an investor who believes that the underlying asset will not move by much in either direction of the spot by the expiry of the options.

Using call options, a butterfly spread constitutes a long position in a call struck at a lower price, a short position in two calls with intermediate strikes, and long a call struck at a higher price. Butterfly spreads are adapted to scenarios where the stock price matures around the intermediate strike. The payoff of a butterfly spread constructed using call options is as follows:

$$\text{Butterfly Spread}_{\text{payoff}} = \begin{cases} 0 & \text{if } S_T \leq K_1 \\ S_T - K_1 & \text{if } K_1 \leq S_T \leq K_2 \\ K_3 - S_T & \text{if } K_2 \leq S_T \leq K_3 \\ 0 & \text{if } S_T \geq K_3 \end{cases}$$

assuming $K_2 = (K_1 + K_3)/2$.

Figure 6.9 shows the profit from a long butterfly that can be constructed by buying one lower striking in-the-money call at 60%, writing two at-the-money calls and buying another higher striking out-of-the-money call at 140%. One buying this butterfly spread receives a positive payoff and pays an initial investment equal to:

$$\text{Butterfly Spread}_{\text{premium}} = C(K - \epsilon) - 2C(K) + C(K + \epsilon)$$

where $C(K)$ is the price of a vanilla call with maturity T and struck at K.

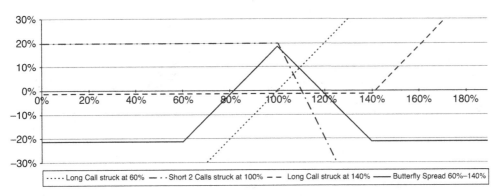

Figure 6.9 Profit patterns of a butterfly spread 60–140% using call options.

The profit patterns drawn in Figure 6.9 are obtained by deducting the butterfly spread premium from its payoff. Note that the maximum payoff occurs when $S_T = K$ and is equal to ϵ. We could give the example of an investor who believes the S&P 500 index will end exactly 5% below its level today in a year from now, so this strategy allows us to make the butterfly spread around the strike $K = 95\%$ and pick an epsilon that reflects how much we want to pay for this structure. In this case, a butterfly spread becomes a bearish product and most importantly, as discussed in Chapter 4, this specific three-option combination enables the holder to capture the curvature of the implied volatility skew. We should also note that the holder of a butterfly spread (Figure 6.10) is bearish on the volatility of the underlying. Low volatility expectations translate to low expectations in the movement in the underlying and, if realized, the butterfly spread will make a profit. This structure can also be replicated using put options as follows:

$$\text{Butterfly Spread}_{\text{premium}} = P(K - \epsilon) - 2P(K) + P(K + \epsilon)$$

where $P(K)$ is the price of a vanilla put with a maturity T and struck at K. That is to say, the holder of a butterfly spread is long the $K - \epsilon$ strike put, short two puts at strike K and long another put at strike $K + \epsilon$.

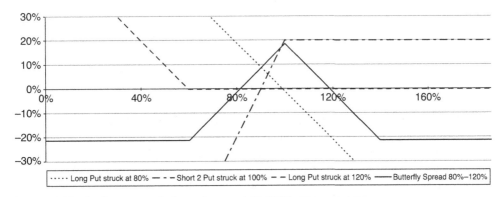

Figure 6.10 Profit patterns of a butterfly spread 80–120% using put options.

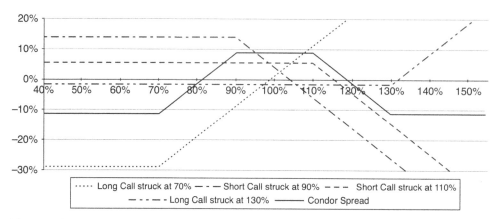

Figure 6.11   Profit patterns of a condor spread using call options.

6.3.2   Condor Spreads

The condor spread is similar to the butterfly spread strategy except that it involves four different strike prices, compared to the three strikes of a butterfly spread. This strategy can be constructed using calls or puts. Like butterfly spreads, condor spreads are entered when the investor thinks that the underlying stock will not rise or fall much by expiration, again bearish on the volatility of the underlying. Using calls, a condor spread constitutes a long position in a call struck at a lower price K_1, a short position in a call with a first intermediate strike K_2, a short position in a call with a second intermediate strike K_3, and long a call struck at a higher price K_4. Condor spreads are adapted to scenarios where the stock price matures around the intermediate strikes. The payoff of a condor spread constructed using call options is as follows:

$$\text{Condor Spread}_{\text{payoff}} = \begin{cases} 0 & \text{if } S_T \leq K_1 \\ S_T - K_1 & \text{if } K_1 \leq S_T \leq K_2 \\ K_2 - K_1 & \text{if } K_2 \leq S_T \leq K_3 \\ K_4 - S_T & \text{if } K_3 \leq S_T \leq K_4 \\ 0 & \text{if } S_T \geq K_4 \end{cases}$$

Note that $K_2 - K_1 = K_3 - K_2 = K_4 - K_3 = 2\epsilon$. One buying this condor spread receives a positive payoff and pays an initial investment equal to:

$$\text{Condor Spread}_{\text{premium}} = C(K - 3\epsilon) - C(K - \epsilon) - C(K + \epsilon) + C(K + 3\epsilon)$$

where $C(K)$ is the price of a vanilla call with a maturity T and struck at K.

Figure 6.11 shows the profit from a long condor spread can be constructed by buying one lower striking in-the-money call at 70%, writing two calls struck at 90% and 110% and buying another higher striking out-of-the-money call at 130%. Note that the maximum payoff is equal to 2ϵ and occurs when $K_2 \leq S_T \leq K_3$. The condor spread strategy is difficult to achieve since the holder has to trade in four different options simultaneously.

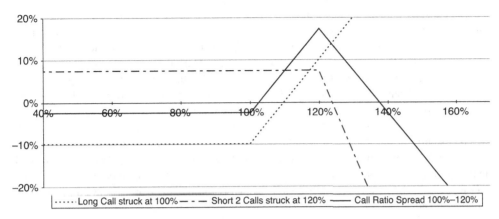

Figure 6.12   Profit patterns of a call ratio spread 100–120%.

6.3.3   Ratio Spreads

The ratio spread is a strategy obtained by combining different quantities of bought and sold calls, or bought and sold puts. Note that the maturities of the negotiated options are still the same. There are four kinds of ratio spreads:

- *Call ratio spread*: Long n calls struck at K_1 and short m calls struck at K_2
- *Call ratio backspread*: Short n calls struck at K_1 and long m calls struck at K_2
- *Put ratio spread*: Long n puts struck at K_2 and short m puts struck at K_1
- *Put ratio backspread*: Short n puts struck at K_2 and long m puts struck at K_1

where $m > n$ and $K_2 > K_1$. Figure 6.12 presents the profit generated at maturity from a call ratio spread strategy. The latter is composed of a long at-the-money call position in the Nikkei index combined with a short position in two out-of-the-money calls on the same underlying struck at 120%. At maturity, if the Nikkei performed negatively, the holder of the call ratio spread would have lost a premium equal to Call(100%, T) $-$ 2 Call(120%, T). Here, the investor is willing to capture the positive performance of the Nikkei but doesn't believe the underlying index will reach 120% of its initial value at maturity date. The premium is much lower than the at-the-money call since it is partially offset by the two sold calls. But in the case where this market scenario is not realized and the Nikkei performs above 120%, the investor is not protected against the upside risk and could lose much more than the initial investment required by the ratio spread. This strategy, which is one of the more complex spreads, is only adapted to a slight increase of the market. The investor is protected against a fallen market but the upside risk remains.

6.3.4   Calendar Spreads

Up to now we have assumed that all the options used to create the spread strategies expire at the same maturity date. A calendar spread strategy, also called horizontal or time spread, is achieved using simultaneous long and short positions in options of the same type (both calls or both puts) of the same strike, but different expiration dates.

Using calls, a calendar spread strategy is constructed through a long position in a call option that matures at T_2 and a short position in a call with maturity T_1 lower than T_2. Both options have the same strike price K. All parameters being constant, we know that the price of a call option increases with maturity. This means that performing a calendar spread strategy requires an initial cost equal to $\text{Call}(K, T_2) - \text{Call}(K, T_1)$. Note that the value of this strategy is in fact equal to the difference between both options' time values since the intrinsic values are the same at any point of time t.

If the investor has a bullish view on the underlying asset and believes the stock price will rise consistently in the long term (which explains why he buys the call maturing at T_2), the chosen strike will then be higher than the initial stock price. Also, the investor believes that the underlying value will still be below the strike in the short term. So he buys a call expiring at T_1 to partially finance the premium paid for the first call. This results in holding a bullish calendar spread.

A neutral calendar spread is said to be a spread with a strike close to the current stock price, whereas constructing the spread with in-the-money calls results in a bearish time spread. Note that calendar spreads can also be created by buying a long-maturity put option and selling a short-maturity put option. The calendar spread strategy can also be used to take advantage of the volatility spread between the two options. And since the time value of the option with the lower maturity decreases faster than the longer maturity option, the investor could be willing to close his time spread position by selling at a higher price than the initial cost.

6.4   OPTION COMBINATIONS

6.4.1   Straddles

The straddle is one of the most common combinations and consists of a long position in a call and a long position in a put on the same underlying asset and having the same strike price K and maturity T. K is often chosen around the actual underlying price. The payoff of the straddle occurs at time T and is described below:

$$\text{Straddle}_{\text{payoff}} = \begin{cases} K - S_T & \text{if } S_T \leq K \\ S_T - K & \text{if } S_T > K \end{cases}$$

The straddle constitutes an interesting strategy for an investor who expects a volatile and large move in the price of the underlying asset, although the direction of this move is unknown. Holding a straddle is characterized by an unlimited profit potential and a maximum loss limited to the net initial debit required to establish the position. The premium paid for creating a straddle is equal to:

$$\text{Straddle} = C(K, T) + P(K, T)$$

where $C(K, T)$ and $P(K, T)$ are, respectively, the prices of a vanilla call and a vanilla put with maturity T and struck at K.

The seller of the straddle gets an initial premium to bear the risks linked to a large move in the stock price. Indeed, the speculative straddle seller expects implied volatility to decrease. Here, the potential loss is unlimited and comes from the fact that the seller is short a call which is always a dangerous position if unhedged. The profit is positive if S_T is inside the range $[K - \text{Premium}; K + \text{Premium}]$; and the maximum profit occurs when S_T is equal to K.

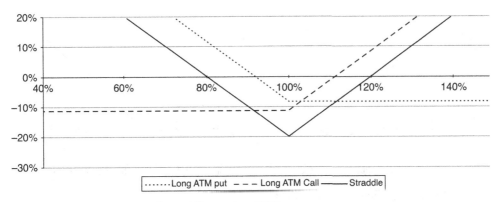

Figure 6.13 Profit patterns of a straddle struck at 100%.

The solid line in Figure 6.13 shows the profit from a straddle realized by combining a long position in a 1-year at-the-money European call on Alpha and a long position in a 1-year at-the-money put on the same underlying. This strategy is adapted to an investor who feels that the stock price of Alpha will move significantly up or down in the next year. Therefore, he pays a premium equal to 19.7% to profit from his expected scenario. Note that the breakeven points are equal to $100\% - 19.7\% = 80.3\%$ and $100\% + 19.7\% = 119.7\%$.

Also, put–call parity says that you can enter into a straddle by buying a call and a put, or two calls and sell a stock or two puts and buy the stock. Note that a straddle is very sensitive to volatility. Indeed, the Gamma and Vega of a straddle are positive and two times higher than the Gamma and Vega of a call. The holder of a straddle is long volatility since this parameter increases the value of the strategy. On the initial date, the Delta of the straddle is also close to zero: the put and the call Deltas cancel each other. At the money the Delta of the straddle is not exactly zero, but close. We see this in more detail in Chapter 16 where we describe trading in straddles as a traditional method for trading volatility, even though this method is trumped by newer volatility products described therein.

6.4.2 Strangles

The holder of a strangle is long a call struck at K_2 and long a put struck at K_1 lower than K_2. Both options have the same maturity T and are often out-of-the-money. The payoff of the strangle is as follows:

$$\text{Strangle}_{\text{payoff}} = \begin{cases} K_1 - S_T & \text{if } S_T \leq K_1 \\ 0 & \text{if } K_1 \leq S_T \leq K_2 \\ S_T - K_2 & \text{if } S_T > K_2 \end{cases}$$

As is the case for straddles, strangles are combinations adapted to investors expecting volatility of the underlying stock to increase. Holding a strangle is characterized by an unlimited profit potential and a maximum loss limited to the initial price equal to:

$$\text{Strangle}(K_1, K_2; T) = C(K_2, T) + P(K_1, T)$$

An investor would prefer to buy a strangle instead of a straddle if he believes there will be a large stock move by maturity, i.e. the investor is even more bullish on volatility. The investor

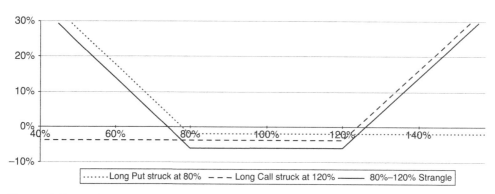

Figure 6.14   Profit patterns of an 80–120% strangle.

would realize a better profit from this strategy since the premium is much lower than the one paid for a straddle. The profit would be negative when the final underlying stock price lies in the range $[K_1 - \text{Premium}; K_2 + \text{Premium}]$. Figure 6.14 shows the profit that could be made by holding a strangle strategy using a call struck at 120% and a put struck at 80%. Both options expire in 1 year and the underlying stock is Vodafone. The dashed lines indicate the profits from the positions in the call and the put taken separately; the profit from the whole strangle strategy shown by the solid line constitutes the sum of the two profits given by the dashed lines. This strategy is interesting for an investor who feels that the stock price of Vodafone will move significantly up or down in the next year. Therefore, he pays a cheap premium equal to 5.9% to profit from his expected scenario. Note that the breakeven points are equal to $80\% - 5.9\% = 74.1\%$ and $120\% + 5.9\% = 125.9\%$.

Strangles also enable investors to trade in volatility. It is interesting to note that a strangle is less sensitive to volatility than a straddle. Indeed, the Vega of out-of-the-money options is lower than the Vega of at-the-money options. Then, the Vega of a strangle, which is the sum of the Vegas of the options composing the strategy, is lower than the Vega of a straddle. The holder of a strangle is long volatility since this parameter increases the value of the strategy.

6.5   ARBITRAGE FREEDOM OF THE IMPLIED VOLATILITY SURFACE

In practice we can only observe European option implied volatilities, of a fixed maturity, at a finite set of strikes. Let's label these strikes as $K_1, K_2, \ldots, K_m$. It is also the case that we can only obtain these skews for a finite set of maturities, and let's call these $T_1, T_2, \ldots, T_n$. Even if the strikes or maturities happened to be very close, the following criteria must be met in order for the surface to be arbitrage free. The reason we place this section in this chapter is because, given a finite set of European options, checking the surface to be arbitrage free involves some of the options strategies described in this chapter.

Firstly, for all maturities T in the above set, there cannot be any negative call spreads. If there was a negative call spread this would imply an obvious arbitrage. This is equivalent to writing that for all j such that $1 \leq j \leq m - 1$ we must have

$$C(K_j, T_i) - C(K_{j+1}, T_i) \geq 0, \quad i = 1, 2, \ldots, n$$

An additional restriction on such spreads is that if we were to divide by the difference in strikes, we must have, for all j where $1 \leq j \leq m - 1$ that

$$\frac{C(K_j, T_i) - C(K_{j+1}, T_i)}{K_{j+1} - K_j} \leq 1, \quad i = 1, 2, \ldots, n$$

As we will see later, one can approximate a binary payoff using a call spread, and the use of the two closest strikes must yield a value less than 1 for these call prices to be arbitrage free. To be clear, we use the reference to call prices and implied volatilities interchangeably as they imply the same thing: each call option has an implied volatility taken from the surface depending on its strike and maturity.

The other consideration is the values of calendar spreads, which too must be positive. So, for all j such that $1 \leq j \leq m$

$$C(K_j, T_{i+1}) - C(K_j, T_i) \geq 0, \quad i = 1, 2, \ldots, n - 1$$

For a more rigorous discussion we refer the reader to Overhaus *et al.* (2007) and Carr and Madan's article on the subject (2005).

In addition, all butterfly spreads must be positive; for all j where $2 \leq j \leq m - 1$, we must have

$$C(K_{j-1}, T_i) - \frac{K_{j+1} - K_{j-1}}{K_{j+1} - K_j} C(K_j, T_i) + \frac{K_j - K_{j-1}}{K_{j+1} - K_j} C(K_{j+1}, T_i) \geq 0 \quad i = 1, 2, \ldots, n.$$

The conclusion of this is that a set of European options, specified as above, will be arbitrage free if all these conditions are met. The market for European options is liquid and we do not expect to find simple arbitrages as such in the market data; however, we should concern ourselves that any model we do use to capture skew observes these conditions or it will not be arbitrage free. The failure of a model's calibration to meet these conditions is a solid criterion to reject such calibration. Any interpolation between the implied volatilities of two consecutive strikes in the above set must also observe these conditions to be arbitrage free.

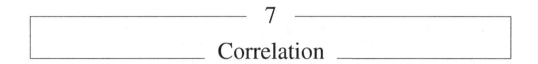

7

Correlation

The web of our life is of a mingled yarn, good and ill together.

William Shakespeare

Many payoffs that exist today are based upon the performance of multiple assets. When an option derives its value from the price of multiple assets, the relationships between these assets become important. Correlation gives us the strength and direction of a linear relationship between different underlyings, and in this chapter we look at the properties of correlation, both realized and implied, together with their measurement and uses. We discuss the correlation risk appearing in multi-asset options and the implications on the pricing and hedging of these options. We see the impact of correlation on the variance of a weighted portfolio, and the required properties of correlation matrices of multiple assets.

Basket options, which can be considered the simplest of typical multi-asset options, are also discussed. These serve as excellent examples to combine the concepts of correlation with previously discussed concepts regarding options and volatility. Quanto options (short for quantity adjustment options) are also discussed. Quanto options are denominated in a currency other than the currency in which the underlying is traded. The chapter ends with a discussion of some methods for trading correlation.

7.1 MULTI-ASSET OPTIONS

The derivatives we have seen so far are all based on a single asset, that is, the payoffs are computed on the basis of the performance of only one underlying asset, and here we introduce multi-asset options. These provide exposure to more than one asset, whether to be used to hedge a position in multiple assets, or to serve as a speculative tool on multiple assets. The creation of such products stemmed from the concept of diversification, and there is now a wealth of products structured on multiple underlyings.

Diversification involves combining multiple assets within a portfolio. Pioneer Harry Markowitz published research on diversification and was awarded the Nobel prize in 1990 for his work (Markowitz, 1952). The central idea is that movements in one asset within a diverse portfolio have less impact on the portfolio and so diversification can lower the exposure to an individual asset. When combining assets of a similar type, the diversification is known as a horizontal diversification. An example of this would be a portfolio of various stocks in the S&P 500 index.

The first product that comes to mind is a call option on a basket of stocks, where the call option's payout at maturity is based on the performance of a (perhaps not equally weighted) basket of stocks (or indices, or both). By adding multiple assets to such a payoff one reduces the level of risk through diversification; the basket payoff's intricacies are discussed below. Although using multiple underlyings as such serves one purpose, we will also see dispersion payoffs in Chapters 8 and 9 where we make use of relationships between the underlying assets for different purposes – for example, yield enhancement or increased leverage.

In addition to all the previous considerations, we now deal with the extremely important concept of correlation and its effects because the value of a multi-asset option does not depend only on the underlying asset's implied volatilities but also on the correlations between these assets. As we saw in Chapter 4, market prices of liquid options can be used to infer the implied volatilities of different individual assets. These implied volatilities contain additional information about future volatility expectations that is not included in historical volatility, and in the multi-asset case we would ideally have a similar *implied correlation*, but we do not. The reason is simple: although we can obtain market quotes for liquid options on many single underlyings, and infer from these the implied volatilities, there is no liquid market for such products in the multi-asset case. Since we can only rarely infer an implied correlation, we must resort to other methods of deciding which correlation to use when pricing multi-asset derivatives. Correlations change dramatically through time, which makes the use of realized (historical) correlations unreliable, and management of correlation risk a difficult task.

Payoffs involving multi-asset options are sensitive to movements in the various underlyings and so the relationships between the underlyings, which are defined using correlations, have an impact on the hedging of any such options. Because such payoffs are non-linear functions in more than one variable, we have cross-Gamma effects. The cross-Gamma terms tell us how the Delta of the option w.r.t. one underlying is affected by a movement in another underlying, and also depend on how we define the correlations between these underlyings.

7.2 CORRELATION: MEASUREMENTS AND INTERPRETATION

7.2.1 Realized Correlation

Realized correlation is the analogy of realized volatility. This is also referred to as statistical and historical correlation. If we use historical data for two variables to compute the realized correlation, then this gives us the strength and direction of a linear relationship between the two variables.

Given two variables X and Y, the realized correlation between them is defined as:

$$\rho_{X,Y} = \frac{\text{Cov}(X,Y)}{\sqrt{\text{Var}(X)\text{Var}(Y)}} = \frac{E((X-\mu_X)(Y-\mu_Y))}{\sigma_X \sigma_Y} \tag{7.1}$$

where Cov is the covariance of X and Y, Var is the respective variance, μ_X and μ_Y are the respective means of X and Y and σ_X and σ_Y are the respective standard deviations of X and Y. This equates to

$$\rho_{X,Y} = \frac{E(XY) - E(X)E(Y)}{\sqrt{E(X^2) - E^2(X)}\sqrt{E(Y^2) - E^2(Y)}}$$

Given a times series of observations of two variables (assets), this formula for the correlation, written in terms of the values at each observation date i, can be computed as

$$\rho_{X,Y} = \frac{\sum_{i=1}^{n}(x_i - \overline{x})(y_i - \overline{y})}{\left[\sum_{i=1}^{n}(x_i - \overline{x})^2 \sum_{i=1}^{n}(y_i - \overline{y})^2\right]^{1/2}}$$

In practice, one computes the correlation between two assets using the two series of daily log returns, not the two series of prices. One can also use the standard returns $S(t_{i+1})/S(t_i) - 1$, and under normal market conditions and assuming there is sufficient data in the period over which the correlation is being computed, the difference can be ignored.

A statistical correlation computed as such will take on values between -1 and $+1$. A negative correlation indicates that, historically, as one variable has moved up the other has moved down. A positive correlation means that historically both variables have generally moved in the same direction. The cases of $\rho = +1$ and $\rho = -1$ indicate perfect positive and perfect negative correlation respectively. The case of zero correlation means the two variables move in a generally random manner comparatively.

Two things must be noted. Firstly, the use of the word 'historical' above is specific. When discussing financial assets, although a historical correlation implies a past relationship between the assets, the same relationship does not necessarily hold in the future. In fact, financial correlations change through time, and these fluctuations can be quite large. Secondly, we must stress that measuring correlation as such gives us information regarding the linear relationship between two variables. Two variables can, for example, have a historical correlation of zero, but not be independent.

When computing historical correlation using the formula above involving two series of data (see Figure 7.1), we must first settle a few things. Assume that we were computing the correlation between two assets for which we had daily price data for as long back as there were records. How far back would we compute the correlation? Assume we had, for example, correlation data dating 5 years back and we wanted to compute a time series of correlation to see how it changed through time. Would we use a rolling time frame of 1 year (and thus have a 4-year series for the correlation) or would we look at how the correlation changed through time based on a 2-year horizon? In addition to these, should we use the daily data or use perhaps data from every 3 days or weekly (5 days?).

To analyse the differences between all of these possibilities we make use of Figures 7.1, 7.2 and 7.3. Firstly, we note that these correlations change through time, and this will be the case for any correlation between financial assets. Table 7.1 gives the correlation between

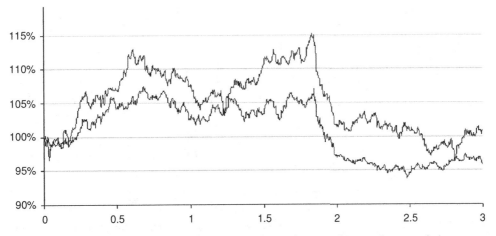

Figure 7.1 Two time series each involving a daily observation over the same 3-year period.

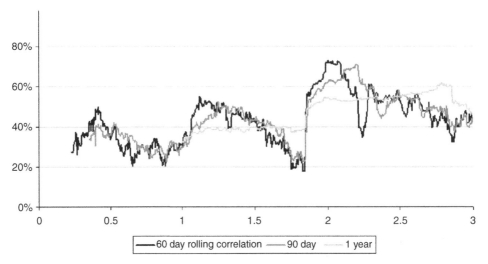

Figure 7.2   The time series of the 60-day, the 90-day and the 1-year rolling correlation. The correlation is computed based on the daily price of the two underlyings in Figure 7.1.

the assets in Figure 7.1. Here we can clearly see different regimes of correlation. During the second year the series appear more correlated compared to the other two. In particular, as both indices crash together before the 2-year point, correlations rise. During a market crash, the realized correlation between various assets could approach 1 and we can definitely witness stocks or indices realizing a correlation of above 90%. October 2008, in the wake of the crash of Lehman Brothers, is a good example.

The bottom row of Table 7.1 shows a significant difference between correlation computed on a daily basis or 3-day basis. In the example of Figure 7.1 this implies that the two series

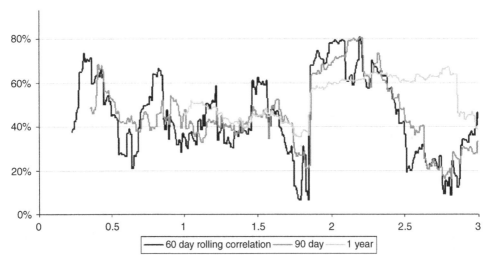

Figure 7.3   The time series of the 60-day, the 90-day and the 1-year rolling correlation. The correlation is computed on the basis of the price of the two underlyings in Figure 7.1 observed every 3 days.

Table 7.1   The realized correlation of the two series in Figure 7.1. The first row corresponds to the realized correlation between 0 and 1 year, the second between years 1 and 2, and the third between years 2 and 3. The first column uses daily observations, and the second uses the same data but only observed once per 3 days.

	Daily series	3-Day series
0 to 1 year	32.56%	46.38%
1 to 2 years	54.32%	59.47%
2 to 3 years	45.70%	38.42%
0 to 3 years	44.47%	88.09%

have the correlated individual daily shocks in the returns, but have far more correlated 3-day returns. This could be the example of the stocks of two quite similar companies.

Before the 2-year point in the time series of Figure 7.1, where we see both assets tank together, the realized correlation spikes upwards. This is what we observe in reality when a global financial crisis impacts all the major indices, such as what we observed in October 2008. In a sharp market decline as such, where indices and stocks all crash together, realized correlations can approach unity.

The most important factor is that the series used to compute the correlations should be aligned – that is, the set of points of the two time series used should have matching dates. This becomes problematic when considering assets in different markets; for example, different countries have different public holidays and one market may be closed while the other is open. The result is a mismatch in the two time series. To avoid these problems one should consider a 3-day or possibly weekly (5-day) series as the sampling points to compute the realized correlation.

We note that in order to obtain a more thorough view of the dependence of two or more variables than a linear relationship between them, one can use copulas. These will be discussed in detail in the context of pricing hybrid derivatives in Chapter 20.

7.2.2 Correlation Matrices

A correlation matrix $\mathbf{M}_\rho$ is a square matrix that describes the correlation among n variables. Let $S_1(t), S_2(t), \ldots, S_n(t)$ denote the time t prices of n assets, and $\rho_{i,j}$ the correlation between assets i and j, then the correlation matrix $\mathbf{M}_\rho$ is given by

$$\mathbf{M}_\rho = \begin{pmatrix} \rho_{11} & \rho_{12} & \cdots \\ \rho_{21} & \rho_{22} & \cdots \\ \vdots & \vdots & \ddots \end{pmatrix} = \begin{pmatrix} 1 & \rho_{12} & \cdots \\ \rho_{12} & 1 & \cdots \\ \vdots & \vdots & \ddots \end{pmatrix}$$

where the second matrix emphasizes two properties of correlation matrices: firstly, that the correlation between any asset and itself is 1, therefore all diagonal entries will be 1; secondly, that this matrix will be symmetric. As is clear from the definition in formula (7.1), the correlation between asset i and asset j must be the same as the correlation between asset j and asset i.

The correlation matrix is also necessarily positive definite. Once the values of the correlation matrix have been decided, the matrix must be checked to see that it satisfies this property. If the correlation matrix we assign is not positive definite, then it must be modified to make it positive definite – see, for example Higham (2002).

Given an index of n stocks or a basket of n assets $S_1, S_2, ..., S_n$ with respective weights $w_1, w_2, ..., w_n$, the realized index correlation (or realized basket correlation) is defined simply as the weighted average of the realized correlation matrix between the components, excluding the diagonal of 1's:

$$\rho_{\text{realized}} = \frac{\displaystyle\sum_{1 \leq i < j \leq n} w_i w_j \rho_{ij}}{\displaystyle\sum_{i < j} w_i w_j} \tag{7.2}$$

The weights w_i have the constraints

$$0 \leq w_i \leq 1 \text{ (for all } i = 1, 2, ..., n) \quad \text{and} \quad \sum_{i=0}^{n} w_i = 1 \tag{7.3}$$

ρ_{ij} is the realized correlation between components i and j, and again, although we may compute each of these separately, the overall matrix of correlation between the components of the index must be positive definite.

Assuming we have computed each of the pairwise correlations ρ_{ij} in the formula using data from a period $[0, T]$, then this represents the weighted-average realized correlation between the n components of the index for the period $[0, T]$. For this to have any meaning, the pairwise correlations must all be computed over the same period.

To compute the sensitivity of an option to a specific correlation pair, one can bump the correlation between them by 1%, check that the correlation matrix is still valid, and reprice the option to see the difference. If we want to see the effect of an overall move in correlations by 1%, we will need to bump the entire matrix of correlations to see what the effect would be on the price if the average correlation increases by 1%. The average (off-diagonal) correlation in such a correlation matrix of n assets is given by

$$\frac{2}{n(n-1)} \sum_{1 \leq i < j \leq n} \rho_{ij}$$

In this case we are interested in the off-diagonal elements as the diagonal elements remain 1 at all times, and increasing each of these elements by 1% will increase this average off-diagonal correlation by 1%. Again, before recomputing the price using the bumped correlation matrix, we should check that this matrix is still a valid correlation matrix. The difference in price (divided by the size of the shift) will give us the overall correlation sensitivity of the option.

7.2.3 Portfolio Variance

Now that we have seen some properties of correlation, we go back to the basis of Markowitz's portfolio theory (Markowitz, 1952) and look at a portfolio of n assets $S_1, S_2, ..., S_n$ to see the implications of correlation on the variance of this portfolio. This allows us to make a link between volatility and correlation.

Let R_i be the usual return of the ith asset. Then the expected return of the portfolio, R_P, is given by

$$E(R_P) = \sum_i w_i \, E(R_i)$$

where w_i is the weight of the ith asset in the portfolio, and the variance of the portfolio is given by

$$\sigma_P^2 = \sum_{1 \le i \le n} w_i^2 \sigma_i^2 + 2 \sum_{1 \le i < j \le n} w_i w_j \sigma_i \sigma_j \rho_{ij}$$

where σ_i is the volatility of the ith asset (and σ_i^2 its variance), and ρ_{ij} is the correlation between assets i and j. Written differently

$$\sigma_P^2 = \sum_{i=1}^{n} \sum_{j=1}^{n} w_i w_j \sigma_i \sigma_j \rho_{ij} \tag{7.4}$$

where $\rho_{ij} = 1$ for $i = j$.

To see the effect of correlation on portfolio variance, take the two-asset case as an example, and assume that both of two assets A and B have an expected rate of return of 5% and each a volatility of 20%. If the correlation between A and B is 0.4, then the above formula gives a volatility of 16.73% for the equally weighted portfolio in A and B. The 20 stock analogy involving a correlation of 0.2 and the same volatility of 30% for all will give an equally weighted portfolio variance of less than half the individual variances.

As long as the correlation in the above formula is less than 1, holding various assets that are not perfectly correlated in a portfolio will offer a reduced risk exposure to a specific asset.

7.2.4   Implied Correlation

Although there isn't an analogy of implied volatility for correlations, we can in practice still define an implied correlation. The usefulness of such implied correlation is subject to debate, but trying to find some method of implying correlations is necessary to say the least. The market for European options on pairs of underlyings or baskets is not liquid so we cannot extract an implied correlation between the underlyings from these prices. However, let us take the case of an index for which we have both European options on the index itself as well as on each of the underlyings composing the index. Then using market quotes, we can infer an implied correlation that is a measure of the dependence between the components of the index.

$$\rho_{\text{implied}}^{\text{index}} = \frac{\sigma_{\text{index}}^2 - \sum_{i=1}^{n} w_i^2 \sigma_i^2}{2 \sum_{1 \le i < j \le n} w_i w_j \sigma_i \sigma_j} \tag{7.5}$$

where n is the number of components, w_i is the ith component's weighting in the index, σ_{index} is the implied volatility of the index and σ_i is the implied volatility of the ith component of the index. In the literature, definitions of implied correlation such as this appear in Alexander (2001). To obtain the implied correlation over a T-day period, we must use the implied volatilities of options with time to maturity T. In this case we make use of ATM volatilities throughout; however, we discuss below the correlation skew that involves implied volatilities of different strikes.

To understand where this came from we go back to the variance of a portfolio and we regard the index as a portfolio of n assets with different weights.

$$\sigma_{\text{index}} = \sum_{i=1}^{n} w_i^2 \sigma_i^2 + 2 \sum_{1 \leq i < j \leq n} w_i w_j \sigma_i \sigma_j \rho_{i,j}$$

The implied correlation of an index is defined as the correlation ρ_{implied} that, when used in place of the $n(n-1)$ individual correlations $\rho_{i,j}$, will result in the same portfolio variance:

$$\sigma_{\text{index}} = \sum_{i=1}^{n} w_i^2 \sigma_i^2 + 2 \sum_{1 \leq i < j \leq n} w_i w_j \sigma_i \sigma_j \underbrace{\rho_{\text{implied}}^{\text{index}}}$$

In a portfolio or basket of stocks for which we apply this formula, all weights are assumed to be constant, whereas in the case of an index, the weights vary as the components of the index vary, thus making this an inexact definition.

However this does still have some implications and uses. Assume that we have a basket of stocks for which we wish to infer an implied correlation. Assume further that these stocks all belong to the same index. The idea is to follow a simple parameterization involving a coefficient λ which relates realized and implied correlations of the index, and in turn use this coefficient and also the realized correlations between the index components to infer specific implied correlations. Firstly, compute the realized correlation of the index in conjunction with formula (7.2), and the implied correlation using formula (7.5), then solve for λ in the equation

$$\rho_{\text{implied}}^{\text{index}} = \rho_{\text{realized}}^{\text{index}} + \lambda \left(1 - \rho_{\text{realized}}^{\text{index}}\right) \tag{7.6}$$

Now take two stocks A and B, both of which are in the same index I, for which we have liquid European options on both the index I and its components and, in turn, obtain the value of λ. With this we can then reapply formula (7.6) and solve for the left-hand side using the realized correlation of A and B on the right-hand side along with the index λ. Assume, for example, that the value of λ implied from the index is 10%, and the realized correlation between A and B was 40%, then using the formula we find an implied correlation of

$$40\% + 10\% \times (1 - 40\%) = 46\%$$

If the index λ was 25%, then this along with a realized correlation of 70% between A and B gives an implied correlation of 77.50%.

Section 7.5 discusses methods for trading correlation, and we will see that it is possible to trade an average implied correlation of index components. Thus, since this can potentially be hedged, using the implied index λ to infer implied correlations for basket subsets of an index will on average reflect the values of the implied correlations that cannot otherwise be inferred. In relevance to pricing, and since this average implied correlation can potentially be hedged, it makes sense that there is some form of implied correlation, and not realized correlation, in the case where there is similar exposure to the correlation pairs between many of the index constituents.

Sell-side desks of multi-asset options will typically be structurally short correlation. This is due to the fact that the sale of many of the multi-asset products we will see result in short positions in the correlations between the underlyings for the seller. The implied correlations seen above, in particular those computed using formula (7.6), will be higher than the realized correlation levels (assuming the implied λ is positive). In the case where realized correlation is higher than implied, one may want to sell correlation at a level at least equal to the realized correlation. Even in the case where the implied correlation is higher than the realized, the seller of a multi-asset option who is to assume upon the sale a negative position in the correlation, may want to increase the level slightly further. This will depend on three factors: firstly, the sensitivity of the option in question to the correlation parameter; secondly, the overall level to which the trader is already exposed to the correlations between the assets of this option; and, thirdly, the level to which the trader needs to be aggressive on the trade.

In the example of the Altiplano option of Chapter 15, the option has higher sensitivity to the correlations between the underlying assets, compared to the basket option described below where this sensitivity is lower. In some cases, such as options on the outperformance of one asset versus another (discussed in Chapter 9), the seller of the option will be long the correlation between the two assets. The decision will then be: At what level should we buy correlation? In all cases, the trader will need to manage unhedgeable or residual correlation risk using dynamic margins which depend on the notional size of the trades and the levels of correlation sensitivity.

7.2.5   Correlation Skew

Assume that we have two assets and that we have implied volatility skews for each of them, and also an implied volatility skew for vanilla options on the basket. To have an implied volatility skew for basket options means that, for a fixed maturity, we can find quotes for the prices of basket options with different strikes. If this were the case and we used formula (7.5) to imply a correlation at each strike where we used the implied volatility for the basket and the two constituents taken from each implied skew at this strike, would the implied correlation be the same? The answer is that it is not necessarily so. This curve, when plotted against the strikes used to compute it at each instance is known as a correlation skew.

Because we have an implied volatility skew for the index as well as each component, the concept of having one implied correlation parameter loses meaning and we may want to look at the correlation skew. Having such a skew can explain at least part of the increase in implied volatilities of OTM puts. The reason is that a lower strike holds a higher implied volatility, but also we expect in this region that if the index is tanking it means that its components are also tanking and thus their correlation will rise. Many exotic products have correlation skew exposure in the sense that as the underlying assets move, the correlation sensitivity can vary significantly.

If we parameterize the skew in the same manner as we did the implied volatility skew, we need the 90% strike, the ATM and the 110% strike options on the index and each component. We can then have a 90–100–110 parameterized correlation skew. To see the impact of correlation skew on a price one needs to use a model that knows about correlation skew in order that it shows this additional risk. This effect can be seen, for example, using a stochastic correlation model (generates a correlation skew). Or, to avoid adding additional model complexity, use the standard correlation and add a price adjustment by estimating the impact of the correlation skew on the price.

On this note, we point out the implying correlations as discussed above may also give rise to a correlation term structure. Using index and component option implied volatilities for different maturities may imply different levels or correlations. What is most important is that whatever correlation we imply, we must use the correct maturities for the relevant implied index and component volatilities. From a modelling perspective, having a correlation term structure is typically less computationally intense than a correlation skew. To go deeper into the concept of a correlation skew, and have a meaningful method to see this in a model, we will need to look at copulas. These are discussed in Chapter 20 in the context of pricing hybrid derivatives.

7.3   BASKET OPTIONS

The basket option has already been mentioned and here we discuss it in more detail. Start with n assets $S_1, S_2, ..., S_n$ and construct a portfolio or *basket* consisting of these underlyings, each with its own corresponding weight. The weights w_i do not need to be equal but must satisfy the criteria laid out in equation (7.3). Define the value of a basket of n assets S_i at time T as

$$\text{Basket}(T) = \sum_{i=1}^{n} w_i S_i(T)$$

where the weights w_i satisfy the criteria of equation (7.3), then the payoff of a call option on the basket (the basket call) with maturity T is given by

$$\text{Basket Call}_{\text{payoff}} = \max\left[0, \sum_{i=1}^{n} w_i S_i(T) - K \right]$$

A basket option is therefore an option whose payoff is contingent on the performance of such a basket. To avoid confusion, the reference to basket options is where the weights of each of the underlyings, upon which the payoff is computed, is known at the outset. This is in comparison with what we see later as a distinct set of options called *Rainbows*, where the weighting is specified at maturity and is based on the relative performance of the various assets. As such, the basket is different from an index in that the weights in a basket stay the same, whereas in an index they can change as the components of the index move.

The logic behind formula (7.4) and the example following it apply to the basket options. The decreased overall variance (and thus decreased volatility) implies that a call option on a basket represents the cheaper alternative to take a view on the portfolio of assets. This involves only one transaction to gain exposure to multiple underlyings and thus lower transaction costs. It is also because of this multi-asset feature, and the problems that could potentially arise from having to deliver multiple underlyings, that multi-asset options are generally cash settled. When pricing an ATM basket call option we only need the ATM volatilities of the respective underlyings. If the product is to be Vega hedged, then ATM options on the various underlyings will be used, and thus the ATM volatilities used in the pricing. We also need a correlation between the underlyings, and, in the case of the basket option, the seller of the option is short this correlation. If we assume that each of the underlyings is log-normal, then we get stuck because the sum (basket) of log-normal random variables is not log-normal; however, we assume that the normal market circumstances can apply the usual portfolio variance of formula (19.1) to approximate the volatility of the basket. The assumptions behind this are discussed in Appendix B, section B.2.

In practice, and for pricing purposes, this is not sufficient; however, it does allow us to look at the effect of correlation. As we can see in the variance formula, the correlations are always

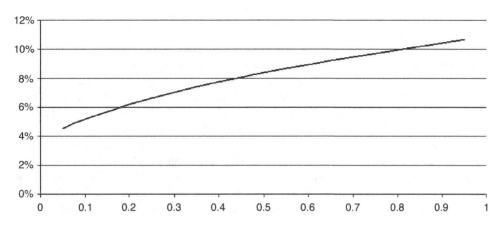

Figure 7.4 The price of an ATM basket call option based on two assets as a function of the correlation between the two assets.

accompanied by positive coefficients and so an increase in correlation implies an increase in the overall basket volatility, as demonstrated earlier. Since call options have positive Vega, the seller of the basket call is thus selling the basket volatility which, in turn, implies that the seller is short the correlation between the underlyings. Note the non-linearity of the basket option's price sensitivity to a movement in correlation through Figure 7.4. If we were to assume that the only impact that correlation has on a basket option is that which it has on the basket volatility, then it is fair to say that the basket call option's correlation sensitivity is given by

$$\frac{\partial \text{Basket Call}_{\text{price}}}{\partial \rho} = \frac{\partial \text{Basket Call}_{\text{price}}}{\partial \sigma_{\text{basket}}} \times \frac{\partial \sigma_{\text{basket}}}{\partial \rho}$$

$$= \mathcal{V}_{\text{basket call}} \times \frac{\partial \sigma_{\text{basket}}}{\partial \rho} \tag{7.7}$$

where σ_{basket} is the volatility of the basket. The last term on the right-hand side is positive but is not a linear function in correlation.

Other methods exist whereby the basket is modelled as a single log-normal asset so that the Black–Scholes formula can be applied. This breaks down to finding the equivalent mean and variance, and thus involves moment matching. One can ask: given a set of variables all of which are log-normal and for which we know the mean and variance, can we find an equivalent log-normal random variable that has the same mean and variance as the weighted basket of these log-normals? In Brigo *et al.* (2004) the authors use a moment-matching method to give a closed formula equivalent log-normal process for the basket.

In practice, we may want to simply apply a simulation-based pricing method. Once the volatilities and correlations are specified, basket options can then be priced using Monte Carlo simulation correlated log-normal random variables. In the case where there is skew dependence, for example an OTM basket call option, skew models will be needed. The seller of an OTM basket call option is short the individual OTM implied volatilities of the underlying assets, and as skew increases these values go down, thus the seller of the OTM basket call option is long the individual skews. The opposite holds in the case of a put option on the basket with respect to skew, but again the seller of a put is short volatility and thus the seller of the basket put is short both the volatilities of the underlyings and the correlations between the underlyings. The seller of a basket call or put option is essentially short the covariance of the underlying assets.

One methodology to handle basket skew is to use an index skew as a proxy for the basket skew. Assuming that a bank wants to sell a skew-dependent option on a basket of banking stocks, then the skew (or a percentage of the skew, 75% for example) of the banking stocks index in which these stocks are present can be used as a conservative proxy for the case where the seller is short skew. One can compare the time series of the volatility of the basket to that of the index to decide the level at which to buy/sell volatility if the basket option's Vega is to be hedged with options on the index. This becomes necessary when dealing with baskets of underlyings for which we do not have liquid individual underlying OTM European options data but still need to price skew correctly. In the case where one has sufficient liquid individual underlying OTM option quotes for the points to which the basket option has Vega exposure, then the calibration of individual local-volatility models to these skews, and a simulation of these correlated variables, will suffice.

7.4 QUANTITY ADJUSTING OPTIONS: "QUANTOS"

7.4.1 Quanto Payoffs

An asset is described as a quanto if it is denominated in a currency other than the one in which it is normally traded. So a quanto option is an option denominated in a currency other than the currency in which the underlying is traded. Cashflows are computed from the underlying in one currency but the payoff is made in another. The idea behind the quanto is that it handles the risk to foreign exchange rates which are found in foreign derivatives (those with underlyings in a non-domestic currency). Quantos are immensely traded, and any of the options we have seen can be changed into a quanto option.

In a European payoff, for example, the strike price is set in the currency of the underlying. Take the example of a European call option on the S&P 500 index which makes its payoff in pounds sterling. Let $S(T)$ denote the price of the index at maturity, then the payoff of the quanto call option is given by

$$\text{Quanto Call}_{\text{payoff}}(T) = \text{FX}(0) \times \max\left[S(T) - K, 0\right]$$

where FX(0) is the exchange rate at time 0, and this is defined as the domestic currency per one unit of the foreign currency. Note that this is fixed in the above payoff. This option gives the buyer exposure to the upside in the index above the specified strike, but without the payout having any exposure to changes in the USD (in which S&P 500 is traded) and GBP (in which the payout is being computed) exchange rate. The payoff can be modified to include the exchange rate at maturity, FX(T), however the option will no longer provide protection against the FX risk. These types of structures are discussed in detail when we look at FX-Equity hybrids in Chapters 17 and 18.

7.4.2 Quanto Correlation and Quanto Option Pricing

Let r_{stock} denote the risk-free interest rate of the currency in which the underlying stock (or index) is traded, and let q denote the dividend yield of the stock (or index) and σ_S its volatility. Denote also by σ_{FX} the volatility of the exchange rate. If we make Black–Scholes assumptions, in particular regarding the log-normality of the underlying process, and also assume a log-normal process for the foreign exchange process, then analytical pricing solutions for quanto European options exist. The result is the same as a Black–Scholes formula for the non-quanto case, using the risk-free rate r_{stock} and dividend yield q, plus what is known as a quanto adjustment which accounts for the quanto effect. The adjustment is added to the dividend yield and is given by

$$-\rho_{\text{quanto}} \cdot \sigma_S \cdot \sigma_{\text{FX}}$$

where ρ_{quanto} is known as the quanto correlation and is the correlation between the underlying equity and the FX rate. Other than the volatility of the underlying equity's price and the volatility of the exchange rate, this quanto correlation will also affect the price of the quanto option – even though it is the fixed FX rate at time 0 that is used in the payoff. Let's be clear on the FX rate and quanto, going back to the example of the call option on the S&P 500 index: when denominated in GBP, the quanto correlation is the correlation between the USD–GBP exchange rate and not the GBP–USD exchange rate. Note that σ_{FX} is the volatility of the FX rate and will be the same for USD–GBP and GBP–USD.

Like many equity–equity correlations, it is hard to correctly obtain an implied quanto correlation from market data. If one has a quote for the price quanto option, then because all other parameters are known we can back out a quanto correlation. For this implied correlation to be useable we would need a liquid market for specific quanto options. In the general case where we cannot imply and hedge the quanto correlation risk, the seller of the quanto option will have to resort to looking at the realized correlation and taking a margin. When computing such a correlation from two time series, we do as before and use data of the log-returns for the asset and the log of the FX rate, not the price and exchange rates themselves.

7.4.3 Hedging Quanto Risk

Firstly, and making use of the above formula, we think about the effect the quanto adjustment has on the forward. As it appears above, applied to the dividend but with a negative sign, it impacts the forward in the opposite way from dividends. An increase in the quanto correlation, the FX volatility or the volatility of the underlying will have the same effect as a decrease in dividends. Lowering dividends increases the forward, and since the seller of a call option, for example, is short the forward, the seller is thus short the quanto correlation and FX volatility. If we think about Delta, the seller of a call option will buy Delta of stock, in order to Delta hedge, and is thus long dividends. Since the quanto adjustment has the opposite effect of dividends, the seller of a quanto call option is short the quanto correlation and FX volatility.

The opposite will hold for the seller of the quanto put option because the seller of a put is long the forward. If we want to think about Delta again, we just need to note that the seller of a put option will go short Delta of stock in order to Delta hedge. Thus the opposite applies in the case of put options. One thing to note is that the volatility of the underlying appears in the adjustment, and although the seller of the put option is short the volatility of the underlying, the quanto effect here has the opposite effect. Generally speaking, the quanto effect will be secondary and the seller of the quanto put will still be overall short the volatility of the underlying.

Leaving the formula aside, we consider how the seller of the quanto call option will Delta hedge. Assume that a trader sells the above call option on the S&P 500 denominated in GBP. Then to hedge, the seller will need to buy Delta of the underlying, which involves selling GBP and buying USD. The seller of the quanto call is thus short the quanto correlation.

In general, when turning a more exotic structure into a quanto option, the general trend that we see among the various structures is that the seller will be long Delta, rather than short, on many more structures. This means that one would expect an exotics desk to be structurally short the quanto correlation between various underlyings and the relevant currencies. Using realized correlation plus a margin is in some ways the best one can do to price this quanto risk; however, the fact that it cannot be hedged in the market means that the seller will have to essentially sit on this risk. In 2008, for example, the Nikkei index's quanto correlation appearing in EUR-denominated quanto options rose significantly and desks suffered losses on this parameter. Although this is an example of where the realized series was misleading and the historical data was not a good predictor of future realized correlation, there was little that could be done. In the future, desks may take a wider margin when selling this quanto correlation.

7.5   TRADING CORRELATION

Here we discuss two of three possible correlation trading strategies. Traditionally one makes use of European options on the index and its components and can trade these against each other in the form of straddles. A more specific and pure correlation trade is the correlation swap. Here we discuss both of these. A third method involves trading variance swaps (or Gamma swaps), again on the index versus the components to get a cleaner exposure than the straddle version. This method, however, will be considered after our discussion of variance swaps in Chapter 16 on volatility derivatives. The other two methods are discussed below.

7.5.1   Straddles: Index versus Constituents

Consider a trade where we go long straddles on an index and short straddles on each of the individual components. Following the formula for portfolio variance and what we have learned about the effect of correlation on the volatility of an index, we see that the holder of this portfolio is long the correlation between the index components. In this case the holder of this position is long the average correlation of the index, defined as above, and not the individual pairwise correlations.

The weights in such a strategy must be specified for the component straddles according to the weights of the index, and will obviously need to be readjusted if the weights change. Straddles are used because a Delta-hedged straddle can provide exposure to volatility, although, as we will see in Chapter 16, trading straddles does not give a pure exposure to volatility. The idea is that by gaining exposure to just the volatility of the index and those of the components, the spread will leave us with an exposure to correlation.

The variance swap, or Gamma swap, provides a purer exposure to volatility, and thus trading spreads between the variance swaps of an index versus those of the components is a more transparent method for trading the average correlation in an index. (See section 16.7 on variance dispersion.)

7.5.2   Correlation Swaps

The correlation swap is an OTC product typically of medium-term maturity between 1 and 3 years. It allows the investor to obtain a pure exposure to the average correlation among a basket of underlyings. If the basket consists of two assets, then the correlation swap provides exposure to the pairwise correlation between the two underlyings. The underlyings of a correlation swap can be any two assets: exchange rates, commodities, equities, etc. – basically any asset for which we have observable price data.

The correlation swap consists of a fixed leg and a floating leg with payments made on the basis of a prespecified notional that we denote $\mathcal{N}_{corr}$. The fixed leg of the swap pays this notional times the strike ρ_{strike} (set out in the contract). The floating leg pays the annualized realized correlation between the underlying assets of the swap, thus the need for price data for each underlying. At expiry, the payoff of the correlation swap is given by the difference in percentage points times the notional. For the payer of the fixed leg this is

$$\mathcal{N}_{corr} \times (\rho_{realized} - \rho_{strike})$$

If the correlation swap is written on a basket of underlyings then the floating leg is the average correlation computed using formula (7.2), where the basket weights are again constrained by the conditions of equation (7.3). Each pairwise correlation is computed using the log daily returns of each underlying. An investor who is short the swap, meaning one who pays the floating level, makes money if the correlation realized is lower that the specified strike level.

The correlation swap thus provides pure exposure to realized correlation, and appeals to investors looking to take a direct view on the future realized correlation and also to those wanting to hedge correlation risk. As discussed earlier, sell-side desks will be structurally short correlation on a book level because of the sale of multi-asset options, the majority of which set the seller of the option short the correlation. Although spread positions in straddles allow one to hedge the average correlation of a basket or index, the risk to pairwise correlations remains, and this can potentially be very large for certain underlyings. The correlation swap provides a method for the sell side to buy back some of the correlation they have sold, providing a counterparty for such a swap can be found. Such counterparties include institutional clients of investment banks, such as hedge funds, who can use the correlation swap to take a view on the future realized correlation compared to its current market price. Ideally one would be able to enter into such swaps for baskets of underlyings for which pairwise correlation exposure is greatest.

The problem with correlation swaps is that they cannot be replicated or priced in a simple and arbitrage-free manner. The strike of the correlation swap would thus generally be some estimation of future realized correlation. Work on correlation swap replication and pricing has been done; for example, Bossu (2005) shows that the fair strike of the correlation swap on the realized correlation of the components of an index is in fact related to the implied correlation (equation (7.5)) of the components. These problems have left the correlation swap market relatively illiquid, with those that are traded generally coming from specific underlyings, for example the world basket of the EuroStoxx50, the Nikkei and the S&P 500 indices.

Assuming that one were able to trade a correlation swap on the underlyings to which a book is most exposed, this is not the absolute solution. On day 1 of selling an option the trader can know the correlation sensitivity of the option. However, this correlation sensitivity changes over time. Going back to the example of the basket option, let's model the basket as one asset and apply a Black–Scholes formula. Just to think about a simple case, we see in equation (7.7) that the basket call option's correlation sensitivity is directly proportional to the Vega sensitivity to the basket volatility. As we saw in Chapter 5, the Vega of a call option is sensitive to movements in the underlying – it is, in particular, a function of moneyness. If we draw the analogy to the basket where we think of the basket's moneyness compared to the strike of the option, we can expect the correlation sensitivity of the option to change as the underlyings move. Thus hedging such correlation risk using a correlation swap – which obviously has a fixed notional – is not the absolute answer to the correlation problem. Better examples of correlation sensitivity arise when we discuss dispersion options – for example, a call option on the best of two assets. Although the correlation swap doesn't provide a complete hedge, it can prove valuable on a book level to at least partially hedge the correlation risk to specific pairs or baskets to which the trader has large short exposures.

Another way to see the basket sensitivity is to note that the seller of the basket call is in fact short the covariance of the assets: both the individual volatilities and the correlation between the underlyings. Generally, the correlation sensitivity of a multi-asset option will move as the volatilities of the underlying assets change. One way to incorporate this is to consider covariance swaps, defined analogously, but involving both the correlation between assets and also their volatilities. However, these will again suffer from the same liquidity problems owing to the lack of a correct replication methodology.

Part II

Exotic Derivatives and Structured Products

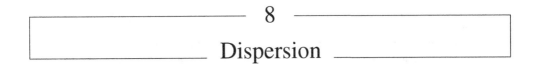

8
Dispersion

May the best from your past be the worst of your future.

In the context of multi-asset options, we often encounter the concept of *dispersion*. In statistics, dispersion – also called statistical variability or variation – is defined by the variability or the spread in a variable or a probability distribution. It measures the extent to which data is spread around a central point. Dispersion effects in multi-asset options appear when its payoff depends on the relative performance of the underlying assets to each other; that is, how far the returns of a sample of assets composing a basket are from each other.

In this chapter, we first discuss the roles of correlation and volatility in dispersion in order to properly understand it. Then, we focus on worst-of and best-of options, analysing the impact of these common features on options pricing. Firstly, the payoff description is detailed through scenarios, then the risks associated with the pricing and hedging of these derivatives are identified and analysed. It is imperative to get a handle on these concepts in order to go further with the exotic multi-asset structures, including hybrids, discussed later in this book.

8.1 MEASURES OF DISPERSION AND INTERPRETATIONS

When discussing correlation in Chapter 7, we left the effect it has on dispersion for the separate discussion here. In the case of basket options, the correlation between the multiple underlyings has an effect on the overall volatility of the basket and thus affects the price. In the case of the basket option, the payoff at maturity is a function of where the basket's value lies, that is the weighted average of the terminal values of the underlying assets. Thus, it is not a function of how dispersed the returns are, as it is an option on the average of such returns. Here we will look at the second effect of correlation, that is, the effect correlation has on the dispersion of the underlyings. In these options the payoff depends directly on how much the underlying dispersed, and we refer to these as *dispersion* trades.

When one says that a basket of assets has a high dispersion, this means that the asset returns are quite different from each other. In other words, a simulation on the stock's returns will result in returns far from each other. Thus, uncorrelated returns result in a high dispersion. If a trader is long dispersion, this also means that he is short correlation since a low correlation implies a high dispersion.

Common examples of measures of statistical dispersion are the variance, standard deviation and interquartile range. Volatility is also a parameter affecting dispersion. In fact, dispersion is an increasing function of volatility: if volatility goes up, the variance of returns goes up, which enhances the likelihood of having returns far from their expected value. When a trader is long dispersion, he is therefore long volatility.

As a result of the sale of multi-asset equity products to clients, the sell-side trader's book positions in dispersion are thus typically structurally long. The majority of these products involve the traders taking short positions in options that have a negative sensitivity to dispersion, and long positions with positive sensitivity. Put differently, the sale of dispersion products involves long volatility and short correlation positions.

We now use these measures of dispersion to structure some derivatives on dispersion. As a first example, consider an option on the dispersion of the individual stocks of a basket over the performance of the equally weighted basket. Let $S_1, S_2, \ldots, S_n$ be the underlying stocks of the basket, and let $R_1, R_2, \ldots, R_n$ be their respective returns at maturity T, defined in the usual manner. The basket return is given by the average of the returns $R_B = \frac{1}{n} \sum_{i=1}^{n} R_i$ and the payoff of the dispersion trade is given by

$$\text{Payoff} = \frac{1}{n} \sum_{i=1}^{n} |R_i - R_B|$$

that is, it is the average of the absolute values of how far each individual return is from the basket return. There is no global floor in this payoff as the absolute values (and their average) are all positive. This measure of dispersion is known as the average absolute deviation.

A second example of an option on dispersion has the following payoff:

$$\text{Payoff} = \max \left[0, \sum_{i=1}^{n} w_i \left(\text{Perf}_i - 1 \right) - \frac{1}{n} \sum_{i=1}^{n} \left(\text{Perf}_i - 1 \right) \right]$$

where

$$\text{Perf}_i = \frac{S_i(T)}{S_i(0)}$$

is the performance of the ith stock, and the weights w_i are

$$w_i = \frac{\text{Perf}_i}{\sum_{i=1}^{n} \text{Perf}_i}$$

After moving the terms around this can be written as

$$\text{Payoff} = \max \left[0, \frac{1/n \sum_{i=1}^{n} \text{Perf}_i^2 - \left(1/n \sum_{i=1}^{n} \text{Perf}_i \right)^2}{1/n \sum_{i=1}^{n} \text{Perf}_i} \right] = \max \left[0, \frac{\text{Variance(Perf)}}{\text{Average(Perf)}} \right]$$

that is, we have a set of individual performances and the option pays on the variance of this set, geared by the inverse of the average.

Relative dispersion, sometimes called the coefficient of variation, is the result of dividing the standard deviation by the mean, and is therefore dimensionless (it may also be presented as a percentage). So a low value of relative dispersion usually implies that the standard deviation is small in comparison to the magnitude of the mean.

One can also have an option on the *range*, which is a measure of dispersion that locates the maximum and minimum (these two values form the range), and a simple payoff with the same notation as above is given by

$$\text{Payoff} = \max_{i=1 \to n} \left(\text{Perf}_i \right) - \min_{i=1 \to n} \left(\text{Perf}_i \right)$$

If the performances are all the same, then the payoff is zero as the range is just one number, which is the case when we have zero dispersion. Again since the maximum will always be greater than (or equal to) the minimum, this payoff is always positive.

8.2 WORST-OF OPTIONS

We now discuss options on the worst-of and the best-of; they serve as excellent examples to describe the effects of dispersion on multi-asset equity options. A *worst-of* option, also known as an option on the minimum, is, as the name suggests, an option on whichever among a basket of assets performs the worst.

8.2.1 Worst-of Call

Payoff Description

Assume that we start with n assets $S_1, S_2, ..., S_n$, then a worst-of call option has a payoff at maturity T given by :

$$\text{WO Call}_{\text{payoff}} = \max\left[0, \min(S_1(T), S_2(T), \ldots, S_n(T)) - K\right]$$

where K is a predetermined strike price. Since this option is a call on a worst-of, it has a lower payoff potential compared to a call option on the same underlying basket, then a worst-of call is cheaper than a vanilla basket call (Table 8.1).

Pricing Formulas for Worst-of Calls

Closed formulas for these options do exist, and although one would typically value these using a Monte Carlo simulation, we present a few of these formulas here. Stulz (1995) gives closed formulas for a worst-of call in the case of two assets, in this case a call option on the minimum of two assets S_1 and S_2. Other articles from the literature discussing this aspect of pricing such options include Johnson's 1987 work on the maximum or minimum of several assets. Under Black–Scholes assumptions, and assuming zero dividends and the same accrual rate for both stocks, we have

$$\text{WO Call}_{\text{price}} = S_1\mathcal{N}_2\left(\gamma_1 + \sigma_1\sqrt{T}, \left(\ln(S_2/S_1) - \frac{1}{2}\sigma^2\sqrt{T}\right)/\sigma\sqrt{T}, (\rho_{1,2}\sigma_2 - \sigma_1)/\sigma\right)$$
$$+ S_2\mathcal{N}_2\left(\gamma_2 + \sigma_2\sqrt{T}, \left(\ln(S_1/S_2) - \frac{1}{2}\sigma^2\sqrt{T}\right)/\sigma\sqrt{T}, (\rho_{1,2}\sigma_1 - \sigma_2)/\sigma\right)$$
$$- Ke^{-rT}\mathcal{N}_2\left(\gamma_1, \gamma_2, \rho_{1,2}\right)$$

where $\mathcal{N}_2(,,)$ is the bivariate cumulative standard Normal distribution, (see Hull (2003) for details and a good way to approximate this). $\rho_{1,2}$ is the correlation between the two underlying

Table 8.1 Scenario observations of the underlying's performances with respect to initial date, note the difference in payoffs at maturity between the ATM worst-of call and the ATM basket call.

	EuroStoxx	S&P 500	Nikkei	WO call	Basket call
Scenario 1	−5%	7%	12%	0%	4.67%
Scenario 2	3%	12%	10%	3%	8.33%
Scenario 3	7%	7%	15%	7%	9.67%

assets, and σ_1 and σ_2 are the respective volatilities of S_1 and S_2,

$$\gamma_1 = \left(\ln(S_1/K) + \left(r - \frac{1}{2}\sigma_1^2 \right) T \right) / \sigma_1 \sqrt{T}$$

$$\gamma_2 = \left(\ln(S_2/K) + \left(r - \frac{1}{2}\sigma_2^2 \right) T \right) / \sigma_2 \sqrt{T}$$

$$\sigma^2 = \sigma_1^2 + \sigma_2^2 - 2\rho_{1,2}\sigma_1\sigma_2$$

Risk Analysis

First of all, the holder of a call option has a bullish view on the underlying stocks. The higher the forward price of the individual stocks, the higher will be the forward price of the worst performing stock, which will increase the option's price. Knowing that interest rates increase the forward price and that dividends and borrow costs decrease the forward price, we can conclude that the worst-of call price is an increasing function of interest rates and a decreasing function of dividends and borrowing costs.

Let's discuss the Delta in the two asset case. Both assets start at 100%, and as they evolve, one of them will perform worse than the other. Looking at the Delta profile, as one of the underlyings becomes the worst-of, then the Delta sensitivity to this asset will increase for the simple reason that the call option is on the worst performing asset.

We also have to consider the cross-Gamma effect: in the case of a worst-of call on two assets S_1 and S_2, both assets start, as always on day 1 at 100%. If stock S_2 stays at 100%, but S_1 moves down by 5% to 95%, what happens to our sensitivity to S_2 given that it did not move? The answer is that in relative terms to it being the worst-of the two, the fact that it stayed the same and is not the best-of, we expect that the further S_1 drops the more the Delta on S_2 will drop.

In the general multi-asset case this is also true. As one asset becomes the worst-of, it picks up Delta and the others lose some Delta. When another name takes over as the worst performer, the primary Delta effect moves to the new asset. The Delta with respect to the previous worst performer can go down even if it has not moved, by virtue of the fact that we now have a new worst performer.

As for the effects of volatility and correlation, a higher dispersion of the returns will likely result in a lower payoff since the income received by the option's holder depends on the worst performing stock. In other words, the worst-of call price decreases if dispersion goes up. This makes one believe that a higher volatility as well as a lower correlation will result in a lower option price. However, the position in volatility is not this obvious when we are talking about a simple worst-of call option. If we keep in mind that volatility increases the price of a call, then the volatility has two opposite effects on the option price. On the one hand, it increases the expected payoff of the call; on the other hand, it increases dispersion which lowers the level of the worst performing stock and thus decreases the payoff's potential.

The seller of a simple call on the worst performing stock must be cautious with its Vega. Most of the time, dispersion's effect is dominant and the trader selling this option would be long volatility. But in some cases, the positive volatility effect on the call offsets the negative volatility effect on dispersion; then the trader selling a worst-of call will be short volatility. This is typical in a high correlation environment. A common occurrence is that the seller is short volatility on one underlying, usually the one with the highest volatility, and long volatility on

Table 8.2 Scenario observations of the underlying's performances with respect to initial date, note the difference in payoffs at maturity between the ATM worst-of put and the ATM basket put.

	EuroStoxx	S&P 500	Nikkei	WO put	Basket put
Scenario 1	−5%	−7%	−12%	**12%**	**8%**
Scenario 2	3%	12%	−10%	**10%**	**0%**
Scenario 3	−7%	7%	−15%	**15%**	**5%**

the others. Knowing the direction and magnitude (and the skew position) of the sensitivities to the implied volatilities of the individual underlyings must be established. Options on the individual underlyings can be used to hedge the Vega sensitivities of the structure to each of their volatilities. As the market moves and assets disperse, their respective Vegas will increase or decrease in magnitude, depending on whether they have dispersed towards becoming the worst-of or not, respectively.

8.2.2 Worst-of Put

Payoff Description

Assume that we start with n assets $S_1, S_2, ..., S_n$, then a worst-of put option has payoff at maturity T given by :

$$\text{WO Put}_{\text{payoff}} = \max\left[0, K - \min(S_1(T), S_2(T), \ldots, S_n(T))\right]$$

where K is a predetermined strike price.

Since this option is a put on a worst-of, it has a higher payoff potential compared to a put option on the same underlying basket. This makes the worst-of put more expensive than a vanilla basket put (Table 8.2).

Pricing Formulas for Worst-of Puts

As in the case of a worst-of call we can rely on several approaches. Following the closed form of the worst-of call on the two assets we saw in the previous section, it is interesting to see one here for the worst-of put. From the price of a call option on the worst-of two risky assets and the price of assets S_1, S_2 and the risk-free rate r, with strike K, it is possible to obtain the price of a call option on the maximum of two risky assets, and the price of a put option on the minimum of two risky assets. Stulz (1995) gives the parity relationship between the worst-of call and the worst-of put as

$$\text{WO Put}_{\text{price}}(K) = e^{-rT} K - \text{WO Call}_{\text{price}}(0) + \text{WO Call}_{\text{price}}(K)$$

To verify this result consider the following two investments:

- *Portfolio A*
  Buy a put on the minimum of S_1 and S_2 struck at K.
- *Portfolio B*
  Buy bonds that pay K at maturity T.
  Sell a call option on $\min(S_1, S_2)$ with zero strike.
  Buy a call option on $\min(S_1, S_2)$ struck at K.

If $\min(S_1, S_2) = S_1 < K$, then Portfolio A pays $K - S_1$, whereas Portfolio B pays $K - S_1 + 0 = K - S_1$. The second case, $\min(S_1, S_2) = S_2 < K$, follows similarly, so A and B are equivalent.

Risk Analysis

Firstly, the holder of a put option has a bearish view on the underlying stocks. The higher the forward price of the individual stocks, the higher will be the forward price of the worst performing stock, which will decrease the option price. Knowing that interest rates increase the forward price and that dividends as well as borrow costs decrease the forward price, we conclude that the worst-of put price is a decreasing function of interest rates and an increasing function of dividends and borrowing costs.

With respect to the Deltas we have an analogous argument to the case of the worst-of call. Consider the position of a seller of a two-asset worst-of put. The seller will go short Delta of stock on day 1 with the respective Deltas. If we assume that S_1 starts to decline and takes the role of the worst-of, then we expect the Delta on it to increase (in absolute value), and at the same time the Delta on S_2 to decrease (again in absolute value).

As for the effects of volatility and correlation, a higher dispersion of the returns will likely result in a higher payoff since the income received by the option's holder depends on the worst performing stock. In other words, the worst-of put's price increases if dispersion goes up. A higher volatility as well as a lower correlation will result in a higher option price. As the market moves, the option will show higher Vega to the volatilities of the underlyings that perform the worst. The magnitude of Vega is also a function of the positions of the asset with respect to the strike; if the worst performing stock is far from the strike and the option far out-of-the-money, then Vega will be less than if the worst-of is near the strike.

The presence of skew, as discussed in Chapter 4, implies that the distribution of the returns of the underlying is skewed with higher probabilities of downward moves than is implied by a flat volatility. In the context of the worst-of put that pays on this downside, a higher implied volatility on the downside will result in a higher price, so an increase in skew will raise the price of the worst-of put.

From the model point of view, and in order to capture the different skew effects, we will need to calibrate a local volatility model to each underlying's implied volatilities. If the option's payoff is only a function of the returns of each underlying at maturity, then it is imperative to get that particular skew correct in the calibration and we would use the exact date-fitting model described in section 4.3.3. The Vega hedge consists of a set of European options on each of the underlyings, and for these to serve as hedging instruments, the model used to price must be calibrated to them so that it shows risk against them. If there is some form of additional path dependency, such as averaging, then we need to use a form of smooth surface local volatility calibration described in section 4.3.3 in order to capture the effect of surface at all dates where the payoff is sensitive. Because this is a multi-asset option we will need to do this for each underlying, and use a correlation matrix that is obtained following the procedures of Chapter 7 and taking into account the trader's position in correlation.

8.2.3   Market Trends in Worst-of Options

Many exotic options traded in the market contain a call feature on the worst performing stock. They are popular since the worst-of feature makes the call option cheaper and thus has a high

Table 8.3   Individual parameter positions for a worst-of option trader.

	Worst-of call seller	Worst-of put buyer
Interest rates	Short	Short
Borrowing costs	Long	Long
Dividends	Long	Long
Volatility	Depends	Long
Correlation	Short	Short
Skew	Depends	Long

leverage potential. Traders at banks are usually selling worst-of call options, and this is one of the reasons they are most of the time long dispersion. Also, an exotic trader is more likely to buy a worst-of put than to sell it, based on the nature of many retail products that use the put feature to enhance yields (see Table 8.3). In this case, the trader is again long dispersion.

Exercise

Let A and B denote two stocks that have an initial price equal to $100. Imagine you can sell a financial product C that pays the holder the minimum value between A and B after 2 years. Would you sell it for $100?

Discussion

To answer this question, there is no need to try to figure out the interest rates, the dividends or the volatility of both stocks. In fact, one needs to know if there is an arbitrage opportunity behind doing this trade. Indeed, if you sell two C products for $100 each, and at the same time buy A and B for $200, this strategy would give the following payout at maturity:

$$A_T + B_T - 2 \times \min(A_T, B_T) \geq 0$$

where A_T and B_T are the stock prices of A and B at maturity T. Therefore, the payoff of this strategy is always positive whereas the cost is null. This means you should definitely sell C for $100.

8.3   BEST-OF OPTIONS

A *best-of* option, also known as an option on the maximum, is, as the name suggests, an option on whichever among a basket of assets performs the best.

8.3.1   Best-of Call

Payoff Description

Assume we start with n assets $S_1, S_2, \ldots, S_n$, then a best-of call option for example has payoff at maturity T given by

$$\mathrm{BO\,Call}_{\mathrm{payoff}} = \max\left[0, \max(S_1(T), S_2(T), \ldots, S_n(T)) - K\right]$$

Table 8.4 Scenario observations of the underlying's performances with respect to initial date; note the difference in payoffs at maturity between the ATM best-of call and the ATM basket call.

	EuroStoxx	S&P 500	Nikkei	Best-of call	Basket call
Scenario 1	3%	−7%	12%	**12%**	**2.67%**
Scenario 2	7%	12%	14%	**14%**	**11.00%**
Scenario 3	−7%	7%	−2%	**7%**	**0.00%**

Since this option is a call on a best-of, it has a higher payoff potential compared to a call option on the same underlying basket, then it is obvious to note that a best-of call is more expensive than a vanilla basket call (Table 8.4).

Pricing and Risk Analysis

Firstly, the holder of a call option has a bullish view on the underlying stocks.

The higher the forward price of the individual stocks, the higher will be the forward price of the best performing stock, which will increase the option price. Knowing that interest rates increase the forward price and that dividends as well as borrow costs decrease the forward price, we conclude that the best-of call price is an increasing function of interest rates and a decreasing function of dividends and borrowing costs.

As for the effects of volatility and correlation: a higher dispersion of the returns will result in a higher potential payoff since the income received by the option's holder depends on the best performing stock. In other words, the best-of call price increases if dispersion goes up. A higher volatility as well as a lower correlation will result in a higher option price. The seller of the option is short dispersion.

The presence of skew means lower volatility on the upside, which is where the best-of call option pays. The market implies a skewed distribution where upside returns have a lower probability than that implied by a flat volatility. More skew amounts to a lower expected payoff for the best-of call, so the seller of this option is long skew.

Exercise

Imagine you are a structurer visiting a client with salespeople from your company. At the end of the marketing presentation, the client is discussing some products that might interest him. He is interested in buying a 6-month European at-the-money call option based on the best performing stock between Merrill Lynch and Morgan Stanley. He wants you to give him an immediate approximate price of this option knowing that you don't have a pricing model in front of you. Assume that the bank sector suffered a violent crash one week ago and you know that the prices of individual 6-month at-the-money European calls on Merrill Lynch and Morgan Stanley are 6% and 8% respectively (prices expressed in percentage of the notional). What would your offer be?

Discussion

The offer price in a scenario such as this constitutes what is known as an indicative price, one that should be as close as possible to the actual price at which the bank is willing to sell such an option. Keep in mind that a best-of call price is higher than the price of the individual calls on each underlying stock since its payoff is higher or equal to the payoff of the call option on the stock that performed the best. Your offer would certainly be higher than 8%, which is the price of the call option on Morgan Stanley.

Thinking about a best-of call price from a correlation point of view, the higher the correlation, the lower the price of a best-of call. Basically, we can now determine the maximum offer we could suggest to the client. The maximum price of a best-of call occurs when correlation between the two underlyings is the lowest. If the correlation $\rho = -1$, this means that we expect one of the stocks composing the basket to go up and the other to go down. In this particular case, we can hedge a short position in a best-of call by selling two calls, one on each stock. So, the maximum price of this best-of call is equal to $8\% + 6\% = 14\%$.

Keeping in mind that the bank stocks crashed one week ago, both realizing large negative returns, and, therefore, that realized correlation is quite high, an indicative offer for this option is around 10%–11%, which seems to be a level that is neither too aggressive nor too conservative.

One can again derive a parity relationship between the best-of call and the worst-of call. By noting that the sum of a best-of call and a worst-of call on the same two assets is equivalent to two standard call options on the two assets:

$$\text{BO Call}_{\text{price}}(K) + \text{WO Call}_{\text{price}}(K) = C(S_1, K, T) + C(S_2, K, T)$$

whatever the position of S_1 and S_2 with respect to each other and to the strike K, the left- and right-hand sides of the equation are equivalent.

8.3.2 Best-of Put

Payoff Description

Assume we start with n assets S_1, S_2, ..., S_n, then a best-of put option has payoff at maturity T given by :

$$\text{BO Put}_{\text{payoff}} = \max\left[0, K - \max(S_1(T), S_2(T), \ldots, S_n(T))\right]$$

where K is a predetermined strike price.

Since this option is a put on a best-of, it has a lower payoff potential compared to a put option on the same underlying basket. This makes the best-of put cheaper than a vanilla basket put (see Table 8.5).

Pricing and Risk Analysis

A parity relationship for the best-of put exists: If BO Put$_{\text{price}}$ and BO Call$_{\text{price}}$ are respectively the prices of a European put and a European call option on the best-of two assets S_1 and S_2,

Table 8.5 Scenario observations of the underlying's performances with respect to initial date, note the difference in payoffs at maturity between the ATM best-of put and the ATM basket put.

	EuroStoxx	S&P 500	Nikkei	Best-of put	Basket put
Scenario 1	−3%	−7%	5%	**0%**	**1.67%**
Scenario 2	2%	4%	−14%	**0%**	**2.67%**
Scenario 3	−7%	−13%	−2%	**2%**	**7.33%**

then again, by a parity relationship, we have:

$$\mathrm{BO}\,\mathrm{Put}_{\mathrm{price}}(K) = \mathrm{e}^{-rT}\,K - \mathrm{BO}\,\mathrm{Call}_{\mathrm{price}}(0) + \mathrm{BO}\,\mathrm{Call}_{\mathrm{price}}(K)$$

The proof of this result is similar to that of the parity relationship between worst-of calls and worst-of puts, and is verified by simply considering the possible outcomes.

With regards to risks, firstly, the holder of a put option has a bearish view on the underlying stocks. The higher the forward price of the individual stocks, the higher will be the forward price of the best performing stock, which will decrease the option price. Knowing that interest rates increase the forward price and that dividends as well as borrow costs decrease the forward price, we can conclude that the best-of put price is a decreasing function of interest rates and an increasing function of dividends and borrowing costs. Table 8.6 summarizes these positions for the seller of a best-of call and best-of put.

With respect to the Deltas we have an analogous argument to the case of the best-of call. Assume that we sell a best-of put, we will go short Delta of stock on the trade date with the respective Deltas. Imagine that S_1 starts to increase and assumes the role of the best-of, we expect the Delta on S_1 to increase (in absolute value), and at the same time the Delta on S_2 to decrease (again in absolute value). Indeed the best-of put starts to be more sensitive to the potentially best performing stock since its payoff is based on its performance.

As for the effects of volatility and correlation, a higher dispersion of the returns will likely result in a lower payoff since the income received by the option's holder depends on the best performing stock. In other words, the best-of put price decreases if dispersion goes up; a higher volatility as well as a lower correlation will result in a lower option price. However, the position in volatility is not this obvious in this case where we are talking about a simple best-of put option. If we keep in mind that volatility increases the price of a put option, then the volatility has two opposite effects on the option price. On the one hand, it is increasing the expected payoff of the call; on the other hand, it increases dispersion which raises the level of the best performing stock and thus decreases the payoff's potential. The position in skew is also not clear and cannot be stated generally, but the option will have sensitivity to skew, one way or another, and a calibration to individual skews is necessary to see this effect when pricing.

Because this is a multi-asset option, calibrating to a set of European options on each of the underlyings must be done individually. Any Monte Carlo pricing simulations must be based on a correlation matrix that is obtained following the procedures of Chapter 7 and taking into account the correlation position of the seller of the option.

8.3.3   Market Trends in Best-of Options

Calls based on the best performing stock are less traded in the market since they are more expensive, thus less attractive to investors. However, exotic traders can sell calls containing a

Table 8.6 Individual parameter positions for a best-of option trader.

	Seller of a best-of call	Seller of a best-of put
Interest rates	Short	Long
Borrowing costs	Long	Short
Dividends	Long	Short
Volatility	Short	Depends
Correlation	Long	Short
Skew	Long	Depends

best-of feature to balance their position with respect to dispersion. Interesting options can be formed that somewhat involve best-of features, for example the Himalaya of Chapter 15 which takes the best returns each period, locks them into a final payout and removes the asset from the basket moving forward. The Himalaya comes under the class of mountain range options that each have some aspect of dispersion in their payoffs. Best-of and worst-of options are special cases of rainbow options that we will see in the next chapter, in which the weights are preset on the basis of performances, e.g. 80% on the best performing and 20% on the second best at maturity. When harnessed in a constructive manner in payoffs, dispersion can be a powerful tool.

9

Dispersion Options

Virtue is more clearly shown in the performance of fine actions than in the non-performance of base ones.

Aristotle

In this chapter we take the concept of dispersion in exotic options a step further, and look at some interesting dispersion-related payoffs: *rainbow options, individually capped basket calls* and *outperformance options*. We make the payoff mechanisms clear for each with the use of scenarios, and then move to a discussion of the risks entailed in pricing and trading each of these options.

9.1 RAINBOW OPTIONS

9.1.1 Payoff Mechanism

The rainbow option pays on a return weighted by the performances of the underlying stocks; that is, the weights are agreed in the contract, but the actual payoff at maturity depends on how the assets performed. Discussions of rainbow options exist in the literature, for example the original article by Rubinstein (1995). Now, taking the example of the world basket,[1] we sell a rainbow call on the basket with weights of 50%, 30% and 20% so that the return at maturity T is given by

$$\text{Ret} = 50\% \times \text{Best return} + 30\% \times \text{Second best} + 20\% \times \text{Third best}$$

and the option is a call on this performance-weighted return.

$$\text{Rainbow}_{\text{payoff}} = \max\left[0, \text{Ret}\right]$$

Consider a specific scenario: Assume that an investor buys a 3-year note containing an Asian rainbow option on the S&P 500 index, the Eurostoxx 50 index and the Nikkei index. The note is denominated in dollars and the investor has a notional of $80 million to put in the note. The rainbow weights are [50%, 30%, 20%].The Asianing return is computed by averaging the returns of the individual stocks from the note's initial date. At maturity, the investor receives 100% of its capital plus a payoff linked to the rainbow option. Tables 9.1 and 9.2 show a returns scenario of the underlying assets and the implied payoff mechanism of the rainbow option. After ordering the stocks in decreasing performance, which are respectively the Nikkei index, the EuroStoxx 50 index and the S&P 500 index, we can now compute the payoff of this rainbow structure:

$$\text{Rainbow}_{\text{payoff}} = (13\% \times 50\%) + (10.33\% \times 30\%) + (9\% \times 20\%) = 11.4\%$$

---

[1] The *world basket* consists of the S&P 500 index, the Eurostoxx 50 index and the Nikkei index.

Table 9.1 Annual observations of the underlying's returns with respect to initial date.

	EuroStoxx 50	S&P 500	Nikkei
Return year 1	9%	7%	6%
Return year 2	15%	12%	14%
Return year 3	7%	8%	19%
Average return	**10.33%**	**9%**	**13%**

At maturity, the investor receives $89,120,000, which is equivalent to 111.4% of the invested capital.

9.1.2 Risk Analysis

The holder of a rainbow option expects a rising market. Therefore, the payoff is higher if the underlying returns go up. Higher forward prices increase the rainbow's price. The seller of this option would be short the indices' forwards, and will need to buy Delta in each of the underlying assets on day 1, and adjust dynamically through the life of the trade to remain Delta neutral. Thus, he would be short interest rates, long dividends and long borrowing costs.

In the example described above, the rainbow weights are [50%, 30%, 20%]. In this case, it is hard to know whether the option's seller is long or short dispersion. The only way to determine the trader's position in volatility and correlation is to compute the option price with different volatility and correlation levels. As such, one can see whether the sensitivities to these two parameters are positive or negative, and accordingly choose which levels to use in the pricer. Typically one bid/asks the levels of these two parameters, and the spread depends on the underlyings and the current state of the market. The option will show sensitivity to the implied volatilities of each of the underlyings, and the set of European options with the maturity of the rainbow can serve as Vega hedging instruments. The skew position is also dependent on the weights accordingly.

However, this is not the case for all rainbow options. For example, in the case of a rainbow option having weights with values far from each other, like [70%, 20%, 10%], the option's behaviour is similar to a best-of call option, then the trader selling this option would be short dispersion, which means short volatility and long correlation. If the rainbow's weights are dispersed, the option's price is higher. A rainbow option paying 80%, 15% and 5% of the best performances is certainly more expensive than one paying 60%, 30% and 10% of the best performances (Table 9.3).

A rainbow note is composed of a zero coupon bond which enables the holder to receive his invested capital back at maturity, as well as a geared rainbow option. When structuring a

Table 9.2 Rainbow weights. This allocation process is associated with the scenario shown in Table 9.1.

	Nikkei	EuroStoxx 50	S&P 500
Return	13%	10.33%	9%
Associated weight	**50%**	**30%**	**20%**

Table 9.3 Individual parameter positions for a rainbow option trader. Note that the cases that are dependent are discussed above.

	Seller of a rainbow	Buyer of a rainbow
Interest rates	Short	Long
Borrowing costs	Long	Short
Dividends	Long	Short
Volatility	Depends	Depends
Correlation	Depends	Depends
Skew	Depends	Depends

rainbow note, if the rainbow option is cheap enough, the structure can offer a higher gearing. Structuring the note with a specific amount to place in the equity portion, various combinations of the rainbow weights can be used to tweak the price to work.

9.2   INDIVIDUALLY CAPPED BASKET CALL (ICBC)

9.2.1   Payoff Mechanism

This product is based on a basket of stocks. For instance, let's take a 3-year maturity *individually capped basket call* based on a basket of N stocks. At the end of each year i, we observe the individual returns Ret(i, j) of the shares j composing the underlying basket:

$$\text{Ret}(i, j) = \frac{S(i, j)}{S(0, j)} - 1, \qquad i = 1, 2, 3, \quad j = 1, \dots, N$$

Then we cap each stock return at Cap% (say 20%). The individual capped returns *Capped_Ret*(i, j) are computed as follows:

$$\text{Capped\_Ret}(i, j) = \min \left[\text{Ret}(i, j), \text{Cap\%} \right]$$

The holder of the option receives an annual coupon, Coupon(i) (floored at 0%) of value of the arithmetic average of the capped returns.

$$\text{Coupon}(i) = \max \left[0, \frac{1}{N} \times \sum_{j=1}^{N} \text{Capped\_Ret}(i, j) \right]$$

Obviously, coupons can be paid periodically (monthly, quarterly, annually) or at maturity of the option, depending on the terms agreed by the contract.

To clarify this payoff mechanism, consider the following scenario: A British distributor decides to buy a 3-year maturity ICBC based on a basket composed of the 10 stocks in Table 9.4. The notional of this option is £30 million. The individual caps are equal to 15% and coupons are paid annually. Table 9.4 shows the individual observed returns and the process through which the coupon values are determined: Note that the maximum annual paid coupon would be equal to Cap (in this case 15%) since $(1/N) \times \sum_{j=1}^{N} \text{Capped\_Ret}(i, j) \leq \text{Cap}$. Then, if the price of an individually capped basket call is higher than Cap, it is worth trying to discover what has gone wrong when pricing this option.

Table 9.4 Scenarios for the 10 underlying stocks' annual returns composing the basket of a 3-year ICBC. Note that the cap is equal to 15%.

Returns	Y1	Capped	Y2	Capped	Y3	Capped
Boeing	−5%	−5%	7%	7%	12%	12%
Carrefour	3%	3%	12%	12%	19%	15%
Electrabel	13%	13%	8%	8%	10%	10%
Exxon Mobil	−2%	−2%	−6%	-6%	0%	0%
Generali	4%	4%	−9%	−9%	2%	2%
General Motors	16%	15%	22%	15%	35%	15%
Gillette	−8%	−8%	−17%	−17%	−21%	−21%
Sony	−1%	−1%	7%	7%	−12%	−12%
Toyota	13%	13%	22%	15%	20%	15%
UBS	8%	8%	18%	15%	15%	15%
Annual coupons	**4.1%**	**4%**	**6.4%**	**4.7%**	**8%**	**5.1%**

9.2.2 Risk Analysis

The buyer of an ICBC has a bullish view on the underlying stocks in the sense that the payoff is higher if the underlyings' returns are positive. Higher forward prices increase the call's price. The seller of this option would be short the stock's forwards and will need to buy Delta in each of the underlying assets on day 1, and adjust dynamically through the life of the trade to remain Delta neutral. The seller is short interest rates, long dividends and long borrowing costs.

Now, would a high dispersion increase the option's price? The answer is a definite no. To price this option, one typically simulates paths using Monte Carlo, and then obtains a price from a large sample of paths. For the sake of an example, consider a smaller number of possible paths, as depicted in Figure 9.1. If dispersion is high, this means that volatility is high and correlation is low. If we take the case of low-correlated stocks, we get a lot of positive returns and a lot of negative returns. If at the same time, volatility is high, this means that we would get returns far from their expected value, and thus more extreme values. When averaging the

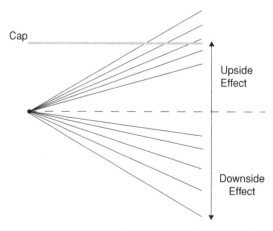

Figure 9.1 Simulations showing the effect of the cap on the dispersion of the underlyings.

Table 9.5 Individual parameter positions for an ICBC option trader.

	Seller of an ICBC	Buyer of an ICBC
Interest rates	Short	Long
Borrowing costs	Long	Short
Dividends	Long	Short
Volatility	Long	Short
Correlation	Short	Long
Skew	Short	Long

returns to determine the option's payoff, the positive large values are capped but the negative values are not floored. This means that the downside effect is more important than the upside effect because of caps applied to individual returns. Therefore, the potential payoff is lower when dispersion is higher. In other words, the seller of this option is long dispersion; which means he would be long volatility and short correlation.

If we think of an ICBC as a basket of covered calls, then it's easy to figure out the skew position. Since the skew makes covered calls more expensive, it also makes the ICBC option more expensive. Therefore, the seller of an ICBC is short skew. The lower the number of stocks composing the basket, the lower the downside effect with respect to the upside effect, and consequently, the higher the ICBC price would be (Table 9.5).

Exercise

Imagine you work on the sell side and are about to sell an ICBC to a client. You already priced the option and are calling him to communicate your offer price. This client has just changed his mind about the product he wants to invest in and says: "Let's slightly modify the payoff mechanism of the ICBC. Instead of averaging the capped returns on the individual stocks, let's take the case where we apply a global cap denoted Cap (equal to the ICBC cap) on the basket's return, which is the average of the individual stocks' returns."

The option we are talking about is called a call on a capped basket and its annual payoff is equal to:

$$\text{CBC}_{\text{payoff}} = \max\left[0, \min\left(\frac{1}{N}\sum_{i=1}^{N}\text{Ret}_i, \text{Cap}\right)\right]$$

Do you think this option is cheaper or more expensive than the ICBC you were about to offer? Moreover, do you believe the risks associated with hedging a *capped basket call* are similar to those associated with the ICBC?

Discussion

Firstly, if we think about the maximum payoffs of both options, they are the same. In the best scenario, the holder would receive Cap% from the ICBC or from the capped basket call. Now, let's have a look at some payoff scenarios depending on the fact that the buyer holds an ICBC or a capped basket call. Through the example illustrated in Table 9.6, the

Table 9.6   Scenarios for a CBC, same as the above ICBC,
only returns here are not capped, just the basket itself is
capped. This demonstrates the higher value of the CBC over
the ICBC for a given set of scenarios.

Returns	Ret. year 1	Ret. year 2	Ret. year 3
Boeing	−5%	7%	12%
Carrefour	3%	12%	19%
Electrabel	13%	8%	10%
Exxon Mobil	−2%	−6%	0%
Generali	4%	−9%	2%
General Motors	16%	22%	35%
Gillette	−8%	−17%	−21%
Sony	−1%	7%	−12%
Toyota	13%	22%	20%
UBS	8%	18%	15%
Annual coupons	**4.1%**	**6.4%**	**8%**

coupons paid by the capped basket call are higher than those paid to the holder of the ICBC.
In fact, this is true in all cases; the price of the ICBC is always cheaper than the price of
the capped basket call because its payoff is lower:

$$\text{ICBC}_{\text{payoff}} < \text{CBC}_{\text{payoff}}$$

since

$$\max\left[0, \frac{1}{N}\sum_{i=1}^{N}\min\left(\text{Ret}_i, \text{Cap}\right)\right] \leq \max\left[0, \min\left(\frac{1}{N}\sum_{i=1}^{N}\text{Ret}_i, \text{Cap}\right)\right]$$

See section B.3 of Appendix B for a demonstration of why this is true.

With this being true, we have to be aware that the ask price of the basket capped call
will be higher than your ICBC's previous offer. It could also be much higher in the case of
a high number of underlying assets as well as a high cap level.

Regarding the risks associated with the capped basket call, the payoff doesn't seem to be
so different, then we can expect to hedge this option in the same way that we are hedging
an ICBC. However, this is not the case at all; this is an example through which we are
going to emphasize the fact that one should be cautious with the Greeks even when option
payoffs seem to be similar.

The *slight* modification the bank's client suggested in the exercise has a big effect on
the risks associated with hedging a position in this option. Firstly, regarding the forward
sensitivity, in the case of a capped basket call, it is obvious that higher stock forwards imply
a higher price. Now, the analysis starts to be interesting when we are talking about volatility
and correlation impacts on the capped basket call price. Recall the dispersion effect on the
ICBC: the dispersion was coming from the idea that the downside effect was more important
than the upside effect when simulating paths. Then, the expected individual capped returns

are lower if dispersion is higher. But in the case of a capped basket call, there are no caps on the individual returns; the cap is global, and so the individual upside paths of the underlyings are not dampened, and the downside paths do not gain relative importance. Thus there is no dispersion effect on the capped basket call. This is an intuitive way of understanding that a capped basket call has risks similar to a simple basket call.

Take a capped basket call payoff:

$$CBC_{payoff} = \max \left[0, \min \left(\frac{1}{N} \sum_{i=1}^{N} \text{Ret}_i, \text{Cap} \right) \right]$$
$$= \min \left[\text{Cap}, \max \left(0, \frac{1}{N} \sum_{i=1}^{N} \text{Ret}_i \right) \right]$$

we are just applying a global cap to the payoff of a basket call. Therefore, a higher volatility increases the capped basket call price since it increases the potential payoff of a basket call. Moreover, a higher correlation increases the volatility of the basket and then increases its payoff. Thus correlation increases the price of a capped basket call.

When a trader sells an ICBC, they are buying the volatilities of the underlying assets, and selling the correlations between them. When selling a capped basket call, they are no longer dealing with dispersion, and the risks involved are slightly simpler, but it is still necessary to know that they are selling the volatilities and correlations. We note that the capped basket call has Greeks that resemble the call spread, for which we know the Vega can become negative depending on the paths of the underlying basket and position of the basket forward.

9.3   OUTPERFORMANCE OPTIONS

9.3.1   Payoff Mechanism

The outperformance option, also referred to as a spread option, is typically European style, and has a payoff based on the positive return of an asset S_1 over another asset S_2. Discussions of outperformance options exist in the literature – for example, Derman (1992), discussing outperformance options, and Margrabe (1978) on the closely related topic of options to exchange one asset for another. At maturity, the outperformance option holder receives a payoff given by

$$\text{Outperformance}_{payoff} = \max \left[0, \frac{S_1(T)}{S_1(0)} - \frac{S_2(T)}{S_2(0)} \right]$$

In other words, for an option based on the outperformance of S_1 versus S_2, the holder will receive money if the performance of S_1 is better than the performance of S_2. In this case, S_1 is said to *outperform* S_2. When the payoff takes the form described above, the outperformance option still makes a positive payout even if both underlying assets decrease in value, as long as S_1 has a negative performance lower in absolute value than the negative performance of S_2. Ideally, the holder of an outperformance option would rather S_1 increase and S_2 decrease, and the payoff would then be higher.

Let's take the example of Adam Alder, an investor who believes that Mexico, as an emerging country, will have a faster economic growth than the USA. He decides to invest in a 3-year

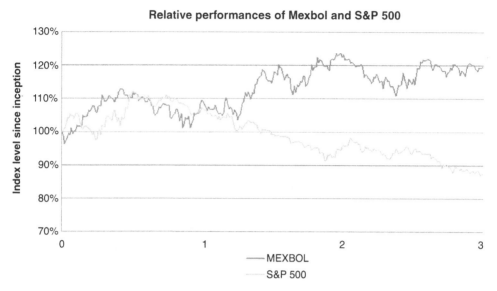

Figure 9.2 Relative performances of Mexbol and S&P 500, plotted against time in years. Note the outperformance payoff at the end of year 3.

maturity outperformance option based on the Mexican Bolsa index,[2] known as Mexbol, versus the S&P 500 index. Then, this option Mexbol vs S&P 500 pays Adam Alder a coupon if the Mexican index outperforms the American index at the end of the third year.

Figure 9.2 shows the relative performances of the Mexbol and S&P 500. This is a scenario where Mexbol outperforms S&P 500, and this means that the option's holder will be paid at maturity. The final level of Mexbol is equal to Mexbol(T)/Mexbol(0) = 119.48%, whereas the final level of S&P 500 is equal to S&P 500(T)/S&P 500(0) = 87.27%. The holder of the outperformance option on Mexbol vs S&P 500 will receive a coupon equal to 119.48% − 87.27% = 32.21% of the option's notional.

9.3.2 Risk Analysis

The seller of this option is essentially short the forward price of S_1 and long the forward price of S_2. The seller will be long the dividends of S_1 because he will have to go long an amount Δ_{S_1} in S_1 to hedge the risk to this underlying, and short the dividends of S_2, again from the Delta hedge, but in this case the hedger of the outperformance will need to go short an amount Δ_{S_2} in S_2.

Moreover, a high dispersion means having performances potentially far from each other. The higher the difference between underlyings' performances, the higher the payoff of this option; so dispersion has an increasing effect on the outperformance option price. The seller of this option is then short dispersion, which means that he is long correlation between the indices and short their volatility.

---

[2] The Mexbol is a capitalization-weighted index of the leading stocks traded in the Mexican Stock Exchange.

Table 9.7 Individual parameter positions for an outperformance option seller.

	w.r.t. asset S_1	w.r.t. asset S_2
Interest rates	Short	Long
Borrowing costs	Long	Short
Dividends	Long	Short
Volatility	Short	Short
Correlation	**Seller is long the correlation between the two indices**	

As is the case for best-of options, outperformance options are another way for an exotic trader to balance his global position in dispersion. Selling such options involves selling volatility, but more importantly, involves buying correlation. This sets it out from the majority of multi-asset options in which the seller is short correlation.

Extending the payoff of the outperformance option, the two assets whose performances are being compared could in fact be baskets of assets B_1 and B_2 which need not be equally weighted (Table 9.7). The seller of the option will still be long the correlations between the two baskets, i.e. long the pairwise correlations between any one element of B_1 and one element of B_2, but will be short the correlations within each basket, i.e. the pairwise correlations between any two elements of B_1 or any two elements of B_2. The sub-basket correlation positions can be seen by recalling the formula for the volatility of a basket, it involves the covariances and thus the correlations, and so an increase in the correlations within a basket raises the overall basket volatility. The seller of the option is short the volatility of each basket and is thus short these correlations.

9.4 VOLATILITY MODELS

In order to capture the skew effects in each of these payoffs, to which all of them are sensitive, we will need to calibrate a skew model, the simplest being a local volatility model, to each underlying's implied volatilities. If the option's payoff is only a function of the returns of each underlying at maturity, then it is imperative to get that particular skew correct in the calibration and we would use the exact date-fitting model described in section 4.3.3. European options with the same maturity as the exotic in question can serve as Vega hedging instruments, but the model must be calibrated to them in order that it shows risk against them. If there is some form of additional path dependency, such as averaging, then we need to use a form of smooth surface local volatility calibration described in section 4.3.3 in order to capture the effect of surface at all dates where the payoff is sensitive.

All these payoffs are multi-asset and are thus sensitive to the correlations between the various underlyings. These correlations must be correctly specified by the criteria laid out in Chapter 7 and by also observing which side of correlation sensitivity the seller of such options is on. For example, in the case of an ICBC, the seller is short correlation and will thus mark correlations accordingly before these are used as inputs to run a multi-asset simulation of each of these calibrated models. In outperformance options the position in correlation is reversed, and again correlations must be correctly specified before simulating the skew model.

10
Barrier Options

Barrier options are options that have a payoff contingent on crossing a second strike known as the *barrier* or *trigger*. The barrier options family includes a large variety of options that are quite popular. They come cheaper compared to traditional options with similar features, offer flexibility in terms of hedging or speculation and higher potential leverage than standard vanilla options.

There are two kinds of barrier option: knock-out options and knock-in options. Knock-out options are options that expire when the underlying's spot crosses the specified barrier. Knock-in options are options that only come into existence if the barrier is crossed by the asset's price. The observation of the barrier can be at any time during the option's life (American style) or at maturity only (European style). We note that the monitoring of the barrier must be clearly laid out in the contractual terms of the option, to avoid any ambiguity or misunderstandings in whether or not a barrier event occurs.

Firstly, we present the payoff mechanism of simple barrier options and some closed formulas to price these options in a flat volatility environment. Barrier options have skew dependency and this must be priced, typically by simulating a skew model. We also discuss the adjustments to be made when monitoring discrete barriers. Some replication arguments are given and we discuss the concept of barrier shifts which are important in the context of hedging barrier options.

Once all these concepts are well understood, we discuss the details of the risks associated with the down-and-in put, which is an option that is commonly used to increase the yields offered by structured products. To conclude we present the shark note as well as reverse convertibles which are examples of funded structured products based on barrier options and dispersion.

10.1 BARRIER OPTION PAYOFFS

10.1.1 Knock-out Options

Knock-out options, also referred to as *extinguishable*, are path-dependent options that are terminated, i.e. *knocked out*, if a specified spot's price reaches a specified trigger level at any time between inception and expiry. In this case, the holder of the option gets zero payout. If the underlying has never breached the barrier during the life of this option, the option holder essentially holds an option with the same features as a European option of the same strike and expiry.

Therefore, the closer the barrier level is to the initial spot, the cheaper the knock-out option would be. Moreover, it is interesting to note that a knock-out option is less sensitive to volatility than a vanilla option carrying the same features. Indeed, a higher volatility increases the probability of expiring in-the-money but also increases the probability of reaching the

Underlying Asset	S&P 500 Index
Notional	$1,000,000
Currency	USD
Initial Spot Price	1,400 points
Strike Price	1,400 points
Initial Date	15/06/2008
Maturity Date	15/06/2009
Barrier (outstrike)	1,820 points
Barrier Monitoring	daily observations
Option Price	1.69% ($16,900)

Figure 10.1   The terms of an up-and-out call option.

barrier and ending with no value. The Vega of a knock-out option is generally lower than the Vega of a comparable vanilla option. This is an important aspect of the appeal of such options.

When knock-outs are defined with the barrier placed in such a way that the option vanishes when it is out-of-the-money, we call these *regular* knock-out options. In these, it is easier for traders to hedge the associated risks. Otherwise, knock-out options are classified as *reverse* and they present higher trading difficulty and risks.

All kinds of barrier options are traded in the OTC market, for example the down-and-out call and the up-and-out put are cheap options that *die* when they become out-of-the-money beyond the barrier. For instance, if the market increases a lot, a fund manager holding a protective up-and-out put would potentially give up his option since he no longer needs to hedge his portfolio of assets at the previous level. This protective barrier option is cheaper than its European counterpart, the protective put.

In the case of knock-out options, an additional feature called a *rebate* can be added to the contract specifications. The rebate is a coupon paid to the holder of a knock-out option in case the barrier is breached.

In the terms described in Figure 10.1, we are dealing with a 1-year 100 call/KO 130 (pronounced 100 call knock-out 130 in the jargon). This means that the option is at-the-money (strike = 100% of the initial spot) and the barrier is at 130% of the initial spot (1,820/1,400 = 130%). From the inception date (15/06/08) until maturity (15/06/09), we make daily observations on the close price of the underlying asset. If it reaches 1,820 points at the end of any day during the life of the option, this up-and-out call dies and the holder receives nothing. In the case where the spot price of the S&P 500 has always been below 1,820 points, the option's holder receives the payoff of an at-the-money vanilla call. For instance, if the spot price is equal to 1,610 on 15/06/09, the holder of this option receives a coupon of 15% (1,610/1,400 − 1 = 15%), which is equal to $150,000. He would have realized a profit of $133,123 (15% − 1.69% = 13.31% of the notional).

The price of a 1-year vanilla at-the-money call option (same features) on S&P 500 is equal to 10.2%. In the example described above, the vanilla call option's holder would have realized a profit of $48, 000 (15% − 10.20% = 4.8% of notional). This shows that the leverage effect of the up-and-out call can be much more attractive than the leverage of a comparable vanilla call for an investor who believes the spot will not reach the outstrike during the investment period. He gets more profit for bearing the risk of knocking out.

In this example, we consider a rebate equal to 0; the premium of a similar up-and-out call with a rebate equal to 3% is 2.48%. If the barrier has ever been breached during the life of the

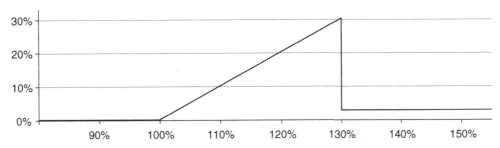

Figure 10.2 Payoff of an up-and-out ATM call option with knock-out barrier at 130% and rebate of 3%.

option, the holder would be paid a coupon of $30,000 (3% of the notional) to compensate for the loss of his premium ($24,800) (Figure 10.2).

In Figure 10.3, we are dealing with a 1-year 100 put/KO 70 (read as 100 put knock-out 70). This means that the option is at-the-money (strike = 100% of the initial spot) and the barrier is at 70% of the initial spot (980/1,400 = 70%). From the inception date (15/06/08) until maturity (15/06/09), we make daily observations on the close price of the underlying asset. If on the close of any day during the life of the option the underlying is at or below 980 points, this down-and-out put dies and the holder receives nothing. In the case the spot price of the S&P 500 has always been above 980 points, the option's holder receives the payoff of an at-the-money vanilla put. For instance, if the spot price is equal to 1,120 on 15/06/09, the holder of this option receives a coupon of 20% (1 − 1,120/1,400 = 20%), which is equal to $200,000. He would have realized a P&L equal to $154,300 (= 20% − 4.57% = 15.43% of notional).

The price of a 1-year vanilla at-the-money put option (same features) on S&P 500 is equal to 9.22%. In the example described above, the vanilla put option's holder would have realized a P&L equal to $107,800 (= 20% − 9.22% = 10.78% of notional). This shows that the leverage effect of the down-and-out put can be much more attractive than the leverage of a comparable vanilla put for an investor who believes the spot will not reach the outstrike during the investment period. The investor gets more profit for bearing the risk of knocking out.

In this example, we consider a rebate equal to 0; the premium of a similar down-and-out put with a rebate equal to 3% is equal to 5.08% (Figure 10.4). If the barrier has ever been

Underlying Asset	S&P 500 Index
Notional	$1,000,000
Currency	USD
Initial Spot Price	1,400 points
Strike Price	1,400 points
Initial Date	15/06/2008
Maturity Date	15/06/2009
Barrier (outstrike)	980 points
Barrier Monitoring	daily observations
Option Price	4.57% ($45,700)

Figure 10.3 The terms of a down-and-out put.

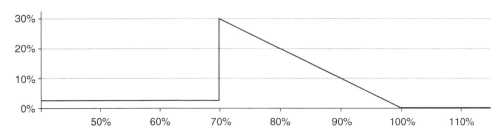

Figure 10.4 Payoff of a down-and-out ATM put option with knock-out barrier at 70% and rebate of 3%.

breached during the life of the option, the holder would be paid a coupon of $30,000 (3% of the notional) to compensate for the loss of his premium.

10.1.2 Knock-in Options

Knock-in options, also referred to as *lightable* options, are path-dependent options that are activated, i.e. *knocked-in*, if a specified spot rate reaches a specified trigger level between the option's inception and expiry. If such a barrier option is activated, the option then becomes essentially European-style and so these options also have lower premiums. If the barrier is never reached during the life of this option, this means that the option's holder paid an initial premium for an option that has never come into existence.

Therefore, the nearer the barrier level to the initial spot, the more expensive the knock-in option would be. Moreover, it is interesting to note that a knock-in option is more sensitive to volatility than a vanilla option carrying the same features. Indeed, a higher volatility can benefit the holder of the option because it increases not only the probability of maturing in-the-money but also the probability of reaching the barrier and being activated. The Vega of a knock-in option is then higher than the Vega of a comparable vanilla option.

When knock-in options are defined with the barrier placed in such a way that the options are activated when it is out-of-the-money, then we call them regular knock-in options since it is easier for traders to hedge the associated risks. Otherwise, knock-in options are classified as reverse and they present greater trading difficulties and risks. Regular knock-in options are the down-and-in calls and the up-and-in puts. The down-and-in puts and the up-and-in calls are reverse knock-in options.

Knock-in options are not as popular because investors are not really willing to pay a premium for a financial asset that doesn't exist and will perhaps never exist. These are still virtual options. However, the knock-in options are an efficient investment to have a position in market volatility.

In the terms described in Figure 10.5, we are dealing with a 1-year 100 put/KI 80. This means that the option is at-the-money (strike = 100% of the initial spot) and the barrier is at 80% of the initial spot (4,800/6,000 = 80%). From the inception date (15/06/08) until maturity (15/06/09), we make daily observations on the close price of the underlying asset. If it has never reached 4,800 points, the option will not be activated and the option's holder would have paid a premium for an asset that never existed. If the spot price of the FTSE 100 index reaches 4,800 points at the close of any trading day during the life of the option, this down-and-in put is activated and the option is equivalent to a vanilla put with the same

Underlying Asset	FTSE 100 Index
Notional	£1,000,000
Currency	GBP
Initial Spot Price	6,000 points
Strike Price	6,000 points
Initial Date	15/06/2008
Maturity Date	15/06/2009
Barrier (instrike)	4,800 points
Barrier Monitoring	daily observations
Option Price	5.84% (£58,400)

Figure 10.5   The terms of a down-and-in put.

strike and maturity. For instance, if the spot price is equal to 4,200 points on 15/06/09, the holder of this option receives a coupon of 30% (1 − 4,200 / 6,000 = 30%), which is equal to £300,000. He would have realized a profit of £241,621 (30% − 5.84% = 24.16% of the notional).

The price of a 1-year vanilla at-the-money put option (with the same features) on FTSE 100 is equal to 7.47%. In the example described above, the vanilla put option's holder would have realized a profit of £225,321. This shows that the leverage effect of the down-and-in put can be much more attractive than the leverage of a comparable vanilla put for an investor who believes that the spot will touch the in barrier during the investment period. He gets more profit for bearing the risk of not knocking in (Figure 10.6).

Figure 10.7 shows the terms of a 1-year 100 call/KI 120. This means that the option is at-the-money (strike = 100% of the initial spot) and the barrier is at 120% of the initial spot (7,200/6,000 = 120%). From the inception date (15/06/08) until maturity (15/06/09), we make daily observations on the close price of the underlying asset. If it has never reached 7,200 points, the option will not be activated and the option's holder would have paid a premium for an asset that never existed. If the spot price of the FTSE 100 index reaches 7,200 points at the

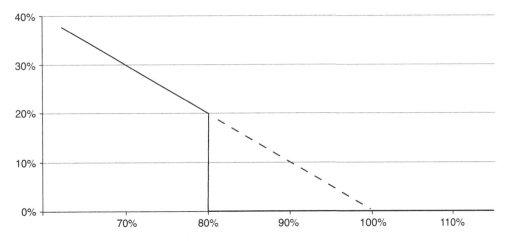

Figure 10.6   Payoff of a down-and-in ATM put option with knock-in barrier at 80%.

Underlying Asset	FTSE 100 Index
Notional	£1,000,000
Currency	GBP
Initial Spot Price	6,000 points
Strike Price	6,000 points
Initial Date	15/06/2008
Maturity Date	15/06/2009
Barrier (instrike)	7,200 points
Barrier Monitoring	daily observations
Option Price	9.79% (£97,900)

Figure 10.7 The terms of an up-and-in call.

end of any day during the life of the option (Figure 10.8), this up-and-in call is activated and the option is equivalent to a vanilla call with the same strike and maturity. For instance, if the spot price is equal to 6,600 points on 15/06/09, the holder of this option receives a coupon of 10% (6,600/6,000 − 1 = 10%), which is equal to £100,000. He would have realized a profit of £2,100 (10% − 9.79% = 0.21% of the notional).

The price of the 1-year vanilla at-the-money call option on FTSE 100 is equal to 10.36%. In the example described above, the vanilla call option's holder would have realized a loss of £3,600. This shows that the leverage effect of the up-and-in call can be much more attractive than the leverage of a comparable vanilla call for an investor who believes that the spot will certainly touch the in barrier during the investment period. He gets more profit for bearing the risk of not knocking in.

10.1.3 Summary

In the case of simple barrier options, there can be eight combinations depending on the option's category (call or put) and the barrier level with respect to the initial spot (up option or down option). Table 10.1 summarizes the description of the eight existing simple barrier options.

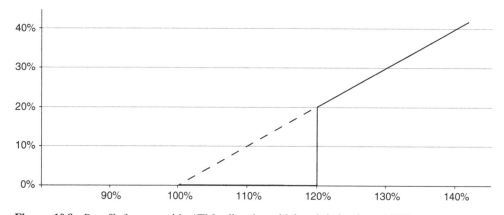

Figure 10.8 Payoff of an up-and-in ATM call option with knock-in barrier at 120%.

Table 10.1 Barrier options summary table.

Option type	Barrier Situated	Barrier's effect on the payoff	
		Reached	Not reached
Down-and-out call	Below spot	No value	Standard call
Down-and-in call	Below spot	Standard call	No value
Up-and-out call	Above spot	No value	Standard call
Up-and-in call	Above spot	Standard call	No value
Down-and-out put	Below spot	No value	Standard put
Down-and-in put	Below spot	Standard put	No value
Up-and-out put	Above spot	No value	Standard put
Up-and-in put	Above spot	Standard put	No value

10.2 BLACK–SCHOLES VALUATION

10.2.1 Parity Relationships

Consider an investor who is long a knock-in option and long a knock-out option with the same barrier level H, the same strike price K and the same time to expiration T. Also assume that the rebate is equal to 0 for the knock-out option. If, during the life of the options, the underlying's spot has ever reached the trigger, then the knock-out option dies and the knock-in option is activated with the same payoff as a vanilla option with strike K and maturity T. If the barrier has never been breached, the knock-in has no value but the knock-out behaves like a vanilla option with strike K and time to maturity T. In other words, being long a knock-out option and a knock-in option with the same features is equivalent to owning a comparable vanilla option independently from the behaviour of the spot with respect to the barrier level. Hence the following arbitrage relationship:

$$\text{Knock-in}(K, T, H) + \text{Knock-out}(K, T, H) = \text{Vanilla}(K, T)$$

10.2.2 Closed Formulas for Continuously Monitored Barriers

In this section, we give closed formulas for the different simple barrier options, as well as the effect of the rebate on the knock-out option valuations. In the literature, closed formulas for barrier options are presented in Haug (2006) and Hull (2003). Here we give formulas and parity relationships for the pricing of the up-and-out call option and the down-and-in put option, and we refer the reader to these authors for more formulas. We note that these formulas assume that the underlying asset's price follows a log-normal distribution, i.e. a Black–Scholes assumption.

Up-and-In Call

The payoff of the up-and-in call is given by

$$\text{UI Call}_{\text{payoff}} = \max[0; S(T) - K] \times \mathbf{1}_{\{(\max_{t \in [0,T]} S(t)) \geq H\}}$$

The closed formula for the price of the continuously monitored up-and-in call is

$$\text{UI Call}_{\text{price}} = S\mathcal{N}(x_1)\,e^{-qT} - K\,e^{-rT}\mathcal{N}(x_1 - \sigma\sqrt{T}) - S\,e^{-qT}\left(\frac{H}{S}\right)^{2\lambda}[\mathcal{N}(-y) - \mathcal{N}(-y_1)]$$

$$+ K\,e^{-rT}\left(\frac{H}{S}\right)^{2\lambda-2}[\mathcal{N}(-y+\sigma\sqrt{T}) - \mathcal{N}(-y_1+\sigma\sqrt{T})]$$

where

$$x_1 = \frac{\ln(S/H)}{\sigma\sqrt{T}} + \lambda\sigma\sqrt{T}, \qquad y_1 = \frac{\ln(H/S)}{\sigma\sqrt{T}} + \lambda\sigma\sqrt{T}$$

and

$$\lambda = \frac{r - q + \sigma^2/2}{\sigma^2}, \qquad y = \frac{\ln\left[H^2/(SK)\right]}{\sigma\sqrt{T}} + \lambda\sigma\sqrt{T}$$

Up-and-Out Call

The payoff of the up-and-out call (Figure 10.9) is given by

$$\text{UO Call}_{\text{payoff}} = \max[0; S(T) - K] \times \mathbf{1}_{\{(\max_{t\in[0,T]}\, S(t)) < H\}}$$

and the parity relationship with the up-and-out call is given by

$$\text{UO Call}(K, T, H) = \text{Call}(K, T) - \text{UI Call}(K, T, H)$$

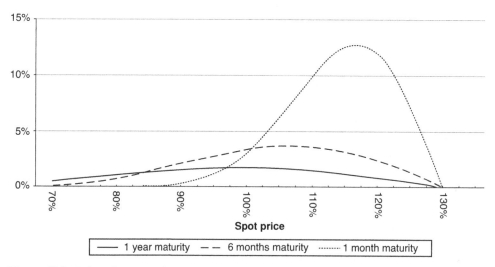

Figure 10.9 Price of an up-and-out ATM call with KO barrier at 130% across spot price. Note the three different maturities.

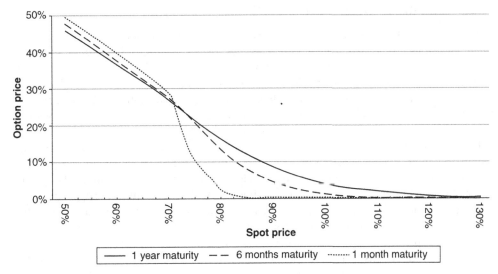

Figure 10.10 Price of a down-and-in ATM put with KI barrier at 70% across spot price. Note the three different maturities.

Down-and-In Put

The payoff of the down-and-in put is given by

$$\text{DI Put}_{\text{payoff}} = \max[0; K - S(T)] \times \mathbf{1}_{\{(\min_{t \in [0,T]} S(t)) \leq H\}}$$

The price of a down-and-in put option is:

$$\text{DI Put}_{\text{price}} = -S\mathcal{N}(-x_1)\,e^{-qT} + K\,e^{-rT}\mathcal{N}(-x_1 + \sigma\sqrt{T}) + S\,e^{-qT}\left(\frac{H}{S}\right)^{2\lambda}[\mathcal{N}(y) - \mathcal{N}(y_1)]$$

$$-K\,e^{-rT}\left(\frac{H}{S}\right)^{2\lambda-2}[\mathcal{N}(y - \sigma\sqrt{T}) - \mathcal{N}(y_1 - \sigma\sqrt{T})]$$

This case is when the down-and-in barrier H is less than the strike K (Figure 10.10).

Down-and-Out Put

The payoff of a down-and-out put is

$$\text{DO Put}_{\text{payoff}} = \max[0; K - S(T)] \times \mathbf{1}_{\{(\min_{t \in [0,T]} S(t)) > H\}}$$

Similar to before, we have the following parity relationship

$$\text{DO Put}(K, T, H) = \text{Put}(K, T) - \text{DI Put}(K, T, H)$$

Note that in this section all the prices are not expressed in terms of percentage of the spot but in currency measure. Therefore, one needs to divide these prices by the initial spot price to get a percentage price.

10.2.3 Adjusting for Discrete Barriers

Here we note that the closed formulas presented above are for a continuously monitored barrier. Many variations on the barrier theme are available. Usually, barrier levels are monitored at discrete fixing times, with barrier observations made periodically. For instance, if barriers are monitored semi-annually, the seller will check whether the underlying's spot reaches the barrier level on the last trading day of each 6-month period starting from inception until maturity date. Barrier observation frequencies can vary a lot (daily, weekly, monthly, quarterly, ...) because these are based on the investor's preference and traded OTC.

In the case of knock-out options, the higher the number of barrier observations, the higher the probability of observing the barrier being breached and the option knocking out. A knock-out option having an annually monitored barrier would be more expensive than a similar knock-out option having a bi-monthly monitored barrier. For knock-in options, this is the opposite. If the number of barrier observations increases, the price of the option is more expensive since the probability of activating it is higher. A knock-in option having a monthly monitored barrier would be cheaper than a similar knock-in option having a weekly monitored barrier.

For up-and-out options, a higher barrier decreases the probability of knocking out and thus increases the up-and-out option price. The seller of this option is short the barrier since a lower barrier would decrease the price of the sold asset. In the case of down-and-in options, a lower barrier level would decrease the probability of knocking in and thus decreases the option price. One buying the down-and-in options would be long the barrier since a higher barrier will increase the value of his holdings. Table 10.2 summarizes a trader's position in the barrier depending on whether he is selling or buying the different combinations of simple barrier options.

Broadie and colleagues (1997) give a discrete barrier monitoring adjustment formula. If one is short the barrier, he should simply replace the barrier by

$$H' = H \, e^{0.5826\sigma\sqrt{T/m}}$$

If one is long the barrier, he should simply replace the barrier by

$$H' = H \, e^{-0.5826\sigma\sqrt{T/m}}$$

Here m is the number of times the asset price is observed (so that T/m is the time interval between observations).

Table 10.2 Relative positions in the barrier for a barrier option trader

	Seller of option	Buyer of option
Down-and-out call	Long	Short
Down-and-in call	Short	Long
Up-and-out call	Short	Long
Up-and-in call	Long	Short
Down-and-out put	Long	Short
Down-and-in put	Short	Long
Up-and-out put	Short	Long
Up-and-in put	Long	Short

Example

Let's take the example of Cherif Zidane, a trader selling a 1-year at-the-money call knocking out at 80% for which the barrier is monitored daily. He can price this option using a closed formula for a continuously monitored barrier option and then apply one of the above correction formulas. Firstly, we need to determine whether Cherif is long or short the barrier. The 100 call/KO 80 is a down-and-out call. A higher barrier level would increase the probability of knocking out and thus decreases the option price. The trader selling this option is then long the barrier. Also, let's assume that the underlying stock implied 1-year volatility is equal to 20%. Using the appropriate formula above for the barrier shift, our new barrier is given by

$$H' = 80\% \times e^{-0.5826 \times 20\% \times \sqrt{1/252}} = 79.4\%$$

Note that in the above formula $T = 1$ representing the 1-year maturity, and $m = 252$ the number of observations during the period (there are 252 trading days per year and we want to have daily observations so $m = 252$ observations in total).

10.3   HEDGING DOWN-AND-IN PUTS

Many structured products use down-and-in puts to obtain enhanced yields or increased participation. The view is non-bearish in the sense that one would not expect the puts to knock in and will just receive the high coupon or participation. These products are good examples of structured products not offering capital protection since the buyer of the structure is in fact selling down-and-in puts at maturity and can lose the money invested. The investor accepts the risk from selling the down-and-in puts to generate extra funding that is used in the structure to increase the yield or participation. In section 3.10 we discussed this in the context of European options, and the same concept holds here, only we now have at our disposal barrier options that allow the downside risk taken to be specifically tailored to an investor's risk tolerance.

10.3.1   Monitoring the Barrier

Traders on the sell side are usually long the down-and-in put at maturity, and have to hedge the risks associated with this position accordingly. Firstly, we analyse the effects of the different market parameters on the down-and-in put price.

If the forward price of the underlying share goes down, then the price of the down-and-in put goes up for two reasons. Firstly, the potential payoff of the put is higher and, secondly, the probability of activating the option increases. The trader taking a long position in the down-and-in put is then short the forward, and will need to buy Delta in the underlying asset on day 1, and adjust dynamically through the life of the trade to remain Delta neutral. The seller will be short interest rates but is long dividends and long borrowing costs.

The risks of a barrier option near the barrier can be difficult to manage. The Delta of a barrier option can jump near the barrier causing hedging problems. When near the barrier, a small move in the underlying can have a large impact on the price of a barrier option. For example, it could be about to knock out and become worthless. So near the barrier, the Gamma, which gives us the sensitivity of Delta to a movement in the underlying asset's price, can be very large; a small move in the underlying will change the value of Delta significantly. One method to smooth out the risks to make them manageable is to apply a *barrier shift*.

If the knock-in barrier is near the initial spot level, this makes the option more expensive because the probability of crossing this barrier is higher. For instance, a 100 put/KI 60 is cheaper than a 100 put/KI 70. The trader buying the down-and-in put is then long the barrier since a higher barrier level increases the option price. Therefore, the trader will apply a shift to the initial barrier when pricing the option in order to compensate for the associated risk. For instance, if one is about to make a bid on a 100 put/KI 60, he can price this option as if the option was a 100 put/KI 58%; in other words, he can apply a barrier shift equal to 2%, which makes the option cheaper for the trader since it is less risky.

The shift will take into account the size of the digital around the barrier and the maximum volume of underlying share that can be bought or sold during one day. This is referred to as a liquidity-based barrier shift, and accounts for the discontinuity in the Delta near the barrier. Depending on the trader's position with respect to the option, he might need to buy or sell a large amount of underlying stock if the barrier is reached. Therefore, the barrier risks are higher if the digital size is high or the daily traded volume is low.

If he is long the barrier, he has to apply a barrier shift that lowers the trigger level. The higher the absolute value of the shift, the cheaper the bid on the down-and-in put would be. In the case of reverse enquiries, a trader buying an option would win the trade if he gives the highest bid price, i.e. most aggressive price. At the same time, his bid should represent the cost of his hedge, i.e. being conservative on risks. The balance between these two is ultimately the difference between the prices seen by an investor from different banks.

In the first days of an option's life, under normal levels of volatility, the underlying is unlikely to breach the barrier level. If one were to simulate paths and monitor the points in time at which the barrier was breached, it is obvious that the knock-in events occur more frequently down the line. One can thus apply a barrier shift that is not constant but is in fact an increasing function of time.

Let's take the case of an investor willing to sell a 100 call/KI 60 for which the barrier is monitored daily. He phones three salespeople from different investment banks to get their bid prices by 4 pm. Let's assume that the three competitors for this trade are willing to charge 50 bp as origination P&L and apply the same levels for the parameters affecting the price of the option (skew, volatility, . . .). Also, they all want to apply a maximum shift of 2% to the 60% knock-in barrier. However, they have different ways of shifting the barrier. Trader number 1 is very conservative and applies a constant barrier shift, as we can see in Figure 10.11.

Trader number 2 is less conservative and decides to apply a linear barrier shift as we can also see in Figure 10.11. At inception date, there is no barrier shift since there is no expected risk around the barrier. He believes that the maximum shift $Shift_{max}$ to be applied would be 2%, which is the shift value at maturity. The barrier shift at time t $Shift(t)$ is computed as follows

$$Shift(t) = Shift_{max} \times \frac{t}{T}$$

and the barrier level to be applied at time t is then equal to

$$Barrier(t) = Barrier(0) - Shift(t)$$

so this shift grows linearly in time from zero (inception) to $Shift_{max}$ (at maturity T).

Trader number 3 uses a curvy barrier in time which is computed from evaluating knock-in scenarios. As we can see from Figure 10.11 he is the most aggressive in his barrier shift. Therefore, his bid is the highest and he wins the trade in this case.

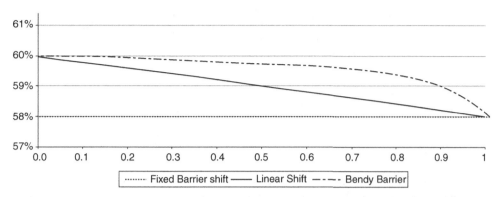

Figure 10.11 Three barrier shift schemes. The barrier is at 60%, and the three schemes represent the effective shifted barrier used in pricing.

10.3.2 Volatility and Down-and-in Puts

The impact of volatility must be considered when hedging the down-and-in put option. A higher volatility increases not only the probability of knocking in but also the potential payoff of down-and-in puts. The trader buying this option is long volatility. This long Vega position can be hedged, at least partially, by buying vanilla put options on the same underlying asset with strikes between the barrier and the spot.

With regards to the skew effect, as we can see in Figure 10.12, the volatility around the barrier is higher than the at-the-money volatility, which makes the probability of crossing the barrier higher. Then the price of the down-and-in put is higher because of the skew. Since the trader buying this option wants its price to go up, he is then long skew (Table 10.3). When the trader is long skew, the question is at what level will he be willing to buy skew? This case we refer to as a *skew benefit* for the buyer, and it usually ranges from anywhere between 70% and 100%, 70% being a conservative approach in the pricing and 100% being aggressive.

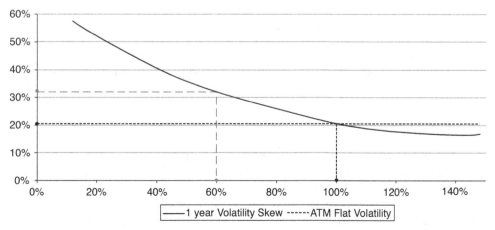

Figure 10.12 Volatility skew for KI barrier at 60%. Note that the volatility corresponding to this barrier level is higher than the ATM volatility.

Table 10.3   Individual parameter positions for a down-and-in put trader.

	DI put seller	DI put buyer
Interest rates	Long	Short
Borrowing costs	Short	Long
Dividends	Short	Long
Volatility	Short	Long
Skew	Short	Long
Barrier	Short	Long

From the model point of view, and in order to capture the skew effects, we will need to calibrate a model to the implied volatilities of options on the underlying, across strikes, with specific attention to the downside skew. If the barrier is monitored continuously we will need to apply a model that gives a smooth calibration through all ends of the surface between short maturities and up to the maturity. This means that one must calibrate to both skew and term structure. The reason is that a continuously monitored barrier option can be triggered at any time up to maturity, and therefore has Vega sensitivity through the different time-buckets. European options with different maturities must now be calibrated so that the model shows risk against them. The Vega sensitivity will change as the underlying moves: if a barrier event is close to happening, i.e. the underlying is trading close to the barrier, then the short-term Vega will increase and sensitivity to the long-term volatility will decrease.

If the barrier is only monitored at maturity, then getting the skew corresponding to that maturity correct is the primary concern and we would use the exact date-fitting model as described in section 4.3.3. For a Vega hedge involving OTM European put options on the same underlying to be meaningful, they must also have been priced correctly by the model. If such instruments are not included in the model calibration, the model will not show risk against them, thus the importance of skew calibration in this case. The cost of hedging the Vega must be included in the price, and because this option pays on the downside – where we expect to see high levels of volatility corresponding to the decline in asset price – we must account for the skew cost.

10.3.3   Dispersion Effect on Worst-of Down-and-in Puts

As is the case for single asset structured products using down-and-in puts, many structures based on multi-assets and dispersion use worst-of down-and-in puts to increase income. Let's take a basket of n assets $S_1, S_2, \ldots, S_n$. The worst-of down-and-in put has a payoff given by

$$\text{WO DI Put}_{\text{payoff}} = \max\left[0, K - \min_{i=1,\ldots,n}(\text{Ret}_i(T))\right] \times \mathbf{1}_{\{(\min_{i=1,\ldots,n;t\in[0,T]}\text{Ret}_i(t))\leq H\}}$$

where $\text{Ret}_i(t) = S_i(t)/S_i(0) - 1$ is the return at time t of the ith asset of the basket. The knock-in event can be triggered by any one of the assets. It is the case more often than not, given the short maturity, that the underlying to trigger the barrier is the worst performing at maturity. Nonetheless, if knocked in, the payoff at maturity is that of a put option on the *worst* performing asset in the basket, irrespective of which element triggered the knock-in. Also note that a worst-of down-and-in put is more expensive than a down-and-in put with the same strike, barrier level and maturity since the potential payoff is much higher. This makes it more effective when used in the context of yield enhancement or for generating income for a higher upside participation, but this obviously involves the investor bearing additional risk.

The risks here are essentially the same as those of a single asset down-and-in put, only here we must account for dispersion. The buyer of the option, typically the sell-side desk, is no longer buying volatility on one asset, but on several, and is short the correlations between these underlyings. This is the consequence of the buyer of the worst-of down-and-in put being long dispersion. The individual Vegas can be hedged by turning to the vanilla market and buying OTM puts on the various underlyings, with strikes between the barrier and the spot. The Vega hedging of the single asset down-and-in put described in the previous section holds here, with the added note that the seller must now trade options on several underlyings to hedge the volatility sensitivity, and this can lead to additional transaction costs.

Depending on the individual volatilities, the Vegas to each of the underlyings can be different. The price of the option is sensitive to all the individual volatilities but will be so much more sensitive to the more volatile underlyings owing to the increased probability that they end up as the worst-of. Therefore, the vanilla puts used in the volatility hedges will be of different notionals. If the barrier is monitored continuously, then the option will have sensitivities in all the time-buckets, and these vary on the basis of market movements in the underlying assets, most notably their position relative to the barrier. If the option is knocked in, it thus becomes a worst-of put, the risks of which were discussed in section 8.2.2.

Moreover, the individual skews increase the option price since, on the one hand, there is a down-and-in barrier and since, on the other, the payoff is based on the worst performing stock. Then being long a worst-of down-and-in put results in a long skew position on the different assets (Table 10.4).

Finally, a higher barrier level would increase the probability of knocking in, which makes the price of the option higher. Therefore, if a trader is long a worst-of down-and-in put, he is long the barrier.

The choice of model breaks down to the same case as the single asset down-and-in put. So again, the choice depends on whether the barrier is monitored throughout the life of the option or just at maturity. If the barrier is monitored continuously we will need to apply a smooth surface local volatility calibration. If the barrier is only monitored at maturity, then getting the skew corresponding to that maturity correct is the primary concern and we would use the exact date-fitting model as described in section 4.3.3. For a Vega hedge involving OTM European put options to be meaningful, they must also have been priced correctly. If the model's calibration does not include such instruments, it will not show risk against them, thus the importance of skew calibration on each of the individual underlyings. Also, because this

Table 10.4 Individual parameter positions for a worst-of down-and-in put trader.

	WO DI put seller	WO DI put buyer
Interest rates	Long	Short
Borrowing costs	Short	Long
Dividends	Short	Long
Volatility	Short	Long
Skew	Short	Long
Correlation	Long	Short
Barrier	Short	Long

is a multi-asset option we will need to do this for each underlying, and run the simulations based on a correlation matrix that is obtained following the procedures of Chapter 7 and taking into account that the seller of this derivative is short correlation. Correlation skew risk may be exhibited by the option, especially if the barrier is far from the spot, and we refer back to the discussion of section 7.2.5.

10.4   BARRIERS IN STRUCTURED PRODUCTS

10.4.1   Multi-asset Shark

Payoff Description

The shark note is a product based on a basket of underlying stocks. Consider a 3-year maturity shark based on a basket of n stocks. At the end of each day, we observe the basket's performance Basket(t), which is the arithmetic average of the individual performances of the shares j composing the underlying basket:

$$\text{Basket}(t) = \frac{1}{n} \sum_{j=1}^{n} \frac{S_j(t)}{S_j(0)}, \qquad t \in [0, T]$$

and the payoff is given by

$$\text{Shark}_{\text{payoff}} = \max\left[0; \text{Basket}(T) - K\right] \times \mathbf{1}_{\left\{\left(\max_{t \in [0,T]} \text{Basket}(t)\right) < H\right\}}$$
$$+ R \times \mathbf{1}_{\left\{\left(\max_{t \in [0,T]} \text{Basket}(t)\right) > H\right\}}$$

so, if Basket(t) has ever been higher than a predetermined trigger H, 160% for example, the first part of the equation is zero, and the holder of the shark gets the predefined rebate coupon R at maturity as well as 100% of the notional invested. Otherwise, the second part of the equation is zero, and the holder of the shark note receives 100% of his investment plus a call option payoff on the basket at maturity:

$$\max\left[0; \text{Basket}(T) - K\right]$$

Barrier observations can be continuous, discrete (daily, weekly, monthly, quarterly, annually) or at maturity of the option, depending on the terms agreed in the contract. The name *shark* comes from the shark fin like shape of the up-and-out call payoff with rebate upon which this structure is based.

Payoff Mechanism

To elaborate on the payoff mechanism, we consider two specific scenarios. An American investor, Kerry Smith, decides to buy a 3-year maturity shark note based on a basket composed of three stocks. The notional of this note is $25 million. Kerry has a bullish view on the underlying stocks, but believes that the composed basket will not have a spot higher than 160% of its initial value during the life of the note. Thus, the outstrike trigger is fixed at 160% and the barrier observations are made daily.

Figure 10.13 shows a scenario in which the barrier is breached by the basket performance. In this case, the holder of the shark note receives his capital back at maturity as well as a predetermined rebate of 6%. Figure 10.14 emphasizes another scenario which shows the individual stocks' performances as well as the basket performance. The barrier has never been

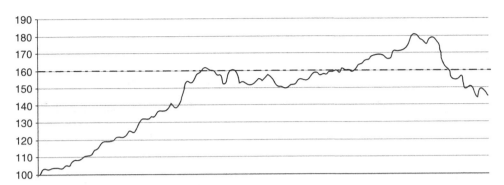

Figure 10.13 Scenario for the basket performance in a shark note. The barrier of 160% has been breached by the basket.

breached by the basket although two underlyings have crossed it. Therefore, Kerry Smith receives a coupon at maturity equal to the return of the basket (51% of notional) plus the 100% of notional from the capital guarantee. This amounts to 151% × $25,000,000 = $37,750,000.

Risk Analysis

The shark note is composed of a zero coupon bond and an up-and-out call option. The zero coupon bond pays 100% of the notional at maturity and the up-and-out call enables the holder to receive a variable payoff based on the underlying basket performance. The seller of the option's risk thus comes from the equity part, and we will discuss the risks associated with the up-and-out call.

Again, the holder of a shark note has a bullish view on the underlying stocks and believes that the performances of the stocks will not be above a specific level. The up-and-out call is

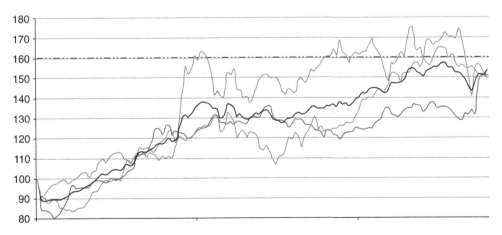

Figure 10.14 Scenario for the individual assets and the basket performances in a shark note. The barrier of 160% has not been breached by the basket. The dark line is the basket performance, and the thinner lines the individual performances of the underlyings.

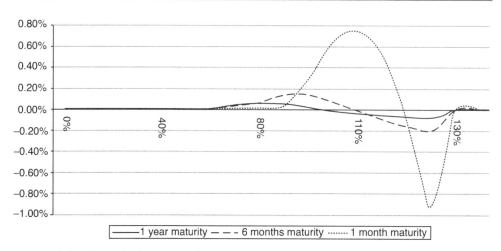

Figure 10.15 Example of the Delta of an up-and-out call with barrier at 130%.

cheaper than a vanilla call option with the same strike and maturity. As we can see in Figure 10.15, the Delta of the up-and-out call is positive as the spot is below the knock-out barrier. But as the spot approaches the barrier, the Delta becomes negative. Therefore, a trader selling a shark note would be short the underlying's forwards at inception. Then, if the spot starts to be close to the outstrike, the trader would be long the underlying's forwards.

The seller's position in volatility is a function of the parameters of the contract. On the one hand, a higher volatility raises the payoff of the call, but at the same time it increases the probability of hitting the barrier, therefore the position in volatility is a function of not only where the strike and the barrier are, but also of the time to maturity. In Figure 10.16 we see the Vegas of three up-and-out calls with different maturities but the same barrier. On day 1, assuming we strike at 100%, our position in volatility is different at $S = 100\%$ for each maturity, and in fact possibly of different sign. Since this is a basket option, correlation has its

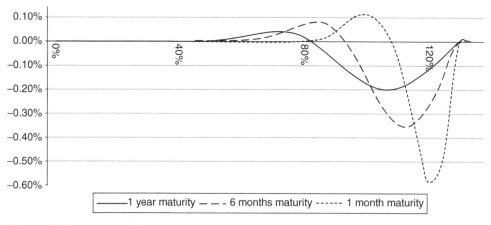

Figure 10.16 Example of the Vega of an up-and-out call with barrier at 130%.

main effect on the volatility. Higher correlation means a higher overall volatility for the basket and the analysis of the position in correlation is the same as that in volatility.

The skew position is also somewhat awkward. The seller is short the ATM volatility, but long volatility near the barrier. The magnitude of the volatility sensitivity near the barrier is a function of the size of the rebate and the location of the barrier. Thus the overall position in skew is not immediately clear and needs to be checked by increasing skew and computing the sensitivity.

Again, the choice of model to use in order to capture the skew is based on the barrier monitoring. In the case described here, we have continuous monitoring of the barrier and we thus need to apply a smooth surface local volatility calibration in order to capture the skew throughout correctly, for each underlying. The Vega is hedged with options on the individual underlyings, and any possible hedging instruments must be correctly priced within the calibration so that the pricing model shows risk against them. Because this is a multi-asset option we will need to do this for each underlying, and run the simulations based on a correlation matrix that is obtained following the procedures of Chapter 7 and taking into account the seller's position in correlation.

10.4.2 Single Asset Reverse Convertible

Payoff Description

As far as yield enhancement products go, the *reverse convertible* is an extremely popular product; it pays a fixed coupon at maturity, contingent on an equity event. Many variations exist, but the main one is the combination of a zero coupon bond and a down-and-in put which the buyer of the reverse convertible is short. In all cases the holder of the reverse convertible receives the predefined coupon. However, in the event of a knock-in, the holder receives at maturity the performance of the stock also. This holds downside risk as the performance of the stock could potentially be large and negative and wipe out both the coupon and part of (or possibly all of) the capital invested, thus the reverse convertible is not a capital protected structure. The key idea being that the investor is willing to accept some downside risk in exchange for an above market coupon; i.e. yield enhancement. The reverse convertible is a good product for the investor who is moderately bullish, as the highly bullish investor can find a better structure to fit his view. The bearish investor should for obvious reasons steer clear.

Here the down-and-in put is monitored continuously but pays on the return at maturity, thus, as we will see in the scenarios, it is possible that a stock can trigger the barrier, but then recover and end above the strike, rendering the put worthless. Typical knock-in levels are 70% or 80% depending on maturity, although these products generally have short maturities.

Payoff Mechanism

Let's consider a set of scenarios. In this example let's set the KI barrier at 80% for a 1-year maturity. Assume interest rates are 4%, the down-and-in put on a specific stock is worth 6.5%, and let's assume that the seller wants to take 50 bp of P&L. Then the coupon the seller can offer the investor is given by

$$\text{Interest from ZCB} + \text{Put Price} - \text{P\&L} = 4\% + 6.5\% - 0.50\% = 10\%$$

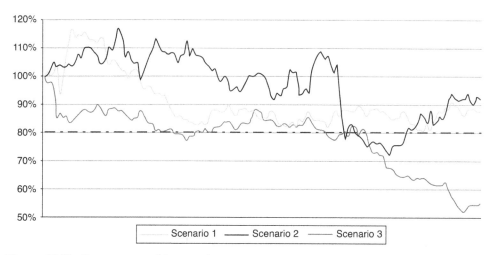

Figure 10.17 Reverse convertible scenarios.

These come from, firstly, the zero coupon bond we buy with the notional amount, plus the down-and-in put (bid) which we have priced, yielding the total amount we have for the coupon. Subtracting out P&L we get the offered coupon. In Figure 10.17 we see the scenarios for a reverse convertible, and the results are given in Table 10.5.

10.4.3 Worst-of Reverse Convertible

The worst-of version is similar to the reverse convertible just discussed in section 10.4.2, only here the equity exposure is on a basket of stocks (or indices) instead of just one. Instead of having a down-and-in put we have a worst-of down-and-in put. That is, the worst-of reverse convertible will bear coupons of enhanced yield provided NONE of the underlyings goes below the prespecified knock-in level H.

In the event of a knock-in, the investor pays at maturity the negative performance (if any) of the worst performing stock. Again these will generally be short dated, and we should note that because of the worst-of put this, too, is not a capital guaranteed structure. As with the case of the regular reverse convertible, this product would be good for the investor who is moderately bullish, as the highly bullish can find a better structure to fit his view.

It is also the case, as seen in Table 10.6, that a stock, as in the reverse convertible, can trigger the barrier, but then all the stocks recover somewhat and the worst ends above the strike,

Table 10.5 Scenarios for a reverse convertible paying a coupon of 10% at maturity. Note that in the third case, the investor has received back less than the 100% invested. This table's results are associated with the returns scenarios drawn in Figure 10.17.

	Lowest return	KI event	KI put payoff	**RevCon payoff**
Scenario 1	81%	No	0%	**110%**
Scenario 2	72%	Yes	8%	**102%**
Scenario 3	52%	Yes	45%	**65%**

Table 10.6 Worst-of reverse convertible scenarios. A knock-in event happens when one of the underlying indices composing the world basket has ever crossed the 70% barrier. The returns here correspond to the final levels of the indices at maturity and the bold column shows the payoff of a worst-of reverse convertible struck at 100% and paying a coupon of 15%. Note that the capital is not guaranteed, as shown in scenario 4.

	KI event	EuroStoxx 50	S&P 500	Nikkei	**WO-ReCon**
Scenario 1	No	85%	102%	72%	**115%**
Scenario 2	Yes	104%	120%	109%	**115%**
Scenario 3	Yes	87%	95%	88%	**102%**
Scenario 4	Yes	85%	45%	75%	**60%**

rendering the put worthless. The presence of dispersion due to the worst-of feature should make this put more valuable than a down-and-in put on just one of the underlyings, all else being the same. Thus, with added value to the put, equity exposure is greater, ceteris paribus, which implies a higher coupon offered in the structure.

In the context of the 2008/09 financial crisis, many investors in reverse convertibles lost money as a large amount of the put options embedded in reverse convertibles knocked in. The result was that unaware investors took hold of the underlying stocks and the losses on these have proved to be substantial. In the secondary market for these products, the note part of some of these structures was also hit owing to the problems involving the issuers, making valuations even lower. Banking stocks were among the favourite underlyings for single and multi-asset reverse convertibles, primarily because the relatively high volatilities of the individual underlyings allowed for enticing coupons. These banking stocks were perceived by many investors to be safer than they in fact were. On the other hand, the result of taking hold of the stock in the reverse convertible is no more risky than holding the said stock.

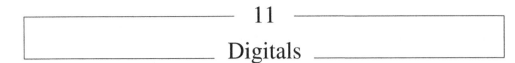

11

Digitals

There are 10 kinds of people in the world, those that understand binary and those that don't.

Digital options, also called binary options, pay a specific coupon when a barrier or trigger event occurs. There are two kinds of digitals: cash-or-nothing options and asset-or-nothing options. In this chapter we look at the European and American digitals on single and multiple underlyings, give examples throughout, and a detailed analysis of the risks involved in these types of trades.

11.1 EUROPEAN DIGITALS

11.1.1 Digital Payoffs and Pricing

The European cash-or-nothing call is an option paying a fixed coupon C if the spot of the underlying at maturity T is higher than the predetermined barrier level H. The payoff is

$$\text{Cash or Nothing}_{\text{payoff}} = C \times \mathbf{1}_{\{S(T)>H\}}$$

or equivalently

$$\text{Cash or Nothing}_{\text{payoff}} = \begin{cases} C & \text{if } S(T) > H \\ 0 & \text{otherwise} \end{cases}$$

Under Black–Scholes, the price of such an option is given by the following formula:

$$\text{Cash or Nothing}_{\text{price}} = C \times \mathcal{N}(d_2) \times e^{-rT}$$

where $\mathcal{N}(d_2)$ is the same $\mathcal{N}(d_2)$ we saw in the Black–Scholes formula for vanilla options in section 3.5. In fact, $\mathcal{N}(d_2)$ is the probability that the spot at time T is higher than the trigger. That is, the derivative of the call price with respect to K is the price of the digital. In much the same way we saw in Black–Scholes that the Delta sensitivity to underlying S is given by $\mathcal{N}(d_1)$; in the case of the digital the price is given by $\mathcal{N}(d_2)$ which is the negative of the derivative with respect to the strike. This is discussed in section 11.1.2; see also section B.4 of Appendix B for derivations. (See Figure 11.1.)

Notice the shape of the price across spot in Figure 11.2 and how it resembles the Delta of a European call option. This is because Delta is $\mathcal{N}(d_1)$ which is also a cumulative distribution function.

The European asset-or-nothing call is an option that pays the value of the underlying asset at maturity if this value is higher than the digital trigger.

$$\text{Asset or Nothing}_{\text{payoff}} = S(T) \times \mathbf{1}_{\{S(T)>H\}}$$

Having a long position in a European asset-or-nothing call, and being short a European cash-or-nothing call for which the coupon is equal to the barrier level, is equivalent to a long position

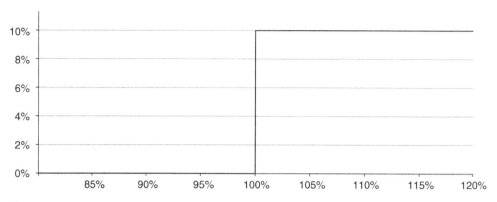

Figure 11.1   The payoff of a 10% digital call option struck at 100%.

in a vanilla call for which strike price is equal to digital trigger. We can then deduct the price
of an asset-or-nothing call from a vanilla call and cash-or-nothing call.

$$\text{Asset or Nothing}_{\text{price}} = Se^{-qT}\,\mathcal{N}(d_1)$$

We can see this if we recall the Black–Scholes price of a vanilla call option given by

$$\text{Vanilla Call}_{\text{price}} = \underbrace{Se^{-qT}\,\mathcal{N}(d_1)}_{\text{Asset−or−nothing}} - \underbrace{Ke^{-rT}\mathcal{N}(d_2)}_{\text{Cash−or−nothing}}$$

In the world of structured products, asset-or-nothing digital options are the less popular of the
two. Cash-or-nothing digitals are used more often because they allow holders to receive fixed
coupons conditionally on the spot price of a specific underlying crossing a predetermined
level. From now on, when discussing digitals, unless stated otherwise, this will implicitly refer
to cash-or-nothing digital options.

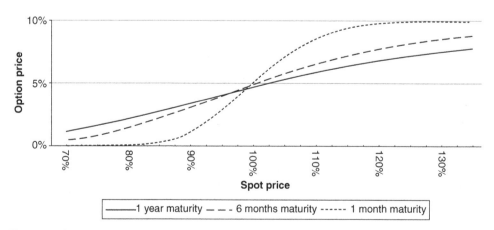

Figure 11.2   The price of a digital struck at 100% for three maturities, plotted as a function of spot
price.

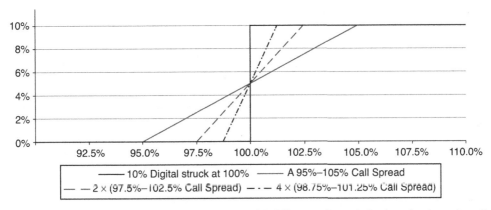

Figure 11.3   A 10% digital and three call spreads with different strikes. Notice how the closer the call spread strikes are to the digital strike, the closer the payoff.

11.1.2   Replicating a European Digital

The digital can be thought of as a *limit* of a call spread. That is, consider a call spread with strikes $K - \epsilon$ and $K + \epsilon$, and a digital struck at K, Digital(K) paying a coupon of $C\%$. In the limit we recognize the mathematical derivative

$$\text{Digital}(K) = \lim_{\epsilon \to 0} \frac{1}{2\epsilon}(\text{Call}(K - \epsilon) - \text{Call}(K + \epsilon)) = -\frac{\partial \text{Call}(K)}{\partial K}$$

To explain this intuitively, in Figure 11.3 we have a 10% digital and three call spreads. Note that to obtain the payoffs in the diagram we need one 95–105%, but we need two of the 97.5–102.5% call spreads and four of the 98.75–101.25% call spreads. This is a demonstration of the above limit in the sense that, as the distance between the call option strikes and the digital strikes, ϵ, gets smaller, we need $1/\epsilon$ call spreads of width 2ϵ to replicate the digital. In the limit, meaning as ϵ approaches zero, the call spread replicates the digital exactly. To see this in our example, the digital size is 10%, so we only need one 10% wide call spread (the 95–105%) to replicate it. Now assume that we split the width of the call spread in two, we need two of the 97.5–102.5% call spreads, and so on.

11.1.3   Hedging a Digital

In practice, one can price and hedge a digital as a call spread, the question is which call spread? The gearing of the call spread required to super replicate the digital depends on how wide we chose the strikes. The term *super replicate* comes from the fact that the call spread over-replicates the digital. In Figure 11.5, the digital at H has zero payoff before H, whereas the call spread has the same payoff of the digital after H, but also has a non-zero payoff before H given by the triangle ACH. The smaller the call spread the less the super replication and thus the more aggressive the price. On the other hand, the smaller the call spread the more difficult the hedging.

For a digital option, Gamma can be quite large near the barrier, and using a call spread means that we obtain less extreme Greeks. The smaller the call spread the larger Gamma, and Vega can get near the barrier. At the barrier they both shoot up and then shoot down while

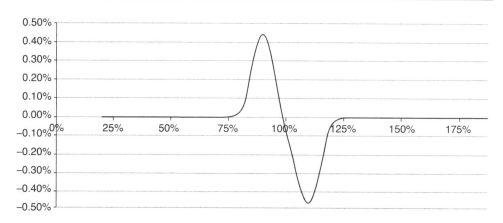

Figure 11.4   The Gamma of a call spread.

changing sign. See Figure 11.4 for the Gamma of a call spread; it, too, changes sign, but is better behaved than that of a digital. Since the plan is to Delta hedge this call spread, we need to make sure that as the underlying approaches the barrier we can still manage to Delta hedge. A large Gamma means that Delta is very sensitive to a movement in the underlying, and if we approach the barrier and our call spread is too tight, then we will need to buy a large Delta of the underlying, which might be difficult in the market. To this end it makes sense that we select the width of our replicating call spreads based on the liquidity of the underlying.

It is possible to reach a middle ground by which we minimize the price of the option by selecting a small enough call spread but also such that the digital can be hedged without problems to do with liquidity. Define MaxDelta as the maximum amount (in the correct currency) that one can trade of the underlying, given data of the daily traded volumes, liquidity that is.

Barrier Shifts

The *barrier shift* is an amount by which the seller of a digital shifts the barrier, while pricing, so that in fact they are really pricing a new digital whose replicating call spread is the hedge of the actual digital. The barrier shift will be chosen so that the resulting *shifted* payoff over-replicates the payoff of the digital by the least amount, but such that the Greeks of the new payoff are manageable near the barrier. We note that, although discussed in this section, barrier shifts apply not only to European digitals but even more so to American digitals and, furthermore, to conditional digitals such as those in autocallable products in Chapter 12. In this section we focus on liquidity-based shifts, while it is possible to do other types of meaningful shifts.

In Figure 11.5, we have a digital of 10% struck at 100%, and we want to specify a call spread to replicate it. The 90–100% call spread does the job, but is in fact an extremely conservative call spread. If we were to assume a new barrier of $H' = 95\%$, then the 90–100% call spread is an approximation of the digital with such a barrier. So instead of pricing a call spread, we simply price a digital with the new barrier defined as the old one minus a shift where

$$\text{Barrier Shift} = \tfrac{1}{2} \text{Width of Call Spread}$$

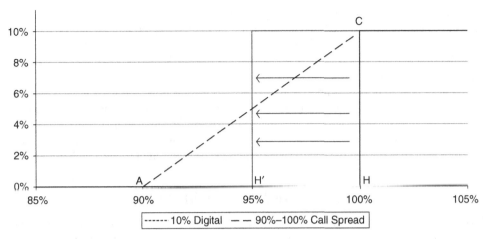

Figure 11.5 Here we have a 10% digital, and a 90–100% call spread. The barrier is shifted from H to H', so that the new digital with barrier H' is replicated by the 90–100% call spread.

In fact here we have used one call spread, and in virtue of the fact that the payoff of the call spread forms the triangle AHC we see in Figure 11.5 for which the sides AH and HC are equal. So the call spread width is the same as the size of the digital, i.e. 10%.

We can do better than this by finding the call spread with the criteria specified above, and we find that the optimal call spread, given MaxDelta, we can trade and to minimize the PV, is given by the call spread around the shifted barrier where

$$\text{Barrier Shift} = \frac{1}{2}\frac{\text{Digital Size} \times \text{Notional}}{\text{MaxDelta}}$$

We multiply by the notional to obtain in the numerator the size of the digital in the option currency, and divide by MaxDelta to obtain the barrier shift with the required properties. That is, if we centre a call spread around the shifted barrier (new barrier = old barrier + shift) we know that we can still Delta hedge the call spread, but at the same time this gives us the smallest call spread (i.e. smallest PV of option) possible from the set of all call spreads. A smaller shift will mean that we might exceed the MaxDelta, and a larger shift will mean we have increased the option price above the necessary amount. Using this formula we know that the gearing on the replicating call spread is given by Digital Size/Barrier Shift, and by using this shift we have over-replicated the digital by the call spread that can still be hedged.

In practice some traders prefer to just take a constant shift of the barrier, and this is again essentially just an additional margin charged for managing the risks if the spot were to approach the barrier. This can also be the more efficient method to use when risk managing a large book.

We note here that the direction one should shift the barrier depends on whether one is short or long the barrier. Take the example of the 10% digital and let it be stuck at 110%. If we raise the barrier further, the option becomes cheaper as the probability of reaching the barrier is lower. The seller is therefore long the barrier and in this case we apply a negative shift to bring the barrier down.

Also, let's note the case of a down-and-in digital, meaning that the digital strike is below the current spot and the digital pays the fixed coupon C; if the underlying is below the barrier at maturity, we will be replicating this digital with a put spread (recall the put spread from

Chapter 6 on option strategies). The same concepts of barrier shifts apply to the size and number of put spreads one needs to hedge the digital. In this case the seller is short the barrier. The higher the barrier, the higher the probability of a knock-in and thus the higher the price, so the seller of the option is short the barrier, and he thus shifts the barrier to the right (a positive barrier shift) to make it more expensive.

Another example of being short the barrier is, for example, the no-touch digital, which we will discuss later. To briefly explain, the no-touch pays the coupon as long as a certain level has NOT been breached. For example, the 120% strike no-touch digital at maturity pays the coupon C if the underlying is not above 120% at maturity. A higher barrier raises the price, therefore the seller is short the barrier and applies a shift to the right to get a higher barrier.

11.2 AMERICAN DIGITALS

American digitals are like European digitals except for the fact that the trigger event is not monitored just at maturity but at any time up to maturity. Typically contracts would specify a monitoring of the trigger on the daily closing prices. It is then much harder to price such options since we don't know when they are going to be exercised. Coupons could be paid if and when such an event occurs, or at maturity of the contract even if the trigger event had already happened.

Reflection Principle

The reflection principle (Figure 11.6) gives us an approximate link between the price of a European digital and an American digital with the same maturity and strike. Let's assume that the log-returns of the underlying are normally distributed, but with mean zero. The symmetry that this introduces (from the symmetric nature of the Normal distribution) in the paths of the underlying means that the paths where the barrier is hit and reflected has the same probability as the path that crosses through the barrier. This implies that the probability of hitting the barrier is exactly twice the probability of ending up above the barrier at expiry (Gatheral,

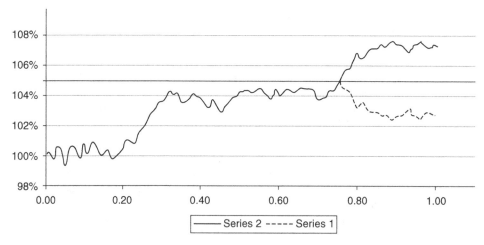

Figure 11.6 An example of a reflected path to illustrate the reflection principle. Barrier is at 105%.

2006). The latter of these two gives us the price of the European digital of the same maturity, and we deduce that the value of the American digital is twice that of the European equivalent. Note that in the example here, the European digital is a digital call and the American digital pays if the barrier is ever hit during the life of the contract.

Exercise

Imagine that you are a structurer visiting a client in Kazakhstan who wants to invest in the local market. He believes a Kazakhstan oil company called KOS is going to perform quite well in the coming years. The client wants to buy from you a digital call option that pays $100 whenever KOS stock price reaches $1. KOS actual spot price is equal to $0.7. You don't have a pricer in front of you and you need to give the client an offer price for this option straight away. At what price would you sell it?

Discussion

First of all, you have to take into account the features of the Kazakhstan market. It is a volatile financial market because of the lack of liquidity. Moreover, the real problem in pricing this option comes from the fact that there is no specified maturity. This option pays a coupon *whenever* the stock price reaches a specified trigger. So it is impossible to compute the probability of striking and then just discounting it.

Now remember, the price of an option is the cost of hedging it. This American digital option is equivalent to 100 American digital options paying a coupon of $1 if KOS spot reaches $1. If the trader selling these options wants to perfectly hedge them, he just needs to buy 1 KOS share for each individual option, so that if the spot reaches $1, he can just sell 1 KOS stock for $1 and pays the coupon to the client. In order to perfectly hedge the initial option paying $100 coupon, the trader should buy 100 KOS shares. Then an upper bound price for this option is $100 \times \$0.7 = \$70$.

In this case, there is no easy way to compute a fair value for this option, but we know that you should sell it for less than $70. So the offer price will depend on the relationship you have with your client as well as how confident you feel trading on the Kazakhstan market.

Upper Bound Price for American Digitals

Assume that you need to give an upper limit to an American digital option paying a coupon C if the spot of an underlying stock reaches K. This option is equivalent to C/K options paying a coupon equal to K if the spot reaches K. The trader selling this option needs to buy C/K underlying shares to be completely hedged. Let $S(0)$ denote the initial spot price; the cost of the hedge is then equal to $C/K \times S(0)$. The fair price of this option should then be lower or equal to $C/K \times S(0)$.

One-Touch vs No-Touch

The *no-touch* digital pays a coupon if a specified barrier is NOT touched throughout an observation period – that is, the underlying stays within a specified range. This is different to the American digitals we saw previously that pay if a barrier has ever been touched, or that is the barrier needs to be touched only once (thus the *one-touch* name). For example, one can have a 1-year maturity no-touch digital that pays an 8% coupon if the underlying never goes below 90%.

What is neat about the no-touch is its relationship to the standard American digital, a parity relationship given by

$$\text{Prob(No Touch)} + \text{Prob(One Touch)} = 1$$

which makes sense because if we fix a barrier and look at any path of the underlying, there can only be two possible outcomes: either the barrier is touched or it isn't, and these two events are complements. Using this parity one can deduce the price of one from the other (note that in the relationship above these are probabilities not prices), by quite simply multiplying both sides by the required coupon and discounting correctly. In section 11.5.1 below we discuss a structure called the *wedding cake*, which is a series of double-no-touch digitals. The term *double* only means that there are two barriers (an upper and a lower).

11.3   RISK ANALYSIS

11.3.1   Single Asset Digitals

If the forward price of the underlying increases, then the price of the digital goes up since there is a higher probability of the digital call option *striking*. These digitals have positive Delta, and the seller of the option will have to buy Delta of the underlying, meaning that the seller will be long dividends, short interest rates, and long borrow costs of the underlying.

If the underlying's forward price is lower than the barrier level, the Vega of a digital call is positive. This means that a higher volatility will increase the probability of the trigger being reached, and thus increase the digital price. If the underlying's forward price is higher than the barrier level, the Vega of a digital will be negative since a higher volatility increases the probability of going out-of-the-money. In Appendix B, section B.4, we derive a simple closed form approximation, in the spirit of the approximations of section 5.9 regarding those for Black–Scholes prices and Greeks, for the Vega position of a digital.

Time to maturity has the same effect on a digital option's fair value as volatility. A trader selling a digital has a long position in volatility, and is also long time to maturity. In this case, this means that digitals with higher maturity are cheaper than digitals with lower maturity. Note that time also has a second effect as we must discount it when pricing, although the effect here is generally larger.

The lower the barrier, the higher the probability of the coupon being paid. In other words, a higher barrier level decreases the digital price. When a structurer prices a digital, he needs to take into account the discontinuity risk around the barrier; therefore the structurer applies a barrier shift whose effect lowers the initial barrier level if selling the digital.

Skew risk is a critical consideration for the seller of a digital. When hedging a short position in a digital, the trader takes an opposite position in a call spread. As discussed in Chapter 6, skew makes a call spread more expensive, and the cost of hedging is then higher. Always remember that the price of an option represents the cost of hedging it; therefore, the skew makes the price of digitals more expensive.

If we consider the digital as a call spread, we can immediately see what is happening. The seller of a call spread is selling volatility at the lower strike call and buying volatility at the higher strike call. In the presence of skew, the volatility the seller is selling is higher and the volatility being bought is lower than in the case of flat volatility. This implies that pricing a digital without skew means that one has not charged correctly for the volatility being sold and paid too much for the volatility being bought. The seller of the digital is clearly selling skew.

One can even write down the price of a digital, using the limit defined in section 11.1.2, and combine it with a parameterization of the skew. That is, the skew, for a given maturity, is the set of implied volatilities of vanillas across strikes, call it $\sigma(K)$ to represent the implied volatility σ at strike K. Then the price of the digital is given by

$$
\begin{aligned}
\mathrm{Digital}(K) &= -\frac{\partial\,\mathrm{Call}(K)}{\partial K} \\
&\quad - \mathcal{N}(d_2)\,\frac{\partial\,\mathrm{Call}(K)}{\partial\sigma} \times \frac{\partial\sigma(K)}{\partial K} \\
&= \underbrace{\mathcal{N}(d_2)}_{Black-Scholes} + \underbrace{Vega \times \mathrm{Skew}}_{Skew\,correction}
\end{aligned} \tag{11.1}
$$

where Skew is the absolute value of the derivative $\partial\sigma(K)/\partial K$. Thus, in the case of skew, we have the correction term to the Black–Scholes price given by Vega × Skew, which makes perfect sense as this says that, should there be a skew, the additional effect is the steepness of such skew times the Vega of a call (think of the digital as a call spread). The above derivation is nothing more than computing a derivative w.r.t. K and noting that the call option's price now depends on K directly as it is the strike, but also that σ is now a function of K.

Beware the Teeny

When pricing a digital, given that one has a fixed amount to spend, it is sometimes the case that the model implies a small probability of the digital paying, the result being that the digital coupon offered may be huge. One must be careful when offering a large digital with a low probability (Table 11.1).

Table 11.1   Individual parameter positions for a digital option trader.

	Digital call seller	Digital call buyer
Interest rates	Short	Long
Borrowing costs	Long	Short
Dividends	Long	Short
Volatility	Depends	Depends
Skew	Short	Long
Barrier	Long	Short

Exercise

Consider two European digitals A and B on the same underlying stock. The options pay the same coupon if the underlying's spot reaches a trigger equal to 160%. Option A expires in 1 year; the other option expires in 3 years. Which one is cheaper and why?

Discussion

For issues concerning Theta, it is always more convenient to think about it in terms of volatility first. Since the trigger level is at 160%, this means both options A and B are deep out-of-the-money. Then volatility increases the price of the digital options. Time to maturity having the same effect on digital prices as volatility, we can say that option B is more expensive than option A.

11.3.2 Digital Options with Dispersion

Again given n assets $S_1, S_2, \ldots, S_n$, and a maturity T, the worst-of digital with coupon C and strike H pays, as the name implies:

$$\text{Worst-of Digital}_{\text{payoff}} = \begin{cases} C & \text{if min } S_i(T) > H, \qquad \text{for } i = 1 \text{ to } n \\ 0 & \text{otherwise} \end{cases}$$

where the minimum over the terminal asset prices is obviously the worst-of. Worst-of digitals are quite popular in the world of structured products. An exotic trader of single asset digitals is usually selling worst-of digitals; therefore, it is important to get used to the different risks involved in trading these products in order to hedge them properly (see Table 11.2).

With respect to forward price sensitivity, we can start by thinking about it in the same way that we did for digitals on single assets, combining this with what we learned about worst-of options in Chapter 8 on dispersion. In fact, higher interest rates, lower dividends and borrow costs will increase the forward prices of the different underlying shares. These will increase the forward price of the worst performing stock and thus make the option more expensive.

For the Vega of a worst-of digital, things get more interesting. As we saw in the discussion of worst-of calls in Chapter 8, the Vega position is not standard for every case. Recall that the seller of a worst-of call is short volatility because of the call option feature, but is buying volatility because it is long dispersion, and the overall position for the worst-of call was a function of the levels of volatility, correlation and the forwards, and can be either long or short in volatility. If we think about a worst-of digital as a worst-of call spread, the first thing to note is that the Vega of a call spread is less than that of just a call, and, again, since we are long dispersion and thus long volatility because of the worst-of feature, overall we expect the seller of the the worst-of digital to be long volatility. In this case, the Vega effect from the call

Table 11.2 Individual parameter positions for a worst-of digital trader.

	WO digital seller	WO digital buyer
Interest rates	Short	Long
Borrowing costs	Long	Short
Dividends	Long	Short
Volatility	Long	Short
Skew	Short	Long
Correlation	Short	Long
Barrier	Long	Short

spread is minimal compared to the effect of dispersion on the volatility position, unlike the case of the worst-of call where the Vega from the call option feature can be more significant.

Since this is a worst-of style multi-asset product, a higher dispersion decreases the price of the worst-of digital and our correlation exposure comes from this dispersion effect. The seller of the worst-of digital is short correlation. As for the skew, we previously saw the skew effect on single asset digitals as well as the skew effect on worst-of products. In the case of worst-of digitals, skew generally makes their price more expensive.

Concerning the trigger effect, it is obvious that a lower trigger level increases the price of the worst-of digitals. When selling these options, a structurer will apply barrier shifts, lowering the trigger level.

Note that the assets composing the underlying basket can have quite different average traded volumes. Recall that the size of the barrier shift (in fact the whole motivation behind it) is based on the liquidity of the underlying – that is, our ability to trade such underlying. In the multi-asset case, which digital barrier shift should be applied? One can be conservative and apply a unique shift taking into account the lowest liquidity (hedged against the highest risk around the barrier). Otherwise, one can apply individual shifts depending on the different stocks' average daily traded volumes.

11.3.3   Volatility Models for Digitals

To correctly price a digital one must use a model that knows about skew. Recall from equation (11.1) the effect of skew on the price of a digital that must be accounted for. If the option's payoff is only a function of the returns of the underlying at maturity, then it is imperative to get that particular skew correct in the calibration and we would use the exact date-fitting model described in section 4.3.3. In fact, using any model that offers the same fit to the skew will price the digital (almost) exactly the same. The reason is that, as discussed above, the digital can be thought of as a limit of a call spread, and capturing the skew means that the implied volatilities of these calls are correct in the model.

If there is path dependency, like the case of the one-touch American digital, then we need to use a form of smooth surface calibration, as described in section 4.3.3, in order to capture the effect of surface through time. Specifically, because the digital can be triggered at any time prior to maturity, the volatility hedge will need to consist of a set of European options with different maturities, i.e. Vega buckets. The American digital will have Vega sensitivity to the volatilities of these Europeans and we need the model to be calibrated to them in order to show risk against them. As such they can serve as valid hedging instruments and the model price will reflect this. As the market moves, the volatility sensitivities can change, for example when the underlying moves closer to the barrier, and thus the model dynamic specified will give different model dependent prices for American digitals.

In the multi-asset cases the calibration will need to be done to each of the respective implied volatility surfaces of the individual underlyings. In the case of the European digital we are concerned with getting the skew correct for each underlying, calibrating to European options of the same maturity as the digital. In the multi-asset case we also need to get the term structure right because an American digital will have a Vega to each underlying and for all buckets. If the digital is on multiple assets, for example a digital call on the worst-of, then again the dispersion effects will mean that these sensitivities change as the underlyings move after inception: sensitivities increase across all the Vega buckets on those underlyings that are performing worst and will decrease on those that are performing better, and are all relative to the position of the spots with respect to the barrier. In the multi-asset case, all payoffs discussed are sensitive to the correlations between the various underlyings. The effects on the digital again depend on the nature in which the multi-asset feature enters, e.g. basket, worst-of, etc. These correlations must be correctly specified by the criteria laid out in Chapter 7 and also by observing the correlation sensitivity of the seller of such options.

11.4 STRUCTURED PRODUCTS INVOLVING EUROPEAN DIGITALS

11.4.1 Strip of Digitals Note

Payoff Mechanism

This structured note is based on the performance of a single asset and its payoff structure is described as follows: At each observation date t, the holder receives a variable coupon equal to:

$$\text{Coupon}(t) = C \times \text{Notional} \times \mathbf{1}_{\{\text{Ret}(t) > H\}}$$

where H is the predetermined trigger level, C is the fixed digital coupon and $\text{Ret}(t) = S(t)/S(0)$ is the return at time t w.r.t. the initial level $S(0)$. This note is capital guaranteed, and the holder receives the following payoff at maturity T:

$$\text{Note}_{\text{payoff}} = 100\% + \text{Coupon}(T)$$

where $\text{Coupon}(T)$ is the final coupon.

Consider the following scenario. After a market crash, an investor believes that the main European stocks will recover their losses and perform by at least 5% per annum for four or five years. The investor then buys a 5-year maturity *strip of digitals* structured note on the EuroStoxx index that has the following payoff: At the end of each year, if the spot of the EuroStoxx index is higher than 105% of its initial level, the investor receives a coupon of 10%. Moreover, this is a capital guaranteed structure since the investor receives his initial investment back at maturity.

In the case described in Table 11.3, the holder of the strip of digitals note receives a coupon of 10% at the end of the second and fourth year since the index value is higher than 105% of its initial value. At maturity, he receives 100% of the notional as well as a coupon of 10% because the value of the EuroStoxx at maturity is higher than 105%.

Table 11.3   A payoff scenario for a strip of digitals note.

	$S(t)/S(0)$	105% barrier reached	Coupon
End of year 1	98%	No	0%
End of year 2	106%	Yes	10%
End of year 3	103%	No	0%
End of year 4	108%	Yes	10%
End of year 5	114%	Yes	**100% + 10%**

Product Structure and Risk Analysis

The non-risky part of this product is a zero coupon bond that redeems 100% of invested capital at maturity. The risky part is in fact a set of different European digitals starting at the start date of the note and having maturities corresponding to the different observation dates. The example of the strip of digitals note described above is in fact composed of a zero coupon bond plus a set of five European digitals having respective maturities equal to 1, 2, 3, 4 and 5 years. The barrier level is equal to 105% of the initial spot of the EuroStoxx index.

To price a strip of digitals, we have to price the individual digitals separately since they are all independent. To do so, we should compute the sum of discounted probabilities of being in-the-money for the different digitals and multiply these probabilities by the coupon paid.

The seller of a strip of digitals note is short the digitals. Therefore, the trader taking a short position in this structure is short the forward price of the underlying share and will need to buy Delta in the underlying asset on day 1, and adjust dynamically through the life of the trade to remain Delta neutral. The seller will be short interest rates, long borrow costs and long dividends, short skew and long the barrier.

The position in volatility is not obvious. In order to check his assumptions on his position in volatility, a trader selling this structure can have a look at the different undiscounted probabilities of being in-the-money and make sure that maturity decreases these probabilities in case he is long volatility or increases the probabilities if he is short volatility.

11.4.2 Growth and Income

Payoff Mechanism

To keep things simple, let's describe the payoff associated with the Growth and Income structure as a note based on a single asset. As is the case for the strip of digitals structure, the Growth and Income note pays the holder periodic coupons depending on the underlying's performances reaching a predetermined trigger H. At each observation date t, the holder receives a variable coupon equal to:

$$\text{Coupon}(t) = C \times \text{Notional} \times \mathbf{1}_{\{\text{Ret}(t) > H\}}$$

where H is the predetermined trigger level, C is the fixed digital coupon and $\text{Ret}(t) = S(t)/S(0)$ is the return at time t w.r.t. the initial level $S(0)$.

This note is capital guaranteed, and the holder receives the following payoff at maturity T:

$$\text{Note}_{\text{payoff}} = 100\% + \text{Coupon}(T) + \max\left[0; \text{Ret}(T) - \left(1 + \sum_{t < T} \text{Coupon}(t)\right)\right]$$

where $\text{Coupon}(T)$ is the final coupon, and the sum inside the payoff is over all coupons paid up to, but not including, T.

The idea behind this product is to add an additional opportunity to capture the final performance of the underlying in case the holder did not receive very much in previous coupons.

Now, let's consider the case of Linda Edgeworth, an investor who has a bullish view on the banking sector. She believes that in the next 5 years Goldman Sachs' stock will not drop below 100% of its current spot price. She decides to buy a 5-year Growth and Income note structure. At the end of each year, we observe Goldman Sachs' spot price; if it is higher than 100% of its initial value, the investor receives a coupon of 8% on a notional of $10 million. At maturity,

Table 11.4   Payoff scenario for a Growth and Income note.

	$S(t)/S(0)$	100% barrier reached	Annual coupon
End of year 1	97%	No	0%
End of year 2	106%	Yes	8%
End of year 3	115%	Yes	8%
End of year 4	131%	Yes	8%
End of year 5	147%	Yes	**131%**

in addition to the fifth year's conditional coupon, if the final performance of Goldman Sachs' stock is higher than the sum of already paid coupons, the investor receives a coupon equal to Goldman Sachs' final performance minus the sum of already paid coupons as well as 100% of its invested capital. In Table 11.4, the investor receives three annual coupons of $800,000 at the end of years 2, 3 and 4. At maturity, the note pays the holder a coupon of $13,100,000. This coupon is computed as follows:

$$\underbrace{100\%}_{\text{guaranteed capital}} + \underbrace{8\%}_{\text{digital breached}} + \max\left[0, \underbrace{47\%}_{\text{perf at maturity}} - \underbrace{24\%}_{\text{coupons paid}}\right] = 131\%$$

Product Structure and Risk Analysis

The Growth and Income note is capital protected since the buyer is long a zero coupon bond having the same maturity as the note plus an option structure. The risky part is composed of a series of digitals paying a predetermined periodic coupon when the underlying stock price is higher than a specific trigger. At maturity, the holder is also long an out-of-the-money European call option with strike level equal to 100% plus the sum of coupons already paid by the digitals.

In the example described above, the risky part consists of five European digitals, each paying a coupon of 8%, triggered at 100% and respectively expiring after 1, 2, 3, 4 and 5 years; as well as a path-dependent 5-year maturity European call striking at 100% + Sum of perceived coupons.

To price the Growth and Income option, we have to price the set of individual digitals as well as the out-of-the-money European call. Concerning digital pricing, the risks are identical to those associated with the strip of digitals described in section 11.4.1. The trader selling these digitals will need to buy Delta in each of the underlying assets on day 1, and adjust dynamically through the life of the trade to remain Delta neutral. The seller is short interest rates, long borrow costs, long dividends. He also has a short skew position and a long barrier position. The volatility position depends on the underlying stock forward price and the digitals' trigger.

Concerning the out-of-the-money call option pricing, one should note that it is not a simple European call since it is now a path-dependent option. The trader selling this call will need to buy Delta in the underlying asset on day 1, and adjust dynamically through the life of the trade to remain Delta neutral. The seller is short interest rates, long borrow costs, long dividends. He is also short volatility since he is selling a call option. The trader selling a Growth and Income note should check the overall position in volatility.

The skew effect is interesting in this case. In fact, skew will decrease the price of the out-of-the-money call, so there is a skew benefit for the buyer. Moreover, since skew increases the price of digitals, this means that skew increases the probabilities of coupons paid. This effect enhances the probability of a higher strike which, in turn, increases the skew benefit on the call since it makes it more out-of-the-money. This is called the second skew effect. Therefore, one should be cautious with respect to the overall effect of the skew but, generally, the skew sensitivity of the digitals is higher in absolute value than that of the out-of-the-money call. Thus, skew usually increases the price of the Growth and Income note.

Extending the discussion of volatility models in section 11.3.3, there is a need for caution. Although the digitals are not path dependent and can be priced by an exact fitting of the skew at the correct dates, the call option is path dependent and needs a smooth fitting across all these dates.

11.4.3 Bonus Steps Certificate

Payoff Mechanism

The *Bonus Steps* certificate is a capital guaranteed structure that pays the holder periodic coupons based on the worst performing stock reaching two specific barrier levels H_1 and H_2. Let's consider an underlying basket with n assets $S_1, S_2, \ldots, S_n$, then a Bonus Steps certificate makes the following periodic payment (Coupon(t)) at each observation date t equal to

$$\text{Coupon}(t) = C \times \text{Notional} \times \left(1_{\{(\min_{i=1,\ldots,n} \text{Perf}_i(t)) > H_1\}} + 1_{\{(\min_{i=1,\ldots,n} \text{Perf}_i(t)) > H_2\}} \right)$$

where C is the fixed digital coupon and $\text{Perf}_i(t) = S_i(t)/S_i(0)$ is the performance of asset i at time t w.r.t. the initial level $S_i(0)$. This certificate is capital guaranteed. The holder receives the following payoff at maturity T:

$$\text{Certificate}_{\text{payoff}} = 100\% + \text{Coupon}(T)$$

where $\text{Coupon}(T)$ is the final coupon.

Now, let's take the case of Alan Grieves, an investor who believes that the American economy is going into a growth period at least for the next 3 years. He has strong expectations on 24 stocks that are very highly rated by most equity analysts. He also believes that none of these stocks will drop below 90% of its initial value. He then decides to invest in a certificate with a payoff based on the worst performing stock to increase his potential upside leverage in the case where no share falls below 90%. He is also aware that everything could happen in the market and wants to have additional protection in case his view on the underlyings is not realized. He therefore specifies a second trigger equal to 75% which enables him to have a lower coupon if one of the 24 underlyings loses more than 10% of its initial value but less than 25%.

Alan calls a structured equity salesperson in an investment bank and says he wants to invest $20 million in a note that has a payoff corresponding to his view on the market. The salesperson discusses the issue with one of the structurers and asks him to price this product and find the suitable coupons to be paid to the client.

Table 11.5   Payoff scenario for a Bonus Steps certificate.

	Worst perf.	75% breached	90% breached	Coupon
End of year 1	72%	No	No	0%
End of year 2	86%	Yes	No	6%
End of year 3	94%	Yes	Yes	100% + 12%

After pricing this product and analysing the different risks, the investment bank offers the client the following 3-year Bonus Steps certificate (Table 11.5).

At the end of each year t,

$$\text{Coupon}(t) = 6\% \times \$20\text{M} \times \left(\mathbf{1}_{\{(\min_{i=1,\dots,24} \text{Perf}_i(t)) > 75\%\}} + \mathbf{1}_{\{(\min_{i=1,\dots,24} \text{Perf}_i(t)) > 90\%\}} \right)$$

Product Structure and Risk Analysis

This Bonus Steps certificate is composed of a zero coupon bond that redeems the holder 100% of the notional at maturity, as well as a risky part composed of a series of different European worst-of digitals starting at the certificate start date and having maturities corresponding to the different observation dates (Figure 11.7).

The example of the Bonus Steps certificate described above is in fact a 3-year zero coupon bond (capital guaranteed at maturity) plus an option that consists of three European worst-of digitals paying a coupon of 6%, triggered at 75%, having respective maturities equal to 1, 2 and 3 years; and another set of three European worst-of digitals paying a coupon of 6%, triggered at 90%, having respective maturities equal to 1, 2 and 3 years. To price a Bonus Steps certificate, we have to price the worst-of individual digitals. To do so, we should compute the sum of discounted probabilities of being in-the-money for the different digitals and multiply these probabilities by the value of the coupon.

The seller of this structure is exposed to the same risks associated with worst-of digitals. The seller will need to buy Delta in each of the underlying assets on day 1, and adjust dynamically through the life of the trade to remain Delta neutral. The seller would be short interest rates, long borrow costs, long dividends, and would also have a short skew position and a long barrier position. The seller would be long dispersion (long volatility and short correlation).

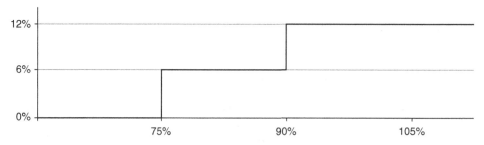

Figure 11.7   Annual payoff of the Bonus Steps certificate structure.

11.5 STRUCTURED PRODUCTS INVOLVING AMERICAN DIGITALS

11.5.1 Wedding Cake

The wedding cake is an option that pays a fixed payout based on the movement of the underlying reference rate within certain predefined barriers. It will typically pay a lower coupon where the reference rate moves within the wider range, or no coupon if it touches the outside barrier levels. See Figure 11.8 for the payoff of a wedding cake structure.

The structure can be thought of as a set of two-sided no-touch digitals. In the example in Figure 11.8, the wedding cake structure pays a 15% coupon at maturity, provided the underlying never went outside the range [95%, 105%]. It pays a coupon of 10% if the underlying goes outside the first range but does not exit from the second range [90%, 110%]. It pays a coupon of 5% if the second range has ever been breached but not the third range [85%, 115%], and it pays zero if the third range has ever been breached.

This can be broken down into three two-sided no-touch digitals in the following sense: start with a digital that pays 5% if the underlying is never outside the range [85%, 115%], add to this a second digital that also pays 5% if the range [90%, 110%] is never breached, and similarly another no-touch of coupon 5% and range [95%, 105%]. Pricing each of these separately and adding them together gives us the price of the structure.

The question now is, does the two sided no-touch introduce any new risks with which we are not already familiar? Well not really. One would want to employ barrier shifts at both sides, in whatever manner one does one's barrier shifting, and definitely account for the skew sensitivity of the trade.

An increase in volatility can increase the probability of the underlying hitting the barriers thus lowering the price, meaning that the seller of the structure is typically long volatility. How sensitive we are to volatility movements will be a function of the size of the ranges and coupons, and can also depend on the forward of the underlying.

This product is an example of the curvature effect of the skew. That is, the skew sensitivities on each side of the digitals cancel each other out somewhat, assuming the skew is relatively non-convex. We refer to section 4.2.1 on volatility skew parameterization and analysis. Here the more positive the curvature, the more the skew begins to impact the price.

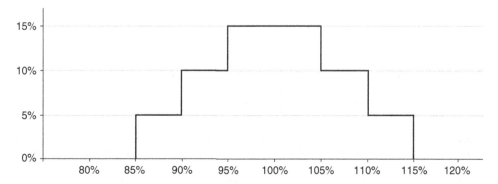

Figure 11.8 The payoff of a wedding cake structure.

11.5.2   Range Accrual

The range accrual pays a coupon at maturity based on the amount of time, typically the number of days, that the underlying has spent within a given range. This can be used to obtain an above market coupon by taking a view on the path of an underlying, or can be used to hedge other risks. The payoff is given by

$$\text{Range Accrual}_{\text{payoff}} = \frac{C}{n} \times \sum_{t \in \{0, t_1, t_2, \ldots, t_n\}} \mathbf{1}_{\{L < S(t) < H\}}$$

where $0, t_1, t_2, \ldots, t_n$ are the days from 0 (start) to T (maturity). $[L, H]$ is the prespecified range. For each day it is in the range, the sum accrues; this is then divided by n, the number of days in the range, to give us the percentage of days it is in the range; this is then multiplied by a coupon. Obviously one specifies in the contract that we are only counting business days – for example, we will consider the days in the range and divide by 252 for a 1-year maturity, representing the number of trading days in the year. It is more important to get the correct number of days the underlying trades between the start and maturity of the option.

As an example see Figure 11.9, where the range is specified at [90%, 110%], and let's assume a coupon of 12%. The underlying spends 144 days within the range, maturity is 1 year (252 trading days) so we have the fraction $144/252 = 57.14\%$, thus the option pays $12\% \times 57.14\% = 6.86\%$.

We can specify this option with a minimum payoff at maturity, a minimum guarantee (MinGtee), for example

$$\text{Range Accrual}_{\text{payoff}} = \max\left[\text{MinGtee}, \frac{C}{n} \times \sum_{t \in \{0, t_1, t_2, \ldots, t_n\}} \mathbf{1}_{\{L < S(t) < H\}} \right]$$

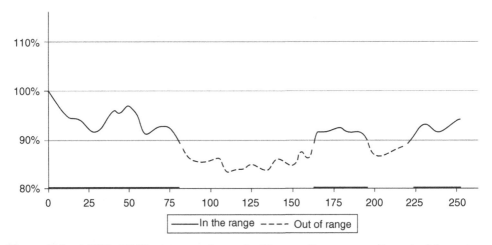

Figure 11.9   A [90%, 110%] range accrual scenario. The wavy line represents the path of the asset on the days it is within this range, the dotted line the days it is out of the range. The horizontal axis is time in days and goes from 0 (start of the option) to 252 (a 1-year maturity) where obviously we only consider days when the market is open. The bold part of the time axis represents the days of accrual. As usual we work with percentages and the asset starts at 100%.

and structure it into a note. Since the payoff is positive in all cases, a minimum value of zero (a global floor) makes no sense. This can also be structured as a swap, where, for example, the investor pays LIBOR plus a specific spread, and the other party pays an equity contingent coupon according to the range accrual.

Obviously the analysis for a range accrual depends on where the range is specified. But generally, with a range similar to the one specified, it is tailored towards the view that one expects relatively flat volatility in the underlying. Taking a range below the spot (or around the spot with more weight on the downside, for example [80%, 100%]) to give it a bearish view, the opposite can be done for a bullish view.

One can think of a range accrual as a set of daily no-touch digitals. To obtain a higher coupon one can introduce a multi-asset component and bring dispersion into the picture. Let's assume that we have N assets and we specify the range accrual as

$$\text{Range Accrual}_{\text{payoff}} = \frac{C}{n} \times \sum_{t \in \{0,t_1,t_2,\ldots,t_n\}} \prod_{j=1}^{N} \mathbf{1}_{\{L < S_j(t) < H\}}$$

The product in the formula means that the indicator $\mathbf{1}$ is only equal to 1 if ALL N underlyings are within the range. For example, the world basket could form our three assets, and the range specified according to a view on the three global indices.

The seller of the range accrual in the multi-asset case specified as above is long dispersion: as dispersion goes up, one of the assets will probably leave the range. The seller is short correlation and long volatility, but caution must be taken as the size of the range and the position of the range can change the effects of these.

If we think about a range accrual as a set of forward starting daily digitals, we can see that because of its path-dependent nature, the dynamics of the model specified will have an impact on the price of the range accrual. If we are concerned with the effect of future volatility implied by the model, we will need to use a stochastic volatility model to capture this. These are discussed at length when we look at cliquets in Chapter 13, and implied smile dynamics in Chapter 15 in the context of mountain range options. Whichever model is chosen must be correctly calibrated to obtain as smooth a calibration through time as possible to European options of different maturities, the Vega buckets.

11.6 OUTPERFORMANCE DIGITAL

11.6.1 Payoff Mechanism

The outperformance digital option is a variation of the outperformance option. Let's consider two assets S_1 and S_2. A digital option based on the outperformance of S_1 vs S_2 is typically a European style option that pays a coupon C at maturity if S_1 *outperforms* S_2. The payoff is as follows:

$$\text{Outperformance Digital}_{\text{payoff}} = C \times \text{Notional} \times \mathbf{1}_{\{\text{Ret}_1(T) > \text{Ret}_2(T)\}}$$

where $\text{Ret}_i(T) = S_i(T)/S_i(0)$.

Now, let's take the example of an English investor who believes that major European stocks will perform better than American stocks in the next couple of years. He thinks the EuroStoxx index will outperform the S&P index but the spread between the performances of these indices will not be very big. He decides to buy a 2-year maturity outperformance digital option on

Table 11.6 Payoff scenarios of an outperformance digital.
Outperformance coupon set at 20%.

	EuroStoxx 50 return	S&P 500 return	Payoff
Scenario 1	93%	85%	20%
Scenario 2	98%	104%	0%
Scenario 3	119%	98%	20%
Scenario 4	76%	75%	20%

EuroStoxx vs S&P that pays him a predetermined variable coupon of 20% on a notional of $20 million (Table 11.6).

11.6.2 Correlation Skew and Other Risks

When pricing and hedging this option, one should be careful because the payoff of an outperformance digital looks similar to that of an outperformance option, but the volatility and correlation sensitivities are quite different. The trader taking a short position in the outperformance digital option described above is obviously short the EuroStoxx index forward price and long the S&P forward price. But it is much more complicated for him to determine his position in volatility and correlation.

If the forward performance of EuroStoxx is higher than the forward performance of S&P, then a higher dispersion decreases the price of the outperformance digital. Otherwise, dispersion increases its price. Therefore, if one is selling an outperformance digital, his position in volatility and correlation depends on the difference between the underlying's forwards.

Correlation, like volatility, has a relationship with the underlying price. In equity markets, for large moves down, we see an increase in correlation. This is what we call correlation skew. Since the position in correlation can potentially change during the life of the option, one should use a stochastic correlation model to capture this effect or to at least be able to notice the existence of such an effect and be able to quantify it.

The issue is linked to convexity – that is, a second-order effect, in much the same way that an ordinary call option has Gamma. In this case it is insufficient to measure a correlation sensitivity by computing a first-order derivative w.r.t. correlation. Since the price is no longer linear in correlation, and this sensitivity may change, the seller should see the second-order effect. The correlation convexity is not something that can be directly or easily hedged, and thus seeing its effect through the use of a correlation skew model is purely to include its effect in the price, if nothing else as a fixed charge for bearing the additional risk. If one knows the magnitude of this effect, then a simple edge can be taken onto the price without the added modelling complexity.

Although this effect is present in the outperformance digital, one must first be sure to take the volatility skew sensitivity of the product into account. The product is a digital and thus carries skew risk and is sensitive to the implied volatility skews of both underlyings. Again, the time fitting will depend on whether we base the payoff on the return at maturity or if we introduce some form of path dependency through averaging, which will introduce sensitivity to the volatility term structure.

12

Autocallable Structures

Our greatest glory is not in never falling, but in getting up every time we do.

Confucius

Autocallables, which are also known as auto-trigger structures, are quite popular in the world of structured products. In this chapter, we look at standard autocallables and several variants on them. Firstly, we discuss autocallables based on a single asset, defining their features and explaining the payoff mechanism. Then, we present the payoffs of *Twin-Wins* and autocallables with bonus coupons, which are both great examples of autocallables with down-and-in put features. The pricing and the risks associated with single asset autocallables are fully covered.

The second part of this chapter deals with the dispersion effect on autocallables. We first describe the payoff of worst-of autocallables as well as the risks encountered when trading these products. Then, we introduce the effect of snowballing coupons as well as the addition of a worst-of down-and-in put feature to the classical worst-of autocallable structure. Finally, we analyse the payoff and the risks associated with trading outperformance autocallables which also deal with dispersion.

12.1 SINGLE ASSET AUTOCALLABLES

12.1.1 General Features

Payoff Description

Consider an autocallable note based on a single asset S, a structure which pays coupons depending on the underlying's performance reaching two triggers H and B, and has a payoff defined as follows: at each observation date t_i, $(i = 1 \ldots n)$ we have

$$\text{Coupon}(t_i) = \text{Notional} \times C \times \mathbf{1}_{\{\text{Ret}(t_i) \geq B\}} \times \mathbf{1}_{\left\{\max_{j=1,\ldots,i-1}(\text{Ret}(t_j)) < H\right\}}$$

where C is a predetermined coupon and $\text{Ret}(t_i) = S(t_i)/S(0)$ is the return at time t_i w.r.t. the initial level $S(0)$.

Since the wrapper is a note, the holder receives back 100% of the notional except that, in this case, the time of payment is not fixed. The notional redemption can be at any observation date, not necessarily at maturity.

$$\text{Redemption}(t_i) = \text{Notional} \times \mathbf{1}_{\{\text{Ret}(t_i) \geq H\}} \times \mathbf{1}_{\left\{\max_{j=1,\ldots,i-1}(\text{Ret}(t_j)) < H\right\}}$$

From the payoff described above, it is important to notice that the holder of the note receives no further payments if H has been breached on one of the observation dates. Then, this note is described as an autocallable since the note *dies* once the barrier H is breached by the underlying at specific observation dates. The autocallable structure doesn't have a fixed maturity. What we call maturity is in fact the maximum duration this product can stay alive.

Table 12.1   Payoff scenarios for a 3-year autocallable note on the CAC 40 index. This table is associated with the scenarios drawn in Figure 12.1.

	Scenario 1	Scenario 2	Scenario 3
Coupon at the end of year 1	8%	8%	8%
Coupon at the end of year 2	8%	8%	0%
Coupon at the end of year 3	100%	108%	108%

H is called the autocall *trigger* or *threshold*. It is a predetermined level above which the autocallable structure expires and the investor receives the notional invested when the structure is a note. The threshold can be fixed during the life of the option or can be variable. In some cases, the threshold can be increasing or decreasing as time goes by.

B is the *coupon trigger*, also called *coupon level*. It is a predetermined level above which the investor receives a periodic coupon. In other words, if the underlying level observed is higher than the coupon trigger, a coupon based on the notional is paid to the investor.

Some autocallable structures are characterized by a coupon trigger equal to the autocall trigger. In this case, we talk about autocallables with knock-out coupons. Indeed, when a coupon is paid, the product autocalls at the same time since the autocall trigger is breached. Therefore, this structure pays a unique coupon at one of the observation dates during the lifetime of the option. In the case of a coupon level different from the autocall trigger, one talks about autocallables with knock-in coupons, as is the case in the payoff described above. Also note that the coupon level is always lower or equal to the autocall level; otherwise the product doesn't make sense.

Payoff Mechanism

Here, we clarify the payoff mechanism by simulating scenarios, shown in Tables 12.1 and 12.2, on a specific case to be more familiar with the behaviour of an autocallable structure.

Consider a retail client of an investment bank who invests $5 million in a 3-year maturity autocallable note on the CAC 40 index (Figures 12.1 and 12.2). Each year, we observe the performance of the underlying index since inception $\text{Ret}(t_i) = I(t_i)/I(0)$. If this return is higher than 70%, the client is paid a coupon equal to $400,000, which is 8% of the notional invested. Moreover, if the observed level of the CAC 40 index is higher than 100%, the structure autocalls and the investor gets back the money he invested. At the end of the third year, if the index level has never been above 100%, the investor gets back the capital he invested.

Table 12.2   Payoff scenarios for a 3-year autocallable note on the CAC 40 index. This table is associated with the scenarios drawn in Figure 12.2.

	Scenario 1	Scenario 2	Scenario 3
Coupon at the end of year 1	108%	8%	8%
Coupon at the end of year 2	–	108%	8%
Coupon at the end of year 3	–	–	108%

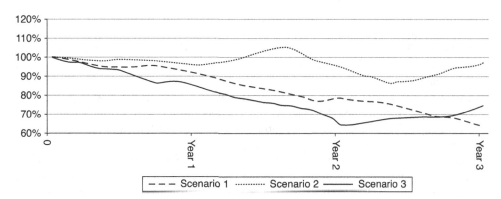

Figure 12.1 CAC 40 index return scenarios. Case where the structure never autocalled.

Risk Analysis

In order to price the autocallable digitals effectively, one can compute the undiscounted conditional probabilities of receiving the coupons. These values can enable one to quickly check whether the pricing makes sense. After these probabilities are computed, they should be discounted and multiplied by the coupons to be received. This gives us the price of the autocallable digitals.

The first digital option is a classical European digital. The undiscounted probability of striking the second year is conditional on not autocalling at the end of the first year. The undiscounted probability of *striking* the third year is conditional on not autocalling at the end of the first and second years. As time goes by, the probabilities of coupons being paid decrease and the value of the last path-dependent digitals can be very small because the conditional probabilities of striking would be low. In this case, the seller must be careful when offering a very large digital with a low probability.

The risks associated with a single asset autocallable structure are similar to those associated with single asset digitals. The risk analysis on digitals having been fully detailed in Chapter 11, we could say that the seller of an autocallable is short the underlying's forward (short interest rates, long dividends and long borrowing costs), short the skew, and long the coupon trigger.

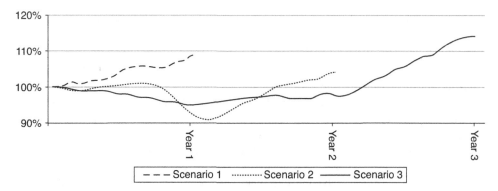

Figure 12.2 CAC 40 index return scenarios. Case where the structure autocalled.

The position in volatility depends on the coupon level and the forward price of the underlying. As already mentioned, the Vega of digitals is positive if the underlying's forward price is lower than the trigger; otherwise, Vega is negative. The Vega hedge will consist of a set of European options with strikes matching (as closely as possible) the autocall trigger dates. The overall volatility sensitivity is split over these Vega buckets, and each of these sensitivities will change as the market moves. If an autocall event is about to happen, the short-term Vega will increase and the Vega in the other buckets will decrease, in line with the higher probability of autocalling. A Vega hedge set at inception will need to be readjusted if the market moves significantly in relation to the autocall triggers.

From a pricing perspective, the autocall structure either autocalls the first year, or tends to stay *alive* until maturity. This means that if the underlying asset doesn't reach the autocall trigger the first year, it is less likely to strike in the next years, which is in line with the decreasing conditional probabilities of autocalling. However, from a utility perspective, autocallables are typically structured to fit a certain price range, and lower probabilities, for the same price, imply higher coupons. If the investors do not get the above market coupon in the first year, they still stand to make coupons in subsequent years. The market could crash during the first year, but recover and trigger the autocall event in a subsequent year.

12.1.2 Interest Rate/Equity Correlation

The autocallable serves as an example of a structure where the correlation between the equity and interest rates has an effect on the price. The autocallable is redeemed at a time in the future that is a function of the path the underlying equity takes. Assume the investor is paying the bank LIBOR in exchange for this equity exposure, then the duration of the swap is dependent on the equity and thus the structure is sensitive to the correlation between interest rates and the equity underlying. In the case where an autocallable is structured to provide equity exposure as part of a note, then the investor is in this case implicitly short the floating leg of an interest rate swap and the same thing holds.

In the case of the autocallable, the pricing of this correlation effect is typically done by taking a small margin. This can be specified by first deciding on the level of correlation and also the length of the trade. To get an idea about this effect we use a hedging argument and analyse the possible cases. Let's start with a 2-year maturity autocallable with a possible autocall date at the end of the first year. Setting aside the equity component that will be Delta hedged using the underlying equity, we look at the interest rate hedge of the seller. The seller of this autocallable will go long zero coupon bonds with respective maturities of 1 and 2 years.

- *First case: Assume that the equity/interest rate correlation is positive.* If the underlying increases, then the probability of early redemption at the first autocall date increases, and to adjust the interest rate hedge accordingly the seller will increase the amount of 1-year bonds held and sell some of the 2-year bonds. Because of the positive correlation in this case between the underlying equity and interest rates, we expect that interest rates will also increase on average, and thus the price of the zero coupon bonds will decrease. Since the bond with the longer maturity decreases more in value than the bond with the shorter maturity (using simple bond maths) the seller nets a loss on the rebalancing of this hedge because the seller is buying one bond but selling the one that decreased more in value.

If the underlying decreases, then the probability of the structure autocalling early decreases. In this case the seller must adjust the interest rate Delta hedge by selling some of the 1-year zero coupon bonds held and buying more of the 2-year bonds. On average we expect that interest rates will also decline because of the positive correlation. This implies that the 2-year bond will increase in value more than the 1-year bond, and again the seller thus nets a loss on the rebalancing of this hedge.

- *Second case: Assume that the equity/interest rate correlation is negative.* If the underlying increases, the opposite happens. We expect the interest rate in this case to decline, on average, and the same rebalancing as the case of increased possibility of early redemption as above will in this case net the seller a profit.

If the underlying decreases, then again the opposite happens: negative correlation means that we expect rates to go up and thus reduce the price of the 2-year bond more than the 1-year bond. The decreased probability of early redemption means the seller will need to buy more of the 2-year bond and sell some of the 1-year bond, thus netting a profit.

The upshot of this analysis is that the autocallable's price should be higher when a positive correlation is assumed between interest rates and the underlying equity, and lower if the correlation is negative. The question thus arises as to whether we should employ a model that includes stochastic rates, and thus be able to enter a value for this correlation and include its impact in the price. Arguments in favour of the use of such models are discussed by Giese (2006) for example, and the impact on pricing is discussed and concluded to be important. However, although using such models allows one to see this impact, they do not give us additional information regarding the hedging of the equity interest rate correlation. If it is agreed that assuming a positive correlation implies that there should be an additional cost, then one can simply add a cost for the interest rate equity correlation to the price and not use such models. Specifically, since the sign of this correlation governs whether there is a cost or a benefit, deciding on which correlation to use and adding a cost accordingly can be done without having to employ a stochastic rates model.

The magnitude of this cost will be a function of the maturity of the structure. If we assume, in the above analysis that the autocallable has a 3-year maturity, with annual autocall dates, then the same hedging argument holds, only the Delta hedge for interest rates will include the 1- and 3-year bonds. The impact of a move in interest rates is greater on a 3-year bond than on a 2-year bond and thus the impact of the correlation is greater the longer the maturity of the autocall structure. If one wants to assume a positive correlation and thus add a cost to this structure, it can easily be set to 10 bp per annum for example, depending on the aggressiveness of the trader, the view on this correlation, the notional size of the trade and thus size of the risk, and the level of competition involved in winning the trade.

The use of stochastic interest rate models and the importance of the correlation between rates and equities becomes more significant when we discuss hybrids in Chapter 17. But generally we can say here that since this correlation cannot be hedged in a straightforward manner, and perhaps not hedged at all, the best thing to do is decide on the level for this correlation and add a cost (or nothing) accordingly. To trade this correlation, and thus hedge this correlation risk, one would need a liquid structure involving equity and interest rates, from which one could extract this correlation by hedging away the other parameters.

Note that, from the investor's point of view, a positive correlation would imply that he is likely to get his above market autocall coupon and his money back in a high interest rate environment. This is a good scenario for the investor.

Underlying asset	Alpha
Notional	$10 million
Currency	USD
Maturity	3 years
Autocall level	110%, 120%
Autocall frequency	Annual
Coupon level	110%, 120%
Coupon frequency	Annual
Coupon value	10% per annum
Participation	250%
Note price	98%
Capital protected	Yes

Figure 12.3   The terms of a 3-year autocallable participating note.

12.2   AUTOCALLABLE PARTICIPATING NOTE

The autocallable participating note (APN) is an interesting structure that offers 100% capital protection and can be used to take advantage of a bull market. Let's consider a share Alpha that is near an all time high. An investor may consider converting a portion of his Alpha portfolio into an autocallable participating note (Figure 12.3), thus locking in the current gains (since the note offers 100% principal protection) yet retaining the ability to profit from continuing appreciation, via an autocallable structure with 250% participation in case the note has never been autocalled.

The note described in Figure 12.3 makes the following payments:

$$\text{APN}_{\text{payoff}}(t_1) = 110\% \times \text{Notional} \times \mathbf{1}_{\{\text{Ret}(t_1) \geq 110\%\}}$$
$$\text{APN}_{\text{payoff}}(t_2) = 110\% \times \text{Notional} \times \mathbf{1}_{\{\text{Ret}(t_2) \geq 120\%\}} \times \mathbf{1}_{\{\text{Ret}(t_1) < 110\%\}}$$
$$\text{APN}_{\text{payoff}}(T) = \text{Notional} \times \left[1 + \text{Participation} \times \max(0, \text{Ret}(T) - 1)\right]$$
$$\times \mathbf{1}_{\{\text{Ret}(t_1) < 110\%\}} \times \mathbf{1}_{\{\text{Ret}(t_2) < 120\%\}}$$

where T is the maturity (end of year 3) and t_1, t_2 are the annual observation dates that occur respectively at the end of the first and second year. $\text{Ret}(t_i) = S(t_i)/S(0)$ is the return at time t_i w.r.t. the initial level $S(0)$. The price of this note is equal to 98% of the notional. This means that the holder will receive 100% of the notional, which is more than the money invested no matter what the performance of the underlying.

It's interesting to note that the APN offers 100% capital protection, multiple lock-in profit levels as well as an uncapped 250% participation in the appreciation of Alpha shares if not autocalled. Compared to holding these shares outright, the investor loses his dividends, in return for 100% capital protection plus autocall coupons at roughly three times the USD interest rate (assuming USD rates are roughly 3%) and 250% participation in the stock upside if not autocalled.

The first scenario (Table 12.3) shows the case of Alpha breaching the first trigger (110%) at the end of year 1. The APN pays the holder of the note a coupon of 10% plus 100% of the notional at the end of the first year. The APN expires at t_1.

In the second scenario, no coupon is paid at t_1 since the first trigger is not breached at this date. At observation date t_2, the return of Alpha is higher than the second trigger (120%), then the holder receives 10% coupon plus 100% of the notional and the APN expires.

Table 12.3 Payoff scenarios for a 3-year autocallable participating note. This table is associated with the scenarios drawn in Figure 12.4.

	Scenario 1	Scenario 2	Scenario 3
Coupon at the end of year 1	110%	0%	0%
Coupon at the end of year 2	–	110%	0%
Coupon at the end of year 3	–	–	126.20%

In scenario 3, the APN doesn't autocall. At t_1, no coupon is paid since the return of Alpha is lower than 110%. At t_2, no coupon is paid either since the return of Alpha is equal to 111.6%, which is higher than the first trigger but lower than the second trigger (120%). At maturity, the return of Alpha is equal to 110.48%; thus according to the payoff formula, the holder receives a payment at the end of year 3 equal to:

$$100\% + 250\% \times \max\left[0, 110.48\% - 100\%\right] = 126.2\%$$

In the case described above (Figure 12.4), the autocall trigger is not fixed, it's increasing: 110% at t_1 and 120% at t_2. Also, the coupon triggers are equal to the autocall triggers. Therefore, this note makes a unique coupon payment. Since the coupon trigger increases, the probability of paying the coupon decreases which decreases the price of the autocallable digitals.

The APN is composed of a set of path-dependent digitals plus a participation in a path-dependent European call. To price this structure, one should price the digitals and add the call price. The price of the digitals is given by:

$$\text{Digital}(t_i) = C \times e^{-rt_i} \times \text{Prob}\,(\,\text{Ret}(i) > H(i)\,\&\,\text{Ret}(1) < H(1)\,\&$$
$$\text{Ret}(2) < H(2)\,\&\, \cdots \,\&\,\text{Ret}(i-1) < H(i-1)\,)$$

Showing the probability that the structure autocalls decrease as time goes by. Therefore the path-dependent digitals become cheaper. Moreover, the step-up trigger decreases the price of the digitals composing the autocall structure. The probability that the APN has never autocalled is a decreasing function of the expected return at maturity. Indeed, if this probability is high, this means that the expected return of the underlying is quite low (since this is the only case where the returns would never reach the coupon trigger). Therefore the path-dependent call at maturity is cheap since it depends on two effects that offset each other.

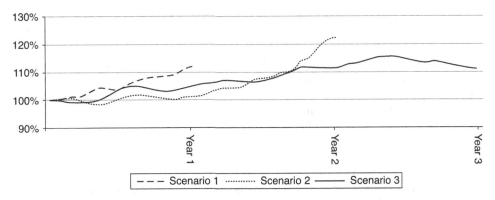

Figure 12.4 Alpha return scenarios for the autocallable participating note described in Figure 12.3.

12.3   AUTOCALLABLES WITH DOWN-AND-IN PUTS

12.3.1   Adding the Put Feature

If the investor believes that the underlying index will not be lower than a specific level at maturity, she can add a put feature to the autocallable structure to increase the potential coupon received. This means that the capital is no longer protected as the holder is short a put option at maturity T.

The put option can be a vanilla at-the-money European put option whose maturity is the maturity of the autocall. But most of the time, the buyer is short a down-and-in at-the-money put option that can be either European or American style. The barrier level is determined depending on the view the investor has on the underlying expected performance.

The down-and-in at-the-money puts with daily monitored barrier are the most popular put features associated with autocallables. We are then going to talk essentially about these options in some examples.

Let's take the example described in section 12.1: if the investor believes that the CAC 40 level will never be below 60% in the next 3 years, he can add a 60% down-and-in at-the-money put feature. He would then be compensated for taking this additional risk by receiving a coupon of, let's say, 12% (instead of 8%) if the underlying return is higher than the coupon trigger.

When a trader sells an autocall with a put feature at maturity, he is short the autocallable digitals and long a path-dependent put option. In order to price this structured product, one should price the autocallable digitals as described above and deduct the price of the path-dependent put option.

In Chapter 10 on barrier options, we analysed in detail the risks associated with down-and-in puts. To briefly summarize, the forward price of the underlying decreases the down-and-in put price. Volatility, skew, and barrier level increase its price. If one is short an autocallable structure with down-and-in put, he would be short the autocallable digitals and long the put. Therefore, he would definitely be short the underlying's forward price and long the triggers (autocallable trigger, coupon trigger and DI put barrier level). However, his overall position in volatility and skew are not immediately clear owing to potentially offsetting effects from the two components.

If the forward price is higher than the coupon level, then volatility decreases the price of the autocallable digitals. This is usually the case since the coupon trigger is lower than the initial spot in most of the autocallable structures with a put feature. A trader selling an autocallable is then usually long volatility with respect to the digitals, and *always* long volatility with respect to the put. Even if this is generally the case, one should always be cautious and check whether the Vega of the overall structure is negative.

As for the skew position, the seller of an autocallable with a put feature has a short skew position with respect to his short position in digitals, but has also a long skew position with respect to his long position in the down-and-in put. Then, he needs to check the overall skew position to know whether he is short or long skew. Priced separately, a conservative trader may take a bid–ask spread on the volatility skew on each direction.

12.3.2   Twin-Wins

A Twin-Wins is a non-principal-protected product linked to a single asset, and has an early redemption feature. In effect, it is an autocall structure with a down-and-in put, with the

Underlying asset	Vodafone
Notional	£10 million
Currency	GBP
Maturity	24 months
Autocall level	105%
Autocall frequency	Semi-Annual
Coupon level	75%
Coupon frequency	Semi-Annual
Coupon value	10% per annum
Knock-in level (daily close)	75%
DI put strike	100%
Upside participation rate	115%
Downside participation rate	55%
Note price	99%
Capital protected	No

Figure 12.5 The terms of a 2-year Twin-Wins note.

potential of capturing the absolute performance of the underlying at maturity. The name *Twin-Wins* comes from the fact that this note enables the holder to get a participation in both the upside and the downside movements of the underlying asset.

Here, we consider the example of a 2-year Twin-Wins note, described in Figure 12.5, making semi-annual payments on observation dates t_1, t_2, t_3 and T.

At each observation date $t_i (i = 1 \ldots 3)$:

$$\text{Coupon}(t_i) = 5\% \times \text{Notional} \times \mathbf{1}_{\{\text{Ret}(i) \geq 75\%\}} \times \mathbf{1}_{\{\max_{j=1,\ldots,i-1}(\text{Ret}(j)) < 105\%\}}$$

The notional redemption can be done at any observation date t_i:

$$\text{Redemption}(t_i) = \text{Notional} \times \mathbf{1}_{\{\text{Ret}(i) \geq 105\%\}} \times \mathbf{1}_{\{\max_{j=1,\ldots,i-1}(\text{Ret}(j)) < 105\%\}}$$

If the structure has not autocalled, the redemption at maturity is determined as follows:

(a) if the underlying closes at or above its initial spot, the note is redeemed at:

$$100\% + 115\% \times [\text{Ret}(T) - 1]$$

(b) if the underlying closes below its initial spot, but has never closed below the knock-in level during the life of the note, the note is redeemed at

$$100\% + 55\% \times [1 - \text{Ret}(T)]$$

(c) if the underlying closes below its initial spot, and has ever closed below the knock-in level during the life of the note, the note is converted into physical shares at strike.

Scenario 1

Vodafone's return is higher than 75% (coupon level) but lower than 105% (autocall trigger) at the end of the first semester (see scenarios in Figure 12.6). At t_1, the investor receives a coupon of 5% (10% p.a.). At t_2, the return of Vodafone is equal to 113.4%; thus the Twin-Wins autocalls and the investor receives a final redemption amount equal to 105% of the notional.

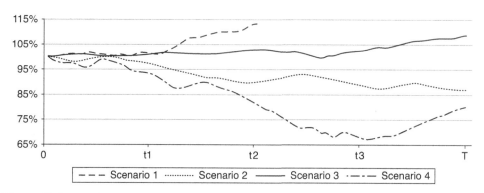

Figure 12.6   Vodafone return scenarios for the Twin-Wins note described in Figure 12.5.

Scenario 2

At the observation dates t_1, t_2 and t_3, the autocall trigger has never been breached. Vodafone returns have always been higher than 75%. Therefore, the note holder receives a coupon equal to 5% of the notional at the end of each observation date. At maturity, Vodafone's return is equal to 87% (lower than 100%). Also, the down-and-in put has never been activated. Then the Twin-Wins holder receives 100% of capital protection plus a coupon equal to $55\% \times (100\% - 87\%) = 7.15\%$ of the notional.

Scenario 3

In this case, the autocall trigger has never been breached at the three observation dates. The three digitals have been activated and pay the note holder a coupon of 5% at the end of each semester date. At maturity, the return of Vodafone is equal to 109%, which allows the Twin-Wins holder to be redeemed at 100% plus a coupon equal to $115\% \times 9\% = 10.35\%$ of the notional.

Scenario 4

The returns of Vodafone have always been lower than 105% which means that the Twin-Wins structure never autocalls. At t_1 and t_2, the holder receives coupons equal to 5% of the notional. At t_3, the note holder receives no coupon since Vodafone's return is lower than 75%. The put has been activated during the life of the option. At maturity, the final return of Vodafone is equal to 80.7%, which is equal to the final redemption. In this scenario, the Twin-Wins holder has lost a part of his capital.

Twin-Wins is an interesting structure in the case where no early redemption has occurred during the life of the note. Indeed, investors can still capture the absolute performance of the underlying at maturity if no knock-in event occurred during the life of the product.

12.3.3   Autocallables with Bonus Coupons

The autocallable with bonus coupon (ABC) is a non-principal-protected product linked to a single asset, and has an early redemption feature. Essentially, the product is an autocall structure with stepping-down trigger levels, and, in addition, a contingent coupon can be paid at maturity even if the autocall level is not triggered.

Underlying asset	Citigroup
Notional	$5,000,000
Currency	USD
Maturity	12 months
Autocall level	98%, 95%, 92%, 89%
Autocall frequency	Quarterly
Coupon level	98%, 95%, 92%, 89%
Coupon frequency	Quarterly
Coupon value	24% per annum
Knock-in level (daily close)	80%
DI put strike	100%
Bonus coupon	20%
Note price	100%
Capital protected	No

Figure 12.7 Terms of an autocallable with bonus coupon note based on Citigroup.

In Figure 12.7, we consider an ABC note based on Citigroup's performance paying quarterly coupons. Note that the autocall trigger and the coupon trigger are the same; the ABC pays only one coupon and then autocalls. At each quarterly observation date $t_i (i = 1, ..., 3)$:

$$\text{Coupon}(t_i) = \text{Notional} \times [1 + C(i)] \times \mathbf{1}_{\{\text{Ret}(i) \geq H(i)\}} \times \mathbf{1}_{\{\text{Ret}(1) < H(1)\}}$$
$$\times \mathbf{1}_{\{\text{Ret}(2) < H(2)\}} \cdots \times \mathbf{1}_{\{\text{Ret}(i-1) < H(i-1)\}}$$

where $C(i) = (24\% \times i)/4$ and $H(i)$ is the trigger level at time t_i. At maturity, the redemption is determined as follows:

(a) If the underlying return is greater than or equal to the final autocall level (89%), the note is redeemed at: 100% + Autocall coupon;
(b) If the final return is below the final autocall level, and the underlying has never closed below the knock-in level, the note is redeemed at: 100% + Bonus Coupon;
(c) If the underlying closes below its initial spot, and has ever closed below the knock-in level during the life of the note, the note is converted into physical shares at strike.

Scenario 1

At the end of the first quarter, the return of Citigroup is higher than the first trigger (see scenarios in Figure 12.8). Then the ABC holder receives a coupon equal to $5,300,000, which is equivalent to 100% plus a coupon of 24%/4 = 6% of the notional.

Scenario 2

In the second scenario, the structure didn't autocall at the end of the first quarter. At t_1, no coupon is paid. The structure autocalled at t_2. The redemption is equal to $5,600,000, which is equivalent to 100% plus a coupon of $24\% \times 2/4 = 12\%$ of the notional.

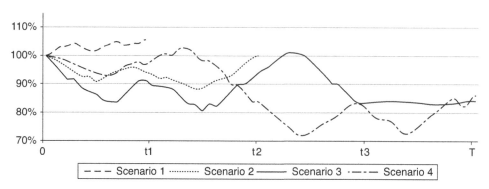

Figure 12.8 Citigroup return scenarios for the ABC note described in Figure 12.7.

Scenario 3

In this case, the autocall trigger has never been breached at the three observation dates. The three digitals have never been activated and the note holder receives no coupon at the end of the observation dates. The knock-in barrier is daily monitored and has never been activated. At maturity, the return of Citigroup is equal to 84.25%, which is lower than the last coupon trigger. Therefore, the note holder receives 100% of the notional plus the bonus coupon equal to 20% of the notional.

Scenario 4

The returns of Citigroup have always been lower than the coupon triggers which means that the ABC structure never autocalls. The knock-in barrier has been activated. The note holder is then long an at-the-money put at maturity. No coupons are paid during the life of the option. The final return of Citigroup is equal to 86%, which is equal to the final redemption. This is a good example where the capital is not protected.

12.4   MULTI-ASSET AUTOCALLABLES

12.4.1   Worst-of Autocallables

Payoff Description

Assume that we start with a basket composed of n assets $S_1, S_2, \ldots, S_n$ then a worst-of autocallable note based on this basket has the following payoff.

At each observation date t_i:

$$\text{Coupon}(t_i) = \text{Notional} \times C \times \mathbf{1}_{\{\text{WRet}(t_i) \geq B\}} \times \mathbf{1}_{\{(\max_{j=1,\ldots,i-1}(\text{WRet}(t_j))) < H\}}$$

H and B are respectively the autocall and coupon triggers.

$$\text{WRet}(t_i) = \min_{k=1,\ldots,n} \left(\frac{S_k(t_i)}{S_k(0)} \right)$$

Underlying assets	KBC, ING, FORTIS, DEXIA
Notional	£10 million
Currency	GBP
Maturity	3 years
Autocall level	100%
Autocall frequency	Annual
Coupon level	60%
Coupon frequency	Annual
Coupon value	25% per annum
Note price	98%
Capital protected	Yes

Figure 12.9 The terms of a 3-year worst-of autocallable note.

Since the wrapper is a note, the holder receives back 100% of the notional whenever the product autocalls. Otherwise, the notional is paid at maturity.

$$\text{Redemption}(t_i) = \text{Notional} \times \mathbf{1}_{\{\text{WRet}(t_i) \geq H\}} \times \mathbf{1}_{\{(\max_{j=1,\dots,i-1}(\text{WRet}(t_j))) < H\}}$$

Let's clarify the payoff mechanism by creating some scenarios on a specific case to be more familiar with the behaviour of the worst-of autocallable structure.

Let's take the example of a Belgian investor who wants to invest in the bank sector in March 2009. Most of the banks suffered from the crisis and their shares dropped significantly. The Belgian investor believes that these banks will recover their losses in the next 3 years. He decides to invest £10 million in a worst-of autocallable on four banks from Belgium and Netherlands. After calling the sales and structuring team of an investment bank, he has been offered the product shown in Figure 12.9, based on a basket composed of KBC, ING, Fortis and Dexia. In the scenario presented in Figure 12.10, the note holder receives annual coupons based on the performance of the worst performing stock. At the end of the first year, all the stocks' performances are above 60% but the worst performing stock is below 100%. Therefore, the first coupon is equal to 25% of the notional and the structure doesn't autocall. At the end of year 2, the product doesn't autocall since there is at least one stock performance below 100%, which is the autocall trigger. However, the worst performance is above 60% (coupon trigger), which makes the second coupon equal to 25%. At maturity, one of the stocks shows

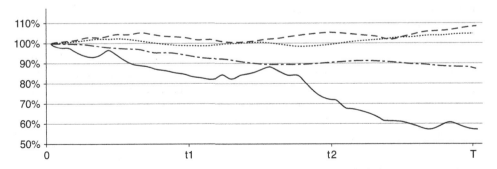

Figure 12.10 Scenario of returns for the underlying stocks of the worst-of autocallable note described in Figure 12.9.

a performance lower than 60%. Then, there is no variable coupon at the end of the third year. The note holder receives 100% of the notional at this last observation date.

Risk Analysis

In order to price the worst-of autocallable digitals efficiently, one can compute the undiscounted conditional probabilities of receiving the coupons. These values enable us to quickly check whether our pricing makes sense. After computing these probabilities, one should discount them and multiply them by the coupons to be received. This gives us the price of the autocallable digitals on the worst performing stock.

As is the case for single asset autocallables, the probabilities of coupons being paid decrease with time and the value of the last path-dependent digitals can be quite small because the conditional probabilities of striking would be low. In this case, one must be careful when offering a very large digital with a low probability – the teeny effect.

A worst-of autocallable note contains a series of path-dependent worst-of digitals. The risks associated with a worst-of autocall are the same as those associated with worst-of digitals which we discussed in Chapter 11. The seller of worst-of autocallables is short the underlying's forwards and will need to buy Delta in each of the underlying assets on day 1, and adjust dynamically through the life of the trade to remain Delta neutral. The seller is short the skew, long the coupon trigger, long volatility and short correlation.

12.4.2   Snowball Effect and Worst-of put Feature

Payoff Description

Where the coupon trigger is equal to the autocall trigger, the autocallable structure *dies* immediately after the coupon is paid. In other words, only one coupon is paid. We can modify the coupon payments by creating snowballing coupons. If the product is still alive at year i, this means that the investor didn't receive the previous periodic coupons. The snowballing structure enables the investor to receive a coupon equal to the sum of all previous coupons if the trigger is reached. The investor is then recovering his losses due to the non-received previous coupons.

One can also add a worst-of down-and-in put feature to the autocallable structure. This happens when the investor is willing to increase the potential coupons received and he believes that all the shares composing the underlying basket will perform above a specific level. This means that the capital is no longer protected as the investor is short a put option at maturity.

As is the case for autocalls on a single asset, the put option can also be a vanilla European put on the underlying basket, with expiry date equal to the maturity of the autocall. Here we are going to consider the case where the investor is short a worst-of down-and-in at-the-money put with European barrier, which means that the knock-in event is determined at maturity only.

Assume that we start with a basket composed of n assets $S_1, S_2, \ldots, S_n$, then a worst-of autocallable note based on this basket has the following payoff:

At each observation date t_i:

$$\text{Coupon}(t_i) = \text{Notional} \times [1 + i \times C] \times \mathbf{1}_{\{\text{WRet}(t_i) \geq H\}} \times \mathbf{1}_{\{(\max_{j=1,\ldots,i-1}(\text{WRet}(t_j))) < H\}}$$

Underlying assets	KBC, ING, FORTIS, DEXIA
Notional	£10 million
Currency	GBP
Maturity	3 years
Autocall level	100%
Autocall frequency	Annual
Coupon level	100%
Coupon frequency	Annual
Coupon value	10%, 20%, 30%
Knock-in level	60%
DI put strike	100%
Note price	99%
Capital protected	No

Figure 12.11 The terms of a 3-year worst-of autocallable note with worst-of down-and-in put at maturity.

If the structure has not autocalled, the redemption at maturity is determined as follows:

(a) If all the assets composing the underlying basket close at or above the knock-in level, the note is redeemed at 100%;
(b) If one of the underlyings closes below the knock-in level, the note is converted into physical shares at strike.

Figure 12.11 shows an example of a contract on a worst-of autocallable structure with snowballing coupons and a worst-of down-and-in put feature at maturity.

Risk Analysis

When we sell a worst-of autocall with a put feature at maturity, we are short the worst-of autocallable digitals and long a path-dependent worst-of put option. In order to price the worst-of autocallable digitals efficiently, one can compute the price of the autocallable digitals separately, as mentioned in section 12.2, and deduct the price of the worst-of put. The probabilities of coupons being paid decrease with time and can be quite small for the last path-dependent digitals. Also note that in the case of snowballing coupons, the digital size increases with time since the potential coupons are higher. Therefore, one must be careful when offering a very large digital with a very low probability of striking (low price compared to the high potential loss).

A worst-of autocallable note with a worst-of down-and-in put is composed of zero coupon bonds, worst-of autocallable digitals and a worst-of down-and-in put. Now that we are familiar with these structures, we can easily analyse the risks associated with a worst-of autocall with snowballing coupons and worst-of down-and-in put. If one is short this structure, he is short the worst-of autocall and long the worst-of put.

Remember, being short the worst-of autocall implies being short the underlying's forwards and long the coupon trigger (which is equal to the autocall trigger in this case). Also, the trader selling these options is long volatility and short correlation. In Chapter 10, we discussed the risks associated with worst-of down-and-in puts. To briefly summarize: the forward price of the underlyings decreases the down-and-in put price; volatility, skew, and knock-in barrier level increase its price; correlation between the underlying assets decreases its price; therefore, one buying a worst-of down-and-in put is short the forwards, long the knock-in barrier, long the volatility, short the correlation and long the skew.

If one is short a worst-of autocallable structure with snowball effect and worst-of down-and-in put, he would definitely be short the forward prices, long the triggers (autocallable trigger, coupon trigger and DI put barrier level), long volatility and short correlation.

The position in skew is more complex to determine since the skew makes the sold worst-of digitals more expensive but also makes the bought worst-of down-and-in put more expensive. Even if the short skew position in digitals has usually more effect on the price than the long skew position in the put at maturity, it is not always the case. Then, we need to be careful and price both skew effects with 100% skew to determine whether we have an overall bid or offer with respect to the skew. After this has been done, we reprice the worst-of autocall with down-and-in put at maturity by applying the correct parameter on skew.

12.4.3 Outperformance Autocallables

Let's consider two assets S_1 and S_2. An outperformance autocall based on the outperformance of S_1 vs S_2 is typically a European style option that pays a coupon C at each observation date if $S_1 - S_2$ outperforms a specific level called a *cushion*. This outperformance structure has an autocall feature that pays a coupon upon early redemption. This note payoff is as follows:

At each observation date t_i:

$$\text{Coupon}(t_i) = \text{Notional} \times [1 + i \times C] \times \mathbf{1}_{\{\text{Ret}_1(t_i) - \text{Ret}_2(t_i) \geq \text{Cushion}\}}$$
$$\times \mathbf{1}_{\{\max_{j=1,\ldots,i-1}(\text{Ret}_1(t_i) - \text{Ret}_2(t_i)) < \text{Cushion}\}}$$

where $\text{Ret}_i(t) = S_i(t)/S_i(0)$.

Outperformance autocallable options are composed of path-dependent outperformance digitals. Indeed, the first digital is a usual outperformance one with a maturity equal to the first observation date. The digitals exist only if all the previous ones didn't strike. There is one and only one coupon payment that also corresponds to the autocall event.

Now, let's take the example of an English investor who believes that HSBC bank will suffer more losses compared to the banking sector in Asia. Most of the analysts agree that for the next 2 years there is a low probability that HSBC will outperform the Hang Seng bank index by more than 35%. Therefore, the investor decides to buy the structure presented in Figure 12.12. Note that, in this case, the autocall trigger is equal to the coupon level, and

Underlying assets	Hang Seng Bank vs HSBC
Notional	£20 million
Currency	GBP
Maturity	24 months
Cushion	-35%
Autocall frequency	Semi-Annual
Coupon value (snowballing)	20% per annum
Note price	100%
Capital protected	Yes

Figure 12.12 The terms of a 2-year outperformance autocallable note.

the coupons are snowballing. At the end of each semi-annual observation i, if the difference between the Hang Seng bank index performance and HSBC performance is greater than or equal to the cushion, the note is redeemed at $100\% + C(i)$, where $C(i) = i \times 20\%/2$. At maturity, the holder receives 100% of the notional invested if HSBC has always outperformed the banking index by more than 35% at the different observation dates.

One should be cautious when pricing and hedging outperformance autocallables since they involve trading outperformance digitals. The risks associated with these structures are quite similar and have been fully covered in Chapter 11. The cushion is important in the risk management process of trading this structure. In the case of the cushion being negative, the outperformance digitals are in-the-money. Otherwise, they are out-of-the-money. Also note that the cushion was implicitly equal to zero when we previously described outperformance digitals.

Part III

More on Exotic Structures

13

The Cliquet Family

I'd rather look forward and dream, then look backwards and regret.

Cliquet options are a popular product in the world of equity derivatives. They are appealing retail products because they provide downside protection while at the same time offer significant upside potential. Cliquet structures are most popular on single indices, but are also structured on stocks, and even baskets of stocks or indices. By introducing various caps and floors, local and global, one is sure to find an attractive yet reasonably priced derivative.

Cliquets are also known as *ratchet* options because they are based on resetting the strike of a derivative structure to the last fixing of the underlying asset. The resetting feature is what makes cliquets unique from the payoffs we have covered so far. This resetting introduces what is known as *forward skew* exposure, as mentioned in Chapter 4. These are truly beautiful derivatives but must be handled with caution.

This chapter introduces cliquets and we look at various versions with different caps and floors, and reverse cliquets. The discussion of cliquets is not possible without going into slightly more detail regarding models than we previously presented. This is due to the additional risks that these products hold. The goal is to explain these without making the discussion too technical.

In the literature, cliquets are discussed in articles including Bergomi (2004) who presents a new model for cliquets, Jeffery (2004) who discusses reverse cliquets, and Wilmott (2002) who discusses cliquets and volatility models. Cliquets also appear in Gatheral (2006) and Overhaus *et al.* (2007).

13.1 FORWARD STARTING OPTIONS

A forward starting option is an option that starts at some (prespecified) time in the future (we call this the strike date), and has a maturity after that date. Since the option starts in the future, we cannot know (today) the price of the underlying at this starting point in the future, and for this reason it is standard to specify a strike price as a percentage of moneyness. For example, we can set the strike to be 100% of the price of the underlying at the strike date, so that the option starts ATM. Forward starting options are typically traded on fixed dollar notionals, not numbers of shares. Let's explain this through a payoff. A forward starting call has payoff

$$\text{Forward Starting Call}_{\text{payoff}} = \max\left[0, S_{t_2} - k\, S_{t_1}\right]$$

or in percentage returns

$$\text{Forward Starting Call}_{\text{payoff}} = \max\left[0, \frac{S_{t_2}}{S_{t_1}} - K\right]$$

where $t_0 < t_1 < t_2$. Here t_0 is the inception date, on which the premium is paid. t_1 is as described above the *strike date*, or the date on which the option's strike becomes set. The

Table 13.1 Strikes for forward starting calls, and the position in which the options start.

	Call option	Put option
$K < 100\%$	Starts $(1 - K)\%$ ITM	Starts $(1 - K)\%$ OTM
$K > 100\%$	Starts $(K - 1)\%$ OTM	Starts $(K - 1)\%$ ITM
$K = 100\%$	Starts ATM	Starts ATM

option, however, is priced and the premium is fixed and paid at t_0. If $t_0 = t_1$ this reduces to a standard call option on S.

This is stating that on t_0 the investor pays for an option that will not strike until t_1. Why is this useful to an investor? From the investors' points of view, a forward starting option can be used if they want exposure to the underlying at the future point t_1 going forward, but not between t_0 and t_1. By buying (or selling) a forward starting option at t_0 they pay (or receive) a fixed price for an option that has a strike contingent on the underlying's level at a future date, whether to hedge or to speculate.

It is true that one can apply a Black–Scholes formula to price such an option, but caution must be taken. The question to be asked here is which volatility does one use to price a forward starting option? We know the implied volatilities of vanilla options, but what about forward starting options? The answer is that one must use the implied forward volatility, and this may not be available with the same liquidity we see in regular vanillas. Ideally at time t_0 we would like to have surfaces for all strikes, strike dates t_1 and maturities t_2, but this does not exist. If it did we would know the prices of all forward starting calls and puts. How about OTM and ITM options? Much like the existence of the skew we see in vanilla options' implied volatilities across strikes, we have what is known as a *forward skew*. Buying or selling forward starting calls or puts gives the investor exposure to this forward skew. Let us take the example of a call spread, only now we look at a forward starting call spread (Table 13.1). Consider the case of an ATM-15% call spread, where the strikes are now represented in terms of returns, not performance. The seller of this call spread is essentially selling the ATM forward starting call and buying the 15% forward starting OTM call (just like the usual call spread of Chapter 6). In the above payoff formula for the forward starting call, the ATM call has $K = 0\%$ and the OTM call has $K = 15\%$. As we shall see, the simplest of cliquet products are built as just a series of forward starting calls, that is, a series of forward starting calls with the same initial date t_0, but where the strike date of the second (or the jth) call is the maturity date of the first (or $(j - 1)$th) call. Not all hope is lost in regard to getting the right forward skews as there exist standardized cliquets for which one can obtain some market consensus data from which one can extrapolate a fairly accurate idea of where the market is pricing forward skew.

13.2   CLIQUETS WITH LOCAL FLOORS AND CAPS

So, now that we know what a forward starting call is, let's look at a sum of forward starting calls and build what is known as a *cliquet* structure.

13.2.1 Payoff Mechanism

Let's start with the example of a cliquet, which has a local floor and a local cap (called an *LFLC Cliquet* for brevity).

$$\text{LFLC Cliquet}_{\text{payoff}} = \sum_{i=1}^{n} \max\left[F, \min\left(\frac{S_{t_i}}{S_{t_{i-1}}} - 1, C \right) \right]$$

where the term $(S_{t_i}/S_{t_{i-1}} - 1)$ is the ith periodic return, C is the local cap and F is the local floor. We call this a *symmetric* cliquet when $F = -C$, that is, the cap and floor are symmetric around zero.

Notice that the denominator of $S_{t_i}/S_{t_{i-1}}$ is $S_{t_{i-1}}$ (the previous period's return) not S_0 (the initial value). These are what we refer to as cliquet style returns. The set of dates $t_0, t_1, \ldots, t_n$ are the initial date t_0 and the n reset dates $t_1, \ldots, t_n$. We call each of the time intervals $[t_{i-1}, t_i]$ a period, and the returns are also known as *period returns* or *period to period returns*.

Following the above definition of a forward starting call option, this is just a sum of such forward starting call options. To be exact, it is in fact the sum of forward starting call spreads. Setting the floor $F = 0$ the holder of the cliquet is long the ATM forward starting calls and short the forward starting OTM calls of strike C (the local cap), each with maturity equal to the resetting period.

Table 13.2 describes the cliquet payoff. In each scenario, there are three yearly returns: initial date to year 1, year 1 to year 2, year 2 to year 3. The call option column gives the payoff of a 3-year regular European call option, and the cliquet is the sum of the capped/floored annual returns. In scenario 1, there is no difference between the two, in the second we notice that the cliquet does not pick up the negative return of year 2, and the overall payoff is higher than that of the call. In the third the cliquet does not pick up the first 2 years of negative returns and has non-zero payoff whereas the ATM call ends worthless out of the money.

We have seen that flooring the annual returns in the cliquet has saved us from potentially bad returns that eat away at the call option. In scenario 4 things start to change, and we see the effect of the cap. Here the cliquet has not picked up the negative return in year 1 but has the significant return of year 3 capped at 10% (the local cap is set at 10%), and the call ends up in the money with a payoff greater than the cliquet. The last scenario clearly tells the story of the local cap. With no negative returns in any year, the call will end in the money (possibly ATM if all are zero), but while the call becomes more and more in-the-money, the cliquet picks up these positive returns only capped. The end result is that the call has a higher payoff.

Table 13.2 Scenario observations of the index performances on the 3 years. Note, each return now represents the return for the specific year only, not from the initial date. That is, for example the second column (year 2) represents the returns between the end of year 1 and the end of year 2. The call option is computed from the initial date to the final date (end of year 3) as a comparison. The cliquet has a local floor of 0% and local cap at 10%, the call is ATM.

	Year 1	Year 2	Year 3	**3-Year ATM call**	**LFLC cliquet**
Scenario 1	0%	0%	5%	**5%**	**5%**
Scenario 2	0%	−2%	5%	**2.9%**	**5%**
Scenario 3	−6%	−5%	10%	**0%**	**10%**
Scenario 4	−2%	5%	13%	**16.28%**	**15%**
Scenario 5	5%	11%	16%	**35.2%**	**25%**

As we can see, the returns are annual from one year to the next, and so to find the return from start to finish (for the ATM call) we use the following formula:

$$\text{Ret}_{\text{call}} = (1 + \text{Ret}_{\text{year 1}})(1 + \text{Ret}_{\text{year 2}})(1 + \text{Ret}_{\text{year 3}}) - 1$$

In conclusion so far, the locally floored cliquet allows the investor to pick up positive annual returns and lock in such profit (we are assuming accrued returns are paid at maturity, although they can be paid annually). This will fit quite naturally into a note structure with capital guarantee, an easily marketable retail product: you collect all positive annual returns capped at 10% but none of the negative returns, and of course your money back at maturity.

13.2.2   Forward Skew and Other Risks

A key risk here that we did not see in previous chapters is the cliquet's exposure to forward skew. Much the same way as a normal call spread has skew exposure, a forward starting call spread has exposure to forward skew, as we saw in the previous section. Cliquet structures have caps and floors, which immediately implies skew dependency. Because cliquets are a series of skew-dependent options, the overall structure will itself be quite skew sensitive, and due to the reset features it is forward skew to which the cliquet is exposed.

In fact, there is exposure to more than one forward skew; taking the example in Table 13.2, the first call spread has exposure to the usual skew, the volatility skew given by the vanilla options surface taken at the required strikes. The second call spread is sensitive to the 1- to 2-year forward skew, and, likewise, the third is sensitive to the 2- to 3-year skew. Obviously, an increase in any of these will increase the price of the cliquet, so the seller of the derivative is short forward skew.

Many of the derivatives we have seen so far can, with some caution, be evaluated using local volatility models. Let us assume that we have calibrated a local volatility model to a set of vanilla options. If we were to simulate the process forward in time, we find that the forward skews it generates begin to flatten out. This can be explained by the fact that, in local volatility models, the volatility is a deterministic function of the underlying price. This dependency of the volatility on the spot results in higher probabilities of the spot moving higher, so as time goes by (or as we simulate forward in time), we find that volatilities and skew go down (thus the flattening out effect). This is cause for serious concern as anyone attempting to price cliquets or any forward skew-dependent derivative with local volatility will almost surely misprice it.

13.3   CLIQUETS WITH GLOBAL FLOORS AND CAPS

Now we introduce global floors and caps to the cliquets we saw in the previous section. The globally floored and globally capped cliquet has the following payoff:

$$\text{GFGC Cliquet}_{\text{payoff}} = \max \left[\text{GF}, \min \left(\text{GC}, \sum_{i=1}^{n} \max \left(F, \min \left(\text{Ret}_{t_i}, C \right) \right) \right) \right]$$

where the term $\text{Ret}_{t_i} = (S_{t_i}/S_{t_{i-1}}) - 1$ is the ith periodic return, C is the local cap and F is the local floor, GC and GF are the global cap and floor respectively. The above payoff is the same locally floored and capped cliquet we saw above, only the total sum of all the cliquets is now capped and floored (that is, globally capped and floored).

The first thing to note is that, in the case of a local floor F set to zero, a global floor of zero (or less than zero) is meaningless as the payoff will be non-negative (a sum of returns each floored at zero). Introducing a positive global floor of, for example, 1% will act as a minimum guarantee for the option, guaranteeing a non-zero payoff of at least 1%, but as previously shown, this makes the option more expensive.

Two popular cliquets are the locally floored globally capped cliquet and the locally capped and globally floored cliquet. With the first, the local floor can be set so that the investor receives no returns below this floor F and the global cap GC serves as a means to make the derivative cheaper than the uncapped version.

Consider, for example, that we are structuring a note, along the lines of the structuring process described in section 3.10. We also have a certain amount to spend on the option after securing the return of 100% capital through a zero coupon bond, and we can set the floor at the required level, for example at 0% and then solve for the global cap that makes the derivative price exactly right to fit into the note structure. The payoff here is a special case of the above general formula (here we have no local cap or global floor)

$$\text{LFGC Cliquet}_{\text{payoff}} = \min\left[\text{GC}, \sum_{i=1}^{n} \max\left(F, \text{Ret}_{t_i} \right) \right]$$

However, one can use the general formula and think of the local cap and global floor to be existent, but set to unreachable levels (for example, $C = 10,000\%$ and $GF = -10,000\%$), this might be applied if one has only a generic pricing template for pricing cliquets and needs to specify these two values. One thing to note is that we must enforce the restriction that $n \times F$ must be strictly less than GC, or else the payoff makes no sense as it will always be equal to GC.

Forward Skew Risk

Again we need to see the forward skew exposure. This cliquet is a nice example involving maximums and minimums for which we can show some manipulations for complex payoff as such. If one looks inside the payoff of the LFGC cliquet above, the term inside the sum can be written as

$$\max\left(F, \text{Ret}_{t_i} \right) = \max\left(0, \text{Ret}_{t_i} - F \right) + F$$

which is nothing but a call (for each i), plus a minimum guarantee of F. How far in- or out-of-the-money the calls are clearly depends on the level of the floor F. Next we manipulate the overall payoff as follows:

$$
\begin{aligned}
\text{LFGC Cliquet}_{\text{payoff}} &= \min\left[\text{GC}, \sum_{i=1}^{n} \max\left(F, \text{Ret}_{t_i}\right)\right] \\
&= \text{GC} + \sum_{i=1}^{n} \max\left(F, \text{Ret}_{t_i}\right) - \max\left[\text{GC}, \sum_{i=1}^{n} \max\left(F, \text{Ret}_{t_i}\right)\right] \\
&= \sum_{i=1}^{n} \max\left(F, \text{Ret}_{t_i}\right) - \max\left[0, \sum_{i=1}^{n} \max\left(F, \text{Ret}_{t_i}\right) - \text{GC}\right] \\
&= nF + \sum_{i=1}^{n} \max\left(0, \text{Ret}_{t_i} - F\right) \\
&\quad - \max\left[0, \sum_{i=1}^{n} \max\left(0, \text{Ret}_{t_i} - F\right) - (\text{GC} - nF)\right] \qquad (13.1)
\end{aligned}
$$

The first equality is just the payoff definition; the second equality makes use of the identity $\min(A, B) + \max(A, B) = A + B$; and in the third we have taken the term GC outside of the last term and it cancels with the first term. In the last equality we have used the derivation done above and removed the floor from the payoffs of the floored call so that we can see each as a call struck at F. Since $\text{GC} - nF > 0$, the second term of equation (13.1) minus the third term is always positive. The term nF appearing here is just n (the number of periods) times F which makes perfect sense in the last equality as from the payoff definition we can directly see that the option will have to pay at least as much as the sum of all the floors, which is $n \times F$.

Having split the payoff as such we can now see two clear things. The second term is just a series of forward starting call options. The third term is a *compound* option (an option on an option) and here it is an OTM call on a series of forward starting call options. It is OTM because we have the constraint that $\text{GC} - nF > 0$ in order that the initial payoff of this cliquet makes sense. Splitting the payoff as such will allow us to see the existence of the two key cliquet risks separately.

The first effect to consider is Vega; the second term is a call option and thus obviously has positive Vega; and the third term, although a compound option, also has positive Vega. If volatility goes up, both of these increase in value. However, since these two have different signs it is not clear which has the greater effect to determine the volatility position. This is compounded by the fact that we do not have a prespecified value for F, different values of F set the first set of call options at different levels of moneyness, which also impacts their Vega sensitivity. Recall from the discussion on Vega in Chapter 5 than an ATM call option has a higher Vega than ITM and OTM call options. This effect is also not clear cut on the compound option.

The appearance of the second term, which involves the sum of forward starting call options, will have forward skew exposure. Whether this is a cost or a benefit is not clear until one specifies the value of F. The reason is that if F is negative, then the call options are ITM, and in the presence of skew this increases the ITM call option volatility, in this case forward skew, thus raising their prices. However, if F is positive, the opposite occurs as these calls will be OTM and the OTM vol is lower in the presence of skew. The third term will also have forward skew exposure, but likewise the position is not clear. It is also the fact that the call options are embedded into another call option in the third term that means the forward skew risk cannot be captured solely by using the forward implied volatility at the correct strike, and here we must apply a model that knows about forward skew.

Another risk to be aware of here is Vega convexity. It comes primarily from the third term and is due to the nature of any compound option. The meaning and interpretations of this risk are discussed below once we have introduced the second cliquet in this family.

Looking at the second structure – the cliquet with local caps and a global floor – do we see anything familiar? This structure is similar to the ICBC structure of Chapter 9, but here instead of having one time period and the returns of several assets, each locally capped, we now have only one asset but a set of returns (due to the resetting). To explain further, let Ret_i, $i = 1, \ldots, n$ be the returns for each of the n periods respectively, then the payoff is given by

$$GFLC\,Cliquet_{payoff} = \max\left[GF, \sum_{i=1}^{n} \min\left(Ret_i, C\right) \right]$$

which resembles the payoff of the ICBC (here returns are taken through time, not over a basket of underlyers). As we saw with the ICBC, the method of using local caps and global floors is an effective method of reducing the price of such a derivative. Here the local caps limit the upside returns, and the global floor acts as a guarantee against a negative overall payout.

Let us consider such a cliquet with a 2-year maturity where returns are computed on a quarterly basis. Specifying the global floor at 0% and the local cap at 5%, we have the following payoff:

$$GFLC\,Cliquet_{payoff} = \max\left[0, \sum_{i=1}^{8} \min\left(Ret_i, 5\%\right) \right]$$

for which we consider a set of scenarios in Table 13.3 which are analysed as follows. In the first scenario the local cap of 5% caps the positive return in Q3 but all the negative returns are picked up. In the second scenario it is clear that the index has performed relatively well, and the cliquet returns 18%.

In this case, an analysis similar to that above will show that the seller of the option is buying volatility and selling forward skew. We now turn our attention to Vega convexity.

13.3.1 Vega Convexity

In addition to the forward skew exposure, we have also to worry about Vega convexity. Just to settle the forward skew risk, all we have to do is note that at each interval $[t_{i-1}, t_i]$ between each two reset dates t_{i-1} and t_i we are capping the returns, that is, the seller of the option is buying volatility at each of these caps. Much like the ICBC, the seller of the option is selling

Table 13.3 Scenario observations of the index performances of the eight quarterly returns for the 2-year globally-floored locally-capped cliquet. The global floor is set to zero and the local cap set to 5%.

	Q1	Q2	Q3	Q4	Q5	Q6	Q7	Q8	GFLC
Scenario 1	0%	2%	7%	3%	−3%	0%	−3.5%	1%	**4.5%**
Scenario 2	2%	3%	2%	−1%	2%	6%	4%	1%	**18%**
Scenario 3	−1%	−4%	−2%	0.5%	−3%	1%	2%	0%	**0%**

skew, only here, due to the reset feature, it is the forward skew of the period $[t_{i-1}, t_i]$ to which the seller is exposed.

Onto Vega convexity, we have touched on the existence of this, but let's look at the details, asking the questions: What is Vega convexity? Or convexity in general firstly? As we saw in the case of vanilla options written on an underlying asset S, the option price is sensitive to movements in said underlying. Not just first order however, we have Delta and Gamma, that is, as the underlying moves our Delta changes. This makes perfect sense as we saw in Chapter 5 on the Greek letters, that, for example, as a call option moves further into the money (i.e. the underlying has increased in price) our Delta increases. Thus the second-order effect, the Gamma – or, as one might call this, the convexity. That is, a call option is convex in the underlying (this is clear from the payoff of a call plotted against S) and convexity is in fact what gives the call options value.

This general term *convexity*, or *price convexity*, is often used to refer to the second-order effect, Gamma. We now want to understand Vega convexity. We know Vega is the sensitivity of our option price to a movement in the volatility of the underlying. Vega convexity, also known as Volga, is the second-order sensitivity, or convexity, of our option price to a movement in the underlying's volatility. Mathematically it is the second derivative of the option price w.r.t volatility. Under Black–Scholes, the Vega of a call (and a put) is given by

$$\mathcal{V} = S\,e^{-qT}\,\Phi'(d_1)\sqrt{T}$$

Now let's turn our attention to the second-order effect of a change in vol. Under Black–Scholes, the Volga of a call (also a put) option is given by

$$\text{Volga} = S\,e^{-qT}\,\Phi'(d_1)\sqrt{T}\,\frac{d_1 d_2}{\sigma} = \mathcal{V}\,\frac{d_1 d_2}{\sigma}$$

As we can see in Figure 13.1, the ATM call has no Vega convexity. If we go back to the approximations in Chapter 5, section 5.9, the formula for approximating the price of the ATM

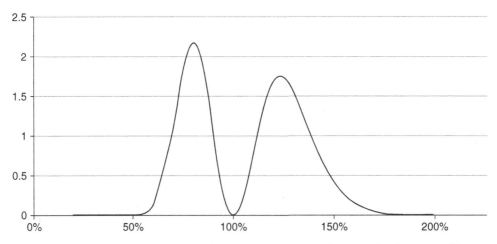

Figure 13.1 Volga of a call option (also for a put option), over strike. Note that the ATM call has no Volga, whereas the OTM and ITM calls pick up Volga but then the very deep OTM and ITM calls lose their Vega convexity.

call is built on the fact that the price is approximately linear in volatility. That is, its Vega is constant and not a function of the level of volatility. So the second derivative w.r.t. volatility must be approximately zero.

As we move away from the money, the OTM and ITM calls start to pick up convexity; however, if we go sufficiently deep in- or out-of-the-money, we see that convexity fades to zero. In these cases the moneyness of the options is so extreme that in the OTM call it drives the price down towards zero, rendering sensitivities negligible, and in the case of the deep ITM call, the price becomes linear in the underlying and has thus lost its convexities.

Now given that we know the prices of call options from the market, we do not need to worry about this when pricing them. In fact we know the implied volatility of these options, which are the values we plug into Black–Scholes to obtain a price. Obviously these are driven by supply and demand, and these convexities are already priced into the call option values.

However, our beloved cliquets do have Vega convexity that will need to be priced. Much the same way that one assumes an underlying stock price to be a stochastic (random) process in order to price options, we will need to introduce the concept of stochastic volatility here. Why? When we model a stock price as a random process it allows us to see the convexity to this stock price (Gamma); if we had assumed it to be deterministic (no randomness in the stock price) our option would have no value (as we would not see the convexity). The same thing applies in the case of Vega convex options, only here we need to allow our volatility (or possibly the variance) to be a random process of its own to enable us to see Vega convexity. For a technical explanation of this, see section A.3 of Appendix A.

Local volatility models do not work in Vega convex situations because the volatility is assumed to be a deterministic function of the underlying's price, thus not a random process of its own. So a local volatility process does not know about Vega convexity, and it will thus not show us such risk when used to price Vega convex payouts. One must be cautious. Obviously the case of Black–Scholes, where volatility is just a constant, is effectively a special case of local volatility and is no use in these situations.

Using a stochastic volatility model for such product allows us to look at a vol-of-vol parameter (the volatility of volatility). Recall, for the volatility to be itself a random process, it must have its own volatility which is known as vol-of-vol. This term is the coefficient of the second derivative w.r.t. volatility (Volga) in a pricing equation.

13.3.2 Levels of These Risks

So now we are faced with two risks: forward skew and Vega convexity. These are present in the cliquets we have seen so far and all the others to come in this chapter. The degree of sensitivity to each of these differs however from one product to the next. Understanding this is the key to pricing these structures correctly.

Starting with the locally floored and capped cliquet, with no global floors or caps, we look at the special case of a symmetric cliquet. From section 13.2.1, this means that the local cap and the local floor are equidistant from the ATM point but on opposite sides; for example, a cliquet with a local floor of -10% and local cap of $+10\%$. What is special about this cliquet is that at the ATM point it does not have Vega convexity. This does not mean that its Vega is not sensitive to volatility movements; on the contrary, Vega even changes sign at this point, but ATM Volga is zero. Figure 13.2 gives the Volga of a call spread which is essentially what this cliquet is, a sum of forward starting -10%, $+10\%$ call spreads. In this case, from a pricing standpoint, we are left with the primary concern of getting the forward skews correct and are

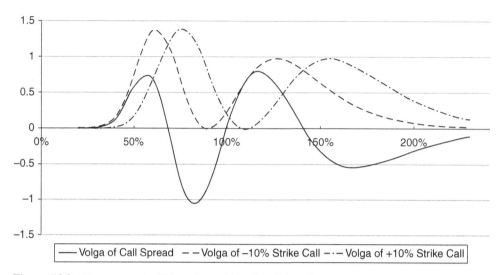

Figure 13.2 Here we see the Volga of a +10% call and that of a −10% strike call (both are positive). The difference between them is the Volga of the call spread, which at-the-money is zero. This assumes zero rates and divs, and a vol of 25% for both call options. Overall this graph might be more confusing than useful as Volga changes sign three times, but what is useful is for us to see that, at-the-money, our symmetric call spread has zero Volga.

not too concerned with the Vega convexity, given it is zero (or very close to it). However, as the market moves the product will begin to exhibit varying levels of Vega convexity.

When the local floor or the cap are positioned differently, introducing asymmetry, as in the case of local floor set to zero and local cap at 5%, we begin to pick up Volga. This happens in much the same way that the Vegas of the two call options in a call spread cancel each other less as the caps and floors become more asymmetric. So, in the case of the 0% locally floored 5% locally capped cliquet, as in the above example, the sellers will be mainly exposure to forward skew, with the Vega convexity, which the seller of the option is short, gradually increasing. Naturally, we also have the usual price convexity to take care of: we have our Delta and our Gamma.

Much like the Vega changes sign for a cliquet, so does the Gamma. If there is a time for one to look at a higher order it is for an option like this for which the Gamma changes sign. The third-order effect, the sensitivity of Gamma to a movement in the underlying's price, is known as *Speed* and defined as

$$\text{Speed} = \frac{\partial^3 C}{\partial S^3} = -e^{-qT} \frac{\mathcal{N}'(d_1)}{\sigma \sqrt{T} S^2} \left(\frac{d_1}{\sigma \sqrt{T}} + 1 \right)$$

The essential idea of this graph will be to notice the point at which the Gamma changes sign to see how sensitive it would be to a movement in either direction of the underlying. As we saw before with Gamma, one will need to compute the two-sided Gamma, that is, the sensitivity to the underlying's price going up, and also (but computed separately) the case when its price goes down.

In conclusion, generally, given the nature of these profiles – especially that the Vega profile can change – we will have to use a stochastic volatility model for such options. In Appendix A, section A.3, we further explain the need for stochastic volatility models.

A question that arises is: Do we have data regarding forward skew to calibrate to? If one is able to obtain broker quotes for some standardized cliquets, or get information regarding the market consensus on specific cliquets, it is possible to conduct a parameterization of the forward skew the same way in which the regular implied volatility skew was parameterized in Chapter 4, and these prices matched during calibration as additional calibration instruments. Ideally we would be able to find the implied volatilities for all forward starting call options of all tenors and all maturities and all strikes and use these, but there is no liquid market for such things as yet. If we were able to obtain 90–110% symmetric cliquets in the market with 1-year resets, then this could be used for the parameterization of the year to year forward skew.

This parameterization can of course be modified as described in Chapter 4 to use the 95–105% skew if the cliquet with these points as caps and floors is available instead of the 90–110% version. Having quotes for the 100–110% cliquet, we will also have information about Vega convexity. For a month-to-month cliquet we would have to use a 98–102% cliquet as caps and floors at 10% apart do not make sense for a monthly cliquet.

13.4 REVERSE CLIQUETS

In this variant on the standard cliquet, the reverse cliquet begins with a headline coupon, and instead of accumulating positive performances in an underlying asset, negative returns are deducted from said coupon. At maturity, the holder of the reverse cliquet receives the part of the coupon that is left after the deduction of the (possibly floored) negative period to period performances:

$$\text{Reverse Cliquet}_{\text{payoff}} = \max\left[0, \text{MaxCoupon} + \sum_{i=1}^{n} \min[0; \text{Ret}_{t_i}]\right]$$

where Ret_{t_i} are the usual cliquet style periodic returns, and MaxCoupon is a large above-market coupon which the bullish investor hopes to collect in its entirety, should the index have a positive performance every month from start to maturity. Here we have set the local cap and the global floor to zero.

We should note that the global floor here plays an important role as there is a very large potential downside should there be continuously large down movements in the index. This floor will be absolutely necessary if one is to fit this option into a principal-protected structure. The upside is that theoretically this option could pay MaxCoupon if there are no negative returns to eat away at said coupon. With capital guaranteed, this makes for an interesting product, and in the structure of section 3.10 the coupon would be adjusted for this option to fit into the structure.

This payoff can be rewritten as

$$\text{Reverse Cliquet}_{\text{payoff}} = \max\left[0, \text{MaxCoupon} - \sum_{i=1}^{n} \max[0; -\text{Ret}_{t_i}]\right]$$

where it is now clear that we are subtracting from the coupon the set of all ATM puts that end in-the-money. In this payoff we have specified the global floor to be zero, and in this case it is clear that the seller of the reverse cliquet is effectively long these puts. Since they are ATM, we find low skew sensitivity, which can potentially increase; however, it is highly convex in Vega and we must tread with extreme caution on this risk from the onset.

Note the scenarios of Table 13.4 with the payout of the reverse cliquet in comparison to the locally floored/locally capped cliquet.

Table 13.4   Scenario observations of the index performances on the 3 years. Note that only the negative returns contribute to the final payoff of the reverse cliquet with headline coupon of 15%. The LFLC cliquet is there for comparison with LC = 10% and LF = 0%.

	Year 1	Year 2	Year 3	LFLC cliquet	Reverse cliquet
Scenario 1	0%	0%	5%	**5%**	**15%**
Scenario 2	0%	−2%	5%	**5%**	**13%**
Scenario 3	−6%	−5%	10%	**10%**	**4%**
Scenario 4	−2%	5%	13%	**15%**	**13%**
Scenario 5	5%	11%	16%	**25%**	**15%**

Reverse Cliquet Risks

The reason the structure appeals to investors in an environment of high volatility is that the seller of the reverse cliquet will be buying volatility at this high level, and is thus able to offer a higher headline coupon to the investor. As volatility goes down, the price goes up, meaning that this would be perfect for an investor wanting to buy an option during a bear market (high volatility) with the view that it is almost over.

With respect to forward skews we can think of this structure as follows. The investor is short ATM puts, but he is also long the global floor that acts like a strip of OTM puts. Thinking about this as a put spread, the seller of the reverse cliquet, who is long the put spreads, is short skew, and forward skew in this case owing to the reset feature. Since this option is highly convex in Vega (and the seller is short Vega convexity) we expect the reverse cliquet to be worth much more under stochastic volatility than local volatility, reflecting not only the flatter skew the local vol generates but, more importantly, the fact that local volatility does not know about Vega convexity. Increasing the global floor up from zero can only increase this Vega convexity further.

Regarding reverse cliquet Vega convexity, the seller of the reverse cliquet will need to buy volatility when volatility increases, and sell volatility when volatility decreases. Assuming that we are in a high-volatility period, we expect to have large negative returns (the puts) that will eat away the headline coupon, thus the seller has a low volatility sensitivity in this environment. The opposite is true in the case of low volatility when the option's Vega is relatively high. This is saying that the Vega of the reverse cliquet is a non-constant function of volatility itself, thus Vega convexity, and there is need for a stochastic volatility model. This is also equivalent to saying that there is a large vol-of-vol effect, and this must be priced to reflect the cost of dynamically hedging this convexity; Vega hedges will need to be adjusted as volatility changes.

We have to deal with forward skew, and in the case of reverse cliquets and in all the cliquet structures to come, it makes sense to additionally calibrate to the cliquets quotes from a broker or data from a consensus of market makers' mid-market prices, if possible. To assume that any model is pricing reverse cliquets correctly, a first step is to see that it is pricing known cliquets correctly to make sure that we are headed in the right direction. This will mean that we have captured the levels at which the market is pricing forward skews (and some convexities) much like those we previously calibrated to the vanilla options market.

14

More Cliquets and Related Structures

If stock markets were like computers, then cliquets would definitely be the best financial products. When the system crashes, you just need to restart to boost the performance.

In this chapter we continue our discussion of cliquets, introduce other cliquet variations and also structures that share similar risks. These include digital cliquets, bearish cliquets, accumulators (cliquets with lock-in features where the option holder locks in returns) and replacement cliquets. We also look into multi-asset cliquets including basket cliquets, best-of cliquets, ICBC cliquets and rainbow cliquets. These bring up the concepts of correlation and dispersion that we have seen in Chapters 7, 8 and 9, in addition to the new risks involved in cliquets. The discussion of Napoleons and lookbacks respectively form the last two sections of this chapter. These will each have various sensitivities, including possibly Vega convexity or forward skew, which must again be made transparent and, in turn, correctly priced. They also present interesting examples for the ongoing discussion of the smile dynamics of pricing models.

14.1 OTHER CLIQUETS

14.1.1 Digital Cliquets

The digital cliquet is an extension of the regular cliquet and the digital options we saw in Chapter 11. Let's start with a simple payoff:

$$\text{Digital Cliquet}_{\text{payoff}} = \sum_{i=1}^{n} C(i)\mathbf{1}_{\{\text{Ret}_{t_i} \geq K\}}$$

where $C(i)$ is the agreed coupon for year i, and Ret_{t_i} is the cliquet style return for the ith period, $\text{Ret}_{t_i} = (S_{t_i}/S_{t_{i-1}}) - 1$. As usual, $\mathbf{1}$ is the indicator function

$$\mathbf{1}_{\{\text{Ret}_{t_i} \geq K\}} = \begin{cases} 1 \text{ if } \text{Ret}_{t_i} \geq K \\ 0 \text{ if } \text{Ret}_{t_i} < K \end{cases}$$

This is just the sum of forward starting digitals. Using these it is easy to describe a retail product: let $K = 0$, then for each year in which the index has gone up on its value at the start of *that* year, you receive a fixed coupon C. The coupons do not necessarily have to be equal, but they must be specified in advance. One can add global caps and floors to make it look like

$$\text{Digital Cliquet}_{\text{payoff}} = \max \left[\text{GF}, \min \left(\text{GC}, \sum_{i=1}^{n} C(i)\mathbf{1}_{\{\text{Ret}_{t_i} > K\}} \right) \right]$$

Since all the digital returns are positive, the global floor will act as a minimum guarantee and the global cap will help to reduce the price.

Considering the risks: if we recall Chapter 11 on digitals, we must be especially cautious about the digital's skew exposure – here, the forward skew. If we were to not account for this

Table 14.1 Digital cliquet scenario observations of the index performances on the 3 years. The digital coupon is set at 6%, and trigger is set to 0%. The LFLC cliquet is there for comparison with LC = 10% and LF = 0%.

	Year 1	Year 2	Year 3	LFLC cliquet	Digital cliquet
Scenario 1	0%	0%	5%	**5%**	**18%**
Scenario 2	0%	−2%	5%	**5%**	**12%**
Scenario 3	−6%	−5%	10%	**10%**	**6%**
Scenario 4	−2%	5%	13%	**15%**	**12%**
Scenario 5	5%	11%	16%	**25%**	**18%**

skew, then we would have a problem as we would be certain to underprice the option. Our hedge in general would be similar to that of the regular digital, only here instead of using a call spread we will use a series of forward starting call spreads, or, even better, use a regular cliquet (with the correct caps and floors). As with any digital we must consider the size of the digital and make sure we can trade the underlying through the strike, i.e. check the liquidity of the underlying and take whatever shifts are necessary to smoothen the Greeks near the digital strike.

In the case of the digital cliquet, the seller of the option is short forward skew, but what about volatility? If we regard the digital as a call spread (which will be necessary for purposes of smoothing the hedge ratios) then whether the seller of the option is long or short volatility will depend on where this digital is struck and the width of the call spreads. (See section 11.1.3 on hedging digital options for more details.)

One thing to note regarding the width of the call spreads necessary is that most cliquets are written on indices, so we are faced with less problems of liquidity as we will always find that trading index futures is more liquid than the underlying stocks.

14.1.2 Bearish Cliquets

Consider the case of an investor who is quite bearish in the short/medium term on global equity indices. An interesting product would be a bearish cliquet, also known as a bearish reverse cliquet because of its payoff, although one should not confuse this with the real reverse cliquet described in section 13.4. Let's start with the payoff:

$$\text{Bearish Cliquet}_{\text{payoff}} = \max\left[0, \text{Coupon} - \sum_{i=1}^{n} \max(0; \text{Ret}_i)\right]$$

where again Ret_i are the periodic cliquet style returns. This can equivalently be written as

$$\text{Bearish Cliquet}_{\text{payoff}} = \max\left[0, \text{Coupon} - \sum_{i=1}^{n} \text{ATM Monthly Calls}\right]$$

This is obviously the case of a cliquet resetting on a monthly basis. The view here is bearish, that is, if the index goes down several months in succession, the investor receives the (full) coupon – as defined, the maximum possible payout is the coupon itself. These would be attractive to investors with a bearish view, and would generally be of short maturity (6 months for example) and serve as a protection product.

Table 14.2 Scenario observations of the monthly index performances over 6 months. Note that only positive returns eat away at the coupon – this is after all a bearish product. In this example we assume a headline coupon of 10%.

	M1	M2	M3	M4	M5	M6	Bearish cliquet
Scenario 1	1%	−1%	2%	0%	1%	1.5%	**4.5%**
Scenario 2	−1%	−2%	1%	−1%	−3%	1%	**8%**
Scenario 3	1%	2%	2%	3%	−1%	2%	**0%**

What is interesting about this structure from the sell side is that the seller of this option is long both forward skew and Vega convexity. To elaborate, the seller of the option is in this case buying forward skew, but the skew sensitivity is not very high; we expect this as the calls appearing in the formula are in fact ATM. We can replace these by OTM or ITM calls depending on the requirements, and this would increase the level of the forward skew sensitivity.

As for the Vega convexity, the fact that such sensitivity is negative (to the seller) means that as volatility goes up the Vega of the option goes down. Intuitively this makes sense as an increase in volatility would raise the calls appearing in the sum, thus reducing the coupon the seller will have to pay at maturity. As a month goes by with the coupon further eaten away (see Table 14.2), there is less and less uncertainty as to how much will have to be paid out at maturity.

14.1.3 Variable Cap Cliquets

We can structure a cliquet so that it has local caps, but at the same time offers the investor something more appealing than a fixed cap. For example, let's assume that the investor wants a −5%, +5% 2-year cliquet with quarterly resets, but is concerned there may be higher returns that she does not want to miss. We can introduce variable caps so that if a return supersedes the cap we take that return as the next quarter's new cap. Any period return to go above the cap (of that period) is capped at the current level of the cap but is then set as the new cap:

$$\text{Variable Cap Cliquet}_{\text{payoff}} = \max\left[0, \sum_{i=1}^{n} \min\left(\text{LC}(i), \max\left(\text{LF}, \text{Ret}(i)\right)\right)\right]$$

where the local cap $\text{LC}(i)$ can vary at each period depending on the returns in the following manner. The first cap $\text{LC}(1)$ is fixed at 5%, for example. The local caps for the subsequent periods are given by

$$\text{LC}(i) = \max\left(\text{LC}(i-1), \text{Ret}(i-1)\right)$$

that is, the cap for any period is the maximum between the last period's cap and the last period's return. We should note that the local cap will always be at least equal to the starting cap $\text{LC}(1)$ so this cliquet will cost more than the same cliquet with the same cap, but is a cheaper alternative than raising the cap and constitutes a great product if one expects several large positive returns.

Naturally with the local caps and floors we have a large forward skew sensitivity, much like the case of the constant cap cliquet in terms of direction, only greater in value. With these and the global floors the seller of the option is again selling Vega convexity and must account for this in the pricing, although again the effect of forward skew is greater than the Vega convexity.

14.1.4   Accumulators/Lock-in Cliquets

This is a cliquet structure in which returns can be locked in as the minimum payout of the option. The payout is as follows:

$$\text{Lock-in Cliquet}_{\text{payoff}} = \max \left[0\%, \sum_{i=1}^{n} \min \left(\text{LC}, \ \max \left(\text{LF}, \ \text{Ret}(i) \right) \right), \ \text{Lock} \right]$$

So this is just a regular globally floored, locally floored, locally capped cliquet, but with an additional embedded lock-in feature. The lock is determined on the basis of accumulated returns, computed as follows:

$$\text{Acc Ret}(j) = \sum_{i=1}^{j} \min \left(\text{LC}, \ \max \left(\text{LF}, \ \text{Ret}(i) \right) \right)$$

that is, Acc Ret at time j is the sum of the locally floored, locally capped cliquet style returns from the start and up to time j. Obviously, the sum of all of them, Acc Ret(n), is what appears in the above payout, which we can write as

$$\text{Lock-in Cliquet}_{\text{payoff}} = \max \left[0\%, \ \text{Acc Ret}(n), \ \text{Lock} \right]$$

One must specify the levels of the lock-in, here for example we set the levels at 10%, 20% and 30%, and define the lock as follows:

(a) If Acc Ret(j) was ever above 30% then the lock is set to 30%.
(b) If Acc Ret(j) was ever above 20% then the lock is set to 20%.
(c) If Acc Ret(j) was ever above 10% then the lock is set to 10%.
(d) Otherwise the lock $= 0$.

That is, if at any point j the returns so far add up to the one above any of these levels, then that level is locked in and the payoff will be at least that much. Since the local floor will be set to a value below zero (for example $\text{LF} = -2\%$, $\text{LC} = 2\%$ for monthly returns on a 3-year lock-in cliquet), the accumulated returns can exceed 10%, but some negative returns can eat away this return. In the case of the lock-in, if accumulated returns ever reach 10% (or 20% or 30%) then the investor is guaranteed at least that percentage. See Table 14.3 for some scenarios to illustrate the payoff of accumulators.

This structure has a higher potential return than the same cliquet without the lock-in as it allows the investor to capture a good run of returns and not have to worry that they may be lost. Obviously this would cost a bit more than the same cliquet without the lock-in, and it too can potentially have zero payoff if all the returns are negative.

14.1.5   Replacement Cliquets

Replacement cliquets, also known as *take-N cliquets*, pay out the sum of all periodic returns where the best, predetermined number, of returns are replaced with a predefined fixed coupon.

Table 14.3 Lock-in cliquet scenarios. The local cap and floor are at 3% and −3% respectively. Lock-in levels are 10%, 20% and 30%. The first **bold** row represents the payoff of the LFLC cliquet without lock-in, the second is the lock achieved, and the third is the payoff of the lock-in cliquet.

Scenario		1		2		3
Month j	Ret(j)	Accum(j)	Ret(j)	Accum(j)	Ret(j)	Accum(j)
Month 1	1%	1%	1%	1%	2%	2%
Month 2	2%	3%	3%	4%	1.5%	3.5%
Month 3	1%	4%	2%	6%	1%	4.5%
Month 4	0%	4%	2.5%	8.5%	2%	6.5%
Month 5	3.5%	7%	1%	9.5%	2%	8.5%
Month 6	1%	8%	1.5%	11%	4%	11.5%
Month 7	−1%	7%	2%	13%	2%	13.5%
Month 8	0.5%	7.5%	2%	15%	−1.5%	12%
Month 9	0.5%	8%	2.5%	17.5%	−1%	11%
Month 10	−1%	7%	1.5%	19%	−2%	9%
Month 11	0%	7%	2%	21%	−4%	6%
Month 12	−2%	5%	−2%	19%	−2%	4%
LFLC Cliq.		**5%**		**19%**		**4%**
Lock-in Cliq.		**0%**		**20%**		**10%**
Accumulator		**5%**		**20%**		**10%**

One can set the returns to be based on the periodic ATM performances of the underlying, and assume that the structure accumulates these returns and pays only at maturity.

This option would be good for someone with a softly bullish view. To understand why, and also be clear on the payoff mechanism, let's write the payoff then look at some scenarios. The payoff itself seems more complicated than it is and can be made clear with the scenarios. Let's assume this to be a 1-year trade with monthly resets and a global floor of 1%. The payoff (with the best five monthly returns replaced by 3%) is:

$$\text{Replacement Cliquet}_{\text{payoff}} = \max\left[1\%, \sum_{i=1}^{12}\text{Ret}^*_{t_i}\right]$$

where the set of returns $\text{Ret}^*_{t_i}$ is the same as the usual $\text{Ret}_{t_i} = (S_{t_i}/S_{t_{i-1}}) - 1$.

In Table 14.4 we show some scenarios for a 6-month option, as this is just to illustrate the point. In the first scenario, the investor has forgone the relatively large positive returns as they have been replaced by 2%. In the second scenario, the replacement mechanism has raised the payout, as two of the three best returns are below 2%. In the last scenario, the replacement did enhance the top three returns, but the large negative returns were the governing factor and the global floor of 1% kicked in to give the return at maturity.

A moderately bullish view is represented here because if we were extremely bullish we would not want the best returns to be replaced by 2% as they may be higher and contribute towards a higher overall payoff. On the other hand, even if none of the returns reach 2% we still replace the best three returns, which can potentially be less than 2%, with 2%. Put, with

Table 14.4   Scenario observations of the monthly index performances over 6 months. Note that the best three returns are replaced by 2%. The **bold** returns are the three that are replaced. The last column is the payout of the replacement cliquet with the global floor set at 1%.

	M1	M2	M3	M4	M5	M6	Replacement cliquet
Scenario 1	0%	1.5%	**5%**	**4%**	**2%**	0.5%	**8%**
Scenario 2	0%	−2%	−1%	**1%**	**1%**	**2%**	**3%**
Scenario 3	−5%	−2%	**0%**	−1%	**1%**	**1%**	**1%**

a minimum guarantee of 1%, into a note structure with capital guarantee, the replacement cliquet may appeal to investors with such a view.

14.2   MULTI-ASSET CLIQUETS

14.2.1   Multi-Asset Cliquet Payoffs

It is possible to restructure almost all the payoffs we have seen regarding correlation and dispersion into cliquet style payoffs like those we have seen so far in these two chapters. Here we mention a few interesting combinations and then discuss the risks involved in moving to multi-asset cliquet structures.

Basket Cliquets

Starting with a basket of N assets, we can structure a cliquet on the basket, meaning that each period's return is computed on the basis of the returns of the basket. We can replace the single asset returns with the basket returns in the cliquets above. One can, for example, structure a GFLC cliquet that pays on the world basket of EuroStoxx, Nikkei and S&P 500 as a retail product that now provides the same benefits as the GFLC cliquet structure in addition to providing exposure to a set of global indices instead of just one index or stock.

Best-of Cliquets

Let's start with a basket of N stocks, then each cliquet is just the return of the best performing asset in that period. At the end of each period i, we observe the individual returns $\text{Ret}(i, j)$ of the shares j composing the underlying basket. Let the maturity be 3 years and the observations made on an annual basis.

$$\text{Ret}(i, j) = \frac{S(i, j)}{S(i - 1, j)} - 1, \qquad i = 1, 2, 3 \text{ and } j = 1 \dots N$$

then the payoff of a locally floored locally capped best-of cliquet is as follows:

$$\text{LFLC BO Cliquet}_{\text{payoff}} = \sum_{i=1}^{3} \max\left[F, \min\left(\max_{j=1,\dots,N} \text{Ret}(i, j), C \right) \right]$$

As before, the seller of the option will be short dispersion (see the section on best-of options in Chapter 8 for details). In addition to the analysis there, the seller is, as expected, exposed to forward skew due to the resetting.

Rainbow Cliquets

We can structure a rainbow cliquet the same way we do a best-of cliquet, only that each period's return is a weighted sum of the best j returns among the N assets. Specifying weights such as 50% on the best, 30% on the second best and 20% on the third best, this cliquet would price, all else being equal, at less than the best-of option and higher than the basket option.

ICBC Cliquets

Put simply, this is an ICBC that resets. The individually capped basket call (ICBC) cliquet is based on a basket of N stocks. Assume that we are interested in a 3-year product with annual resets. At the end of each year i, we observe the individual returns $\text{Ret}_j(i)$ of the shares j composing the underlying basket:

$$\text{Ret}_j(i) = \frac{S_j(i)}{S_j(i-1)} - 1, \quad i = 1, 2, 3 \text{ and } j = 1 \ldots N$$

Then we cap each stock performance at Cap% (say 20%). The individual capped returns $\text{Capped Ret}_j(i)$ are computed as follows:

$$\text{Capped Ret}_j(i) = \min\left[\text{Ret}_j(i), \text{Cap\%}\right]$$

The holder of the option receives an annual coupon, $Coupon(i)$ (floored at 0%) of value of the arithmetic average of the capped returns.

$$\text{Coupon}(i) = \max\left[0, \frac{1}{N} \times \sum_{j=1}^{N} \text{Capped Ret}_j(i)\right]$$

Of course, the coupon can be paid periodically (monthly, quarterly, annually) or at maturity of the option, depending on the terms agreed by the contract.

14.2.2 Multi-asset Cliquet Risks

When discussing the basket, ICBC, best-of and rainbow cliquets, some of the risks are similar to those of the regular versions (non-cliquet style returns). Obviously here, with the new risks of Vega convexity and forward skew, we will need to go into details, but the common risks will be similar.

In the best-of version the seller is short dispersion. The effect of correlation on the rainbow, as before, lies somewhere between the best-of cliquet (high correlation sensitivity) and the basket cliquet (lower correlation sensitivity). This means that the seller of the rainbow could be long or short correlation, whereas the seller of the best-of is long correlation and short volatility. In the ICBC the seller is short the correlations between the assets and long their volatilities. For the basket cliquet the seller is short both correlation and volatility.

In the cliquet case there is forward skew exposure, but the forward skew positions are the same as the cases of the regular skew exposure in the regular case. The seller of an ICBC cliquet, for example, is short forward skew. There is Vega convexity in each of these products, much like the single asset cliquet versions, only here we will also see cross Vega terms, that is, the effect a move of one volatility has on the Vega of the others. This is picked up with the use of a multi-asset stochastic volatility model. With this, one would have to calibrate the parameters of the correlation between the different volatilities, and this cannot really be implied from the market; so one would simply see what the effect is on the specific option and then take a conservative spread on these values. Correlation between the underlyings themselves is handled as normal.

14.3 NAPOLEONS

14.3.1 The Napoleon Structure

The Napoleon is a structure that pays a coupon at maturity, which is a pre-agreed headline coupon plus the worst period return. It is more probable than not that this worst return will be negative and thus the coupon at maturity is expected to be less than the headline coupon. However, to the bullish investor this can be appealing as the headline coupons are generally large and definitely above the market rates. Writing a payoff we have

$$\text{Napoleon}_{\text{payoff}} = \max\left[0, \text{MaxCoupon} + \min_{i=1,\dots,n}\left(\text{Ret}_{t_i}\right)\right]$$

where Ret_{t_i} is the usual cliquet style period return, and in this case it does not necessarily have to be those of one asset.

In the example scenarios of Table 14.5, notice that in scenario 1, even though the Napoleon has paid a substantial coupon for the 5-year trade, given the index's performance in the first few years, it seems that there may have been better products to buy, for example one of the above cliquets. In scenario 2 the extremely bad return in year 4, which corresponds to some sort of market crash, has eaten away a large chunk of the coupon. In scenario 3, all the annual returns are positive, albeit small, and the Napoleon's payoff in fact exceeds the 50% coupon. In the final scenario we see that although the index's performance is relatively poor throughout, there was no large negative annual return and the Napoleon has a nice payout. This should emphasize the nature of the Napoleon in terms of which views it expresses.

As in the case of the reverse cliquet above, the seller of a Napoleon will need to buy volatility when volatility increases, and sell volatility when volatility decreases. If we assume that we are in a high volatility period, we expect that a large negative return will eat away the headline coupon, thus giving a lower volatility sensitivity in this environment. The opposite is true in the case of low volatility when the option's Vega becomes quite high. This is saying that the Vega of the Napoleon is a function of volatility itself, thus we have Vega convexity and the need to use a stochastic volatility model. This is also equivalent to saying that there is a large vol-of-vol effect, and this must be priced to reflect the cost of hedging this convexity:

Table 14.5 Scenario observations of the annual index returns over 5 years. See the worst returns in **bold**. We assume a headline coupon of 50% for the Napoleon

	Year 1	Year 2	Year 3	Year 4	Year 5	Napoleon
Scenario 1	15%	13%	19%	7%	**−11%**	**39%**
Scenario 2	15%	8%	6%	**−34%**	5%	**16%**
Scenario 3	2%	4%	9%	**1%**	4%	**51%**
Scenario 4	13%	−9%	**−10%**	−5%	−9%	**40%**

Vega hedges will need to be adjusted as volatility changes, especially so when volatility rises significantly during a market decline.

The volatility hedging instruments are European options of different maturities, ideally going out to the maturity of the Napoleon, and the stochastic volatility model must be calibrated to these correctly to show the risk against them. The Napoleon has Vega distributed along the time-buckets, and depending on how the term structure of volatilities changes, the Vega sensitivity in the different Vega buckets will change. The effect of skew for a Napoleon depends on the size of the coupon, and the seller of the Napoleon is generally long skew. So, in addition to the term structure, one must calibrate to the OTM European options that can also serve as hedging instruments. We refer to Chapter 4 for discussions of trading the skew and its convexity with combinations of European options.

14.3.2   The Bearish Napoleon

One can modify the payoff of the Napoleon to make it into a bearish structure. By taking the best period return and subtracting it, this now suits someone with a bearish view

$$\text{Bearish Napoleon}_{\text{payoff}} = \max\left[0,\ \text{MaxCoupon} - \max_{i=1,\dots,n}\left(\text{Ret}_{t_i}\right)\right]$$

in that only positive returns can now eat away at the headline coupon. What is interesting in this product from the pricing perspective is that the large Vega convexity cost the seller must charge for the regular Napoleon is now reversed and, in fact, is a Vega convexity benefit for the buyer. How much of this benefit the seller chooses to offer is a function of his aggressiveness and the state of competition. Similar to most bearish structures, these will generally only be bought on much shorter maturities than the regular Napoleons.

14.4   LOOKBACK OPTIONS

14.4.1   The Various Lookback Payoffs

There are several different types of lookback options, and the first question one must ask when encountering the term *lookback options* is "which lookback is this referring to?". As the name suggests, a lookback option's payoff at maturity depends on some value reached by the underlying asset's price during the life of the option and at maturity: looking back at this value, in hindsight, the payoff is computed. An example of this is the lookback call where the payoff depends on the maximum level reached by the underlying, so the payoff is given by $(\tilde{S} - K)^+$, where $\tilde{S}$ is the maximum stock price over the life of the option, with K as the fixed strike price. This lookback we shall refer to as the "Max spot lookback". Lookback structures have been placed in this chapter because they can carry some forward skew risk and have sensitivity to smile dynamics.

Other lookbacks include the put version of the above option that now involves the minimum over the life of the option. It is also possible to have a floating strike lookback option. The floating strike lookback call option in this case pays the difference between the asset price at maturity and the floating strike that is the minimum value reached by the underlying during the life of the option. The idea is that the investor is buying the underlying at maturity at the lowest value it attained throughout the life of the option, compared to the standard call option where the investor is buying the underlying at a fixed strike price. A similar argument holds

Table 14.6 Lookback scenarios.

	Minimum	Maximum	Final
Series 1	99.19%	110.40%	105.46%
Series 2	98.83%	116.28%	116.28%
Series 3	94.12%	104.81%	99.12%

for the lookback put in comparison to the European put option, only the investor here is selling the underlying at a more favourable price than the standard put.

These possible features imply that the lookback is a path-dependent option in the sense that the payoff of the derivative is dependent on the path followed by the underlying asset and not just its final value. If we assume that the lookback option is monitored continuously, then there exist closed formulas for the lookback option (see Garman, 1989 and Goldman *et al.*, 1979). The price of the lookback is obviously sensitive to the frequency at which the maximum (or minimum) is observed (continuously, daily closes, weekly, monthly,...) and a formula by Broadie, *et al.* (1998), analogous to that discussed in the chapter on barrier options, serves as a correction to move from continuous monitoring to discrete monitoring.

The minimum, maximum and final value of each of the series in Figure 14.1 are given in Table 14.6; and the prices of the maximum spot lookback call (with strike at 100%), the floating strike lookback call, and the European ATM call are given in Table 14.7.

14.4.2 Hedging Lookbacks

To understand the lookback structure's risks, let's first consider a hedging argument. A standard hedging argument for the max spot lookback is that the seller of the option buys two call options with the same strike as the lookback. In the literature, hedging arguments of this nature for the lookback were first proposed by Goldman *et al.* (1979) and appear in texts such as Gatheral (2006). Considering various scenarios we first note that if the underlying never goes above the strike then both the lookback and the call options expire worthless. If and when the underlying reaches the strike, then the call options are ATM. If the underlying then goes above the strike,

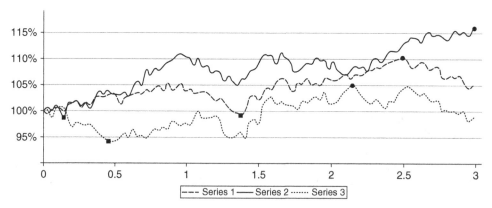

Figure 14.1 Path scenarios for three underlying assets over a 3-year period. The boldly stressed points represent either the maximum or the minimum of each series.

Table 14.7   Lookback payouts.

	Scenario 1	Scenario 2	Scenario 3
Max spot ATM lookback	10.40%	16.28%	4.81%
Floating strike lookback	6.27%	17.45%	5.00%
European ATM call	5.46%	16.28%	0%

let's say by an amount ΔK, then the lookback gains value because the spot price used to compute the payoff at maturity will be at least the value of $\tilde{S} = K + \Delta K$ and the payoff at this stage is at least $(K + \Delta K) - K = \Delta K$. Since the two call options were ATM, using what we learned about the Delta of call options in Chapter 5 we know that Delta of an ATM call is close to 0.5, which means that as the spot increases by an amount, say ΔK, we expect the value of the call to increase by $0.5 \times \Delta K$. This means that if we hold two call options then, combined, they will increase by an amount $2 \times 0.5 \times \Delta K = \Delta K$, the same amount as the increase in the lookback. At this point we immediately sell the two calls, locking in this value, and then buy another two calls struck ATM which is now $S = K + \Delta K$. The argument continues as such in that the same thing holds: if the spot goes up further, we lock in the value by selling the two calls and buying two new ATM calls. In reality, Delta is not 0.5 and this is a slightly simplistic argument. The real amount of call options needed to be held is slightly below 2, however this does allow us to look further at the structure to think about the other risks. To see the skew position we must discuss the concepts of sticky strike and sticky Delta.

14.4.3   Sticky Strike and Sticky Delta

The sticky strike and sticky Delta models were introduced by Derman (1999). In the sticky Delta model, we assume that the implied volatility skew is related to specific strikes in that the shape of the skew will not change as the underlying moves. In the sticky Delta model the whole implied volatility skew moves with the underlying. For example: if a 100 strike call has a Delta of 0.56 and the ATM implied volatility is 20%, and if the underlying moves downwards and the 95 strike option now has a Delta of 0.56, then we expect the skew to move in line with this and see the implied volatility of the 95 strike option at 20%. These two models serve mainly as toys in the sense that neither is a real reflection of what one observes in the market. In fact what one observes is somewhere between these two.

14.4.4   Skew Risk in Lookbacks

Applying these two models to the lookback, and following the hedging argument using the two call options, we can see that if we assume any one of the sticky strike or sticky Delta models, we see a skew benefit for the investor (seller of the option is long skew). In the sticky strike case, as the spot increases to $K + \Delta K$ and we sell the two call options and buy two new ones ATM, we see that in the presence of skew, the two new call options we buy are priced with a lower implied volatility (the skew has not moved). Lower implied vol in the presence of skew means a lower cost to buy the two new call options and thus the skew benefit. In the case of sticky Delta, the two new options we buy are also ATM, meaning that we expect them to have the same Delta as the previous calls we bought, the same implied volatility (sticky

Delta), and in this case we see little skew effect. If we assume the reality to be a blend between these two possible models, then the skew benefit becomes apparent.

The lookback can carry forward skew risk. Consider the case of the floating strike lookback. Here the strike is not determined at the onset and the payoff at maturity is computed on the basis of observations of the underlying (discrete or continuous) and thus carries some forward skew risk. It is not an explicit forward skew risk as in the case of cliquets: the lookback is sensitive to how the implied volatility skew evolves, i.e. smile dynamics. If we were to compare the price of a lookback option under local volatility with its price under stochastic volatility, we would see that the lookback is cheaper under the latter. This is because a stochastic volatility model propagates some forward skew in its dynamics, whereas local volatility's forward skew fades, as discussed previously. Less skew generated by the model means less skew benefit to the option buyer, which means a higher price.

How much forward skew and how serious the difference in price is between the stochastic and local volatility models is a function of the fraction of the maturity of the option over which we observe and compute the floating strike. Take, as an example, a 3-year lookback where the floating strike is computed as the minimum value of the spot reached during the first month. The effect will be much less, due to less sensitivity to the assumed smile dynamics, than if the lookback strike were taken to be the minimum level reached throughout the life of the option. It would be prudent to price such an option with both models to gauge this effect before making a price. The analysis presented here extends to options that contain lookback features as just part of the payoff.

Product Example: Lookback Strike Shark

As a product example consider a lookback strike shark (knock-out call with rebate as in section 10.4.1 of Chapter 10). This would serve as a product for the investor who is bearish in the short/medium term and bullish in the long term. As an example, one can consider a 3-year product where the lookback strike is specified as the lowest monthly close during the first year. Adding the lookback feature allows one to tailor additional views into many of the products we have seen.

15

Mountain Range Options

The man who moved the mountain began by carrying away small stones.

Originally marketed by Société Générale in the late 1990s, the *mountain range* is a series of path-dependent options linked to a basket of underlying assets. In this chapter, we present some of these options, discussing their payoffs as well as the risks associated with these mountain range options. This chapter provides us with not only the chance to present some interesting examples of quite popular products, but to also bring together many of the concepts we have covered so far. The examples shown in this chapter include some of the most popular mountain range options in the market for equity derivatives. In the literature, these are discussed by Quessette (2002), and specific products by Overhaus (2002) and Overhaus *et al.* (2007).

15.1 ALTIPLANO

The *Altiplano* option is a multi-asset derivative with a payoff based on the returns of n assets $S_1, S_2, \ldots, S_n$ composing the underlying basket. It entitles the holder to receive a large fixed coupon C at maturity T, provided that none of the assets in the basket have fallen below a predetermined barrier denoted L, during a given time period. This observation period is usually started at the inception date and ends at the maturity date; but can also be a specific time sub-period $[t_1, t_2]$ of the option's lifetime. If, however, one of the components in the set of chosen underlyings crossed the downside barrier, then the payoff is computed differently, usually by a participation in a call-type payout. Here, we consider the most common case where the Altiplano holder receives the payoff of an Asian call option even though the call can be European style. The Altiplano option payoff is given as:

$$\text{Altiplano}_{\text{payoff}} = \phi \times \text{Participation} \times \max\left[0, \text{Asian Perf} - K\right] + (1 - \phi)C$$

where K is the strike price associated with the call option and ϕ is a binary variable equal to the condition set for the index value given as:

$$\phi = \begin{cases} 1 & \text{if } \min_{1 \leq j \leq n,\, t_1 \leq t \leq t_2} \left(\frac{S_j(t)}{S_j(0)}\right) \leq L \\ 0 & \text{otherwise} \end{cases}$$

and

$$\text{Asian Perf} = \frac{1}{n \times N} \sum_{j=1}^{n} \sum_{i=1}^{N} \frac{S_j(i)}{S_j(0)}$$

where $S_j(i)$ is the closing price of stock j observed at time i.

In the case described above, the coupon is paid if the worst performing stock has always been higher than the lower trigger during the barrier observation period. Note that more complicated variants pay the option holder a coupon if a specified number of underlying assets did fall below the barrier level. Also, the participation in the call payout can vary depending

Underlying basket	5 European Blue Chip Stocks
Tenor	5 years
Currency	EUR
Notional	10 Million EUR
Barrier (daily observations)	80%
Coupon	150%
Call type	Asian
Averaging	Semi-annual
Strike	100%
Participation	115%
Note	99%
Capital protected	Yes

Figure 15.1   The terms of an Altiplano structure.

on the number of assets that break the trigger. The 5-year Altiplano note shown in Figure 15.1 offers the investor an attractive payoff at maturity. Indeed, this structure based on the worst performing stock on a basket of five underlying European "Blue Chips" pays the holder the following payout. If all the stocks in the basket have always been above 80% of their initial level, the note holder receives 250% of his initial investment at maturity, which represents a 20.11% annualized rate of return. Otherwise, 115% participation in the basket-averaged positive performance is paid instead. Figure 15.2 shows two different stocks' return scenarios; the dashed lines indicate the basket performance whereas the solid lines constitute the worst stock performance registered over time. On the left, we have a scenario where the lower barrier of 80% has never been crossed during the life of the note. Here, the note holder receives a unique payment at the end of the fifth year equal to 25,000,000 euros (150% in addition to the 100% redeemed capital).

In the second scenario, at least one of the stocks composing the basket has been below 80% of its initial level. In this case, the Altiplano note pays the holder 115% participation in an Asian call payoff based on the basket performance. At the end of each semester, the performance of the basket is observed and computed by taking the arithmetic average of the stocks' performances with respect to initial date. At maturity, the Asian return is calculated as the average of the eight observed basket performances. Here, this return is equal to 111.22%

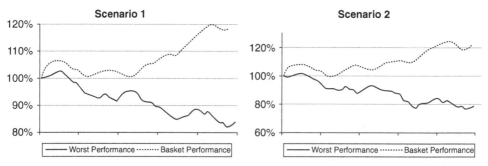

Figure 15.2   Two scenarios showing the basket performance as well as the worst performance observed during the life of the note.

of the basket initial level. Therefore, the buyer of the Altiplano note receives a coupon of $12.90\% (= 115\% \times 11.22\%)$ plus 100% capital protected.

Altiplanos are sometimes considered to be Parisian basket options due to their barrier and Asian characteristics. Indeed, we can think of this derivative as a cross between worst-of digitals and European or Asian style down-and-in call options for which the barrier observations are based on the worst performing stock, whereas the payoff depends on the basket performance. Note that this structure is adapted to a bullish view on the stocks composing the underlying basket.

15.2   HIMALAYA

The *Himalaya* is a type of growth product that is usually linked to a basket of n shares or indices $S_1, S_2, ..., S_n$. In the literature these are discussed by Overhaus (2002). The structure pays a coupon at maturity, based on the arithmetic average of the performance of the n_b best underlying assets in each specific period during the term of the product. Once a share or index has been selected as one of the best performers in a particular period, it is then removed from the basket for all subsequent periods. At each observation date $t_i (i = 1, \ldots, N)$, the n_b best performing stocks in the basket are removed from the latter for subsequent periods and their performances are frozen. Note that the basket at time t_i is composed of $n - n_b \times (i - 1)$ assets. The Himalaya option payoff at maturity T is given as:

$$\text{Himalaya}_{\text{payoff}} = \text{Participation} \times \max\left[0, \frac{1}{n}\text{Running Perf}(T) - K\right]$$

where K is the strike price and

$$\text{Running Perf}(t_i) = \text{Running Perf}(t_{i-1}) + \sum_{j=1}^{n_b} \frac{S_{t_i}^{(j)}}{S_0^{(j)}}$$

Note that Running Perf$(0) = 0$ and $S_{t_i}^{(j)}$ is the spot price of the jth best performing stock in the basket at time t_i.

In the example shown in Figure 15.3, the holder buys a 4-year Himalaya note that is capital protected and offers him an unlimited profit potential. The underlying basket is composed of four sector indices. At the end of each year, the best performing underlying is removed from the basket and its performance is frozen, i.e. locked in. At maturity, the holder receives 100% of

Underlying basket	4 sector indices
Tenor	4 years
Currency	USD
Notional	$ 1,000,000
Strike	100%
Observations (frequency)	Annual
Strike	100%
Participation	120%
Note	100%
Capital protected	Yes

Figure 15.3   The terms of a Himalaya structure.

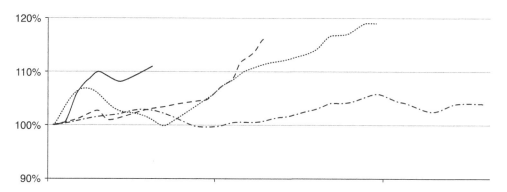

Figure 15.4 Scenario showing the returns of four underlying sector indices as well as the *freezing* mechanism process of the Himalaya structure.

its investment plus a participation of 120% in the positive arithmetic average of the four frozen performances. For example, the Himalaya can be structured on various sectors, so that it freezes the performance of a specific sector when it is performing well, locks in this performance and gives time to other sectors to perform later. Another example we see in Chapter 19 on hybrids uses the Himalaya across different asset classes to pick up the different cycles between the asset classes. In Figure 15.4, we see a scenario showing the underlying sector indices' returns as well as the freezing process behind the Himalaya concept. It is important to keep in mind that the best performances are only observed at the end of each period. At the end of the fourth year, the investor receives 100% of his invested capital plus 120% participation in the frozen basket. Here, the arithmetic average of the frozen performances is equal to 112.57% and the strike price is equal to 100%. Therefore, the Himalaya note pays the buyer an amount equal to $1,150,800, which corresponds to 100% plus $1.2 \times 12.57\%$ of the notional.

Himalayas are quite popular because investors can earn an unlimited profit on a structure that looks like a best-of structure. The Himalaya option is adapted to a bullish view on the underlying assets composing the basket. The seller of this option has a short position on the underlyings' forwards, and will need to buy Delta in each of the underlying assets; he is long dividends and long borrowing costs. However, the option sensitivities with respect to volatility and correlation are much less trivial.

Let's take the example shown above to determine the answer. The idea is to consider the Himalaya option either as a series of best-of options or as a series of worst-of options. Indeed we can regard this Himalaya option as a series of best-of options having respective maturities of 1, 2, 3 and 4 years, knowing that the options based on best performing stocks have a lower maturity. On the other hand, we can consider this Himalaya option as a series of worst-of options having respective maturities of 4, 3, 2 and 1 years, knowing that the options based on worst performing stocks have a higher maturity. Because of the maturity effect, the worst-of impact is more important than the best-of impact. This means that we should look at this Himalaya option as a series of worst-of options. The seller of the option, as this conclusion implies, is long dispersion which is a long position on asset volatility and a short position on correlation between the different sector indices.

However, this is not always the case. Now let's consider a 4-year maturity Himalaya option based on 10 underlying stocks. Like an Asian option, the Himalaya is a call on the average performance of the best stocks within the basket. At the end of each year, the best performing stock is removed from the underlying basket and its performance is frozen. The option holder receives the positive arithmetic average of the frozen performances. In this case, the Himalaya option is considered as a series of best-of options since the frozen performances are respectively the performances of the best performing stock out of 10, 9, 8 and 7 stocks. A trader selling this option is then short dispersion, which means that he is short volatility and long correlation.

Therefore, the Vega as well as the correlation sensitivity depends on the contract specified. It is also interesting to note that this structure is the first one to replicate a strategy from the management of mutual funds, where one typically sells the stocks in a portfolio that have performed best each year. Indeed, when a stock performance is frozen, the seller of the Himalaya gets rid of it since it no longer has any impact on the payoff. More modelling details are discussed in the section below on pricing mountain range products. We also revisit Himalayas in the context of hybrid derivatives in Chapter 19. In this context, the underlyings are selected from different asset classes, and the Himalaya thus provides an excellent way to benefit from the different cycles of the different asset classes, locking in returns.

15.3 EVEREST

The *Everest* structure typically gives the holder, at maturity, a minimum of 100% of the sum invested in addition to a bonus linked to the worst performing stock from a basket of assets. The maturities of the Everest structure tend to be quite long, possibly greater than 10 years, and the basket has a large number of assets, typically greater than 10. The holder of an Everest note receives the following payoff at maturity T:

$$\text{Everest}_{\text{payoff}} = \text{Notional} \times \left[\text{Coupon} + \min_{j=1,...,n} \left(\text{Ret}_j(T) \right) \right]$$

where $\text{Ret}_j(T) = S_j(T)/S_j(0) - 1$. When investing in an Everest note, owing to the nature of the payoff, capital is guaranteed, and it is interesting to note that the coupon can have a value greater than 200%. While this presents an attractive feature for the investor, the seller must be cautious when risk-managing this product and we discuss the associated risks below.

Consider an investor who wants to invest $10 million in a 100% guaranteed capital structure that offers an attractive payoff linked to a basket of shares on which he is bullish. He can invest in a 10-year Everest structure associated with his basket of 11 international "Blue Chip" stocks that gives a payoff at maturity of 200% plus the positive or negative performance of the worst-of between initial date and maturity date. Or equivalently

$$\text{Notional} \times \left[200\% + 100\% \times \min \left(\frac{S_1(T) - S_1(0)}{S_1(0)}, \ldots, \frac{S_{11}(T) - S_{11}(0)}{S_{11}(0)} \right) \right]$$

In Figure 15.5, we can see four scenarios showing the returns of the worst performing stock at maturity. Table 15.1 clarifies the payoff scenarios of the Everest structure according to the four cases drawn in Figure 15.5. For instance, the performance of the worst-of in the first scenario at the end of the tenth year is equal to 34.26% of its initial level. This means that the holder of the Everest structure receives a unique payment at maturity equal to $200\% + (34.26\% - 1) = 134.26\%$ of the notional. This corresponds to an annualized rate of return equal to 2.99%. As we can see through the different case scenarios, Everest can potentially offer an unlimited investment performance as the underlyings are usually chosen on the basis of consistent growth potential. For instance, if the worst performing stock shows

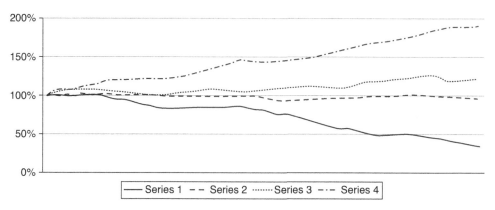

Figure 15.5 Four scenarios showing the worst performing stock returns in a basket of 11 underlying assets.

a zero percent performance after 10 years, the investor could get twice his initial investment, which is equivalent to 7.18% annualized rate of return. The worst case scenario for an investor would correspond to the spot of one of the underlying stocks finishing with no value. Then the investor receives a final payment equal to $200\% + (0\% - 1) = 100\%$, which shows that 100% of the capital is guaranteed.

As for the risks associated with trading Everest options, the payoff is based on the worst performing stock; lower stock forward prices imply lower potential payoff. Therefore, a trader selling Everest notes is short the forwards, and will need to buy Delta in each of the underlying assets on day 1, and adjust dynamically through the life of the trade to remain Delta neutral. He is short interest rates and long the dividends and borrowing costs. On the other hand, a higher dispersion decreases the level of the worst performing stock. The seller of Everest structures is long dispersion, that is, long volatility and short the correlation, between the stocks composing the underlying basket. More details are discussed below in the section regarding pricing mountain range options.

15.4   KILIMANJARO SELECT

The *Kilimanjaro Select* structure is a type of multi-asset Growth and Income product since it pays the note holder fixed periodic coupons C, most of the time higher than the market rate of interest, as well as a final coupon at maturity depending on the performance of the shares that constitute the *heart* of the underlying basket. Throughout the life of the note, the worst

Table 15.1 Payoff scenarios for a 10-year Everest note based on 11 international Blue Chips. The results in this table are associated with the scenarios drawn in Figure 15.5.

	WO level at maturity	Note payoff	Annualized RoR
Scenario 1	34.26%	134.26%	2.99%
Scenario 2	96.36%	196.36%	6.98%
Scenario 3	123.48%	223.48%	8.37%
Scenario 4	190.47%	290.47%	11.25%

performing shares are removed from the basket at different observation dates. At maturity, the basket is composed of $n - m$ shares where m stands for the number of removed shares. Ultimately, the m best performers composing the basket at expiry date are also removed from the underlying basket. The remaining $(n - 2m)$ shares that constitute the final basket Basket_f are the so-called *heart* of the basket. Note that the performances of the underlyers are computed with respect to the initial date of the structure, and the nature of the asset-removing process again makes this a dispersion trade. The note holder of the Kilimanjaro Select receives the following payoff at maturity:

$$\text{Kilimanjaro}_{\text{payoff}}(T) = \text{Notional} \times \left[\text{Basket}_f(T) - K \right]$$

where K is the strike price and

$$\text{Basket}_f(T) = \frac{1}{n - 2m} \sum_{j=1}^{n-2m} \frac{S_{f,j}(T)}{S_{f,j}(0)}$$

Here $S_{f,j}(T)$ is the spot price at maturity of the jth share composing the heart of the basket.

It is also interesting to understand that this structure is not capital protected. Indeed, the final basket can have a negative performance, which can imply a negative rate of return.

Take an investor who wants to put £10 million in a 6-year Kilimanjaro Select note. An investment bank is willing to sell him this structure with the following features:

- At the end of each year and until maturity, the holder receives a fixed coupon equal to £600,000, which corresponds to 6% of the note notional.
- The underlying basket is composed of 10 stocks. At the end of each year, the worst performing stock is removed from the basket. This process is continued until the end of the fourth year. Four years after the initial date, the underlying portfolio is composed of six remaining stocks. At maturity, after observing the returns of the remaining underlying shares, the four best performing stocks are removed from the basket. Let $\text{Share}_{f,1}$ and $\text{Share}_{f,2}$ denote the two remaining stocks that constitute the heart of the underlying portfolio.
- At maturity date, the note holder receives a final coupon depending on the performance of the final basket:

$$\text{Notional} \times \frac{1}{2} \left[\frac{S_{f,1}(T)}{S_{f,1}(0)} + \frac{S_{f,2}(T)}{S_{f,2}(0)} \right]$$

where $S_{f,i}(t)$ is the spot price of share f,i at time t.

In Figures 15.6 and 15.7, we can see two separate scenarios showing the returns of the underlying stocks throughout the life of the note described above. These graphs emphasize the stock selection mechanism of the Kilimanjaro Select. Indeed, the solid lines represent the returns of the shares that constitute the final basket. Table 15.2 clarifies the payoff of the Kilimanjaro structure according to the cases drawn in Figures 15.6 and 15.7. In the first scenario, the final level of the two shares that compose the final baskets are equal to 111.11% and 115.93%, which makes the payoff at maturity equal to 113.52% of the notional. And since the note holder receives six annual fixed coupons of 6%, this makes the annual rate of return equal to $6\% + (113.52\%^{1/6} - 1) = 8.14\%$. In the second scenario, the stocks that constitute the heart of the basket underperformed and their final levels are equal to 58.98% and

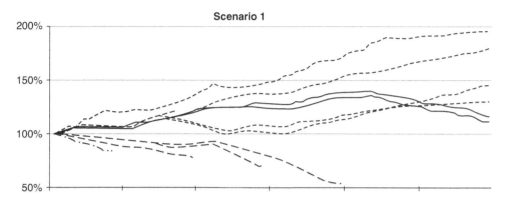

Figure 15.6 Scenario 1 showing the returns of the underlying stocks as well as the stock selection process of the Kilimanjaro Select structure.

72.62% of their initial spot. Therefore, the Kilimanjaro Select pays the buyer a final amount of £6,580,000, which is 65.80% on the notional. In this case, the annual rate of return is negative; the Kilimanjaro Select is not capital guaranteed. The percentage of protected capital is equal to the sum of the coupons received (here 36%) which constitute a fixed income no matter how the underlying stocks' returns behaved.

15.5   ATLAS

The Atlas note is a capital guaranteed multi-asset product. Indeed, this growth structure makes a unique payment at maturity T where the holder receives 100% of the invested capital plus a variable coupon linked to the basket of n assets $S_1, S_2, \ldots, S_n$, and computed as follows. At maturity, the n_1 worst performing stocks as well as the n_2 best performers are removed from the underlying basket. The payoff at maturity is based on the average performance since

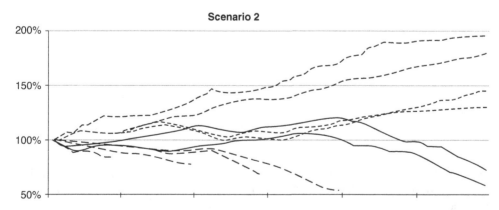

Figure 15.7 Scenario 2 showing the returns of the underlying stocks as well as the stock selection process of the Kilimanjaro Select structure.

Table 15.2   Payoff scenarios for a 6-year Kilimanjaro note based on 10 underlying stocks. The results in this table are associated with the scenarios drawn in Figures 15.6 and 15.7.

	Scenario 1	Scenario 2
Sum of received annual coupons	36.00%	36.00%
Final level of Share$_{f,1}$	111.11%	58.98%
Final level of Share$_{f,2}$	115.93%	72.62%
Kilimanjaro Select redemption at T	**113.52%**	**65.80%**
Annual rate of return	**8.14%**	**−0.74%**

inception of the remaining stocks composing the heart of the basket:

$$\text{Atlas}_{\text{payoff}} = 100\% + \max\left[0, \frac{1}{n - (n_1 + n_2)} \sum_{j=n_1+1}^{j=n-n_2} \frac{S_j(T)}{S_j(0)} - K\right]$$

where K is a predetermined strike price, j represents the jth stock given by the iteration counts, and the terms n_1 and n_2 are constrained by the condition $n_1 + n_2 < n$.

Take the example of a 6-year Atlas note based on 10 underlying stocks. The holder invests a notional amount equal to \$1 million. This structure generates the following payoff:

- At the end of year 6, the three worst performing stocks as well as the four best performing stocks are removed from the underlying basket. Let Share$_{f,1}$, Share$_{f,2}$ and Share$_{f,3}$ denote the three remaining shares composing the final basket.
- At maturity, the note holder receives a unique payment depending on the performance of the final basket

$$\text{Atlas}_{\text{payoff}} = \text{Notional} \times \left(100\% + \max\left[0, \frac{1}{3}\sum_{i=1}^{3} \text{Perf}_{f,i}(T) - 100\%\right]\right)$$

where $\text{Perf}_{f,i}(t) = S_{f,i}(t)/S_{f,i}(0)$, and $S_{f,i}(t)$ is the spot price of Share$_{f,i}$ at time t.

Figure 15.8 shows a scenario drawing the underlying stocks' returns throughout the life of the note described above. This graph emphasizes the stock selection mechanism of the Atlas structure. Indeed, the solid lines represent the returns of the three shares that constitute the final basket. Here, the levels of the remaining stocks at maturity are equal to 93.27%, 111.11% and 115.93%; which makes the final basket performance equal to 106.77%. The strike price being equal to 100%, then the note holder receives a coupon equal to \$1,067,700 which corresponds to 100% + (106.77% − 100%) = 106.77% of the invested notional.

15.6   PRICING MOUNTAIN RANGE PRODUCTS

In this section we look into the pricing intricacies of mountain range options, discussing the risks they entail and the models needed to capture these. Using what we have learned through the earlier discussions, the first risk to think about is the Delta. One must take into account any digital risk involved in these options and base a price on the ability to Delta hedge large digitals. Recalling the discussions of hedging digitals, the liquidity of the underlying assets comes under question, and the option's price must reflect the cost of hedging.

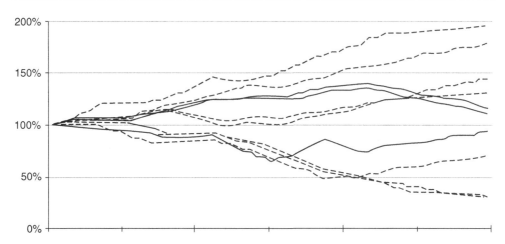

Figure 15.8 Scenarios showing the returns of the underlying stocks as well as the stock selection process of the Atlas structure.

The complicated multi-asset nature of these products means that it is unlikely that one can find closed form solutions. Even if we had closed formulas for the fair values of these options under Black–Scholes assumptions, these formulas would be almost totally useless because mountain range options are notoriously sensitive to skew, and using a flat volatility would lead to serious mispricing. Thus, although we assume that the pricing method will have to involve a Monte Carlo simulation, the question is: Which model do we need to simulate?

Because these payoffs are quite skew dependent, the bare minimum we need is a skew model. Given the multi-asset nature of these products we would need to calibrate to the skews of each of the underlying assets. The dates to which we want to calibrate will be at least those that have a significance to the payoff (for example, the dates where the Himalaya's underlyings are assessed and the best are removed). Ideally, we want to have a smooth calibration through time, with emphasis on the calibration on these dates (so as to not over smoothen the calibration overall at the cost of the fit being of lower quality at these points). Our ability to do so will depend on how good our skew model is. The significant dates will serve as maturity dates for vanilla options that can be used to hedge the Vega and possibly the Gamma (if too large) of these options. The prices of these vanillas must thus be reflected in the calibration of the model, in order for these exotic products to correctly show risk against them, and allow them to serve effectively as hedging instruments. Vega hedges will need to be rebalanced depending on how the markets move and the relative dispersion on the underlying assets' prices – meaning that the seller will have to adjust their Vega dynamically as the market moves, and the price must reflect the cost of hedging.

Assuming that we need skew, the simplest thing would be to look to a local volatility model. In the case of mountain range options however, we find that these models fall short, and we will in fact need to price and compute hedge ratios for these options using a stochastic volatility model. Why is this? In the previous two chapters regarding cliquets, we had explicit forward skew risks that needed to be priced, as well as Vega convexities. In the case of mountain range options, though we do not have explicit forward skew risk as we have with cliquets, these options are extremely sensitive to the implied smile dynamics of the model. A stochastic volatility will also allow us to pick up any Vega convexities that also need pricing, although the main concern is smile dynamics.

So what do we know about smile dynamics? We explicitly saw in Chapter 13 that local volatility models do not generate forward skews, and can thus not be used for products with explicit forward skew dependence. Local volatility models are, in the case of mountain range options, also not useful, particularly because the smile dynamics generated by local volatility models are not realistic, and in fact these dynamics can be the complete opposite of what we observe in the market. By smile dynamics we refer to the phenomena of how the skew moves as the underlying moves: if the underlying moves in one direction, how should the skew move? We already touched upon this in the discussion of lookback options in Chapter 14, and saw the concepts of sticky strike and sticky Delta in regards to movements in the skew. The lookback, and also the range accrual that can be regarded as a set of forward starting digitals, do not carry explicit forward skew, but will be sensitive to how the skew moves as the underlying does. In the case of mountain range options, it is key that we use a model with correct smile dynamics, and to this end we must use a stochastic volatility model.

Discussions about smile dynamics in the literature appear in the context of models such as the SABR model of Hagan *et al.* (2002) in which this particular flaw in local volatility models is pointed out, and the need for a stochastic volatility model emphasized in order to obtain correct smile dynamics. Wrong smile dynamics have a serious impact on the prices and hedge ratios, and because of the complicated nature of the mountain range payouts – particularly the sensitivities to implied volatility skews as we move through time – our price will be off, as will our hedge ratios (drastically!) if we have the wrong dynamics. We see the SABR model in more detail when we discuss interest rates in Chapter 17, and although this model is not the best suited for equities, the concept of smile dynamics it raises is equally serious in the context of these exotic equities.

In these exotic options, it is important to understand how the Vegas change with respect to other parameters. We already know about Vega convexity from Chapter 13, and this is the sensitivity of Vega w.r.t. volatility. Vanna, on the other hand (another higher order Greek), is the sensitivity of Vega to a move in the underlying's price. This is represented by the cross term involving the cross derivative of the option's price w.r.t. the volatility and to the underlying's price. As the spot changes, how does this affect our Vega? This is Vanna. In a mountain range option, and particularly when an underlying's path can result in it being removed from the basket, we expect the Vega to be sensitive to a movement in the underlying. While stochastic volatility models know about Vega convexity, they also allow us to price this Vanna term. Vega hedges for mountain range options can be very unstable, and the cost of dynamically adjusting them must be reflected in the price. In Appendix A, section A.3, we discuss more technical details and see why these terms appear in the pricing equation under stochastic volatility.

Other than these issues, the multi-asset nature of these products introduces correlation risk. All these payoffs are multi-asset and are thus sensitive to the correlations between the various underlyings. More importantly than knowing that this risk exists is the fact that, in mountain range options, it can be particularly pronounced. For example, the Altiplano option has high correlation sensitivity that is much higher than a basket option's sensitivity.

These correlations must be correctly specified and computed by the criteria laid out in Chapter 7. However, in the case of some mountain range options, for example the Himalaya, the option's correlation sensitivity to a correlation pair can change near or at the monitoring date. From a day 1 pricing perspective, one can firstly monitor whether the seller is short or long the various correlation pairs and take a spread over or below the computed correlation levels. Additionally, because this may change, the trader will most likely be unable to hedge away this risk entirely, if at all, and a margin should be taken for any residual risks.

The stochastic volatility process for each underlying will need to be correlated with each other, and we face problems with the calibration of the volatility to volatility processes. Recall that the stochastic volatility model has two sources of randomness, one from the underlying asset's price being modelled as a random variable and the second from the volatility (or variance), which is also random. The question arises: How do we calibrate, or at least meaningfully interpret, the correlations between two volatility processes? This can be done by simply taking a conservative value to use in the pricing, depending on their effect on the price, or avoided all together. The more important correlations to worry about are those between the processes for the underlying assets' prices. A realistic modelling approach would be to use copulas to connect the independently calibrated processes of each underlying asset. Copulas, which are discussed in detail in Chapter 20, offer a way of having a joint distribution, consistent with each underlying's distribution, and offer a range of rich correlation structures.

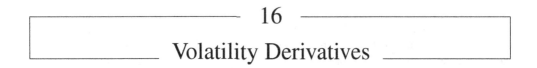

16
Volatility Derivatives

Never swap horses crossing a stream.

As the name implies, volatility derivatives have payoffs that depend explicitly on the volatility of the underlying assets on which they are written. These payoffs are designed to provide the investor with a way to take a direct and clean view on volatility, whether for speculation or hedging purposes, without being exposed to movements in the underlying. There is now a liquid OTC market for products such as the variance swap, and we have also seen the rise of volatility indices, such as the CBOE's VIX, which is used as a measure of the implied volatility of the S&P 500 index options. There is a lot of literature on the subject of volatility derivatives and we refer to these contributions as we develop the various aspects of the chapter.

16.1 THE NEED FOR VOLATILITY DERIVATIVES

One aspect of the demand for such products comes from the generally negative correlation that is often seen between an index (or stock) and its volatility, as discussed in Chapter 4 on volatility and skew. This negative correlation makes a volatility product an excellent choice for diversification, especially in the light of the recent increase in the correlations among assets on a global level. As we saw, volatility generally increases as the market declines, and being able to directly buy volatility as a downside hedge definitely has appeal. This demand has been met with supply from the sell side in certain contracts, particularly the variance swap. This is attributed to the existence of robust hedges for such contracts, and today there exists a liquid OTC market for variance swaps on major indices.

Following the variance swap, investors' appetites have increased for more tailored views and we saw the emergence of a new generation of volatility derivatives such as corridor and conditional variance swaps, Gamma swaps and options on realized variance. One can also now trade futures and some options on the volatility indices. In addition to these, one can build structures using what we know about volatility derivatives combined with some of the previous payoffs we have seen. Volatility derivatives can be tailored to hedge specific volatility risks and can also be customized investments in volatility. With the increase in the liquidity and range of products, it is fair to consider volatility derivatives as an asset class of their own.

16.2 TRADITIONAL METHODS FOR TRADING VOLATILITY

Here we review some of the strategies seen before and study their potential (or lack thereof) as a means to trade volatility. Essentially we streamline the analysis to show that the traditional methods do not provide a pure exposure to volatility, justifying the necessity for the variance swap and subsequent volatility derivatives. Traditional methods revolve around Delta-hedged options in the sense that by hedging the exposure to movements in the underlying one can isolate volatility exposure. One buys (sells) options whose implied volatility is less (greater) than the anticipated realized volatility.

First let's consider the case of a straddle. As we saw in Chapter 6, the (ATM) straddle is a combination of an ATM call and an ATM put, and since the buyer (seller) of both the call and the put is long (short) volatility, the buyer (seller) of a straddle is long (short) volatility. Thus the straddle provides a method for the investor to take a view on the future realized volatility of the underlying, and also on changes in implied volatility.

The initial Delta of a straddle is close to zero, but as the underlying moves, the trade will begin to pick up Delta, and can incur high transaction costs and liquidity issues while keeping the straddle position Delta neutral. In order to see only the volatility risk, we would have to consistently Delta hedge the position to approximately remove the risk to movements in the underlying's spot price. In addition, given that both the call and the put are at-the-money, the initial cost in going long a straddle can be quite high. This method can be made cheaper by buying strangles, but with strangles one would need the underlying to move by a larger amount in order to make money. Recall that the strangle is the combination of an OTM call and an OTM put. Sadly, neither of these provide a pure exposure to volatility.

In the case of a regular call option, if the investor is able to Delta hedge away the underlying price risk, then a large proportion of the P&L from this strategy comes from the difference between the volatility the underlying realizes throughout its life and the volatility used to price and hedge the option.

$$P\&L = [V(S(0), \sigma_i) - V(S(0), \sigma_h)] e^{rT} + \int_0^T e^{r(T-t)} \left(\sigma_h^2 - \sigma_t^2\right) \frac{S(t)^2}{2} \Gamma(t, \sigma_h) \mathrm{d}t$$

where σ_i is the implied volatility that was used to price the option; σ_h is the volatility that the trader uses when computing her Delta; and $\Gamma(t, \sigma_h)$ is the Gamma of the option at time t computed using the volatility σ_h, as discussed by Carr and Madan (1998). As we saw in the discussion of Gamma in section 5.2 (in particular the discussion of Figure 5.7 on page 73), the Gamma of a vanilla at a time t prior to maturity is a function of the level of the underlying. Thus, the above integral implies that this P&L is still a function of the path of the underlying and the transition of time. An additional drawback is that a call option's Vega decreases when the underlying moves away from the strike in either direction. This lowers the method's potential as a way to gain exposure to volatility, without taking a view on the path of the underlying. The upshot of this is that we need a vehicle that will provide pure exposure to the volatility of the underlying irrespective of its path, and one that does not require Delta hedging.

16.3 VARIANCE SWAPS

The variance swap allows the investor to obtain a pure exposure to the volatility of the underlying, unlike Delta-hedged options which still have path dependency. Variance swaps pay the difference between the future realized variance of the price changes of the underlying, and some prespecified strike price that we label as K_{var}. Its fair strike at inception is determined by the implied volatility skew, but its final payout is a function of the realized variance. It thus allows one to take a clean view on the levels of implied volatility being high or low relative to the expected realized volatility. Also, because of its nature as a pure volatility product, it serves as an excellent vehicle for speculation on volatility and also as a hedging instrument.

16.3.1   Payoff Description

The variance is defined as the annualized variance of log stock returns, and the strike price K_{var} of the variance swap is referred to as the variance swap rate. At inception, this strike is chosen to be the *fair variance* strike so that the present value of the swap is zero, that is, one enters into a variance swap with no initial cashflow.

Different types of variance swap contracts can be specified, but daily log-returns are typically used, based on the closing price of the underlying. The realized variance $\text{RV}_0(T)$ or simply $\text{RV}(T)$ between time $t = 0$ and time T is given by

$$\text{RV}(T) = \frac{A}{N_{\text{E}}} \sum_{i=1}^{N_{\text{A}}} \ln^2\left(\frac{S(t_i)}{S(t_{i-1})}\right) \tag{16.1}$$

where A is the annualization factor, typically set to 252 in contracts, representing the number of trading days per year (generally the number of sampling points per year); N_{E} is the expected number of sampling points given by the number of trading days; and N_{A} is the actual number of trading days where $0 = t_0, t_1, \ldots, t_{N_{\text{A}}} = T$ between time $t = 0$ and T. The numbers N_{A} and N_{E} will coincide as long as there are no market disruptions, but although N_{E} is known and specified at the outset, the payoff at expiry will have to be a function of the actual number of days N_{A}. As such, we have quoted realized variance in annual terms over the life of the contract $[0, T]$. It is imperative that these specifications are clear in the term sheet of the contract and that scenarios such as trading being halted mid-session are covered. The payoff of the variance swap at expiry is given by

$$\text{Variance Swap}_{\text{payoff}} = \left(\text{RV}(T) - K_{\text{var}}^2\right) \cdot \mathcal{N}$$

where K is quoted as the square root of variance. For example, a 320 variance strike K_{var}^2 would be denoted by $K_{\text{var}} = 17.89$ so that this can be interpreted in volatility terms. $\mathcal{N}$ is the notional of the variance swap and, like other swaps, this is the amount on which the payoff is computed without this amount ever changing hands. That is, the payoff at expiry is the above difference which is settled in cash, however, some intermediate payments may be specified, depending on counterparty risks.

For a variance swap this notional is known as the *variance notional*, and is specified in terms of a volatility notional (Vega); for example, $100,000 per Vega or volatility point. The standard practice for determining the variance notional, $\mathcal{N}$, appearing in the above payoff, is calculated as

$$\mathcal{N} = \frac{\text{Volatility Notional}}{2 \times K_{\text{var}}} \tag{16.2}$$

The reason for doing this is so that a one-point move in realized volatility is approximately equivalent to the variance swap payoff moving by the specified volatility notional. Using the example so far, the variance notional in this case is $100,000/(2 \times 17.89) = \$2,795$, and the holder of this variance swap receives \$2,795 for every point by which the realized variance $\text{RV}(T)$ exceeds the strike price K_{var}^2.

One thing to note is that the definition of realized variance here differs from the usual statistical definition seen in Chapter 4 on volatility, as in this case we have not subtracted the mean when computing the variance that we assume here to be zero. This makes the payoff of the variance swap additive in the sense that a 6-month variance swap can be split into two 3-month variance swaps.

16.3.2   Variance vs Volatility Swaps

At first it may seem strange to see a discussion of volatility swaps within that of variance swaps, since a volatility swap should allow the investor to directly trade the volatility (and not the variance) of the underlying asset. However, the variance swap is the more popular product owing to several advantages over the volatility swap. A volatility swap is defined much the same way as the variance swap, only the floating part of the volatility swap is the square root of realized variance.

$$\text{Volatility Swap}_{\text{payoff}}(T) = \left(\sqrt{\text{RV}(T)} - K_{\text{vol}} \right) \cdot \mathcal{N}$$

So, in fact, it is a forward contract on the future realized volatility of the underlying. Again one can define the fair strike for a volatility swap, the *fair volatility*, so that the swap's present value is zero at the start. At expiry, the holder of a volatility swap receives (or pays) the difference between the realized volatility and the prespecified volatility swap strike, times the notional amount.

So why is the demand for variance swaps greater? Simply put, variance swaps are a much more natural hedging instrument. Taking the example of the Delta-hedged call, it is the *variance* that appears in the P&L formula, not the *volatility*. Keep in mind that variance is scaled by time, giving it an additive property (Carr and Madan, 1998), whereas volatility, which is the square root of variance, loses this property of linearity. Consider the following trade: we buy a variance swap with a 2-year maturity, and sell a variance swap with a 1-year maturity. This allows us to take a view on the expected 1-year variance in 1 year's time. This is in fact one way of trading forward variance using variance swaps. Or, assume that we enter into a 2-year variance swap and in 1 year's time decide to unwind the position, we can simply at that point in time take the opposite side in a 1-year swap thus completely offsetting the original position. These are possible due to the additive property of variance swaps, which a volatility swap lacks.

Another reason, now for the seller of a variance or volatility swap, is that there exist robust replication strategies for variance swaps. As we will see in the next section dealing with pricing, there are model-independent results that allow for the replication (and thus pricing) of a variance swap but only approximate formulas exist for volatility swaps. Again it is the linear property of the variance swap that allows for the development of such formulas and the non-linearity of the volatility swap that causes problems.

One can apply a model, for example Heston's stochastic volatility but this requires specifying the dynamics of the volatility. The advantage of this is that one can value both of these in closed form (see section A.3.1 in Appendix A), however, such pricing does not necessarily enlighten us on how to hedge these contracts. All in all, volatility swaps are less useful as hedging instruments, and are also more difficult to price making the variance swap the more popular product in equity markets.

16.3.3   Replication and Pricing of Variance Swaps

To value a variance swap one must evaluate the portfolio that replicates it, and the value of fair variance is the initial cost of such a portfolio. In the literature, related work on this dates back as far as Neuberger's paper (1990). The rise of the variance swap can be largely attributed to the fact that it can be robustly replicated, thus both priced and hedged, using a linear combination of European options and a dynamic position in futures. Since the replicating portfolio consists of vanilla options, one does not need specific modelling assumptions to find the fair value. As long as we can trade European options on an underlying along enough strikes, and with the same maturity as the variance swap, and can also trade futures, then we can replicate the variance swap on this underlying.

The variance swap can be replicated by a portfolio of long positions in OTM options for all strikes (zero to infinity) weighted by the inverse of the square of the individual strikes plus a dynamically adjusted forward position in the underlying. Since the replication portfolio contains European options, the valuation at inception is sensitive to changes in the implied volatilities of these options. Thus we must make sure that whatever model we do use ultimately knows about the implied volatility skew and prices these Europeans correctly. Given we require a full range of strikes, one must be cautious when calibrating the skew in the wings as these have an impact on the pricing of the variance swap, particularly so on the downside.

Written explicitly, the price of the variance swap is the sum of the components of the replicating portfolio given by

$$\text{Variance Swap}(T) = \frac{2}{T}\left[rT - \ln\left(\frac{F_T}{S(0)}\right) - \left(\frac{S(0)}{F_T}e^{rT} - 1\right)\right.$$
$$\left. + e^{rT}\left(\int_0^{F_T}\frac{dK}{K^2}\text{Put}(K,T) + \int_{F_T}^{\infty}\frac{dK}{K^2}\text{Call}(K,T)\right)\right]$$

where F_T is the ATM forward (Demeterfi et al., 1999) The first term is the cost of rebalancing the position in the underlying, the second is a short position in a log contract paying $\ln(F_T/S(0))$ at expiry. The third is a short position in $1/F_T$ forward contracts struck at F_T, and the two integrals are the long position in strips of OTM puts and calls respectively with a weighting of $1/K^2$. This replication is made possible by applying the result of Breeden and Litzenberger (1978), that, with some assumptions, any twice differentiable payoff can be replicated using a strip of European options.

In practice, the sum of the two integrals is approximated discretely as

$$\sum_{i=1}^n \frac{\text{Put}(K_i,T)}{K_i^2}(K_i - K_{i-1}) + \sum_{i=n}^N \frac{\text{Call}(K_i,T)}{K_i^2}(K_i - K_{i-1}) \quad (16.3)$$

where we have discretized the set of strikes over which we take the strip of options. In the above price of the variance swap, the term F_T could have actually been specified to be another value, but the forward is a good place to switch from calls to puts (indeed OTM options are more liquid). As for volatility swaps, although approximations do exist, there is not a similar model-independent result. See Appendix A, section A.3.1, about Heston's model as an example where one can price both volatility and variance swaps when one has made a modelling assumption.

From a theoretical point of view, these formulas allow for the replication of variance swaps, but from a practical point of view, some problems can arise. We require a whole strip of European options, and although we may be able to get these for indices, they are not generally available for single stocks. One could use American options on stocks to get the values of European options to resolve this problem, but we will still have the problem of not being able to find quotes for listed options for all the required strikes. If we apply the approximation involving the sums and lack a specific strike, it is possible to use a form of arbitrage-free interpolation between two strikes to obtain the required value, and possibly also the extrapolation of deep OTM implied volatilities. Recall section 6.5 regarding the requirements for arbitrage freedom of an implied volatility skew. Since the replication requires an entire strip of options, executing the hedge can be quite expensive in terms of transaction costs, and in fact accounting for the aforementioned problems can at least partly explain the difference between the theoretical value of a variance swap and the OTC market quotes.

Note that the above formulas do not contain a correction for dividends. One can modify the way the variance is computed to adjust for dividends to come and account for the jump in the stock price due to the dividend payments. Owing to the uncertainty of future dividends, one should take precautions.

We can get a quick price for the fair strike of a variance swap, and if we assume that the skew is linear in strike, an approximation is given by

$$K_{\mathrm{var}} \approx \sigma_{\mathrm{ATMF}}\sqrt{1 + 3T \times (\mathrm{Skew})^2} \qquad (16.4)$$

where σ_{ATMF} is the ATM forward volatility, T is the maturity, and Skew is the slope of the implied volatility skew, as appearing in Demeterfi et al. (1999), and more recent market research articles such as Bossu et al. (2005). If we assume that the skew is log-linear of the form $\sigma(K) = \sigma_{\mathrm{ATMF}} - \beta \ln(K/F)$ where F is the forward price, which is a much more realistic parameterization, we can use the following approximation

$$K_{\mathrm{var}} \approx \sqrt{\sigma_{\mathrm{ATMF}}^2 + \beta\sigma_{\mathrm{ATMF}}^3 T + \frac{\beta^2}{4}\left(12\sigma_{\mathrm{ATMF}}^2 T + 5\sigma_{\mathrm{ATMF}}^4 T^2\right)}$$

where σ_{ATMF} is the at-the-money forward volatility, T is the maturity, and β is the slope of the log skew curve. This takes account of the convexity in the implied volatility skew, as opposed to the assumption that it is just linear. However, both these approximations lose accuracy when the skew is steeper.

16.3.4   Capped Variance Swaps

Consider the variance swap in the event of the underlying defaulting. The variance as defined above will shoot to drastic levels in such an event, and so being short a variance swap could result in an unlimited loss. For this reason variance swaps, on single stocks in particular, are often capped. Not only does this take care of the potentially huge downside, but it also reduces the contribution of the deep OTM puts for which there is limited liquidity. Recall that this is one reason for a discrepancy in the market quotes vs the theoretical value. A typical cap would be at 250% of K_{var}^2, and the payoff of the capped variance swap is given by

$$\text{Capped Var Swap}_{\mathrm{payoff}} = \min\left[\mathrm{RV}(T), 2.5K_{\mathrm{var}}^2\right] - K_{\mathrm{var}}^2$$

Moving around some terms, this is equivalent to

$$\left[\left(\mathrm{RV}(T) - K_{\mathrm{var}}^2\right) - \left(\mathrm{RV}(T) - 2.5K_{\mathrm{var}}^2\right)^+\right]\mathbf{1}_{\{\text{No Default}\}} + 2.5K_{\mathrm{var}}^2\mathbf{1}_{\{\text{Default}\}}$$

Notice that the term $\left(\mathrm{RV}(T) - 2.5K_{\mathrm{var}}^2\right)^+$ is the payoff of an OTM call option on realized variance. By imposing caps on variance swaps, the sellers of such contracts have essentially bought OTM calls on realized variance, as discussed in Overhaus et al. (2007). This has spurred the development of a new set of volatility derivatives: options on realized variance, discussed below in section 16.5.

16.3.5 Forward Starting Variance Swaps

In a forward starting variance swap the variance is calculated between two future dates T and T' (T is the start date and T' the maturity). Here the forward starting realized variance is given by

$$\text{Forward Starting RV}(T) = \frac{252}{N} \sum_{i=n}^{N} \ln^2 \left(\frac{S(t_i)}{S(t_{i-1})} \right)$$

where $T = t_n, t_{n+1}, \ldots, t_N = T'$ are the trading days between T and T'.

From a pricing perspective, the forward starting variance swap is the calendar spread of two variance swaps with the correct notionals, starting at time $t = 0$ and with respective maturities T and T'. This is possible thanks to the additive property of the variance swap, as pointed out by Carr and Madan (1998), and thus the forward starting variance swap is not more difficult to price and hedge than the regular variance swap (albeit there are two swaps now) and the contract itself provides the investor with an instrument to trade future volatility.

16.3.6 Variance Swap Greeks

The variance swap is the answer to obtaining volatility exposure without being exposed to the path of the underlying. The Gamma of the variance swap at time t is

$$\Gamma_{\text{var swap}}(t) = \frac{2}{T} \cdot \frac{1}{S(t)^2}$$

which means that the cash Gamma $\Gamma_{\text{cash}} = \Gamma \times S(t)^2/100$ is actually constant. That is, the cash Gamma of a variance swap is not a function of the price of the underlying or time, meaning that it has a constant cash Gamma that depends only on the replicating portfolio's initial value. This is in line with the idea behind the variance swap that the level of the underlying does not impact the P&L from a position in a variance swap. Essentially, once one sets up the replicating portfolio, the derivation of Greeks will follow. For more on their derivation see Demeterfi *et al.* (1999).

The Vega of a variance swap is given by

$$\mathcal{V}_{\text{var swap}}(t) = \frac{2}{T}\sigma(T - t)$$

which is linear in volatility σ. The second derivative with respect to volatility shows the positive Vega convexity seen in variance swaps. The variance Vega (sensitivity to the variance σ^2) is given by

$$\mathcal{W}_{\text{var swap}}(t) = \frac{T - t}{T}$$

This is saying that the sensitivity of the variance swap to variance itself is equal to 1 at time $t = 0$ and is equal to zero at maturity T. This makes perfect sense as at time $t = 0$ the variance swap, by construction of the payoff, should have a one to one sensitivity to variance.

The Theta of the variance swap is

$$\theta_{\text{var swap}}(t) = -\frac{1}{T}\sigma^2$$

which also stays constant over time (it is not a function of t). Therefore the variance swap bleeds time value at a rate proportional to variance, and at maturity, it has bled exactly σ^2: the initial variance.

Combining the Theta and Gamma, as seen in section 5.6 in Chapter 5 on Greeks, we see the same classic result of Black–Scholes theory

$$\theta + \frac{1}{2}\Gamma S^2 \sigma^2 = 0$$

that the decrease in the option's value through time (Theta) is offset by positive Gamma.

From the setup of the replicating portfolio, as skew increases, the value of the variance swap increases (the fair strike increases) meaning that the seller of the variance swap is short skew. One can obtain an approximate skew sensitivity by using the approximation in equation (16.4).

16.4   VARIATIONS ON VARIANCE SWAPS

As we saw, variance swaps are an excellent way to trade volatility and we have understood the demand for this product as well as the reasons for the willingness to supply such product. While investors have grown used to this product, the appetite has grown for similar contracts that offer a more tailored exposure to volatility. The next generation of products discussed here include corridor variance swaps, conditional variance swaps and Gamma swaps. These allow investors to target specific exposures to the implied volatility skew and the term structure of volatility, and can also be used as vehicles for dispersion trading. Additional motivation for such products comes from the need to resolve some of the aforementioned problems involving hedging variance swaps, and to also offer better prices than traditional variance swaps do. We discuss these three products under this section as they all have the distinct advantage of having replication portfolios similar in nature to the variance swap albeit different.

16.4.1   Corridor Variance Swaps

As the name implies, corridor variance swaps pay realized variance when the underlying is within a corridor, let's call this corridor or range $[L, U]$. That is, when computing the realized variance to be used in the final payout of the swap, one only includes returns when the underlying is within the prespecified range, the rest are taken to be zero. In the literature, pioneering work on corridor variance swaps has been done by Carr and Lewis (2004), specifically the work on replication formulas.

The (corridor) realized variance to enter into the final payout of the swap is given by

$$\text{Corridor RV}(T) = \frac{252}{N} \sum_{i=1}^{N} \mathbf{1}_{\{L < S(t_{i-1}) \leq U\}} \ln^2 \left(\frac{S(t_i)}{S(t_{i-1})} \right)$$

Specifying a corridor allows the investor to gain exposure to the volatility of an asset that is contingent on its price. Immediately it is clear that this is a generalization of the variance swap since, taking $L = 0$ and $U = +\infty$, the underlying is always within the range and we get the payoff of the usual variance swap. We can also see that because of the specification of a corridor, the fair strike of the corridor variance swap is always less than (or equal to in the case above) that of the corresponding regular variance swap. Like the variance swap, payment is made at maturity, and the corridor variance swap is struck at its fair strike, which again means that there is zero cost to enter into the swap.

Two popular types of corridor variance swaps are the up-variance and the down-variance swaps. An up-variance swap is a corridor variance swap where the lower bound of the corridor is some fixed number L and the upper bound is $+\infty$. In contrast, the down-variance swap has a corridor from a bound U down to zero, that is, over the range $[0, U]$. Being careful about some details, which we discuss below, it makes sense that a down-variance swap plus an up-variance should equal the regular variance swap. So if we can price an up-variance swap (with range $[L, +\infty)$), we know that the corresponding corridor down-variance swap is given by the difference between a regular variance swap and an up-variance swap. Also, one can define the corridor variance swap with corridor $[L, U]$ as the difference between two corridor up-variance swaps, with lower bounds L and U.

These two corridor variance swaps allow the investor to take views on the implied volatility skew. Consider an investor who believes that the implied volatility skew will steepen; he can take a view on this by buying a down-variance swap and selling an up-variance swap. Also the opposite position would allow a view on the flattening of the skew. Since the implied volatilities of OTM puts are generally greater than the OTM calls, the ATM corridor down-variance will be more expensive than the ATM corridor up-variance. Thus the cost of entering such trades is a function of the bound (where the down-variance ends and the up-variance starts) and the view one takes. A corridor down-variance swap can be used as a hedge for market crashes, but one must note that the contribution of a daily return to the payout is contingent on the previous day's close being in the range. Thus, if a crash occurs in one day (the price going from a level outside the down-variance corridor to a level within it) it will not contribute to the accrued realized variance.

The replication portfolio for a corridor variance swap is similar in weighting to the variance swap, but the strip of European options needed is restricted to the specified corridor of the swap; with some adjustments. This means that the number of options needed for the static position is less and the hedge thus cheaper and easier to execute. For example, an up-variance swap does not have exposure to the strike region of deep OTM put options that cause problems in the case of the usual variance swap and impact the price. One can tailor a corridor variance swap around a specific view on the path of the underlying and gain exposure to volatility where required and for a better price than a simple variance swap. The condition that $L < S(t_{i-1}) \le U$, in particular the "less than or equal" in the computation of corridor realized variance is what allows this additive property. For the replication formulas of corridor variance swaps we refer the reader to Carr and Lewis (2004) where the problem of corridor variance replication is tackled.

16.4.2 Conditional Variance Swaps

Similar to corridor variance swaps, conditional variance swaps have a payoff contingent on the underlying being within a specified corridor. However, when computing the variance in the case of the conditional variance swap, any variance accrued outside the corridor is not counted; that is, the variance accrued is divided by the total number of days the underlying spends in the corridor, in contrast to the corridor variance swap in which such returns are counted as zero and the returns are summed up and divided by the total number of trading days. The conditional realized variance is given by

$$
\text{Conditional RV}(T) = \frac{252}{\sum_{i=1}^{N} \mathbf{1}_{\{L < S(t_{i-1}) \leq U\}}} \sum_{i=1}^{N} \mathbf{1}_{\{L < S(t_{i-1}) \leq U\}} \ln^2 \left(\frac{S(t_i)}{S(t_{i-1})} \right)
$$

where $[L, U]$ is the specified corridor. The sum appearing in the denominator, $\sum_{i=1}^{N} \mathbf{1}_{\{L < S(t_{i-1}) \leq U\}}$, is always less than N. It is equal to N when the underlying never leaves the range, and in this case the payoff is exactly that of the regular variance swap.

This specification is what separates the conditional variance swap from the corridor variance swap and can be interpreted financially as follows: If an investor is long a corridor variance swap, then he is at risk that the underlying trades outside the corridor. He thus accrues less realized volatility since the amount accrued is divided by the total number of trading days. With a conditional variance swap, however, these returns are not considered at all and if the underlying trades outside the corridor this is reflected in the denominator, which only counts the days spent inside the range. This means that the investor is purely exposed to the volatility accrued in this range. So the risk lies in the underlying trading within the corridor, at a low volatility. The investor is essentially taking a view on the path of the underlying's price falling within a range, as well as what the volatility of the underlying will do in such a range. In the conditional variance swap, the amount of time spent in the range is not as important as the same consideration for a corridor variance swap, as here a key consideration is knowing what the underlying will do once in such a range.

To illustrate this point, consider the example of a holder of a corridor variance swap and a conditional variance swap, both with range $[L, U]$ and maturity 6 months. Assume, though an extreme example, that the underlying only spends 2 days in the range. The corridor variance swap has a very low variance since whatever the underlying did in these 2 days, the total variance will be divided by 126 (number of trading days in 6 months). In contrast, the floating part of the conditional variance swap is the sum of the variance accrued on these 2 days divided by 2 (number of days in the range), a big difference. So the conditional variance swap is more about what the underlying does once in this range, and in the example here the payoff can be large or small depending on what it does during these 2 days inside the range.

As with corridor variance swaps, there exist conditional down-variance swaps and conditional up-variance swaps. The conditional down-variance swap can be used as a hedge against a market crash, but as with the corridor variance swap, the underlying has to be in the corridor at the previous day's close for a return to contribute – meaning that it does not accrue if the crash occurs in one day. A conditional down-variance allows the investor to take a view on the levels of volatility in the event of the market declining. For example, if we consider an investor who believes that if the market does decline it will do so with a lot of volatility, then going long a conditional down-variance swap is a good way to express this. As before, one can bet on the steepness of the skew by taking opposite positions in conditional up-variance and conditional down-variance swaps. The conditional variance swap can again be replicated and involves only Delta hedging after the initial static hedge. For a discussion of replication formulas for conditional variance swaps, we refer the reader to the product note (Allen *et al.*, 2006).

16.4.3   Gamma Swaps

As we saw, the variance swap has a constant cash Gamma, that is, the Gamma exposure is not a function of the underlying's price. The Gamma swap is a variance swap whose notional is proportional to the level of the underlying, and is designed to have a constant Gamma. In contrast to the variance swap that has a constant cash Gamma, this is thus useful for the investor who thinks in terms of units of the underlying and not the cash value of such units in the portfolio. The payout has the same features as the variance swap, but the realized *Gamma* variance used to compute the payoff is given by

$$\text{Gamma RV}(T) = \frac{252}{N_F} \sum_{i=1}^{N_A} \frac{S(t_i)}{S(t_0)} \ln^2 \left(\frac{S(t_i)}{S(t_{i-1})} \right)$$

which makes it immediately clear that the Gamma swap introduces an exposure to the underlying's level not seen in the variance swap. That is, the exposure of the Gamma swap to the underlying's price means that it is exposed to the correlation between the underlying's price and its volatility.

The first advantage over a variance swap is seen in the case of a default: as the stock price drops to zero, the realized Gamma variance does not shoot to infinity. As the stock price $S(t_i)$ appearing in the term $S(t_i) \backslash S(t_0)$ in the above sum goes to zero, it takes the entire term appearing in the sum to zero. This characteristic of Gamma swaps means that there is no need to impose caps in order to handle this eventuality. At the expense of introducing exposure to the underlying's level, the Gamma swap dampens the weight on large downward moves (which have large positive square returns). Therefore the Gamma swap should have a lower fair strike than the corresponding variance swap, reflecting the fact that it generally has lower payoffs.

Much like the variance swap, one can replicate, and thus price and hedge, the Gamma swap using a strip of European options. The fair strike of a Gamma swap, $K_{\text{Gamma swap}}$, at time $t = 0$, is given by

$$K_{\text{Gamma swap}} = \frac{2 \, e^{2rT}}{T \, S(0)} \left[\int_0^{F_T} \frac{dK}{K} \text{Put}(K, T) + \int_{F_T}^{\infty} \frac{dK}{K} \text{Call}(K, T) \right]$$

That is to say, the Gamma swap can be replicated by a continuous strip of puts and calls, each weighted by the inverse of the relevant strike.[1] As before, F_T is the ATM forward, and these integrals will have to be approximated by a sum resembling that of equation (16.3). This is different to the weights of the variance swap, which are the square of the inverse of the strikes. Thus the weighting on the deep OTM puts is reduced, making the Gamma swap easier to hedge with respect to the corresponding variance swap.

One can trade the implied volatility skew by taking positions in Gamma and variance swaps. For example, consider the investor who believes the skew will decrease (flatten), this view can be played by going long a Gamma swap and short a variance swap. When hedged, a combination as such sets the investor short downside variance and long upside variance, and this can be reasoned as follows: if the market drops, we pick up negative Vega (the variance swap generally pays more than the Gamma swap), but if the market goes up, we pick up

---

[1] Proven by applying the result of Carr and Madan (1998). More discussions on Gamma swaps can be seen in Lee (2008) and Overhaus *et al.* (2007).

positive Vega (the Gamma swap here pays more than the variance swap). Gamma swaps can also be used as a tool for dispersion trading, discussed below in section 16.7.

16.5   OPTIONS ON REALIZED VARIANCE

As investors have adapted to using variance swaps, options with realized variance as the underlying have emerged. A call option on the realized variance has payoff

$$\text{Call on RV}_{\text{payoff}}(T) = \mathcal{N} \times \max\left[0, \text{RV}(T) - K^2\right]$$

and likewise the put option on realized variance

$$\text{Put on RV}_{\text{payoff}}(T) = \mathcal{N} \times \max\left[0, K^2 - \text{RV}(T)\right]$$

where $\text{RV}(T)$ is the realized variance of an asset between time $t = 0$ and time T, given by equation (16.1), and K^2 is the strike price. $\mathcal{N}$ is the notional amount, specified in currency units per variance point.

Since realized variance can potentially reach quite high levels, the seller may want to impose a cap on realized variance before its inclusion in such a payoff. Specifying the cap in terms of volatility points, the payoff is

$$\text{Call on Capped RV}_{\text{payoff}}(T) = \max\left[0, \min\left[\text{Cap}^2, \text{RV}(T)\right] - K^2\right]$$

Although the variance swap and some of its variations have the distinct advantage that they are replicable in a model-independent manner, the option on realized variance, along with the volatility swap, does not have such formulas. This means that to price these options one has to specify a model, although under some assumptions one can find useable formulas: Carr and Lee (2007), under the assumption of a symmetric skew,[2] show that one can find replication formulas for options on realized variance. We also refer the reader to the paper by Sepp (2008), in which the analytical pricing and hedging of options on realized variance are discussed assuming Heston's stochastic volatility model with jumps.

Option payoffs involving realized variance are convex in volatility, and when a model must be used to value them in the absence of a replication strategy, then stochastic volatility models are a natural choice. The Vega convexity coefficient, i.e. the vol-of-vol parameter, plays an important role in such payoffs, because depending on the type of option and the trader's position, they can be long or short vol-of-vol to a large extent.

The variance swap itself can serve as a part of the set of hedging instruments for such options, since its payoff is linear in realized variance. If variance swaps are to serve as hedging instruments, then variance swap curve calibration is also a requirement so that the model shows risk against these instruments. Transaction costs of any possible dynamic hedge must be factored into the price.

16.6   THE VIX: VOLATILITY INDICES

The VIX is the Chicago Board Options Exchange (CBOE) Volatility Index which measures the implied volatility of the S&P 500 index. It is commonly used as a measurement of the market's expectation of short-term volatility and, specifically, it estimates the implied volatility

---

[2] A smile, meaning zero correlation between the underlying and the volatility.

of the S&P 500 over the coming 30 days. For this reason it is sometimes referred to as the fear index: a high VIX level implies low confidence in the market, and vice versa. It is computed in real time using a weighted average of options on the S&P 500 across strikes, and thus it incorporates information about the skew. This is known as the new VIX as there was a previous VIX that used only ATM options and was thus not as informative (see Carr and Wu, 2006). A formal reference for the VIX is the CBOE's official documentation (CBOE, 2006).

The idea behind such an index is that it can be replicated by a portfolio of options that will not be affected by movements in the underlying, but only by movements in volatility. In fact, the VIX is an approximate quote for the fair strike of a variance swap on the S&P 500 index with maturity T

$$K_{\text{VIX}}^2 = \frac{2e^{rT}}{T} \left[\sum_{K_i \leq F_T} \frac{\Delta K_i}{K_i^2} \text{Put}(K_i) + \sum_{K_i > F_T} \frac{\Delta K_i}{K_i^2} \text{Call}(K_i) \right] - \frac{1}{T} \left(\frac{F_T}{K_0} - 1 \right)^2$$

where K_0 is the first strike below the forward index level F_T, and the term

$$-\frac{1}{T} \left(\frac{F_T}{K_0} - 1 \right)^2$$

helps to improve the accuracy of this approximation. The choice of the variance swap, but not the volatility swap, is for the same reasons discussed earlier in the chapter – in particular, the existence of a model-independent replication strategy.

The VIX is quoted in terms of percentage points as $\text{VIX} = 100 \times K_{\text{VIX}}$. Since it is not quoted in a dollar amount there are not ETFs or other liquid instruments that track the VIX like traditional equity indices. However, there are futures and traded derivatives on the VIX; as of 2004, it has been possible to trade CBOE Volatility Index (VIX) futures. The typical contract size is $1,000 times the VIX, and is cash settled on the final settlement date. These provide an excellent tool to trade implied volatility independently of the level of the underlying, whether for hedging purposes, diversification or speculation.

Similar volatility exists on other indices, for example the VSTOXX which is the Dow Jones EuroStoxx 50 volatility index, on which futures are also traded. The same applies to the new VDAX, and the VSMI volatility index of the SMI.

16.6.1 Options on the VIX

In 2006 the CBOE introduced options on the VIX, and so far there are call options, put options and even digital options. These provide tools for the investor to take views on the level of the VIX, much the same as a traditional call option allows on an index or stock. For example, assume that the VIX has been at relatively low levels as the market has been climbing, and that 6-month VIX futures are also pointing to expected low levels. For an investor who believes that this will change over the next 6 months, and that the VIX will rise, a call option on the VIX is an easy way to express it. If the VIX does rise, this will realize a profit for the investor, but with the traditional payout of a call option this can potentially end OTM and have zero payoff. After the market crash of the 2008/09 crisis, the VIX hit unreached levels, and options on the VIX would allow one to express a view that the VIX would decrease.

In the light of the negative correlation between the S&P 500 and the VIX, using options on the VIX one can form the following views: The investor who is bearish on the S&P and bullish on the VIX can go long VIX futures or long call options or call spreads on the VIX, depending on whether or not she wants the optionality feature. For the investor who is bullish on the S&P 500 and bearish on the VIX, a short position in VIX futures or a long position in VIX put options or put spreads would fit. A call option on the VIX can also be used as a hedge for the investor against a large downward movement in the S&P 500.

16.6.2   Combining Equity and Volatility Indices

Consider an equity portfolio to which we add volatility as a diversifying asset. The negative correlation that exists between equities and their volatilities can be utilized to form payoffs that benefit from both increases in equities but also increases in volatility during market declines. Firstly, consider an equity index, for example the S&P 500 index, and its volatility index, the VIX; and, secondly, decide on the type of payoff in which one is interested. Forming a basket of the S&P 500 and the VIX, one will find a low overall volatility because of the large negative correlation between the two. Some form of rainbow payoff at maturity can be formed, the extreme case being a best-of option.

In order to capture the negative correlation between these two we will need to settle on a reasonable frequency for the observations: for example, quarterly observations. The payoff at maturity can use the average returns of each of these, computed using the frequency dates. The frequency of the observations will have an impact on the price, and is one degree of freedom if structuring such an option with price constraints. The second degree of freedom is the rainbow weights, 80% and 20% for example, corresponding to the best-of the two and the worst-of the two, respectively (these are 100% and 0% in the case of a best-of payoff). This is just one example of how one can benefit from volatility as an additional asset class.

16.7   VARIANCE DISPERSION

Regarding an index as a basket, we can write the variance of the index as the weighted sum of the constituents' volatilities and pairwise correlations:

$$\sigma_I^2 = \sum_{1 \le i \le n} w_i^2 \sigma_i^2 + 2 \sum_{1 \le i < j \le n} w_i w_j \sigma_i \sigma_j \rho_{ij}$$

where n is the number of constituents. Assuming that we knew the values of, and were able to trade, the variances on the left-hand side and the variances (and volatilities) on the right-hand side, then the only remaining factors in this equation are the pairwise correlations. To this end, trading options to implement a strategy of gaining exposure to these correlations, by trading all other components of the equation, will incur the same issues we saw in section 16.2 on traditional methods for trading volatility. However, if one makes use of the advances in volatility trading vehicles, this simplifies things by removing the need for Delta hedging and allowing one to gain direct exposure to the volatilities.

When variance swaps are used in this fashion this is known as a variance dispersion trade. By going short variance swaps on each of the individual components of an index and long a variance swap on the index itself, one obtains a long position in correlation. The notionals of each of the variance swaps must be chosen so that the trade is Vega neutral, and we know the Vegas of each of these. It does not necessarily have to be an index, it can be a basket, and all one needs is the ability to trade a variance swap on the basket and on its individual components. One can almost replicate the payoff of the correlation swap of section 7.5.2 by trading Vega neutral variance dispersion, (see Bossu, 2005), though not perfectly.

Variance dispersion can be used by a sell-side derivatives desk that is structurally short correlation – as the result of the sale of many multi-asset structures – in order to buy back some of this correlation. Although it will not replicate the correlation swap exactly, it is the case that correlation swaps between single stocks are very liquid, whereas there is a market for variance swaps on the components of major equity indices.

The Gamma swap is actually the best vehicle to use in the case of variance dispersion, because the proportion of an individual asset in the basket increases when its value increases, as discussed by Roger Lee (2008). If we recall, the variance weighting in the Gamma swaps increases linearly in the underlying's price, making it ideal for the variance dispersion trade.

The reason for the use of spreads of index vs components variance or Gamma swaps as such to gain correlation exposure is because of the transparency they give. The fact that they provide a purer exposure to volatility than traditional methods (such as straddle trading, discussed above) means that when such a trade is in place one can see their P&L from the trade clearly, for example, if the trade has made five correlation Delta points. In addition, trades involving variance swaps can be easily unwound as we saw, and this can add to the appeal of such a strategy.

Part IV
Hybrid Derivatives and
Dynamic Strategies

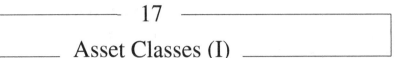

17

Asset Classes (I)

Everything has its beauty but not everyone sees it.

Confucius

A hybrid derivative is a multi-asset derivative whose underlyings do not belong to the same asset class. The structures introduced in previous chapters are focused around equities, although much of the analysis regarding structuring and risk analysis can be extended to other asset classes. In the case of hybrids we again have to think about the effects of volatility and correlation. On the side of volatility, different asset classes have different volatility structures and can have very different implied volatility skews compared to equities. Also, the different asset classes have different futures and forward curves. The issues of liquidity and transaction costs also arise and must be understood for each asset class.

In this and the next chapter on hybrid derivatives we present these other asset classes and explain the intricacies in each of them. By describing the markets, the forward curves, the vanilla derivatives and then some exotic derivatives that exist in each, we can then translate this understanding to combine these asset classes with each other in a meaningful manner in Chapter 19. Understanding these asset classes will also allow us to extend all the analysis done so far on various structures to all the asset classes, individually, and ultimately combined. The chapters on hybrid derivatives also provide us with tools for tackling dynamic strategies involving multiple asset classes in Chapter 21.

The most obvious motivation for the use of hybrids is that products structured on multiple asset classes can provide a valid source of diversification. While we have already seen volatility as a valid diversifier for an equity portfolio owing to its negative correlation with equity, we can also find low correlations, if not negative correlations, among the other asset classes. Correlation structures are discussed in Chapter 19 where we describe some examples of macro-economic views that can be structured into hybrid derivatives and used for purposes of diversification or yield enhancement.

Other than equities, we discuss the following major asset classes:

1. Interest Rates
2. Commodities
3. Foreign Exchange (FX)
4. Inflation
5. Credit

Hybrid derivatives enable an investor to take a view on combinations of these asset classes whether for speculative purposes or even as a hedging strategy for multi-asset class exposures. This chapter covers interest rates and commodities and Chapter 18 covers FX, inflation and credit.

17.1   INTEREST RATES

We have already touched upon interest rates in Chapter 1 when we discussed basic instruments. In this section we go into more detail, in particular with respect to the aspects of interest rate derivatives that we will later use to construct multi-asset derivatives. The section will cover forward rate agreements and swaps, explaining constant maturity swaps (CMS). We discuss bonds, yield curves and interest rate swaptions. This leads us to a discussion of the SABR model that is now a market standard in interest rate derivatives. The section ends with a discussion of some popular interest rate exotics.

This section is by no means a comprehensive discussion of interest rate derivatives; it is designed to arm us with the knowledge and tools that are necessary to understand hybrid derivatives, although much more can be said. The interest rate products described here are standard, and for more elaborate discussions on interest rate markets and derivatives we refer the reader to Brigo and Mercurio (2006) and Rebonato (2002).

17.1.1   Forward Rate Agreements

A forward rate agreement (FRA) is an OTC contract that specifies an interest rate that will be paid or received as part of an obligation that starts at a future date. The relevant dates and the notional amounts will also be specified in the contract. A typical contract involves two parties exchanging a fixed rate for a floating one equal to some reference rate that underlies the contract, typically LIBOR or EURIBOR. Payments are calculated on the basis of the notional amount, and it is the difference between the fixed and floating legs that is ultimately paid. The party receiving the floating leg (who is paying the fixed rate) is said to be long the FRA, and the party paying floating is short the FRA. These are important as a swap is a combination of FRAs.

Let $R_{ref}(t)$ denote the reference rate at time t and R_{fixed} the fixed rate. On the effective date, T_{eff}, the payment made by the FRA is the netted amount given by

$$\text{FRA}_{payoff}(T_{eff}) = \text{Notional} \times \frac{(R_{ref}(T_{eff}) - R_{fixed}) \cdot d}{1 + R_{ref}(T_{eff}) \cdot d}$$

d is the day count fraction, which is given by the day count convention of the relevant currency on which the FRA is written. It defines the number of days in the year over which interest rates are calculated. As a fraction, for GBP this is typically 365, while for EUR and USD it is 360, and d is given by the number of days divided by 365 (or 360).

The fixed rate R_{fixed} is the rate at which both parties agree. Both the fixed and reference rates are those that begin to accrue on the effective date T_{eff}, and in turn are paid on the termination date of the contract. The discount factor, which is represented in the denominator, is specific to the case where – because the payments are known on the effective date – they are paid on such a date.

Consider a simplified example to illustrate the contract where party A enters into an FRA with counterparty B such that party A will receive a fixed rate of 3% for 1 year on a notional amount of $10,000,000 in 2 years' time. Party B will receive a floating rate, the 1-year LIBOR in this example, which is determined in 2 years' time on the effective date. The same notional applies to the 1-year LIBOR rate prevailing at that point in time and is used to compute the net payments needed to be made.

In 2 years' time, according to the FRA contract, and assuming that the 1-year LIBOR is 3.2%, which is higher than the agreed fixed rate of 3%, party A who is paying the fixed portion will have to make a net payment of $(3.2\% - 3\%) \times$ Notional $= \$20,000$ to party B. Here we ignored the day count fraction and did not discount.

The reference rate to be used in computing the net payment depends on the difference between the effective date and the termination date. For example, if the FRA has an effective date in 3 years and termination date in 3.5 years, then the USD 6-month LIBOR rate would be specified in the FRA contract. Similarly, an FRA with an effective date in 4 months and termination date in 5 months would use the USD 1-month LIBOR rate.

17.1.2   Constant Maturity Swaps

An interest rate swap is an OTC instrument in which two counterparties agree to exchange a stream of interest payments for another stream of cashflows. In a typical fixed for floating interest rate swap, one party makes payments based on a reference rate (the floating leg of the swap) in exchange for the other party making payments based on a fixed rate (the fixed leg of the swap). The fixed rate in such a swap is computed so that the swap has a net present value of zero at initiation, and, as such, the fixed rate is called a swap rate.

These swap rates form the swap rate curve, also known as a swap curve or LIBOR curve. This curve must be related to the zero coupon yield curve. The swap curve gives the relationship between swap rates at different maturities. In some cases, particularly in emerging market currencies, where sovereign debt is not liquidly traded, a swap curve can sometimes be more complete, and can thus be the better indicator of the term structure of interest rates in such currency.

Consider a swap, of maturity T, between two counterparties: A will pay a fixed interest rate on a notional in currency C, and B will pay the floating leg on the same notional in the same currency C, indexed to reference rate. Party A pays fixed and receives floating and is thus said to be long the interest rate swap. For example, the swap can involve exchanges of cashflows on a quarterly basis where the floating leg is given by the prevailing 3-month USD LIBOR plus a spread of 25 bp.

A constant maturity swap (CMS) is a swap in which the buyer is able to fix the duration of the cashflows he will receive in the swap. In the swap described above, the floating leg is reset on a quarterly basis to the LIBOR rate prevailing at the time, whereas in a CMS the floating leg is fixed against a point on the swap curve on a periodic basis. That is, the floating leg is reset with reference to a market swap rate rather than a LIBOR rate. The second leg of the swap is typically a LIBOR rate but can be a fixed rate or even another constant maturity rate. Again the structure of these can be based on a single currency or as a cross-currency swap. The value of the CMS depends on the volatilities of different forward rates and also the correlations between them. As such, pricing a CMS requires an interest rate model or at least what is known as a convexity adjustment (Brigo and Mercurio, 2006).

As an example of a CMS, consider an investor who believes the 3-month USD LIBOR rate will fall with respect to the 5-year swap rate. To play this view the investor can go long the constant maturity swap that pays the 3-month USD LIBOR and receives the 5-year swap rate. The 5-year swap rate here can be specified to be a point even further down the curve, thus allowing one to take a view on the longer section of the yield curve. The CMS thus also serves as a tool for hedging exposures to the long end of the yield curve, and in the case above where the investor receives the 5-year swap rate, a CMS as such will hedge against a sharp increase in this 5-year swap rate.

17.1.3   Bonds

Continuing the Chapter 1 introduction to bonds, we discuss here various types of bonds and then bond price sensitivities. A bond is a debt instrument in which the issuer will need to pay the holder interest, usually in the form of a coupon, and repay the notional on the maturity date of the bond.

Government Bonds

When a national government issues a bond it is known as a government or sovereign bond, and these are denominated in the currency of the relevant country. Interest from some government bonds is generally considered to be risk free, although there are cases where governments have defaulted on their sovereign bonds. In the US, Treasury securities, denominated in USD, are the least risky USD investments.

Such bonds may carry a low default risk, but do carry other risks. For example, if an investor buys a 5-year Treasury bond in USD and receives interest plus her money back in 5 years, the notional amount received back may be worth less owing to depreciation in the USD w.r.t. other currencies and also the risk of inflation. When we discuss inflation in the next chapter we see government issued bonds that are inflation-indexed and as such protect investors from exposure to inflation.

Bond Futures

Bond futures, which are traded on a futures exchange market, are contracts in which the holder is obliged to buy or sell a bond at a specifically agreed point of time in the future and for a specific price. Being traded on an exchange, these contracts are standardized and their trading regulated. As with trading any future, we are exposed to price fluctuations between the initial trade date and the exercise date of the futures contract. That is to say, the price of a bond can fluctuate like anything else, and although a bond may be purchased and its interest payments may be safe, its price between the initial agreement of a futures contract and exercise date can vary by a significant amount.

Bond Market Indices

A bond market index is a weighted index of bonds or other interest rate instruments. Like a stock market index, a bond index is used as a method to measure the composite value of its constituents. As an index it can also serve as a benchmark for comparison with other bond portfolios. However, bond indices are generally more complex than stock market indices and harder to replicate. It is still possible, however, to replicate such an index using bond futures. A Treasury bond index, for example, is a portfolio of outstanding Treasury bonds and notes.

Floating Rate Notes

A floating rate note (FRN) is a bond in which the coupon varies according to a reference rate, for example LIBOR plus a constant spread. A typical FRN has quarterly coupons and, at each payment date, the value of the reference rate is monitored and added to the agreed spread. For example, the quarterly coupon can be the 1-month USD LIBOR plus a spread of 30 bp.

Inverse Floating Rate Note

An inverse floating rate note (IFRN) again offers a variable coupon, but in this case the coupon has an inverse relationship with a specified reference rate. An instrument as such is designed to offer a higher coupon as the reference rate declines. The price of a typical bond is inversely proportional to the interest rates used in computing its value – as rates go up the value of the bond in the market goes down. The inverse floater is designed so that as short-term interest rates fall, both the bond's yield and value increase. The opposite holds for such a structure if rates were to rise and the inverse floating rate note's value would decrease accordingly. As an example of the formulation of the inverse floating rate:

$$\text{Floating Rate} = \underbrace{6\%}_{\textit{fixed rate}} - \underbrace{2}_{\textit{gearing}} \times \underbrace{6\text{m USD LIBOR}}_{\textit{reference rate}}$$

Bond Price Sensitivities

The *duration* of a financial asset refers to the sensitivity of this asset's price to a movement in interest rates. In the context of bonds, duration is the percentage change in the price of the bond with respect to interest rates, i.e. the absolute change in the price w.r.t. interest rates, divided by the current bond price. Duration is measured in years and is between 0 and T years, where T is the maturity of the bond. For small movements in interest rates, duration gives the first-order effect, i.e. linear effect, as the approximation of the drop in price of the bond with an increase of 1% per annum in interest rates. A bond with 10-year maturity and a duration of 5 would fall in price by approximately 5% if interest rates increased by 1% per annum.

The second-order effect, or bond *convexity*, measures the sensitivity of the duration of the bond to a change in interest rates. This is used similarly to the way the *Gamma* of a derivative, or book of derivatives, is used. If the duration of a book of bonds is low, but the overall convexity is still high, then a movement in interest rates will have a large impact on the duration of the book. If that book has both low duration and convexity, then it is far better hedged against large interest rate movements. The concept of Taylor series expansions discussed at the start of Chapter 5 applies, and we can write the change in the price of a bond $\Delta(P)$, where $P = P(r)$ is the bond price written as a function of (flat) interest rates, in terms of the first- and second-order terms of the series:

$$\frac{\Delta(P)}{P} = -D\Delta(r) + \frac{C}{2}(\Delta(r))^2$$

where D is the bond duration and C is the bond convexity.

17.1.4   Yield Curves

A yield curve is a plot of the interest rate yields of bonds of different maturities versus these maturities, and yield curves are widely monitored. The bonds used to form a yield curve must all be of the same credit quality. For example, the highly looked at yield curve of US Treasury securities of different maturities. The significance of this yield curve is that owing to the government's influence in this curve it is often used to infer future information about economic growth.

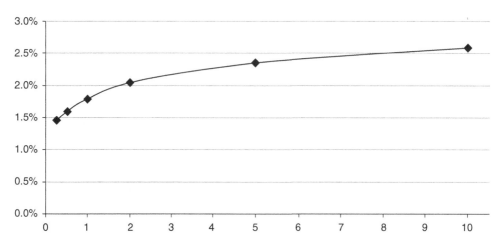

Figure 17.1 A typical yield curve. The 3-month, 6-month, 1-year, 2-year, 5-year and 10-year rates are plotted. Notice the upward-sloping nature of the curve as well as how this increase slows down as maturities get longer.

Yield curves are typically upward sloping with the longer maturities accompanied by higher yields, although this increase in yield by maturity slows down as the maturities increase (see Figure 17.1). An upward-sloping curve generally reflects that the market expects higher interest rates in the future. Because the Federal reserve controls short-term rates,[1] an upward-sloping yield curve indicates that the market believes Fed policy will be favourable to financial markets. The steeper the yield curve, the more positive this is believed to be.

The opposite case, where we see a downward-sloping yield curve, is when the short-term interest rates are higher than the longer term rates. This is also known as an inverted or negative yield curve. This type of yield curve reflects that there are market expectations for lower rates in the future. This is primarily because high short-term interest rates can imply that the government is trying to slow down the economy.

We may also see a humped shape yield curve. Assume the hump peaks at the 2-year point, then such a curve will indicate that the market expects rates to rise over the next 2 years but then decline.

Yield curves can make parallel shifts, and this is when all the points along the curve rise (or fall) by the same amount. This generally signals a change in economic conditions and expectations regarding inflation. We come across these when structuring macro-economically meaningful multi-asset options. A non-parallel shift of the yield curve is when the various points move by different amounts.

One can structure options to take a view on any of the yield curve shapes or moves, specifically the flattening or steepening of the yield curve, and movements up and down in the yield curve. One can also take a view not only on the slope of the yield curve but also on its curvature. With regards to the slope, one can have a yield curve option on the spread between two rates on the yield curve corresponding to two different maturities. Based on how these rates are chosen, the option will pay off when the yield curve either flattens or steepens.

---

[1] The Fed controls the federal funds rate. This is the rate that banks charge each other for overnight loans of reserves.

In the example of the CMS above, receiving the 5-year swap rate for example in a constant maturity swap allows for the view that rates will rise in the future as a result of a steepening of the yield curve. The opposite holds and one can pay the swap rate in a CMS with the view that the long-term swap rates will not end up as high as the market is currently implying through the yield curve. When an investor receives the 7-year CMS, for example, and pays a floating rate of, say, LIBOR plus a spread, then the exposure is primarily to the slope of the yield curve and not to its level. This means that such a structure is not sensitive to parallel shifts in the yield curve.

17.1.5   Zero Coupon, LIBOR and Swap Rates

In this subsection we establish the relationships between some of the interest rate concepts we have seen so far. Firstly, the relationship between a zero coupon bond $B(t, T)$ at time t and maturity T, and the instantaneous interest rate r_t.

$$B(t, T) = E\left[e^{-\int_t^T r_s ds}\right]$$

Here we point out the difference between zero coupon bonds and discount factors. Discount factors are not random as we can always get the current discount factors $D(T)$ by stripping the yield curve (Hagan, 2003). $D(T) = B(0, T) =$ today's discount factor for maturity T. However, zero coupon bonds $B(t, T)$ will remain random until the present time reaches time t.

The spot LIBOR rate at time t and maturity T is

$$L(t, T) = \frac{1 - B(t, T)}{(T - t)B(t, T)}$$

in terms of bonds $B(t, T)$.

A forward LIBOR at time t, with expiry T_{i-1} and maturity T_i, is

$$F_i(t) = \frac{1}{T_i - T_{i-1}}\left(\frac{B(t, T_{i-1})}{B(t, T_i)} - 1\right)$$

This is a market rate, and is the underlyer of the forward rate agreement contracts discussed above. The Treasuries used to form a yield curve only have a finite number of maturities, and to see the yield at a maturity for which no Treasury security is available one will have to interpolate the yield curve. When doing so it should be checked that the forward rates computed as described here are all positive to ensure that the interpolation of the yield curve is arbitrage free.

A swap rate described above can also be written in terms of bonds. Let $S_{\alpha,\beta}(t)$ be the swap rate at time t with tenor $T_\alpha, T_{\alpha+1}, \ldots, T_\beta$.

$$S_{\alpha,\beta}(t) = \frac{B(t, T_\alpha) - B(t, T_\beta)}{\sum_{i=\alpha+1}^{\beta}(T_i - T_{i-1})B(t, T_i)}$$

This is a market rate and it underlies interest rate swaps discussed above. At time t these are all known from the bond prices $B(t, T)$.

17.1.6   Interest Rate Swaptions

An interest rate swap option (called a swaption) is an option that gives the holder the right but not obligation to enter into an underlying swap. Which leg of the swap the holder of a swaption can potentially enter into is determined by the type of swaption: the owner of a payer swaption has the right but not obligation to enter into a swap where they pay the fixed leg and receive floating. A receiver swaption gives the opposite: the right but not obligation to enter into a swap where they pay the floating leg and receive fixed.

Swaptions are OTC derivatives but there exists an interbank swaption market. Typically swaptions are valued using Black's model, and from the swaption market one can obtain implied swaption volatilities. One key difference between a swaption and an option on a stock is that two swaptions of the same maturity (the option) can be on two swaps of quite different tenors. So for swaption volatilities there are not only volatilities for swaptions of different maturities but also different volatilities for underlying swaps of different tenors. The dominant factor in the swaption market is the time to expiry of the swaption compared to the tenor of the underlying swap.

Black's model (see Black, 1976) is specifically designed to have as underlying a forward contract on a swap – a forward swap rate. Instead of having a call option on a spot rate, we have a call option on a forward rate. In 1976 Black applied this model to price calls and puts on physical commodities, forwards and futures, and applying it to the case of European swaptions the underlying is a single forward swap rate:

$$\text{Call Option}_{\text{price}} = e^{-rt_{\text{set}}} [f\mathcal{N}(d_1) - K\mathcal{N}(d_2)]$$

$$\text{Put Option}_{\text{price}} = e^{-rt_{\text{set}}} [K\mathcal{N}(-d_2) - f\mathcal{N}(-d_1)]$$

where f is the current underlying forward rate and K is the strike price. The values of d_1 and d_2 are

$$d_{1,2} = \frac{\log f/K \pm \frac{1}{2}\sigma_B^2 t_{\text{exp}}}{\sigma_B \sqrt{t_{\text{exp}}}}$$

This resembles the Black–Scholes formula but has some key differences, in particular, forward prices exhibit a different form of randomness to spot prices. In the above formula the discount factor is taken between time zero and the settlement date t_{set}. The time parameter used in computing d_1 and d_2, which in turn gives the value inside the brackets, is the expiry date t_{exp}.

The volatility σ_B will be chosen from the swaption implied volatilities in the market. Typically in the swaption market there are ATM swaption implied volatilities for various swaption maturities and various tenors of the underlying swaps. A swaption is quoted by the maturity of the option, the tenor of the swap, whether the swap is a receiver or payer swap, the strike and the implied volatility. For example, a 1 into 2 receiver at 5.4% for 16.8%. The 1-year represents the maturity of the option, the 2-year is the tenor on the underlying (receiver) swap, the option is struck at 5.4% and has an implied volatility of 16.8%.

Using an ATM volatility to price an OTM European swaption would require an adjustment (Figure 17.2). Black's model is popular because it is extremely fast, and recently we saw the emergence of the SABR model that is the simplest extension of Black's model that accounts for skew and has decent implied dynamics. To manage a book with potentially thousands of swaptions, speed is a key factor, and the SABR model is as instantaneous as Black's model. We discuss SABR in a section of its own below.

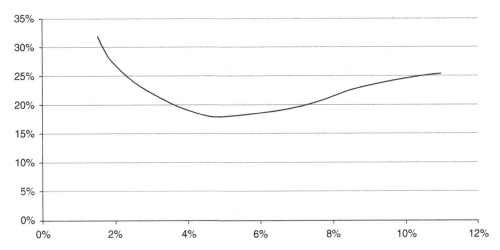

Figure 17.2 The implied volatility smile of a European swaption. Deep OTM call option implied volatilities tend to flatten out the deeper one goes OTM. The smile shape is different to the equity skews.

17.1.7 Interest Rate Caps and Floors

An interest rate cap is an OTC derivative that makes a payment to the holder when a specified short-term interest rate rises above a specified *cap* rate. Interest rate cap maturities typically range from 1 year to 7 years, and the derivative makes periodic payments where, at each such payment date, the difference between the underlying reference rate and the cap rate is paid. Consider, for example, a 2-year cap in which each quarter a payment is made in the amount by which LIBOR exceeds 1.5%. The premium for the cap is usually paid up front.

The interest rate cap is a series of interest rate *caplets*, one for each period up to the cap's maturity. A caplet is simply a European call option on the reference rate with strike rate equal to the cap. The payoff of a caplet on a rate L struck at K is

$$\text{Caplet}_{\text{payoff}}(T) = N \cdot \alpha \cdot \max(L(T) - K, 0)$$

where N is the notional value exchanged and α is the day count fraction corresponding to the period to which L applies. This is essentially a call option on the LIBOR rate observed at time T.

The interest rate cap allows its holder to limit a floating rate exposure to interest rates rising. By buying an interest rate cap on the rate to which the investor is exposed, he receives payments when the rate exceeds the cap rate (the strike). The longer the maturity of the cap the more it offers this protection, but the more expensive it is.

An interest rate floor is defined similarly as a series of *floorlets*, each of which is a put option on a reference rate, typically LIBOR. The buyer of the interest rate floor receives payments on the maturity of any of the individual floorlets; the reference rate is below the specified floor.

Both the caplets and floorlets are valued using Black's model, and again the relevant implied caplet volatility will be used.

17.1.8   The SABR Model

The SABR model was pioneered by Hagan *et al.* (2002). SABR stands for Stochastic Alpha, Beta and Rho, as these (along with a parameter v) are the parameters that form the model. The SABR model deserves a subsection of its own; in fact it deserves a whole lot more. The key point is that although in equities, for example, there is no real market standard for managing skew risk, in interest rates and FX there is: it is this SABR model. Broker quotes for swaption volatilities of different moneyness can be quoted in terms of SABR parameters.

SABR models a single forward rate, allowing for both local volatility and stochastic volatility. As such it allows for the modelling of swaption implied volatility smiles. The motivation behind its creation was to find an extension of Black's model that allowed for smiles and skews but also offered correct smile dynamics. One key feature of this model is that the prices of European options can be computed in closed form using the SABR formula that gives the correct implied volatility to use in Black's formula. This makes the model as quick as using Black's formula, only with the added advantage that it knows about volatility smiles and also offers correct smile dynamics which, in turn, gives stable hedge ratios.

The SABR formula is based on an approximation and this can lead to troubles, these are discussed in Appendix A, section A.3.2. Mainly, it assumes a small vol of vol, which may be reasonable in interest rates or foreign exchange but not so much so in equities or commodities. The SABR formula is given by

$$\sigma_B(K, f) = \frac{\alpha}{(fK)^{(1-\beta)/2}\left\{1 + \frac{(1-\beta)^2}{24}\log^2 f/K + \frac{(1-\beta)^4}{1920}\log^4 f/K + \cdots\right\}}.$$

$$\left(\frac{z}{x(z)}\right) \cdot \left\{1 + \left[\frac{(1-\beta)^2}{24}\frac{\alpha^2}{(fK)^{1-\beta}} + \frac{1}{4}\frac{\rho\beta v\alpha}{(fK)^{(1-\beta)/2}} + \frac{2-3\rho^2}{24}v^2\right]t_{\text{ex}} + \cdots\right.$$

where

$$z = \frac{v}{\alpha}(fK)^{(1-\beta)/2}\log f/K$$

and $x(z)$ is defined by

$$x(z) = \log\left\{\frac{\sqrt{1-2\rho z + z^2} + z - \rho}{1-\rho}\right\}$$

where f is the forward price. The first thing to note is that although this formula appears complicated, it is in fact closed form, and it involves nothing more than computing logarithms and powers of the various parameters. This is the original form of the SABR model, and is the volatility parameter that is plugged into the Black–Scholes formula to return the prices of European options at the relevant strikes. Note that in the above formula the dots indicate the left-out higher-order terms that are typically ignored when the formula is implemented and used. When the parameters are calibrated to an implied volatility skew across strikes, the set of SABR parameters: α, β, ρ, v gives a parameterization of this skew.

To explain the parameters we start with β. This parameter is specified within the range $0 \le \beta \le 1$, and appears above mainly as an exponent of f. This is because, in the model from which this formula came, β in fact represents the power parameter of a specific type of local volatility. When $\beta = 0$ the underlying forward is normally distributed, and when $\beta = 1$, the underlying forward is log-normally distributed. The case where β is in between represents a dynamic for the forward that is neither Normal nor log-normal.

The β parameter is typically chosen first and set to be constant, for example, if we like to model our forward as a log-normal random variable, we set $\beta = 1$ and work with the rest of the parameters. In the case where $\beta = 1$, the model is a simple stochastic volatility extension of Black's formula in that the underlying forward is modelled as log-normal in both cases, but in SABR the volatility is also modelled as a log-normal random variable compared to Black's case where it is just a constant.

The α is a volatility-like parameter for the forward (West, 2005). Its volatility ν is thus the vol-of-vol, and ρ is the (instantaneous) correlation between the underlying and its volatility. α thus controls the height of the ATM implied volatility level. The correlation ρ controls the slope of the implied skew and ν controls its curvature.

17.1.9 Exotic Interest Rate Structures

Here we discuss some popular interest rate exotics, specifically range accruals, target redemption notes and CMS steepeners. The selection of an interest rate structure, exotic or not, can be to hedge a specific set of cashflows, or to take a speculative view on interest rates. The exotics case can allow for a more tailored hedge or a more specific view.

Callable Features

Compared to equities, we can find some long-dated structures, although longer structures in interest rates tend to have callable features. In a callable interest rate swap, for example, the payer of the fixed rate has the right to end the swap at some specified set of dates in the future (possibly only one date). In exchange for this right, the investor paying the fixed leg in such a swap would expect to have to pay an above-market rate.

These break down into European and Bermudan style callable features. For a fixed for floating swap to be European style callable, it means that the payer of the fixed leg has one date in the future at which the swap may be terminated. For example in a 7-year swap callable after 2 years the payer of the fixed leg has one and only one opportunity, at the 2-year mark to decide whether or not to terminate the swap. If not called at this point in time, the swap will remain active till its prespecified maturity, here the 7-year point. During these first 2 years the payer of the floating leg will receive an above-market fixed rate, but if rates decline then the payer of the fixed leg will most probably cancel the swap.

In a Bermudan style callable swap, the payer of the fixed leg is given the right to call the swap at a set of dates in the future. For example, a 7-year swap where the payer of the fixed leg can cancel the swap on an annual basis on or after the second year. Similar to the European case, if rates move against the payer of the fixed leg it may be cancelled at one of these dates. The Bermudan case obviously adds more flexibility, and the right to a Bermudan callable feature will cost more than a European version; however, the Bermudan feature is the more popular of the two.

Range Accruals

Range accruals are relatively popular. Similar to the range accrual we saw in section 11.5.2, the range accrual in the interest rate case pays a coupon proportional to the number of days that an underlying reference rate stays within a prespecified range. A coupon as such can be paid as an exotic coupon in a swap where the investor pays a fixed (or even a floating amount) and receives this range-dependent coupon. The range accrual coupon can also be used in a floating rate note.

There are also interest rate digitals where a digital call option makes a payment if a reference interest rate is above a specified barrier. Or even a digital that makes a payoff if the reference interest rate at maturity is within a specified range.

Target Redemption Notes

A target redemption note (TARN) pays a set of coupons that are linked to a reference rate, with the possibility of early redemption. The coupons are computed, typically using an inverse floating LIBOR rate such that once the sum of all coupons paid reaches a *target* amount, the note is redeemed at par. For example, consider a 7-year TARN with annual coupons in which the coupons of each year T_i are computed, based on the formula

$$\text{Coupon}(T_i) = 2 \times \max\left[0, 4\% - L(T_i)\right]$$

where $L(T_i)$ is the USD 12-month LIBOR at time T_i. The coupons are paid annually until either the note reaches maturity or the sum of all coupons paid has reached the target amount of 14%. In both cases the notional is returned as the note is redeemed at par. The appeal of such a note is the possibility that the investor may get his money back at par plus the target coupon in what could be a relatively short amount of time.

CMS Steepener Options

A CMS steepener option, also known as a CMS spread option, pays a coupon based on a multiple of the spread between two CMS rates. The most popular of these is the option on the 30-year to 10-year CMS rate spread. The 10-year to 2-year and 30-year to 2-year structures are also popular. The maturity of an option on such a spread does not have to be nearly as long; for example, one can have a 1-year option on the 10-year to 2-year CMS rate spread. If the yield curve was to steepen, the spread between these two CMS rates would increase. A product as such can be appealing in an environment where the yield curve is flat or even inverted, and a CMS steepener option as described provides a leveraged play on the view that the yield curve will steepen.

17.2   COMMODITIES

Moving to our next asset class, here we discuss commodities. The idea is to understand commodities as an asset class of their own. Commodities can be broken down into categories:

- Energy, which includes crude oil
- Precious metals, which includes gold
- Industrial metals, which include copper
- Agricultural products, which include wheat

There is additionally the category of Livestock and Meat.

These can be split into two categories: hard commodities and soft commodities. Hard commodities are those whose supply is limited to the finite availability of natural resources;

these include metals such as gold and energy commodities such as crude oil. Soft commodities include agricultural products and livestock that are affected by other factors such as the weather.

In this section we want to understand the properties of commodities, in particular those with significance to commodity derivatives. This entails understanding the forward curves and the volatilities of each. For more details we refer the reader to the comprehensive books by Geman (2005) and Schofield (2007).

The rise in commodity investing, which has been made even easier through commodity derivatives, comes from the broad range of possible commodities that are accessible through financial markets, in addition to the general belief that commodities markets are not strongly correlated to equity markets. Commodities are also an interesting asset class as they are believed to serve as an inflationary hedge. Commodities were in fact involved in some of the first derivatives where farmers tried to secure certain prices for their crops that were yet to be produced. Although such derivatives were originally designed for risk management purposes, today investing in commodities is done by many people with no such risks.

The Chicago Board of Trade (CBOT), the first established exchange, offers standardized commodity contracts. The CBOT along with the Chicago Mercantile Exchange (CME) are two of the largest exchanges in the world offering commodity contracts. In addition to trading in standardized commodity contracts, there are many ETFs that provide exposure to commodity prices directly, for example ETFs that track the spot price of gold. As such an investor can take a view on the price of gold without having to take hold of the physical commodity himself. Commodity indices such as the GSCI and the DJAIG can also be accessed through ETFs.

In addition to the expansion in commodity derivatives, both vanilla and exotic, there has been a rise in the appearance of commodities as an asset class in multi-asset derivatives: hybrids. An investor can add commodities to such a derivative in combination with other asset classes for diversificational benefits, as a hedge for a multi-asset class exposure that involves commodities and to even take a combined view on commodities along with another asset class.

Although commodities are generally believed to be negatively correlated to equities, in an environment such as that of the credit crunch of 2008, it is possible that owing to supply and demand and the global impact of the credit crunch, commodities such as oil also fall as equities do. The point of this chapter is to explain this asset class and then explain in the subsequent chapter how to structure and price hybrid derivatives involving commodities, not to discuss investment ideas in commodities.

17.2.1   Forward and Futures Curves, Contango and Backwardation

The forward curve is the plot of forward prices with maturity T versus this maturity, and similarly for a futures curve. A futures contract is basically a standardized forward contract, while futures are traded on an exchange, forwards are done OTC. The word *nearby* refers to how close the forward contract is to expiry. The first nearby is the closest to expiry, the second nearby is the second closest to expiry, and so on. As the first nearby expires, the second nearby contract becomes the first nearby, and so on.

An upward-sloping curve, which means that the price for the future delivery of a commodity (or asset in general) is higher than its current spot price, is referred to as *contango*. This means that the amount the market charges for the delivery of an asset in the future is more than what would be charged to receive delivery of the asset today. *Backwardation* is the opposite case where the forward curve is downward sloping, i.e. the price of future delivery of the commodity is lower than its current spot price. It is also possible to see humped forward curves.

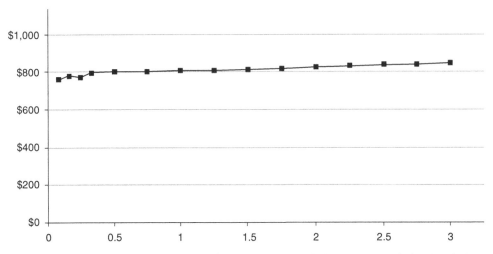

Figure 17.3 A typical futures curve for gold. Notice the curve is in contango, and also that the long end of the curve is more stable than the short end. Although the curve is bumpy at first, we still say it is in contango as the first few nearbys are cheaper than the longer term futures.

The short end of a commodities forward curve is affected directly by supply and demand in the short term, and thus this end of the forward curve often looks less stable than the longer end of the curve, which is generally smoother. When the short end of the curve is higher than the long end – that is, we are in backwardation – it generally means that the commodity in question is in short supply (compared to demand). When in contango and the short end of the forward curve is lower than the long end, it means that the commodity is generally in good supply. A hump at an intermediate point along the forward curve reflects the market's expectation of a high demand at that point in time, and multiple humps can represent a seasonal change in demand (for example, natural gas in the winter).

As an example, assume the spot price of gold is $800 per ounce. If the futures price for the delivery of gold in 3 months is $780, where payment is made on delivery, then this implies that gold is currently in short supply. The lower futures price means that the market believes that delivering gold today will be more costly than delivering it in 3 months' time, thus the backwardation. Someone who believes that in 3 months the delivery of gold will cost more than $780 can enter into the futures contract for the delivery of gold at $780 in 3 months' time, thus taking a view on the forward curve.

If the 3-month futures price for gold were $850, it reflects a healthy supply of gold today, with the view that the delivery of gold in 3 months' time is worth more than the spot price. Again a view can be taken that this futures curve will not be realized by taking the opposite side of a forward contract. In fact, the use of gold as an example is not the best as backwardation rarely occurs in the forward curve of gold. Figure 17.3 gives an example of a typical futures curve for gold.

Figure 17.4 gives an example of a futures curve for crude oil. There are several different types of crude oil: West Texas Intermediate (WTI), for example, is a type of crude oil often used as a benchmark for oil prices. WTI futures are traded on the New York Mercantile Exchange (NYMEX) where one can obtain a futures curve up to 6 years in maturity.

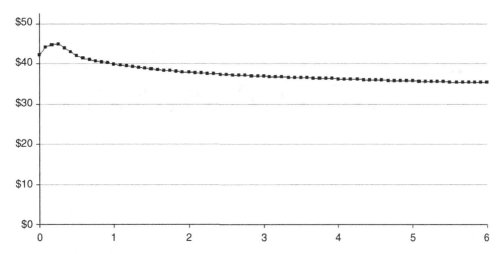

Figure 17.4 An example of a futures curve for crude oil. Notice that the curve is in contango in the start then goes into backwardation as the long-term futures are worth less than the near-term futures contracts.

To understand the case of backwardation we explain the existence of a *convenience yield* in commodities. This yield is nothing more than an adjustment to the cost of carry, which is the cost of taking on a financial position. In the case of equities there is no cost of storage but interest rates and dividends both appear in the computation of the non-arbitrage price of the forward contracts on a stock. Buying a forward contract on a stock would involve interest payments to pay for borrowed funds when buying on margin. Dividends have an opposite effect as the opportunity cost of the decision to buy a forward instead of the stock itself. The inclusion of rates and dividends reflects this in the price of forwards in the equity case. In the case of commodities, a convenience yield should be included as an adjustment to the cost of carry to account for the fact that the physical commodity itself cannot be shorted and that its delivery today might be a necessity for which a market participant is willing to pay a premium. The convenience yield is defined as the premium that a consumer is willing to pay to be able to attain the commodity now rather than at some time in the future (Schofield, 2007).

The forward price, which also serves as an approximation of the futures price, including the cost of carry, is

$$F(T) = S(0)e^{(r+s-c)T}$$

where F is the forward price, T is time to delivery, S is the spot price, r is the risk-free interest rate, s represents the cost of storage, and c is the convenience yield. The value of such a convenience yield is affected by the demand for a commodity. The case where there is a shortage of a commodity with respect to the demand for it will be reflected in a high convenience yield. In the case where there is an abundance of supply for a commodity, this yield shrinks to zero.

The convenience yield helps to explain the reason behind backwardation. In the case of oil, and generally for the energy market, delivery might be a necessity, and penalties high for not

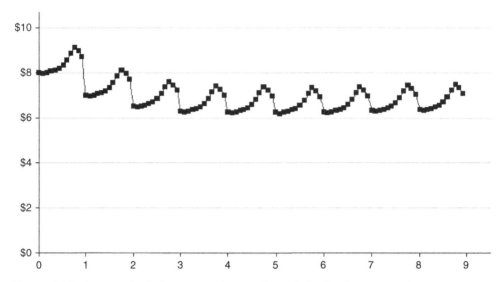

Figure 17.5 An example of a futures curve for natural gas. Notice that the curve goes between contango and backwardation during each season. In this curve the maturities start at a point during the summer season, and the curve peaks during each winter.

delivering. Obtaining oil today will carry a higher convenience yield, reflecting the premium on the price for the delivery of the spot today.

One can ask the questions: Is it possible to arbitrage the futures curve in the commodities market? Is it possible for the oil futures curve to remain in backwardation? The answers are: commodities have a non-arbitrageable forward. When the curve is in backwardation, the shorter dated contracts are worth more than the longer dated ones, making the latter seem cheap or incorrectly priced. To take advantage one would need to buy the longer dated contracts and short the front end of the curve. Firstly, the spot market can be quite illiquid and the asset hard to obtain and thus quite difficult to short. If one were to sell a contract at the front end of the curve and buy the long end, then the commodity itself would need to be obtained and delivered in order to honour the obligation of the first contract. If the commodity is not readily available in the spot market, then this forward curve is non-arbitrageable and can remain in backwardation for this reason. In the case where one does take physical delivery of the commodity, storage and other costs will be incurred. As such, and since the market for these contracts is driven by participants' fair value of future delivery, a given slope of the curve will account for these factors and not allow for an arbitrage.

17.2.2   Commodity Vanillas and Skew

Since commodity futures and forwards are more liquid than the asset's spots, these forwards and futures are used as the underlyings in commodity derivatives. From a hedging perspective, the illiquidity of commodity spots and the resulting lack of shorting ability, make hedging with spots not feasible.

A call option on a commodity, for example, will give the holder the right but not the obligation at the maturity of the option to buy a commodity future at the agreed strike price.

The underlying future will also be of an agreed maturity. In a manner similar to how we previously specified strike prices as a percentage of the current spot, the strike of an option on a commodity future can be specified as a percentage of the price of the underlying future at the time of pricing.

Pricing an option on a spot price of a seasonal commodity can also add complexity. For example, one would expect the spot price for natural gas to be higher in winter. A seasonal effect must be priced into the derivative and a Black–Scholes log-normal assumption for the spot price is unreasonable. However, since the seasonality effect is already priced into the forward curve, it makes sense to price derivatives on points of this curve compared to using the spot price. Figure 17.5 provides an example of a futures curve for natural gas.

In Black (1976) he modelled forward price instead of the spot price, which solved the aforementioned issue. We have already seen Black's model in section 17.1.6 in interest rates, his paper was written to address this issue. Black's model is also the standard in commodity markets for pricing European options on physical commodities, forwards and futures.

Commodities will also exhibit some form of skew in the implied volatilities of European options. This is the volatility that, when used in Black's model, gives the correct price of the European option, and again implied volatility is the market's consensus of future volatility. The commodity volatility surface consists of the implied volatilities of options on futures, for which we have one option maturity for each futures contract maturity. The option's maturity is typically only a few days after the date the futures contract is set to expire.

This term structure is downward sloping most of the time. Volatility in commodity markets is closely linked to issues of supply and demand. If the supply of a commodity is struggling to keep up with demand, volatility will rise. In the short term, supply and demand fluctuations have a large impact on volatility causing it to be very high in cases where there is a supply shortage, whereas the longer dated implied volatilities are governed more by long-term expectations regarding the economy and are generally lower. Long-term factors, such as the mining of limited resources and even the weather, can play a role depending on the commodity.

With respect to moneyness, the implied volatilities surface will have decreasing liquidity in European options struck away from the ATM point. Commodity implied volatilities also imply that commodity returns are positively skewed compared to equities in which returns are negatively skewed. For example, in oil, greater uncertainty is generally associated with higher oil prices. Market participants, particularly in industries, who rely on having oil in order to conduct business, will need to hedge the upside risk of price increases to which they are adverse. Those producing oil will want downside protection in order to protect profits in the event that oil prices may decline; however, upside hedging sees more demand and comes with higher implied volatilities.

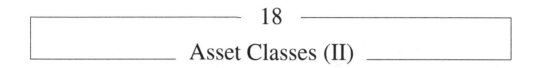

18
Asset Classes (II)

No complaint, however, is more common than that of a scarcity of money.

Adam Smith

Continuing the discussion of asset classes, in this chapter we discuss foreign exchange (FX), inflation and credit, each as a separate asset class.

18.1 FOREIGN EXCHANGE

The foreign exchange market, often referred to as FX, encompasses everything to do with currency trading. Again, we focus in this section on understanding the underlying market, FX forward curves, FX vanillas, FX implied volatility smiles and some FX exotics. For a more detailed account of FX derivatives we refer the reader to Wystup (2007).

The FX market is highly liquid with many quite different parties acting as market participants, from corporations, to speculators and even governments. To define an exchange rate, one must specify two currencies: a domestic and a foreign. These are not related to geography but simply define a standard by which values will be measured. An exchange rate is defined as the amount of the domestic currency required to buy one unit of the foreign currency. A transaction in FX will involve the exchange of an amount of one currency for an amount in another currency; for example, exchanging euros for US dollars.

To be clear on notation, we use the convention of foreign–domestic where, for example, the exchange rate between the euro and the US dollar is written as EUR–USD and represents the amount of US dollars needed to buy one euro. The USD–EUR exchange rate is the inverse of this where the domestic currency is taken to be the euro. If the EUR–USD is 1.4356 then the USD–EUR is the inverse of this, given by $1/1.4356 = 0.69657$.

18.1.1 Forward and Futures Curves

Futures are standardized forward contracts that are traded through an exchange, and these are the more popular choice among currency speculators; many futures positions are closed out before they reach expiry. An FX future is a contract that allows the holder to buy or sell a currency for a specific price at a specific date in the future. Forward contracts in FX are traded OTC and are the more popular choice for parties hedging FX exposures. FX forward contracts do not need to be settled with the delivery of the foreign currency, and can be cash settled in the domestic currency. If the investor actually wanted to take hold of an amount of foreign currency, then the contract can be specified so that it is settled in the foreign currency.

The FX forward rate is affected by the interest rates in both the domestic and foreign currencies. In fact the most important factor in determining an FX forward rate is the spread between the two interest rates. If we recall the concept of the cost of carry – that is, the cost of taking on a financial position, including the opportunity costs – in the case of FX we can expect the buyer of an FX forward to be long interest rates in the domestic currency and short

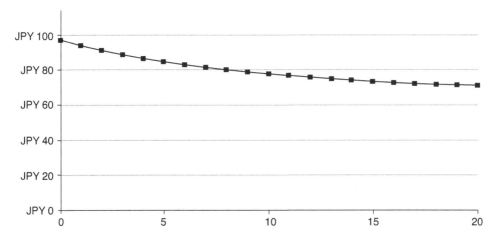

Figure 18.1 A USD–JPY forward FX curve. Notice that the curve is in backwardation, reflecting the case where interest rates in Japan are relatively lower.

interest rates in the foreign currency. The FX forward, which delivers an amount of a currency at time T is given by the formula

$$F(T) = S \, e^{(r_d - r_f)T} \qquad (18.1)$$

where S is the FX spot price, r_f is the risk-free rate on the foreign currency, and r_d is the risk-free rate in the domestic currency. This formula is explained by understanding the effect of interest rates and what is known as interest rate parity.

Different countries usually have different interest rates, and this means that money in one currency can grow at the local risk-free rate, which is different to how it would grow at the risk-free rate in another currency. This must be reflected in the price of an FX forward or there would be an arbitrage opportunity, and interest rate parity relates FX forward prices to interest rates in the form of a non-arbitrage condition. Assume that an investor borrows money in one currency and converts it to another currency in which the risk-free rate on interest is made on this amount. An FX forward, that would be used to lock in an exchange rate at a future date to convert this money back to the original currency, must be priced so that the risk-free returns from such a trade match those in the original currency.

Formula (18.1) describes this parity in the case where we assume continuous compounding on interest. When both interest rates are equal, the forward price must equal the spot price. When rates are different, and depending on which is higher, the forward curve can be in contango or backwardation. Different interest rate term structure shapes can also impact the shape of the forward curve and it is not necessarily smooth. Figure 18.1 shows a USD–JPY forward curve in backwardation. The bigger the difference between the two rates, the steeper the slope of the forward curve.

Carry Trades

A carry trade is a play on the interest rate differentials between two currencies that involves the FX rate. Assume that a forward curve is quite steep, reflecting a large interest rate differential, then an investor can enter into a carry trade that involves selling the currency with the lower interest rate and buying the currency with the higher interest rate. The play on the FX rate is that the investor is paying the lower risk-free rate on the money borrowed, and receiving the higher interest rate yield in the second currency, thus netting a profit.

This is not an arbitrage strategy as it will only be profitable if the currency does not move against the investor. If the currency does not move then at the end of the investment period the investor can change money back to the original currency and pay off the loan in that currency, having netted the profit from the difference in interest rates. If the currency with the higher rate were to depreciate relative to the currency in which the investor is borrowing, then when the time comes to exchange the money back to cover the original loan, the value in the original currency will be lower and it is possible to make a loss.

The opposite can also happen where the investor makes additional gains if the currency with the higher yield appreciates. One can put on a carry trade and continuously net the interest rate differential, and close out the trade once the FX rate moves in the wrong direction; however, exchange rates can jump suddenly in the wrong direction leaving the investor with an immediate loss. Since the forward price is governed by interest rate parity, it is not possible to hedge this FX risk completely and a view must be taken on the exchange rate between the two currencies.

A typical currency to borrow in is the Japanese Yen because interest rates in Japan have been very low. An investor can borrow money in JPY paying very little interest and exchange yens for another currency with a high interest rate that can be in excess of 10% per annum. Carry trades can also involve borrowing in a low-yielding currency and investing in a high-yielding asset other than a bond, but again the same risk remains, in addition to the risks the asset in question also adds that its yield will not be paid.

18.1.2   FX Vanillas and Volatility Smiles

FX options are mostly OTC and are highly liquid – particularly those written on a forward rate. Exchange-listed FX options exist, and although these greatly reduce counterparty credit risk, the OTC market is much bigger. An FX option is a derivative in which the holder has a right but not the obligation to exchange money from one currency to another at a fixed strike rate and specified maturity date, both specified in the terms of the option.

If we take a call option in USD on one unit of a stock for a fixed strike price, then this strike price is the amount of dollars that will be paid for one unit of the stock if the option is exercised at maturity. An FX option involves the exchange of two notionals in different currencies, and the strike is given by the ratio of these notionals. As FX can be confusing, we will clarify by use of an example.

Assume that an investor buys 1,000,000 options with a GBP–EUR strike at 1.3464, where these options give the holder the right but not the obligation, at maturity, to sell GBP 1,000,000 and buy EUR 1,346,400 (1.3464 × 1,000,000). The GBP notional of the trade is GBP 1,000,000, and the EUR notional of the trade is EUR 1,346,400 so that the ratio of the two is equal to the strike price. If the investor decided on a different strike for the option, then one of these notionals must change in order that the new strike is still the ratio of the two notionals. To set the option ATM, the strike would have to equal the current spot exchange rate between the two currencies, and if one notional is fixed then the second notional will have to be set so that the ratio of the two matches the spot.

In the above option, if the EUR appreciates w.r.t. the GBP, then the GBP–EUR exchange rate has decreased (the amount of EUR needed to buy one GBP has gone down). The holder of the above option has the right to sell GBP 1,000,000 and receive EUR 1,346,400 at a time when the EUR has appreciated, which means that GBP 1,000,000 is currently worth less than EUR 1,346,400. Such an option is thus a put option on GBP, and it is the market convention to quote an exchange rate strike using the terminology of a GBP–EUR strike in reference to the put option that increases in moneyness as EUR gains w.r.t. the GBP. It also acts like a call option on the EUR. The opposite option can be specified where the put is on the EUR (call on GBP) and the strike, assuming the same notionals, will be the inverse of the previous strike, i.e. $1/1.3464 = 0.7427$, and this would be referred to as a EUR–GBP strike.

The premium charged for entering into an FX option depends on how many contracts are being bought. This premium can be computed using the Garman and Kohlhagen (1983) model, which is essentially an extension of the Black–Scholes model that accounts for the two interest rates. As such, the model, like Black–Scholes, assumes that the exchange rate is log-normally distributed. The idea is to use this model to obtain the value of one contract and the premium can thus be computed by multiplying the cost of one contract by the number of contracts.

Following the same notation as before, let r_d denote the risk-free rate in the domestic currency, and r_f that of the foreign currency. The domestic currency refers to that in which the option will be denominated. Caution must be taken when specifying the spot and strike. As the strike and spot of a call option on a stock will be specified in terms of dollars per stock, the strike and spot in the FX case must also be specified in terms of the same units.

In the above example involving GBP and EUR, the call option will be denominated in GBP and the EUR–GBP strike price will be used for a call option. The strike and the spot must be specified in the same units: here we are using the number of domestic currency units per unit of foreign currency. It is the domestic currency that is exchanged for the foreign currency at maturity if the option is exercised. If we denote the spot and strike by S and K, then the values of calls and puts under the Garman and Kohlhagen model are given by

$$\text{FX Call Option}_{\text{price}} = S\,e^{-r_f T}\mathcal{N}(d_1) - K\,e^{-r_d T}\mathcal{N}(d_2)$$

The value of a put option has value

$$\text{FX Put Option}_{\text{price}} = K\,e^{-r_d T}\mathcal{N}(-d_2) - S\,e^{-r_f T}\mathcal{N}(-d_1)$$

where

$$d_1 = \frac{\ln(S/K) + (r_d - r_f + \sigma^2/2)T}{\sigma\sqrt{T}}$$

and

$$d_2 = d_1 - \sigma\sqrt{T}$$

and the parameter σ, which should be used, is the implied volatility. Much like the previous cases we have seen, the market for vanilla options is driven by the premiums at which market makers are willing to trade, and the observed implied volatilities represent the consensus of all views. The implied distribution for FX will not be log-normal, but using the correct implied volatility obtained from the market in the above formula will yield the market price of the option.

The implied volatilities in the case of FX typically exhibit smiles, not skews. This means that ATM options will have lower implied volatilities than both ITM and OTM call options. This is the market's way of pricing a premium on FX options struck away from the money to include the risk that an exchange rate can have extreme moves in either direction. The

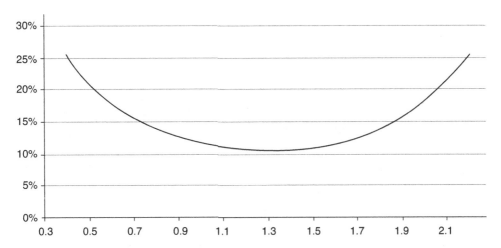

Figure 18.2 An example of an implied volatility smile for the EUR–USD. The smile is (almost) symmetric.

existence of the smile means that the market believes such are more probable than a log-normal distribution implies. An extreme move in an exchange rate between two currencies is the result of a depreciation of one currency w.r.t. the other, and the smile in FX markets prices this uncertainty in both directions (Figure 18.2). The implied volatility smile is not necessarily symmetric, and a steeper skew on one side can reflect more uncertainty in one of the currencies.

FX vanilla options must satisfy a put–call parity relationship. This is the equilibrium relationship that must exist between the prices of put and call options on the same underlying and with the same strike and expiry.

$$C(K, T) - P(K, T) = S\,e^{-r_f T} - K\,e^{-r_d T}$$

from this the parity of the Deltas of the call and put is

$$\Delta_{\text{call}} - \Delta_{\text{put}} = e^{-r_f T}$$

which for small maturities, and low foreign interest rates, we have $\Delta_{\text{call}} - \Delta_{\text{put}} \approx 1$.

Risk Reversals

The risk reversal is an option strategy that involves a call and a put. A long risk reversal consists of a long OTM call option and a short position in an OTM put option, both with the same maturity but different strikes. The strikes are specified in terms of the Deltas of the two options (Figure 18.3). In a typical risk reversal, the Deltas of both the call and put are chosen to be 0.25. As such it would be referred to as a 25-Delta risk reversal, and the market quotes the 25-Delta risk reversal as it gives information regarding expectations on the currencies composing the underlying exchange rate through the skewness of the implied volatility surface.

The risk reversal expresses the difference in the implied volatilities of the OTM call and the OTM put. By showing a higher implied volatility for either the call or the put, and thus implying a higher price for such an option, this tells us the direction in which the market expects the underlying to move. If the volatility of put options is higher, it means that the implied

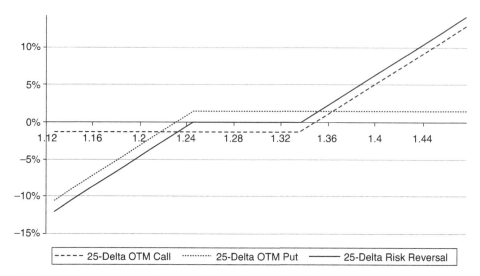

Figure 18.3 The payout of a risk reversal. It combines calls and puts in what is usually referred to as a collar.

distribution of returns is skewed in its expectation of a possible large downward movement and small but more frequent upward movements, much as for the case of the equity skew. This case is referred to as a negative risk reversal. In a positive risk reversal the opposite holds and the market places higher volatilities on call options, suggesting that the distribution is skewed in the opposite manner, and reflects expectations of large possible upward movements but with low frequency, compared to smaller downward movements of higher frequency – the opposite of the equity case. Risk reversals on a currency pair can change sign over time, and thus the FX market is said to have a stochastic (i.e. random) skew.

Risk reversals are typically quoted by giving the Delta of the call and put, a volatility spread that gives the bid–ask spread on the derivative, and an indication of which is higher between the volatilities of the calls and puts (i.e. which is favoured). Though the 25-Delta risk reversal is somewhat of a standard, one can obtain a quote for a risk reversal with any Delta, for example a 10-Delta corresponding to the risk reversal formed from Europeans with a Delta of 10%. For example, a 1-month 25-Delta risk reversal on USD–EUR can be quoted at 0.2/0.3 with EUR calls favoured over EUR puts, Here, 0.2 and 0.3 correspond to spreads over some mid-volatility, typically the ATM volatility, and these give the bid–ask spreads for the risk reversal in question. Assuming this mid-level to be 10%, then this quote means that the trader is willing to do two things: firstly, to buy the 25-Delta USD put (EUR call) for $10\% + 0.2\% = 10.2\%$ and sell the 25-Delta USD call (EUR put) for 10%, and, secondly, to sell the 25-Delta USD put (EUR call) for $10\% + 0.3\% = 10.3\%$ and buy the 25-Delta USD call (EUR put) for 10%. The favouring of the EUR call over the EUR put means that the trader is bid–asking the EUR call price at 10.2–10.3%, and leaving the EUR put volatility at the mid level of 10%.

Straddles, Strangles and Butterfly Spreads

Straddles and strangles are also option strategies that are constructed using European options, and these were discussed in Chapter 6. Both of these, like the risk reversal, are quite popular in FX and there is a liquid market for them in many currencies. In fact, these are also standard in the sense that it is quotes from these, like the risk reversal, that are used to give information regarding the market's view on the underlying currencies through their implied volatilities. Again the strikes of the European options composing these products are specified in terms of their Deltas.

A straddle position consists of two long positions, one in a call and one in a put. If we recall, a straddle can be constructed at a strike that is specified so that the Delta of the straddle is zero at initiation. In the case of FX, the ATM straddle refers to the straddle that is struck at a strike for which the Delta of the position is zero. As in the case of equities, this strike will be at or very close to the forward price, and it is this zero Delta feature that made the straddle a traditional method for trading volatility in equity derivatives. A European option comprising a straddle must, of course, have the same maturity.

Going long a strangle, one is again long two call options but with different strikes. A 25-Delta strangle is composed of a long position in a 25-Delta call option and a long position in a 25-Delta put option. The strangle, combined with knowledge of the ATM straddle implied volatility, gives us a measure of convexity. The reason is that these two combine to give a butterfly spread.

Butterfly spreads, often referred to as *Flys* in FX, are another options strategy, and also one that we have seen in section 4.2.1 of Chapter 4 under the discussion of convexity of implied volatility skews, and section 6.3.1 of Chapter 6 under option strategies. A risk reversal contains two options and it gives us information regarding which way the market is skewed, whereas the butterfly spread involves three European option strikes and gives us a measure of the convexity of the smile. In FX, the butterfly spread will involve European options struck ATM and at the two strikes corresponding to a specific Delta for each European option on either side.

Butterflys that are constructed from straddles and strangles take an inverted shape to those we saw before. Figure 18.4 shows the payoff of a short position in a butterfly

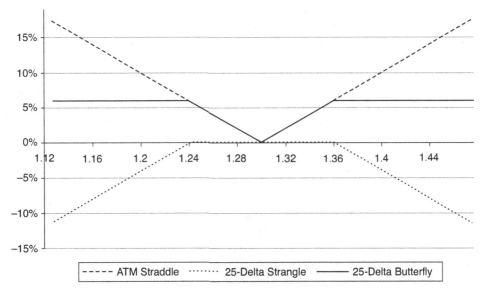

Figure 18.4 The payout of a short position in a butterfly spread. This is formed using an ATM straddle and a 25-Delta strangle.

spread as the combination of a long position in an ATM straddle and a short position in a strangle.

The method for quoting a butterfly spread, other than the maturity and Delta specification of the away-from-the-money options involved in its construction, is again a volatility spread. For example, a 1-month 25-Delta strangle quoted at 0.2/0.38 implies that the trader is willing to buy 25-Delta strangles at a volatility spread of 0.2% over the implied volatility of the ATM (zero Delta) straddle. It also means that she is willing to sell the 25-Delta strangle for a volatility of 0.38% over the same ATM straddle. The ATM straddle's implied volatility will govern whether the trader would rather buy or sell the strangle. If it is closer to the 0.2% then she favours buying the strangle over selling it; if closer to the 0.38%, then selling the strangle is favoured, and if it is right in the middle of this spread, i.e. 0.29%, then the trader is equally willing to buy or sell the strangle.

Garman–Kohlhagen, SABR and Smiles

When quoting Deltas for any of the options above, these always refer to the Black–Scholes Deltas that are computed using the implied volatilities of the quotes. To be correct, it is the Garman and Kohlhagen formula that is used. This allows for a standard method of computing the strikes of the above options and agreeing on Deltas. It is key to have a standard method to compute the Delta if this is to be exchanged as part of the transaction. So the 25-Delta call with an implied volatility of 10% is the call option whose strike is such that when this strike and implied volatility are used in the Garman and Kohlhagen formula, and the Delta is computed, it will be equal to 0.25.

To capture the smile, one has to venture beyond the Black–Scholes framework. A local volatility can be used, although the SABR model discussed in section 17.1.8 is a market standard in FX. Since most vanilla contracts in FX are written on forward rates, the SABR model, which models a forward rate, lends itself perfectly to the pricing and risk management of a portfolio of FX vanillas. Further details on the SABR model appear in section A.3.2 in, Appendix A.

The parameters of the SABR model have direct links to the discussed options. The volatility parameter, α, will control the level of the smile, and this volatility level is known through the market's quotes for ATM straddles. The correlation ρ between the underlying and the volatility controls the skew, $\partial\sigma(K)/\partial K$, which in the FX market we know through quotes of risk reversals. The vol-of vol parameter ν controls the smile's curvature, $\partial^2\sigma(K)/\partial K^2$, for which we also have the market values of strangles. Calibrating a SABR model to these points will give us the set of parameters that capture the market information of level, skew and curvature of the implied volatility smile. The β parameter can be used in the calibration, and as the local volatility parameter of the model it controls the deterministic skew; however, it is usually specified in advance based on *a priori*, and held constant. For example, the case of $\beta = 1$ refers to log-normal dynamics for the underlying and all other parameters are calibrated with this β fixed.

What makes this model significant is not only the intuitiveness of its parameters and their interpretations, but the dynamics generated by this model are consistent with what is observed in the market regarding how the skew moves as the underlying moves, $\partial\sigma_{\text{ATM}}/\partial S$. As such, the model yields much more realistic hedge ratios. The benefits that were clear in the interest rate case also hold here in that this model is essentially a closed form extension to Black–Scholes, is lightning fast, and serves as an excellent tool for risk managing a portfolio of European options in FX.

18.1.3   FX Implied Correlations

The nature of exchange rates means that in certain cases one can compute the implied correlation between two exchange rates. Consider two exchange rates with the same domestic
currency, for example the EUR–USD and the JPY–USD, then we know the EUR–JPY exchange rate as the quotient of these two. Call the two exchange rates of common domestic
currency R_1 and R_2, and their quotient $R_3 = R_1/R_2$. Assume that we have implied volatilities
for each of these three exchange rates, obtained from vanilla options on each, then applying
the Black–Scholes assumption of log-normality of these rates, we know that the quotient of
two log-normals is also log-normal.

$$\ln\left(\frac{R_1}{R_2}\right) = \ln R_1 - \ln R_2$$

both of $\ln R_1$ and $\ln R_2$ are normally distributed (recall a log-normal random variable is one
whose logarithm is normally distributed), and their difference thus also normally distributed.
On the one hand, we know the implied volatility of R_3 from the market, but we also know it must
be a function of the volatilities of R_1 and R_2 according to the above equation. Working with
variances, we know $\mathrm{Var}(\ln R_3) = \sigma^2(R_3)$ on the one hand, but also from the FX relationship
above that

$$\begin{aligned}
\mathrm{Var}(\ln R_3) &= \mathrm{Var}(\ln R_1/R_2) \\
&= \mathrm{Var}(\ln R_1) + \mathrm{Var}(\ln R_2) - 2\mathrm{Cov}(\ln R_1, \ln R_2) \\
&= \sigma^2(R_1) + \sigma^2(R_2) - 2\rho_{1,2}\,\sigma(R_1)\sigma(R_2)
\end{aligned}$$

Substituting the market value of $\mathrm{Var}(R_3)$ into this equation and solving for $\rho_{1,2}$ we find that

$$\rho_{1,2} = \frac{\sigma^2(R_1) + \sigma^2(R_2) - \sigma^2(R_3)}{2\,\sigma(R_1)\sigma(R_2)}$$

where the right-hand side of this equation is all implied from the vanilla markets of each of
the three exchange rates.

Wystup (2002) gives a geometric interpretation of this and describes how the same concept
can be extended to multiple currencies. The key observation is that because of the nature of
the FX market and in light of the above formulas, FX correlation risk can be transformed into
a volatility risk, and hedging this correlation risk is thus possible by using adjusted Vegas.
This can be extremely useful when handling baskets of currencies.

18.1.4   FX Exotics

FX exotics, like the other asset classes, can be used for tailoring specific market views, hedging
specific FX risks, or even be structured to offer higher yields or better diversification. Digital
options and barriers are especially popular in FX, and it is possible to find broker quotes for
some barrier and digital options, making them more liquid in comparison to their counterparts
in different asset classes. Many different types of barrier options exist in FX and below we
mention a few of them.

An interesting example of a barrier option is the *Parisian* barrier. This is a knock-out option,
where the option knocks out only if the underlying spends a certain amount of time above
(or below, depending on the position of the barrier) the barrier. As such, this differs from the
simple barrier that knocks out if the underlying crosses the barrier at any point in time. The

idea behind the Parisian barrier is that if the underlying is close to the barrier, a short spike in the underlying won't cause the option to knock out (or knock in). For example, consider an up-and-out ATM call option that has a Parisian barrier at 125%, monitored daily, and of length five business days. Then the call option will only knock out if the barrier spends five or more days above this 125% barrier.

The Parisian barrier option will obviously be worth more than the simple barrier and will increase in price the longer the length of time the underlying has to spend beyond the barrier. A key feature of the Parisian barrier option is that its Greeks are far smoother at the barrier than the simple barrier option case, and as such alleviate some of the related issues that arose in Chapter 10. An interesting variation on the barrier option would be to decrease the participation in the call option above for each day the underlying spends beyond the barrier. For example, the call option can start with 100% participation and decrease by 12.5% each day the underlying spends beyond the barrier.

It is of course possible to structure a basket option where the underlying assets are all exchange rates. These will typically have a common domestic currency and the specification of different foreign currencies gives the different exchange rates in the basket. The analysis of baskets in Chapter 7 generally holds, and the addition of multiple assets helps to lower the overall volatility of the basket, compared to the volatility of a single underlying. For example, the basket can consist of differently weighted emerging market currencies' exchange rates with the EUR.

Forward skew-dependent payoffs such as cliquets are also found in the FX market. The cliquet style and related payoffs seen in Chapters 13 and 14 can be structured with FX rates as underlyings. The issues regarding forward skew and Vega convexity will still hold, but depending on the style of cliquet, the skew effect may be different, as it will, even for regular digitals, compared to equities, because of the presence of a smile.

Variance and volatility swaps are also traded in FX, and these are the same payoffs we saw in Chapter 16. Again these are essentially forward contracts on the future realized variance (or volatility) of an FX rate. The general model free replication results will still hold for the payoff of variance swaps on an FX, however the effect of skew may be slightly different to equities because of the FX smile. The formulas will also change to allow for foreign interest rates instead of dividends. The methods for trading skew using corridor and conditional variance swaps will also be different for this reason. Volatility derivatives in FX again serve the purpose of providing pure exposure to volatility, and as such allow an investor to trade the volatility of an FX rate directly.

18.2 INFLATION

This section deals with inflation as an asset class. The inflation market may not be as liquid as the previous ones, but it does have many uses, and it is a market that has witnessed considerable growth recently and does not appear to be losing momentum. In this section we discuss inflation and focus on the inflation products that exist from inflation swap and bond to inflation derivatives, with the ultimate goal of combining other asset classes with inflation in multi-asset class payoffs. In the literature, pricing inflation derivatives and related products are discussed, among others, by Hughston (1998). Inflation products and in-depth uses and motivations are covered extensively in Deacon *et al.* (2004).

18.2.1   Inflation and the Need for Inflation Products

Inflation is the increase in the price of a basket of goods and services over time. The basket in question is a weighted collection of goods and services that serves as a representative for a whole economy. Essentially, when inflation occurs, the general price of goods rises, which means that the purchasing power of a specific currency is lower, meaning that the real value of a unit of currency is lower. Deflation is the opposite phenomenon referring to the case where the same basket of goods has declined in price.

An inflation rate is a measurement of how inflation has changed over a period of time. To have an inflation rate there must be an inflation index – that is, the dynamically weighted basket as above that is modified to continuously reflect the general price of goods and services in an economy – and these are referred to as "Consumer Price Indices" (CPIs). The percentage changes of such an index are a measurement of the inflation rate, and the main CPI indices of specific countries are typically computed by government agencies – for example, the UK RPI (retail price index), the US CPI, and the Eurozone's HICP. Such indices are widely monitored because the inflation rate is a key consideration for many financial decisions, including the interest rate policies of central banks. These indices are not directly tradeable, but are accessible via futures markets on such indices (for example, futures contracts on the CPI trade on the Chicago Mercantile Exchange). The price of these futures is informative because their prices represent some form of market consensus regarding the index itself. Some inflation index futures are, however, not very long dated.

In the context of inflation, it is key to define the terms *nominal* interest rate and *real* interest rate. The nominal interest rate is a rate of interest that has not been adjusted to account for inflation. Take a government bond that pays 4% per annum, then the rate of 4% is a nominal rate of interest. Assume that an investor purchases such a bond and collects the 4% on top of the notional back after the first year, then it is not necessary for the buying power of the amount of money he currently holds (104% of the notional amount) to have gone up by 4%. If the rate of inflation that same year were 1.5%, then it means the buying power of the new notional is in fact 1.5% less. The real interest rate is (approximately) the difference between the nominal interest rate and the inflation rate for the same period. The real interest rate is thus the inflation-adjusted nominal interest rate, in this case given by $4\% - 1.5\% = 2.5\%$.

Many investors are concerned with the buying power of their money, and even in the case of, for example, a capital guaranteed note, with redemption of at least 100%, the 100% of notional is in fact worthless in real terms if the currency has witnessed (positive) inflation. When inflation occurs, the time value of such a notional is in fact decreasing, and many investors want to be protected against these inflation risks. The need for inflation products thus arises, and the client base is quite large because many investors need to have inflation-linked returns. For example, a large corporation that must give annual salary increases equal to the inflation rate, does not know in advance what the rate of inflation will be for the upcoming year(s), and thus needs a method of hedging this risk. Other examples would be investors who want to take a direct view on an inflation rate going up or down, and need a method of expressing such speculative views.

18.2.2   Inflation Swaps

In a typical inflation swap, two counterparties exchange cashflows where one party pays a fixed (or possibly floating) rate in exchange for a floating rate that is linked to a measure of inflation such as a CPI index. The inflation swap, like other swaps, is entered into at zero cost, which means that the fixed rate side of the swap reflects the market's consensus on inflationary expectations. Inflation swaps are typically computed on the basis of compounded rates, meaning that the payer of the fixed leg will pay a compounded fixed rate on the swap dates and receive the cumulative rate of change in the inflation index. For example, a 5-year swap at a fixed swap rate of 1.78% will pay the rate of 1.78% compounded, on the notional, in exchange for the compounded change in inflation, thus hedging the notional from inflation in exchange for the fixed cost. This is known as a zero coupon inflation swap, and is a fundamental building block in inflation markets.

A different inflation swap would be the year-on-year inflation swap. In this swap, the payer of the fixed rate at the end of each year will pay an amount equal to the notional times this fixed rate, and receive the annual period to period return of an inflation index given by

$$\text{Notional} \times \left(\frac{\text{CPI Index}(n)}{\text{CPI Index}(n-1)} - 1 \right)$$

where n goes from 1 up to the number of years specified in the contract of the swap. This type of swap would be better suited to an investor who needs to receive annual payments linked to the inflation rate that was realized during that year in order to meet some obligation. Additionally it is useful to a speculative investor who believes that the current market consensus on the fair swap rate is high and is willing to pay inflation and receive fixed with the view that inflation will be lower than anticipated.

The case of deflation is also included in the swap, as described above, in that if inflation decreases over one or more years, then the return on the index will be negative and the payer of the fixed leg will end up paying both legs of the swap. To avoid this, a floor can be introduced into the floating leg payments.

18.2.3 Inflation Bonds

Instead of offering a nominal rate of interest that is common to most bonds, an inflation bond's rates are based upon real interest rates. The nominal rate appearing in bonds does not account for inflation and is thus generally higher than the real interest rate yields offered on inflation-linked bonds. Inflation bonds are not new as many sovereign entities have issued inflation-linked bonds for many years. These are known as inflation-indexed bonds, where the notional is indexed to inflation. In the UK, inflation-linked gilts are linked to the UK RPI, and in the US, for example, there are Treasury inflation-protected securities that are linked to the US CPI. OTC inflation-linked bonds offered by some corporations will have a yield that is just the rate of a government issued inflation-linked bond plus a spread corresponding to the creditworthiness of the issuer.

18.2.4 Inflation Derivatives

Inflation swaps and bonds allow investors to gain exposure to inflation, or transfer inflation risk, but more tailored views or needs regarding inflation may be required. This has spurred the development of inflation derivatives that allow parties to transfer inflation risk in many different forms. It is possible to trade options on some CPI indices, although many of these are OTC and one has to rely on broker quotes for prices.

Inflation caps and floors are a good way to take a leveraged view on inflation. Payment from an inflation cap, like the interest rate cap, comes from a series of inflation caplets. The cap can be based on the year-on-year inflation rate, and each caplet has a payoff based on an inflation index I, and the payoff of the ith caplet is given by

$$\text{Caplet}_{\text{payoff}}(i) = \max \left[0, \frac{I(t_i) - I(t_{i-1})}{I(t_{i-1})} - K \right]$$

where the index i runs over all maturity dates for the caplets. Each of these payoffs is essentially a call option on the inflation rate with strike K. The payoff will be multiplied by a notional amount. Other than the first, the caplets based upon year-on-year inflation are forward starting. If the periods over which the caplet is taken are unequal, then the strike can be specified differently as $K \times (t_i - t_{i-1})$ to reflect this. Inflation floors and floorlets are the put option analogy of caps and caplets.

A caplet, as such, is related to the yields of a coupon paying a year-on-year inflation-linked bond if these rates are floored to avoid negative coupons from deflation. Quotes for inflation caps will exhibit an inflation implied volatility smile where looked at across strikes, and this will need to be captured by a modelling assumption to price more elaborate inflation-linked derivatives whose hedges rely on caps of different strikes. The smile can be explained as normal by the market's supply and demand for options of different strikes. Quotes involving implied volatilities will again correspond to prices through Black's model.

The inflation cap can be based on the zero coupon inflation swap, and in this case the caplets are just call options on the zero coupon swaps and are typically spot starting. The more popular option involving the zero coupon inflation swap is the inflation swaption, that is, the analogy of the interest rate swaption. In an inflation receiver swaption, the holder has the right to pay the floating leg of an inflation swap, and in the payer inflation swaption the right to enter into an inflation swap and pay the fixed leg.

18.3   CREDIT

Credit generally refers to borrowing power. In a transaction where one party lends money to another, credit risk arises, and this is the risk that the debtor will be unable to repay the amount of money, the interest charged on it, or both. The borrowing power of an individual or corporation is based upon how much credit risk the party lending the money will have to assume in the transaction. It is the party that owed (or will be owed) money that is subject to this risk and the greater the credit risk, the more the lender will want to be compensated for lending money. Both the ability and the willingness of the borrower to repay are factors.

Credit ratings are used to assess the creditworthiness of an entity, be it an individual, a company or even a country. Credit rating agencies use the levels of assets and liabilities, and the entity's financial history when allocating a rating. Credit ratings will in turn be used by a lender to assess the risk of lending money to such an entity, giving an idea about the borrower's ability to meet whatever obligations there are within a financial transaction.

Credit derivatives are financial contracts involving two counterparties that derive value by removing (at least part of) the credit risk from a financial instrument, and allowing it to be transferred between the two parties. The financial instrument whose credit risk underlies the credit derivative need not involve the two counterparties of the credit derivative itself. These have allowed for tailored solutions for the previously unhedgeable credit risk involved in many facets of business. The credit market witnessed huge growth in recent years, but certain aspects of the credit market were to blame for starting the crash of 2008.

The key instruments in the credit markets are

- Bonds with default risk
- Credit default swaps (CDS)
- Collateralized debt obligations (CDO).

18.3.1 Bonds and Default Risk

In a bond, the issuer must repay the principal to the holder at maturity. The coupon offered on a bond will reflect the issuer's creditworthiness because the holder of the bond has essentially loaned the notional to the issuer, and the coupon will reflect the risk the holder is taking on by buying the bond. The idea behind a bond is that it offers a return but at a lower volatility to an equity for example; however, bonds are not risk free: the buyer still runs the (credit) risk that the issuer of the bond will be unable to repay the notional at maturity (or perhaps not even the interest on the bond).

A higher credit risk of an issuer will generally be reflected in a higher yield on the bonds being issued. Treasury bonds are considered the safest of all bonds because they carry a low probability of default. Other bonds will offer a higher yield, of which the spread over the rate of government bonds will be a function of the risk involved in loaning the money to the issuer along with the length of time the money is to be loaned. The greater the maturity of the bond, the greater the risk of default on the bond and thus the higher the spread. Figure 18.5 gives an example of some yields of bonds of differently rated issuers.

A corporation, for example, may issue a bond that is not backed by collateral, but in the event that the corporation does default, a liquidation follows, and bond holders receive money

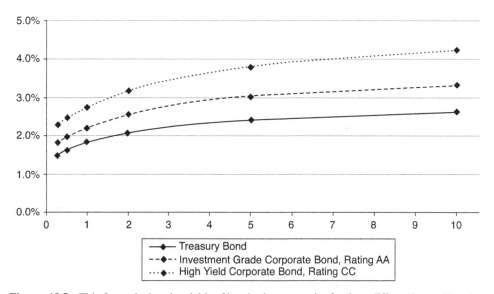

Figure 18.5 This figure depicts the yields of bonds along maturity for three differently rated bonds.

based on seniority. In some cases they may receive all their money, in others only cents on the dollar. The greater this risk, the greater the investor (holder) in the bond will expect to be compensated through higher coupons on the bond.

Junk bonds are higher yielding bonds that are rated as "below investment grade" by the relevant credit-rating agencies. For a bond to be investment grade at the time of issuance, the credit-rating agencies must rate the issuer as likely to be able to meet all related obligations. Junk bonds do not fall into this category, and are judged at the time of issuance to be more risky than investment grade bonds. The higher yield on such bonds reflects this.

18.3.2   Credit Default Swaps

A credit default swap (CDS) is an OTC credit derivative based upon the debt of a company, a sovereign entity, and possibly a credit index such as the iTraxx or the Dow Jones. The buyer of the CDS makes some form of payment to the seller (this leg is known as the premium leg), in exchange for a payoff in the event the issuer of the underlying debt defaults (known as the default leg). In the event of default, the holder of the CDS on debt in the form of a bond, has bought the right to sell the bond, at par, to the party who sold the CDS protection.

The price of a CDS that insures a notional amount of a specific debt, is given by the percentage of this notional that the seller of the CDS will receive, on an annual basis, in exchange for offering this protection. This percentage is referred to as a CDS *spread*. The annual payments typically continue until either the CDS contract expires, or a default occurs.

A CDS can thus serve as a tool for managing credit (default) risk by protecting invested notionals from the event of a default. For example, if an investor is long a corporate bond, then a CDS can provide a hedge that offsets the losses incurred if the issuing corporation defaults on the bond. A *negative basis trade* is a single-name credit trading strategy in which the investor buys both a bond and the CDS on the same name. When the CDS spread is less than the spread on the bond, the investor receives a spread while being protected from default risk.

The CDS spread on the debt of an issuing entity will generally be greater the less creditworthy is the issuer. Vice versa, as an entity's creditworthiness increases, the CDS spread on its debt will decrease. The greater the CDS spread of an entity, the greater the market perceives the possibility of the entity defaulting. For example: the cost of protecting $1,000,000 of debt issued by a corporation can be 25 bp per annum, which means that the buyer of a CDS on this notional of debt will have to pay the seller of the CDS $2,500 per year. If this corporation were to be downgraded by the rating agencies, then this CDS spread will increase, reflecting the greater risk in insuring its debt. CDSs thus allow an investor to take a speculative view on an entity's creditworthiness and the probability that he will or will not default. This is also made easier because CDS contracts can be cash settled.

CDS Indices

The popularity of CDSs has spurred the development of tradeable CDS indices that are standardized credit securities, compared to CDSs that are OTC derivatives. These indices allow for exposure to multiple credits, and can thus be used to hedge credit risk or take speculative positions in a range of credits. The standardization of these indices is key to enhancing their liquidity, allowing for investors to take positions for small bid–ask spreads. This makes trading a CDS index the more cost-efficient method to hedge or take a view on a basket of CDSs, compared to buying all the CDSs separately.

The composition of a CDS index is designed to offer specific exposure to underlyings from a sector, region or similar credit quality. Each has an index methodology, typically focused on the liquidity of the underlying CDSs. Based upon the triggering of a specific credit event on one of the names, it may be removed from the index. Futures are traded on such indices, through an exchange, and these are cash settled on expiry. Additionally, OTC derivatives are traded on the CDS indices. Two examples of such indices are the iTraxx and the CDX. For a comprehensive discussion of credit derivatives we refer the reader to O'Kane (2008).

19

Structuring Hybrid Derivatives

Where there is no strife there is decay: The mixture which is not shaken decomposes.

Heraclitus

In this chapter we combine the asset classes we have seen so far, and give examples of various hybrids. A hybrid product serves as an investment vehicle with a specific payoff and risk profile that is based upon underlyings from various asset classes, compared to a multi-asset equity derivative whose underlyings are from the same asset class. The functions of hybrid derivatives are no different to the equity derivatives seen throughout the book, with assets from multi-asset classes now replacing multiple equities, and the standard breakdown of uses for hybrid derivatives follows suit. Hybrids can serve various purposes including diversification, yield enhancement, serve as speculation vehicles for multi-asset class views and as hedging instruments for multi-asset class risk. It is possible to combine these asset classes in a suitable payoff to serve any of these purposes. In the literature, Overhaus *et al.* (2007) discuss hybrid derivatives with a focus on pricing models, and Hunter and Picot (2005/2006) discuss the functionality of hybrid derivatives.

We have at our disposal the wealth of possible structures and multi-asset payoffs addressed in the previous chapters, many, if not all, of which can be extended to work on multiple asset classes – with some caution and a dose of common sense. The possible range of investors is thus quite broad. Hybrids can be structured for retail clients of banks seeking features such as capital protection, yield enhancement or risk reduction. Institutional investors can also obtain hybrid products to express their macro-economic views in a single instrument through a multi-asset class option – however specific these views. Additionally, any corporation or portfolio manager with multi-asset class exposures can use hybrid derivatives to hedge multi-asset class risk in an efficient manner and through a single derivative.

Following suit with all the multi-asset options we have seen so far, the investor might be taking a view on a set of paths for assets of various asset classes, but in different structures the investor can be long or short the forwards of the underlyings, their volatilities and the correlations between them. In an outperformance option, the long investor is short the forward of one underlying and long the other, and also short the correlation between the underlyings of the outperformance. In a basket call option, for example, the buyer of the option is long both the volatilities of the underlyings, the correlations between them and the forwards of the underlying assets. A hybrid derivative can be constructed to express a view on any one or more of these.

We break the chapter down into sections, each based upon one of the motivations behind the creation of hybrid derivatives. Multiple examples involving possible structures are given in each section.

19.1 DIVERSIFICATION

In Chapter 7 we discussed the concept of horizontal diversification, which involves the use of multiple assets of a similar type. When combining assets from different asset classes, we now refer to this form of diversification as *vertical*. A *horizontal* diversification can reduce the risk to one single asset, but when considering multiple stocks, for example, its effectiveness is weakened when all such stocks are impacted in the same manner by economic events, and adding additional stocks to a portfolio of stocks will not reduce this risk.

The risk reduction obtained from adding multiple assets to a portfolio is not only dependent on the individual asset volatilities, but also on the correlations between these assets. Recall the approximate formula for the variance of a portfolio:

$$\sigma_P^2 = \sum_{i=1}^n \sum_{j=1}^n w_i w_j \sigma_i \sigma_j \rho_{ij}$$

By selecting assets from multi-asset classes one can find assets that have relatively low historical correlations, compared to those observed among equities. Although there is no guarantee that these correlations will stay low, they do provide a more diversified portfolio than the horizontal diversification case. In recent years, globalization and other factors have contributed to the increases in the correlations between various assets from both different and identical asset classes. However, there exist economic reasons as to why we expect certain asset classes to be affected very differently by economic events, and their cycles to look quite different. As such, using multi-asset classes to diversify, should over time offer enhanced and consistent returns, while reducing the overall risk.

19.1.1 Multi-asset Class Basket Options

The simplest multi-asset class option that serves this purpose is the basket option discussed in section 7.3 of Chapter 7, where the option's payoff is contingent on the performance of a basket of assets, here from multi-asset classes. The effects of volatility and correlation on the basket option hold even if the assets are from different asset classes. The more non-perfectly correlated assets we add, the more the overall volatility of the basket is reduced and the price of a basket call or put option decreases accordingly. The volatility of the returns of an asset will affect that of the basket and thus the decision to add it as an additional asset class depends on this volatility. The choice to add an additional asset class to such a basket to enhance this diversification effect will also be based on its correlation with the remaining elements of the basket. The seller of a call or put option on a basket will be short both the volatilities of each of the components and the correlations between them. The weights of individual assets in the basket option do not have to be equal, but their sum must be unity.

Even if an investor were bullish on the US economy, buying a single option on the S&P index, or even a basket option on a number of US stocks, the risk of a market crash that would decrease all such equities still remains. This risk can only be removed by adding an additional asset class, for example gold. The basket of the S&P 500 index (equities) and the USD price of gold (commodities), in different weights even, will lower the volatility compared to both individual options. The correlation between gold and equities is not necessarily negative, but gold, which is generally considered to be a safe haven, will offer quite different returns to equities, particularly during a crash in equities.

A basket option combining the two, along with some form of averaging to capture the possible different market regimes and include these quite possibly different returns, would be a much more diversified bet. A simple capital protected structure combined with the call option on just the S&P 500 would not cost the investor any money. However, the downside of possibly not getting any return above the 100% guaranteed notional is lowered at the cost of a perhaps lower return, should the equity markets rally in a big way.

Another example can be to combine an equity index (EuroStoxx50), a commodity index (Dow Jones AIG commodity index), and a bond index (iBoxx). These three possible underlyings have very different return structures and volatilities, making them an interesting combination to have in a diversification instrument. Allowing for some averaging will allow the basket to pick up these differences more easily.

The correlations between equities and interest rates go through periods of different levels, but historically bonds exhibit a low correlation to equities. Bonds are typically used along with a portfolio of equities to lower the overall volatility and benefit from this low correlation, which allows for diversification. Additionally, bonds will still provide some income, compared to using just cash. Though the potential returns from bonds are lower than returns from the other two asset classes, the inclusion of bonds will help to generate at least some return in the event that equities perform quite poorly.

The correlation between equities and interest rates is affected by many things, including inflation and the business cycle. The addition of the commodity index serves as an inflationary hedge in the basket. Historically, commodity indices are positively correlated with inflation, but not strongly correlated with either bonds or equities, and as such the basket is quite well diversified.

Additionally, one can enter inflation directly into the payout of the basket as an additional asset to enhance diversification. Inflation has low to negative historical correlations with equities, although inflation does exhibit strong correlations to commodities such as oil. Alternatively, the deal can be structured to include some form of inflation bond, in addition to a capital guarantee feature to also protect against rising inflation.

19.1.2 Multi-asset Class Himalaya

The Himalaya structure described in section 15.2 of Chapter 15 on mountain range options, allows the investor to lock-in the performance of an asset before it is subsequently removed from the basket. This type of payoff can be quite well suited to assets that have very different return structures because it will allow the investor to pick up these different returns as the market cycles change. This can be more suited to investors who are looking for a different exposure and possible set of returns on the options than the simple basket.

An example would be a 3-year Himalaya option for the investor who believes that a bear market will persist in the short–medium term (oil to possibly outperform US equities and bonds), but is bullish long term (US equities and bonds to outperform oil), and wants to obtain a return each year above a fixed market rate. Additionally, the USD–EUR rate can be added (USD to appreciate), in relevance to its historically negative correlation with oil prices, adding diversification. The Himalaya on a basket of the four assets of US equities, US bonds, USD vs EUR (USD to appreciate), and oil, works by taking the assets with the best return each year, locking in this return, and removing this asset from the basket. Payments can be made annually to make this into an income product, or the returns paid at maturity as some weighted average. Other mountain range options from Chapter 15 can also be structured to include multi-asset classes instead of just multiple equity underlyings.

19.2   YIELD ENHANCEMENT

The next possible use for hybrids would be to benefit from the possible low correlations between some assets from different asset classes in order to enhance yields. The idea behind yield enhancement is to form a payoff of multi-asset classes that increases the leverage to offer a higher expected return but with increased risk. Investors seeking higher yields in light of the low interest rate environment currently observed in the global economy can turn to hybrids as a possibility. The possible set of enhanced yields will obviously be a function of how much additional risk is taken, but we differentiate between an investor seeking a higher yield through hybrids and an investor who is taking an aggressive and specific view on multi-asset classes.

Again we have at our disposal many yield enhancing payoffs from the multi-asset equity cases discussed in previous chapters. Other than explicit dispersion payoffs we also have the entire mountain range option that could potentially be extended to include multi-asset classes. These serve a different purpose to diversification and use multiple assets in order to increase leverage as discussed in Chapters 8 and 9. Barriers and digitals on multi-asset classes can also provide enhanced yields. We also make use of callable features that can make the prices of such options more favourable to the buyer, and thus a callable feature can allow for an increased participation for the same price as the non-callable version with a lower participation.

19.2.1 Rainbows

The rainbow, discussed in Chapter 9 under dispersion options, pays a weighted average of the performances of a basket of underlying assets where the weights are specified according to how the assets performed during the life of the option. These lie between basket options and best-of and worst-of options – depending on how the weights are distributed. For example, a 50%, 30%, 20% rainbow that pays 50% of the best performing asset, 30% of the second best, and 20% of the third lies between a best-of option (100% on the best performing) and the equally weighted basket option. This will be priced higher than the basket option but offers a better return, reflected in this higher premium, and still serves the purpose of diversification.

To leverage the rainbow payout to serve yield enhancement is to make it a more leveraged instrument than the diversifying basket option. Lower weights can be placed on the best performing in order to lower the price and increase leverage. In this case the rainbow behaves more like a worst-of option, and the resulting lower price can allow for a higher participation rate and lead to potentially enhanced returns in exchange for the increased risk.

To have a 3-coloured rainbow option, the underlying basket will need to consist of at least three different assets. For example, a retail product providing emerging market exposure along with some asset class diversity can be constructed by adding a rainbow option to a capital guaranteed note. Taking Brazil as an example of an emerging market that has performed well in recent times, especially with respect to similar economies, one can have a 50%, 30%, 20% rainbow option on a basket consisting of the Brazilian equity index the Bovespa, the Brazil Real versus the USD (BRL to appreciate w.r.t. the USD), and a commodity such as oil (WTI futures, for example). This provides a diverse exposure, and will definitely be cheaper than the sum of single options on each of the underlyings, but will have a higher expected yield than the basket option.

To use the rainbow as a yield enhancer, for example, consider a bullish view on the global economy to recover with equities to rise, real estate to rise and oil to rise. This view can be structured into a leveraged payoff by taking a 25%, 35%, 40% rainbow on the basket of these three, for example the S&P 500, the EPRA real estate index and WTI futures. The 25% weighting on the best performing, compared to the 40% weight on the worst, makes this rainbow behave more like a worst-of option. This rainbow will thus be cheaper than the call option on the basket (assuming equal weights) and participation in it could be increased to offer higher leverage for the same cost. A more extreme leveraging would be to simply take 100% weight on the worst-of, making it a worst-of option.

The correlations and volatilities in this example would be higher than the above basket, and the return structures more similar. The seller of a rainbow option, however, is not necessarily short correlation. A higher correlation adds to the overall volatility of the basket of underlying assets, however it also increases the effect of dispersion; the net effect depending on the weights of the rainbow. The discussion of Chapter 9 holds in regard to volatility and correlation in rainbow options. The skew effect must also be looked at, especially because now the assets included may have very differently behaving implied volatility skews – or smiles. This is discussed in further detail when modelling multi-asset class skews in the next chapter on the pricing of hybrid derivatives.

19.2.2   In- and Out-barriers

Adding barriers to payoffs as we saw in Chapter 10 can also reduce the price and offer a similar yield but with higher risk reflected in the decreased premium. A simple knock-out call option is cheaper than its vanilla counterpart, reflected in the higher risk that the option will knock out. An investor willing to take potentially enhanced yields in exchange for a view that the underlying will follow a specific path, can include barriers to decrease prices and increase leverage.

We refer to the case of an in-barrier for the barrier option in which the barrier is triggered by an underlying that is included in the final payout (for example, a call option on a basket with a knock-out clause on one of the underlyings), and the out-barrier for the case where the option's knock-out (or knock-in) clause is specified on an asset not included in the payout (for example, a knock-out call option on S&P 500 that knocks out if interest rates breach a certain barrier). Interesting examples of both can be constructed using multi-asset classes.

An example of a hybrid derivative with a knock-out in-barrier can be obtained by adding the knock-out feature on the first basket example of equities and gold. The barrier can be specified on the basket or on one of the individual assets; for example, a 3-year basket option that pays the weighted average performance of the basket of S&P 500 and gold, as long as the price of gold does not go above 140% of its price at the onset. The addition of the barrier decreases the price of the option reflecting the added knock-out risk, and the participation can be increased and the potential yield thus enhanced, in exchange for this additional risk.

A hybrid option with an out-barrier can, for example, be an ATM call option on the S&P 500, with a knock-out barrier on gold. The investor is bullish on US equities, but also believes that even if gold increases it won't go above 130% of its initial value during the life of the option. As long as gold never breaches this barrier on any of the observation periods for the barrier, the option is still alive. The more frequent the observation on gold, the more possible the barrier will be breached and the S&P 500 call option knocked out, and the cheaper the option. Lowering the barrier closer to the 100% level has the same effect.

19.2.3   Multi-asset Class Digitals

Digital options can be structured to involve a digital view on multi-asset classes. For example, an option that pays a fixed coupon of $X\%$ if both oil and equities are above their current levels in a year from now represents a bullish view on both asset classes. At maturity T the payoff is given by

$$\text{Double Digital}_{\text{payoff}} = X\% \times \mathbf{1}_{\{\text{S\&P }500(T) > \text{S\&P }500(0)\}} \times \mathbf{1}_{\{\text{Oil}(T) > \text{Oil}(0)\}}$$

In this payoff the digital strike for each asset is the same; we are comparing time T prices of the assets with time 0 prices. When this is the case, the payoff is in fact a worst-of digital, which has been discussed in Chapter 11. The strikes, however, need not be equal, and one could compare with 110% of the time 0 price for example, of one asset or both.

The higher the correlation between these two assets, the more chance the option has of ending in-the-money, and the seller of the option is thus short this correlation. The seller is short or long the individual volatilities depending on the position of the forwards. This option will be worth less than the sum of two individual ATM digital call options, so taking the combined view will allow for enhanced leverage. The oil section of the hybrid could be based upon the price of WTI futures, of a specific maturity, increasing during the life of the hybrid. The investor would as such be taking a view on the forward curve. The same analysis of digitals involving multiple equities holds here with regard to the impact of forward price movements on the digital, with attention to the possibility of different smiles and skews.

19.2.4   Multi-asset Range Accruals

By bounding one or more of the underlyings in a range and considering a range accrual on one or more of the possible asset classes, we can again enhance leverage. For example, a payoff can consist of a fixed coupon, paid at maturity, multiplied by the percentage of days that each of two assets spend within their individually specified range. By subjecting the coupon to two assets, the potential coupons, being range bound, will be relatively higher. For example, consider an investor who believes that US equities will rise but not by more than 20%, and that the USD could appreciate versus the EUR but not gain more than 15% against the EUR in the next year. Instead of buying options with barriers or outright digitals, the investor can play both ranges through a double range accrual that only accrues on the days when both these underlyings are within their respective ranges. The leverage will be quite high, and the offered coupon that is multiplied by the percentage of days that both are within the range, would look quite appealing.

Callable Dual Range Accrual: Oil and Equities

Adding a callable feature to an option, where the option is callable by the seller, will make the price more favourable for the buyer. In the case of a callable range accrual on two assets, a more appealing coupon can be offered based upon the same ranges. The idea of the callable feature is the same as the autocallable option of Chapter 12 in that the investor hopes to obtain an above-market fixed rate coupon and the structure to be called in order to get his money back early.

Take an investor who believes that a recession will persist for some time and also believes that oil and equities will stay bound within the 90–115% range for at least the next year and possibly up to 18 months. A semi-annually callable dual range accrual of 18-month maturity will capture this. The investor pays LIBOR in exchange for this potentially above-market coupon, computed semi-annually and paid on maturity, or an earlier date if called.

19.3   MULTI-ASSET CLASS VIEWS

To construct some of the hybrid derivatives seen so far, some market views on multi-asset classes were necessary. Here we describe some slightly more detailed views as examples for which we structure hybrids offering the exact required exposure. The hybrid derivative can be structured as a cheaper alternative to expressing each asset class view separately.

ICBC–CMS Steepener Hybrid

As a first example, consider an investor who is bullish on a specific basket of stocks and also believes that the yield curve will steepen, specifically the difference between the 30-year and 10-year CMS rates. A cheap structure to express the bullish view on the basket is the ICBC of section 9.2 in Chapter 9 where the returns of each stock in the basket are capped from above at a fixed cap, and the returns are then averaged to form the payout. Additionally, the view on the yield curve can be expressed through a CMS steepener option described in section 17.1.9. Combining both of these into a best-of option allows the investor to express this view in a combined manner that is cheaper than two separate views, and in one payoff that will offer a return even if one of these two parts ends out-of-the-money. A payoff for such an option with maturity T could look like

$$\max\left[0, \ \frac{1}{N}\sum_{j=1}^{N}\min\left[\text{Ret}_j(T), \ \text{Cap}\right], X\% \times \left(\text{CMS}_{30y}(T) - \text{CMS}_{10y}(T) - K\right)\right]$$

where $\text{Ret}_j(T)$ is the return of the jth stock among the N stocks of the basket, Cap is the prespecified cap rate and this first part makes up the equity part of the hybrid. In the second component, the two rates are just the time T 30-year and 10-year CMS rates. X is to add increased gearing to the interest rate section of the hybrid, and K is the strike for the CMS steepener, which can be specified so that this part of the option also starts from zero. The zero at the start of the payoff acts as a global floor.

The option contains one parameter for each section that can be modified either (a) to reach a specific overall price for the hybrid, or (b) to increase the potential upside on one of the parts at the cost of lowered potential upside in the other, in the case where we want the price to remain the same. The cap of the ICBC serves as this parameter in the equity part, and the strike of the CMS steepener for the rates part. The gearing of the CMS can also be modified for this purpose. Even though this is a best-of option, and best-of can be expensive (compared to a basket option on the same underlyings), the cap on the ICBC can greatly reduce the price contribution of the equity part (compared to a capped basket call), and the strike and gearing on the CMS part can reduce the interest rate part by lowering the participation or setting it out-of-the-money.

Equity Reverse Geared Basket of Oil and CHF

An investor believes that instability in the middle east in the next year will cause oil prices to rise. Additionally the investor thinks that the CHF (Swiss franc) will appreciate with respect to the EUR, because the Swiss franc has historically been considered a safe haven during times of uncertainty. The investor also expects that this may have a negative impact on US equity markets, and is willing to include an equity view as part of a gearing on an option on the

CHF–EUR rate and oil.

$$\left(200\% - \min\left(\frac{\text{S\&P }500(T)}{\text{S\&P }500(0)}, 100\%\right)\right) \times \max\left[0, \frac{\text{Ret}_{\text{oil}}(T) + \text{Ret}_{\text{FX}}(T)}{2}\right]$$

For the investor, this option provides a tailored interpretation of the suggested view. The reverse gearing adds the investor's view that equities may decline, and the participation according to the above payoff is bounded between 100% and 200%, where the higher participation corresponds to a decrease in the S&P 500. The equity gearing will enhance the leverage of this view, and depending on the premium the investor is willing to spend, the basket can be made into a rainbow (whether moving towards a best-of or a worst-of) on the oil and FX rate part of the hybrid. One can set the oil and FX part of the hybrid to be written on an oil future and an FX forward so that the option is more in line with the liquid vanilla options of each of these.

Tail End of Economic Cycle: Equity – Inverse Floating Rate Hybrid

An investor believes that we are at the tail end of an economic cycle, and wants to take the view that, over the next 2 years, equities may still perform well but that equities will begin to fall at some point and this will be accompanied by a decrease in interest rates. The investor expects a weakening of the economy and interest rate cuts by the US Federal Reserve. The investor also believes that at this point rates could stay low for at least another year.

A 3-year cliquet style trigger option can be constructed where the S&P 500 is observed on a quarterly basis, and if a quarter has a negative return, the investor is then entered into an interest rate inverse floater on the USD 3-month LIBOR. The inverse floater will accrue on a quarterly basis, with a coupon that is inversely related to this reference rate. At the point where the negative equity return occurs, the equity exposure is cancelled while quarterly returns are locked in in a period-to-period cliquet style. The investor continues to accrue returns from the inverse floating rate till maturity.

The equity part involves an ATM quarterly cliquet and the structure locks in positive returns, up till the first negative one, and a cap can be included to cheapen the structure if necessary. The reverse floating part of the structure can be floored at zero and have a quarterly coupon of the form

$$\text{Floating Rate} = \max[0, 5\% - 2 \times 3\text{-month USD LIBOR}]$$

where the components are as described in the inverse floating rate note of section 17.1.3. The 5% fixed rate and the gearing of 2 can be adjusted to better fit both the view of the investor and modify the price if needed. The floor in the payout turns this into a geared put option on the LIBOR rate, which is just a geared interest rate floor. The floor can also be adjusted to increase the leverage on the interest rate part.

Emerging Market Currencies, Equities and Default

An investor believes that several emerging market countries will run into serious problems in the next 2 years, primarily because their currencies and equity markets have declined severely, and that a big portion of their large amount of debt accumulated recently is in USD, against which their currencies have declined. The investor is quite bearish on their equity indices and currencies, and wants to take such a view. Additionally, the investor believes that some of these countries will be unable to repay these debts and will default, under which scenario the investor wants to receive an additional income for each default on sovereign debt that occurs among the countries of the corresponding basket of emerging market indices.

A downside put on the basket or a rainbow style modification would capture the downward view on the equities and exchange rates, and a fixed coupon can be specified additionally for each default that occurs. The basket put or rainbow can be struck OTM to lower the cost of the structure and in turn possibly serve to enhance participation.

Oil-Geared Equity Outperformance

The investor is more bullish on the Eurozone than the US in the next 4 years, and believes that the EuroStoxx50 will outperform the S&P 500 over this period and, additionally, that oil prices will rise. Making use of the outperformance payoff, we can structure an outperformance option of the EuroStoxx50 versus the S&P 500 and gear it by the price of oil. The payoff for a maturity T will look like

$$\frac{\text{Oil}(T)}{\text{Oil}(0)} \times \max\left[0, \frac{\text{S\&P 500}(T)}{\text{S\&P 500}(0)} - \frac{\text{Stoxx50}(T)}{\text{Stoxx50}(0)}\right]$$

19.4 MULTI-ASSET CLASS RISK HEDGING

Last but not least we describe how hybrid derivatives can be used as a single instrument to hedge risks from multi-asset classes. An investor looking to hedge a portfolio covering multi-asset classes would typically hedge each of these separately; however, depending on the nature of the portfolio, it may be possible to hedge with just one hybrid option. The hybrid derivative will cost less than the sum of the individual hedges and still provide the required hedge for the portfolio of multi-asset classes as a whole. This is not magic: the reality is that hedging each asset class separately is an over-hedge that does not account for correlations in the returns of the various assets.

Protective Multi-asset Class Puts

Consider an investor who holds a portfolio of commodities and equities, and wants to protect the value of the portfolio against a decline in its value. A fall in the price of either can potentially lower the value of this portfolio, and the traditional hedge would be to buy protective puts on each asset class component. The inclusion of put options reduces the overall portfolio risk because the puts will offer downside protection when the market moves against the long portfolio.

The cheaper but equally effective hedge is to buy a hybrid that serves as a put to protect the entire portfolio of these two asset classes, instead of the two separate puts. As long as correlation is less than 1, which it generally will be, the hybrid hedge will be cheaper and involves only one transaction. The strikes of the put options in the naive hedge on each component are chosen according to how much risk the investor is willing to take on the long portfolio, and the amount of put options is a function of the weights of the underlying components of the portfolio. Likewise, the weights in the hybrid hedge reflect those of the portfolio and the hybrid hedge on the portfolio will again be struck at the level beyond which the investor wants to hedge the downside of the entire portfolio.

For example, assume that the investor is long a portfolio of equities and commodities, and is not willing to lose more than 30% of the portfolio's value, then he can buy a hybrid put option on the weighted basket of the components of the portfolio with a strike of 70%. If the value of the portfolio drops by more than 30% then the investor can exercise the right from the put option to sell the portfolio at 70% even if it has dropped further. The notional of the hybrid put will need to match that of the portfolio for this to work, and the investor cannot lose more than 30% on this portfolio.

Inflation and Downside Equity Protection

Payoffs can also be constructed to protect the portfolio of an equity investor from inflation risks. If the equity portfolio performs well but inflation is high, then the effective rate of return will be less. Additionally the investor wants to protect the portfolio from downside risk, in which scenario inflation is not the primary concern. A best-of option combining a call option on an inflation index and a put option on the equity portfolio will provide a hedge for whichever of these two scenarios occurs. An example of a payoff would be

$$\max \left[0, (K - 100\%) - \text{Portfolio}_{\text{Ret}}(T), \text{Inflation}_{\text{Ret}}(T) \right]$$

where T is the maturity of the option and represents the duration of time over which this hedge applies. The notional of the trade should match that of the portfolio, and the gearing of both parts of the hybrid kept the same in order that the protection is in line with the portfolio's value.

The first part involves the put feature on the equity portfolio, which only ends in-the-money if the performance of the portfolio is lower than the strike. In the event where it does decline beyond this strike, the investor can sell the equity position at the strike K at maturity, and not lose more than the difference $100\% - K$. If the equity portfolio were above the strike, and ideally above the ATM point, any excess returns would be unaffected by inflation because the put feature is out-of-the-money and the positive performance (if any) of inflation is paid through the structure to hedge this risk.

20

Pricing Hybrid Derivatives

Common sense is that which judges the things given to it by other senses.

Leonardo da Vinci

In this chapter we discuss the pricing of hybrid derivatives. We have already seen various structures in the discussion of asset classes and here we discuss the various risks and modelling issues by providing modelling frameworks for each asset class. In the discussion of each asset class we came across the market standards, and Black's formula came up more than once as the standard formula for which market-implied volatilities are quoted accordingly. In this chapter we venture into the models that allow for more elaborate options in the various asset classes to be priced. The focus is kept on the models and exotic products that are of direct relevance to the pricing of hybrid derivatives that involve more than one asset class, drawing on Chapter 19 for examples of structures.

As always, when we specify a model, we are exposed to model risk. As discussed in Chapter 4 in the context of volatility models, the choice of which models to use depends on the different risks involved in the option. If the payoff exhibits convexity to the price of one of its underlying assets' prices, then we should take the underlying's price to be a random process. Again, the model inputs must be correctly specified, and will be those that are relevant to the hedging of the option. We point out that what we have learned regarding hedging throughout the book is applicable to hybrid derivatives. Additionally, the liquidity of the various assets from each asset class, and the ability to trade individual options within these asset classes is also paramount to one's ability to Delta, Vega and Gamma hedge an option.

A general problem with pricing hybrid derivatives is that correlations between the various asset classes cannot be implied from liquid instruments and is very difficult to hedge. Understanding how each of these correlations affects the price of a hybrid is important, specifically the magnitude of the correlation sensitivity of the hybrid and whether the seller of the hybrid is long or short these correlations. As always, the price of the derivative must reflect the cost of hedging it. The parameters used in the model will be chosen while bearing in mind any residual risks that cannot be hedged, and technical margins based on these risks will need to be taken. We also discuss copulas that are increasingly popular and can be necessary in hybrid derivatives. Copulas allow us to formulate multi-variate distributions using separate processes for each asset class, allowing for different types of dependence to be modelled. Under copulas, assets can be correlated in more meaningful ways, and the result is more meaningful hedge ratios.

20.1 ADDITIONAL ASSET CLASS MODELS

20.1.1 Interest Rate Modelling

There is more than one approach to interest rate modelling. The decision of which approach will depend on the structure and risks entailed in the product being priced. Possible choices of which rate to model include the short rate, LIBOR rates and forward LIBOR rates. In the market we know today's yield curve, the prices (implied volatilities) of both swaptions and interest rate caps and floors, and these can all serve as calibration instruments. If an instrument, for example an OTM swaption, is to be used in the hedging of an exotic option, then it must appear in the model's calibration in order that the model shows risk against it and includes this in the pricing. The two modelling frameworks we discuss here are short-rate models and market models.

Short-Rate Models

The price of a zero coupon bond $B(t, T)$, at time t and maturity T, is related to the instantaneous interest rate r_t by

$$B(t, T) = E\left[e^{-\int_t^T r_s ds}\right] \qquad (20.1)$$

The rate r_t is known as the short rate, and is the interest rate prevailing over a very small period of time. One can think of the short rate as the interest rate cost of borrowing money from time t to time $t + dt$, where dt is a small increment. A short-rate model describes the evolution of this short rate r_t as a random variable.

The dynamics of a short-rate model are given by its drift and volatility function; these uniquely specify the first and second moments of the process. In short-rate models, the drift is often taken to be mean-reverting so that the process reverts to a long-term mean, reflecting the view that interest rates are mean-reverting. The volatility function specifies whether the process in question is normal, log-normal or something else (for example, a square root process).

In equation (20.1) the relationship between the short rate and bonds means that if we specify a process for the short rate, then the prices of all such bonds are given by the paths of this short-rate process. Bond prices are thus a function of the parameters of the model, and one step in the calibration of short-rate models is to make sure that the prices of bonds generated by the model match as closely as possible those observed in the market through the yield curve. Time dependence is often introduced to the drift of short-rate processes to allow for perfect fits to the initial yield curve.

Time dependency in the volatility structure is also necessary in a single-factor short-rate model in order that it can also be calibrated to a set of ATM swaptions or caps, in order to complete the calibration. One-factor short-rate models do suffer from the fact that with a single driving source of randomness, forward rates are perfectly correlated in the model; a contradiction to market observations. This renders such models unsuitable for pricing interest rate structures that are sensitive to the correlations between forward rates. Including additional factors by allowing the drift or the volatility to be random is necessary to calibrate such a model to an entire swaption cube (strike and maturities). The additional factor will allow for a richer volatility structure and allow us to calibrate to swaptions or caps of different strikes should this be necessary.

Despite the fact that the short rate itself is not observable in the market, these models have the distinct advantage of being quite tractable, making them handy for risk management purposes. Additionally, these models lend themselves to tree implementations that in turn allow for the pricing of more exotic structures. For example, the Bermudan swaption of section 17.1 can thus be priced using backward induction through a tree implementation of a short-rate model. Structures that involve early exercise features like American and Bermudan style options are priced as backward-looking structures.

One starts at the maturity of the option and works backwards in order to find the optimal exercise points of the option making the pricing of early exercise features possible. Trees allow for this, whereas Monte Carlo implementations, that are by nature forward looking, are not best suited for pricing options with early exercise features, although adjustments can be made.

A commonly used short-rate model is the Hull–White model (see Hull and White, 1990). Technical details of this model and some extensions of it are given in Appendix A, section A.5.

LIBOR Market Models

Market models are a quite different class of models, and in these the variable being modelled is directly observable in the market. The most successful of these is the LIBOR Market Model, abbreviated to LMM and also known as BGM after (some of) its pioneers (Brace *et al.*, 1997; Jamshidian, 1997). In an LMM the underlying variables modelled are a set of forward LIBOR rates, all of which are observable in the market, compared to the short rate that is not.

Additionally, these forward LIBOR rates are the underlyings of liquidly traded interest rate derivatives which means that their volatilities are also observable and can be implied from such options. The modelling assumption of the log-normality of each of the forward rates means that the prices of vanilla options will be given by Black's formula, and the LMM thus consistent with the market standard for the pricing of such options (caps, floors and swaptions). Short-rate models, on the other hand, do not offer such features.

A LIBOR rate $L(t, T)$, expiring at time t and paying at time T is the underlying in a caplet, a series of which forms the interest rate cap described in section 17.1.7. The LMM consistently models a whole set of n forward rates $L_i(T_i, T_{i+1})$, $i = 1, ..., n$, each corresponding to a different period. Black's formula for caps is recovered from the model for each of the forward rates being modelled, and the implied volatilities of the corresponding options are readily available to serve as calibration instruments. The key difference between the LMM and Black's model is that the LMM can consistently model an entire set of forward rates, compared to Black's model that takes a single forward rate as the underlying.

This modelling framework can also be applied to model forward swap rates, and the model in this case recovers Black's formula for European swaptions. The forward swap rate is again observable, and European swaptions are liquidly traded instruments, making calibration to interest rate swaptions instead of caps also possible.

The LMM lends itself in a more natural way than short-rate models to being calibrated to many traded instruments. The framework models a whole set of forward rates, each as a random process, and needs the correlations between these forward rates to be specified. This is also a key difference between the LMM and short rate specifications: The forward rates in a short-rate model are perfectly correlated, whereas the LMM allows for a *de-correlation* of such rates making it much more realistic, and applicable to exotics that are sensitive to the correlations between forward rates. The choice between using swaptions or caps in the calibration depends on the instruments with which we want the model to show risk and be consistent, in order to correctly price an exotic structure.

Pricing using an LMM is done using Monte Carlo simulation and the model is thus well suited for structures that are forward looking. At any point in time the simulation includes the history of each path up to that point, and thus its relevance to the exotic structure in question.

The LMM framework, in its simplest form, does not capture the interest rate skew. Stochastic volatility and local volatility extensions of the LMM do exist (see, for example, Rebonato,

2007). An interesting combination is that of the SABR model with the LMM, particularly because the SABR model is a market standard for quoting implied volatility skews in swaptions or caps. Making the LMM consistent with the SABR pricing formula will allow for a stochastic volatility extension of the model that will combine the benefits of both these models.

Interest Rate/Equity Hybrids

The interest rate modelling framework choice depends on the interest rate part of the hybrid derivative. We use the two equity/interest rate hybrids described in section 19.3 of Chapter 19: the equity/inverse floating rate hybrid, and the ICBC–CMS steepener hybrid. In both cases one will need to allow for randomness in both the interest rate and the equity, but in a quite different manner in each case.

The equity/inverse floating rate hybrid of section 19.3 is a 3-year structure which, from the onset, is a quarterly cliquet, with a local floor ATM and a local cap. The returns from the cliquet are locked in up until the point where the underlying equity index has a negative quarterly return, at which point the structure switches to accruing quarterly returns based on an inverse floating rate. If we floor the inverse floating part at zero, then the interest rate part is reduced to a set of interest rate floorlets. These are just geared put options on the relevant LIBOR rate, in this hybrid taken to be the USD 3-month LIBOR rate. The floating interest rate part for each quarter is given by

$$\text{Floating Rate}(t_i) = \max \left[0, 5\% - 2 \times \text{3-month USD LIBOR}(t_{i-1}, t_i) \right]$$

$$= 2 \times \max \left[0, 2.5\% - \text{3-month USD LIBOR}(t_{i-1}, t_i) \right] \qquad (20.2)$$

Adjusting this by the day count function is the payoff of a twice geared floorlet, each quarter.

This is a hybrid structure on equity and a USD short-term interest rate, and because it is a forward-looking structure, it can be priced using Monte Carlo simulation of a correctly calibrated model. On the equity side, we are dealing with a cliquet style payoff, which means that we immediately have forward skew risk (recall the discussion of Chapter 13), thus making the simulation of the equity path non-trivial. Some form of stochastic volatility will be needed in this case, and the calibration made consistent with a non-interest rate related quarterly cliquet. It is imperative that the forward skew risks and Vega convexities of the cliquet part of the hybrid are priced.

The interest rate part is forward looking and involves forward LIBOR rates thus making it suited to treatment with a LIBOR market model. The interest rate floor quotes are obtained from the market, with the correct strike corresponding to that of the floating rate payoff of equation (20.2), and their implied volatilities used to calibrate the LMM.

The two processes will need to be correlated and, as in the case of the autocallable swap of Chapter 12, we decide what to do about interest rate/equity correlation. The buyer of the structure is essentially playing on this correlation in that he expects declining equities to be accompanied by a decline in rates. If correlation decreases between interest rates and equities then the chance of these two moving in opposite directions and against the client increases. The seller of the structure will need to price into these correlations the fact that it is difficult to hedge interest rate/equity through liquidly traded instruments. This correlation cannot be implied from the market for the same reasons, and historical estimates are the best starting point. Risk-related margins will need to be taken.

The ICBC–CMS steepener hybrid described in section 19.3 is a best-of option between the ICBC component on a basket of underlying equities, and the (geared) spread between the

30-year and 10-year CMS rates. The main risk in the equity part of this hybrid is volatility skew, as the ICBC is quite sensitive to the equity skew. A local volatility model for the equity processes will be sufficient to capture and price this effect sufficiently. Equity correlations must also be dealt with as in the standard ICBC discussed in Chapter 9.

As for the CMS steepener part of the hybrid, spread options are sensitive to implied volatility smiles or skews, and this must be captured by the interest rate model. A constant maturity swap spread option is an example of an option that is sensitive to the correlations between the forward rates, suggesting that a LIBOR market model is better suited. The LMM used will have to be one that knows about skew, meaning either a local volatility or stochastic volatility extension thereof. In this case it may be possible to use a two-factor short-rate model on the basis that it allows for a calibration to a swaption implied volatility cube (strikes and maturities), but also allows for some de correlation in the forward rates. From a modelling perspective, combining this with a local volatility process for each of the equities may be simpler.

The correlation between the equities and the two CMS rates is specified keeping in mind the nature of the best-of payoff, discussed in Chapter 8. On the one hand we know that the seller of this option is short the correlations between the various equity underlyings, because of the nature of the ICBC payoff, as discussed in Chapter 9. In a simple best-of option the seller is long the correlation between the two underlyings, but here, the second part of the option consists of a spread payoff. The correlations between the equity underlyings and each of the CMS rates thus affect the payoff in opposite ways. The seller of the hybrid option will be long the correlation between the first CMS rate and the equities, and short the correlations with the second CMS rate of the spread. Again, margins need to be taken on these correlation parameters.

20.1.2 Commodity Modelling

Black's model greatly simplifies commodity modelling, but is not applicable to the spot price. Additional effects such as seasonality must be priced when modelling commodity spot prices. This depends on the commodity itself, but for examples such as oil, a model of the spot price must include information regarding the convenience yield described in section 17.2.1. This yield varies considerably as supply and demand for the physical commodity change. Modelling the convenience yield as a constant will not capture the varying forms of the futures curve, and the resulting models will be unrealistic. Thus, models such as Gibson and Schwartz (1990) involve two factors: one for the oil spot price, and one for the convenience yield. The short end of the futures curve is somewhat de-correlated with the longer end of the curve, reflecting short- and long-term expectations, and multiple factors can better explain this de-correlation.

Mean reversion similar to the case of short-rate models can be used, and seasonality effects built into models to make them more realistic. Additionally, oil spot prices for example can exhibit large jumps, suggesting the need for a jump model. Jump models, like stochastic volatility models, will allow for a calibration to the volatility skew observed in the vanilla options market. It is possible to combine all these features in models, but at the cost of greater complexity.

A commodity exotic such as a digital is very sensitive to skew. A digital on the price of oil is sensitive to the volatility skew implied by vanilla options. The implied returns are positively skewed, which means that there is a skew benefit in the digital, compared to a skew cost in the equity case. The double digital of section 19.2.3 involves a digital on oil and one on equities. The skew of each has a different impact on the price of the hybrid because the markets are different in nature, and in a product like this, it is key to capture both these skews. Liquidity-based barrier shifts can be taken on each to smoothen out the Greeks near the barrier to ensure that one can hedge. The nature of digital contracts, on single or multiple underlyings, as discussed in Chapter 11, emphasizes the importance of liquidity in the underlying assets.

The correlation between oil and equities is again a quantity that cannot be implied or hedged efficiently. The historical correlation between WTI futures and the S&P 500 index may be historically low, but it changes through time and there are points where this correlation has increased far beyond its long-term average. The seller of the structure is short the correlation between oil and equities, and as usual a margin needs to be taken over the historical correlation.

20.1.3   FX Modelling

During the discussion of FX vanillas we saw the Garman and Kohlhagen formula, which is the Black–Scholes equivalent for FX, and to quote FX vanillas in terms of their Deltas, this model is used. To manage the presence of the FX smile, the SABR model can be used for a book of vanilla options. Other stochastic volatility models are also popular, for example Heston's model discussed in Appendix A (A.3.1) and Bates's model in section A.4. In both these, it is the spot FX rate that is modelled, and the variance of the spot rate modelled as a random variable. Additionally Bates's model allows for jumps in the underlying spot rate, and the addition of jumps is the main difference between Bates's and Heston's models. Once calibrated to vanillas, each of these models gives the same prices for such options, but different hedge ratios depending on the model assumptions.

FX markets exhibit what is known as a stochastic skew, as we saw, meaning that the way implied returns from the market are skewed (positively or negatively), as observed through the quotes of risk reversals, can change sign. Models such as Carr and Wu (2007) are designed to pick up this additional risk. A change in the skewness of the implied returns can have a large impact on the prices of barrier options and digitals. Pricing in this additional risk factor can thus be important. Since European options are involved in the hedging of such instruments, it is important that the model used for pricing these captures the possible changes in the skew.

When moving to exotic FX structures, things get more complicated. Particularly in callable long-dated FX structures, the options are sensitive to movements in the interest rates of both currencies of the FX. The longer the maturity of the structure, the greater this sensitivity. As we saw in Chapter 18, the FX forward is a function of the spot FX rate, and also the spread between two interest rates geared by the time to maturity. The effect of the drift involving this interest rate spread has a greater effect on the long-term evolution of the FX process than, for example, allowing its volatility to be stochastic.

As such, for long-dated callable FX structures, and all interest rate/FX hybrids, one must use a model that allows for randomness in not only the FX rate, but also the two interest rates. In particular, the interest rate part of the model will need to be calibrated to at least capture each of the yield curves correctly, and a Hull–White style model for each of these would work. Interest rate volatility also impacts and the volatilities of the interest rate part must be calibrated to interest rate volatilities, for example using interest rate swaption-implied volatilities. The FX part will need to capture the information given by the vanilla surface. The modelling choices regarding the interest rate curves and their calibration, as well as the FX process and its calibration, will have a huge impact on the hedge ratios given by the model.

Composite Options

A composite option is an option on a foreign underlying with a strike in the domestic currency of the investor. As the option is priced in the domestic currency, it pays in the domestic currency if exercised. Consider a call option on an underlying S, then a composite call option involving an exchange rate FX has the payoff

$$\text{Composite Call}_{\text{payoff}} = \max\,[0,\,S(T) \times \text{FX}(T) - K]$$

where $S(T)$ is denominated in the foreign currency, the FX rate converts this into the price of the underlying in the domestic currency, and the strike K is in the domestic currency. This is different to the quanto option described in Chapter 7 where the FX rate is fixed up front. The holder of the composite option is thus still exposed to currency movements, but benefits from having fixed the strike in his domestic currency.

For example, consider a call option on Microsoft (denominated in USD) with a strike of 15.6 GBP, designed for a GBP investor. At maturity T the payoff of the composite option is determined by the product of the USD–GBP exchange rate at time T and the price of Microsoft's stock price at time T. If Microsoft is trading at USD 24 at maturity and the exchange rate is 0.7 (that is, 0.7 GBP to buy 1 USD) then the product is 16.8 and the option expires in-the-money and pays $16.8 - 15.6 = 1.2$ GBP. If the stock price were 25 USD and the exchange rate 0.6, then the product is 15 and the option expires OTM and worthless.

The pricing of the quanto option involves using a quanto adjustment to the risk-neutral drift, but with no change in the volatility used. The composite, on the other hand, is essentially a call option on a product basket of both the exchange rate and the underlying equity. If we assume that both the equity and the FX are modelled using Black–Scholes assumptions, in particular log-normality for both, then the product of the FX rate and the equity can also be modelled by a log-normal process. A Black–Scholes formula applies where one used the risk-free rate of the foreign currency, and a volatility given by

$$\sigma_S^2 + \sigma_{\text{FX}}^2 + 2\,\rho_{S,\text{FX}} \cdot \sigma_S \cdot \sigma_{\text{FX}}$$

This volatility we recognize as the approximate volatility for a standard basket option where the sum, instead of the product, of the underlyings, is taken. In this case the volatility of the product is exact for the product of two log-normals. The volatility of the product, which is used in the composite option's pricing, contains both volatilities because the composite option has risk to both the FX rate and the underlying equity.

The risk-neutral drift is taken to be the domestic rate of the investor, for the simple reason that the drift of the product of two log-normals is the sum of their drifts. These are given by $r_{\text{domestic}} - r_{\text{foreign}}$ for the exchange rate, and r_{foreign} for the risk-neutral drift of the underlying equity in its denominated currency (here this is the foreign currency). Adding these two, the r_{foreign} cancels out, and we are left with just r_{domestic}. This means that the expected growth of the product of these two is the risk-free rate of the domestic currency.

This isn't really a hybrid product, but it does combine the two asset classes in a payoff, and again we see the appearance of a two-asset-class correlation. In general this correlation is hard to imply and to hedge, unless one is able to obtain a quote for a relatively liquid stock/currency composite pair. The seller of both the composite call option and the composite put option is short the FX volatility, the volatility of the underlying equity, and the FX/equity correlation. Any more elaborate combination of FX and equities must be studied accordingly. The ability to trade the underlyings to Delta hedge is as always key, i.e. the question of liquidity. To hedge Vega or Gamma one must be able to trade options on the individual underlyings. The correlation structure is again analysed and residual risk factors built into the price.

20.2   COPULAS

A copula is defined as "something that connects or links together". In a statistical context, the word copula refers to a function that combines two or more univariate distribution functions to form multi-variate distribution functions, allowing for different types of dependence to be modelled. Applying a copula method to finance, the univariate distributions in question will be those of financial variables.

The dependencies obtained through a copula are much more realistic when interpreting the correlated behaviour of these financial assets, compared to using standard correlation coefficients. The standard correlation, as defined in Chapter 7, measures linear dependencies between two random variables.

If two variables are independent, then their correlation must be zero. The opposite is not true, however: two variables with a zero correlation are not necessarily independent. Two random variables can have a strong dependency on each other, i.e. far from being independent, but have a correlation of zero. Figure 20.1 depicts the discrete time series of two variables that have a correlation coefficient of zero, but obviously some form of dependency exists between them.

The importance of copulas in hybrid derivatives, and multi-asset derivatives in general, is that copulas provide a method of expressing joint distributions between assets, allowing for the simulation of these variables, and thus the pricing of multi-asset options. Hybrids present an interesting set of applications because of the quite different dependencies that are observed between the various asset classes. In this section we aim to explain the theory behind copulas and their importance. In the literature, some interesting discussions of the theory and uses of copulas in finance are discussed in, among others, Cherubini *et al.* (2004), Overhaus *et al.* (2007), Nelsen (1999), Schmidt (2007), and Trivedi and Zimmer (2007).

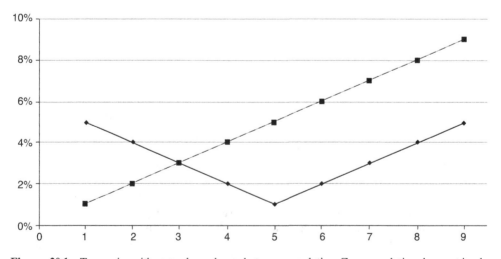

Figure 20.1 Two series with some dependency, but zero correlation. Zero correlation does not imply independence.

As we have seen, the correlation between the various asset classes can rarely be implied or hedged, and the specification of this correlation has an impact on both pricing and hedging. Although the traditional correlation does provide information regarding how different assets behave with respect to each other, it doesn't allow us to specify different behaviours for different parts of the distribution. A copula does precisely this, and modelling with copulas can thus provide more meaningful hedge ratios. For example, in the cases of out-barriers, the Greeks with respect to the variable on which the payoff is written, Delta, Vega, etc., are sensitive to movements in the asset on which the barrier knock-out clause is written. As such these Greeks will be affected by the method by which the two assets are correlated, and the more meaningful hedge ratios can result from using copulas.

20.2.1   Some Copula Theory

Let's start with the simplest case where we have only two random variables X and Y to consider. Assume that each of these has its own probability distribution, represented by two functions f_X and f_Y; these are our two univariate distributions. From these we know the cumulative distribution functions of each, denoted by $F_X(x)$ and $F_Y(y)$ for X and Y respectively. By definition, $F_X(x) = \Pr(X \leq x)$, i.e. the probability that the variable X is less than or equal to x, and in terms of the probability distribution function is given by

$$F_X(x) = \int_a^x f(s)\,\mathrm{d}s$$

where a is the lower bound over which the distribution is defined. An important property of the CDF is that, being a probability itself, means that it will take a value between 0 and 1. So how does one formulate a joint distribution $J(x, y) = \Pr(X \leq x, Y \leq y)$ out of these, where $J(x, y)$ preserves the marginal distributions of both X and Y? The answer is the copula.

Firstly, consider a uniform distribution defined on the interval $[0, 1]$. This has a probability distribution function equal to the constant 1 on the interval $[0, 1]$ and 0 everywhere else. Now, regard the CDF of the random variable X above (and the same thing for Y) as a transformation of the distribution of X given by the above integral. This connects the probability distribution of X with the CDF of X. If we assume X and Y to be continuous random variables, and their CDFs both strictly increasing, then the variables $U = F_X(x)$ and $V = F_Y(y)$ are both uniformly distributed on the interval $[0, 1]$.

So, starting with the two distributions, one for X and one for Y, we are able to transform these to uniform distributions on $[0, 1]$. A copula is only a joint distribution function of two random variables, defined on $[0, 1] \times [0, 1]$, such that both marginal distributions are also uniformly distributed on the interval $[0, 1]$. The random variables on which the copula acts are the two transformed random variables. The selection of a copula (out of many possible functions satisfying the requirements of copulas) will specify the dependency between X and Y. Note that the copula described is a 2-dimensional one, which we work with for simplicity, although the general theory is extendible to more than two random variables.

The concept of the copula was pioneered by Sklar (1959). Sklar's theorem, in simplified form, tells us that if $J(x, y)$ is a joint distribution function of two random variables X and Y, and the marginal distributions computed from $J(x, y)$ are given by $F_X(x)$ and $F_Y(y)$, then there exists a copula C such that $J(x, y) = C(F_X(x), F_Y(y))$. The converse also holds: given any two uniform marginal distributions $F_X(x)$ and $F_Y(y)$, and any copula function C, then the function $J(x, y) = C(F_X(x), F_Y(y))$ is a joint distribution function for X and Y, and it preserves their marginal distributions.

The main point from this is that the existence of the copula that gives the joint distribution is not dependent on the individual marginal distributions. This means that, in theory, whatever the distributions of X and Y, one can apply a copula to obtain a joint distribution. Also, any joint distribution function can be expressed as a copula. So through the copula, a joint distribution is formed by two separate parts: the marginal distributions of both variables, and the choice of dependency specified independently by our choice of copula.

20.2.2   Modelling Dependencies in Copulas

The standard correlation coefficient measures the strength and direction of the linear relationship between the random variables, but does not provide information about how the relationship between the two variables changes as we traverse the distribution. A copula, on the other hand, allows us to impose dependencies of different strengths between the random variables based on different sections of the distributions.

We have seen a simple example of this in equity markets. We generally see different regimes of correlation: relatively low correlation during periods of relative stability, and spikes in correlations during market crashes. The copula allows us to translate this into a model by imposing a stronger dependency between two stocks of an index on this tail in the two distributions. This is known as tail dependence, and can only be accomplished through the use of a copula. Recall that the tail of a single distribution corresponds to extreme events; and the equity market prices the higher probability of an extreme event through the skew, giving a distribution with a fatter tail than the log-normal one. Pricing an exotic structure on a single asset would generally involve capturing this through a skew model, but moving to the two (or more) asset case where we may need to capture the dependency at the part of the distribution where these fat tails occur. Given two (or more) such distributions, each representing one asset, a copula will allow us to model dependencies between extreme events in both.

An important feature of copulas is that the dependence captured by a copula is invariant under increasing and continuous transformations of the marginal distributions. This means that a copula used to join two variables X and Y can also be used on their logarithms $\ln X$ and $\ln Y$, for example. The idea is that if two variables are transformed by increasing transformations (the logarithm for example), then the transformed versions give the same information as the original variables. So specifying a dependency between X and Y, or their logarithms, is in essence the same. This means that we can work with logarithms and returns should we need to, instead of using prices for example when doing applications. The same concept does not apply to the standard coefficient: the correlation between two asset prices and the two assets' returns (or log-returns) is not necessarily the same.

In order that a copula be useful, we must specify a parametric form for it. Recall, the copula is a joint distribution function acting on $[0, 1] \times [0, 1]$ (in the case of two variables) such that both marginal distributions are uniform. As it turns out, we have at our disposal a whole range of possible parametric forms that will satisfy the criteria to be a copula. The choice of which parametric form depends on where we want to stress dependency, and below we give different copulas, each of which stresses a different part of the distribution.

We start by specifying a bivariate joint distribution J that has a useable parametric form. For example, the bivariate Normal distribution leads to what is known as the Gaussian copula described below. Our copula function C, acting on two variables u and v in $[0, 1]$, is given by

$$C(u, v) = J_{X,Y}\left(F_X^{-1}(u), F_Y^{-1}(v)\right) \tag{20.3}$$

Let's elaborate on what this formula is saying. Firstly, X and Y are the two random variables for which we are introducing dependencies using the copula. In this formula, $F_X^{-1}(u)$ represents the inverse function of the CDF $F_X(x)$ of the random variable X. We assume that the CDFs of the random variables we are modelling are strictly increasing and continuous, which means that they have an inverse. The CDF $F_X(x)$ maps the domain where X is distributed to $[0, 1]$, and so its inverse $F_X^{-1}(u)$ maps this back, and takes as an argument a value u in $[0, 1]$. Similarly, $F_Y^{-1}(v)$ is the inverse of the CDF of our second variable Y, again acting on $[0, 1]$.

Equation (20.3) comes from the earlier point where the joint distribution was defined by the copula as $J(x, y) = C(F_X(x), F_Y(y))$, combined with the use of the inverse function: if $u = F_X(x)$ then $x = F_X^{-1}(u)$. Both inverse CDFs go from $[0, 1]$ to the domain of their respective random variable, and the joint distribution $J_{X,Y}$ then acts on these. As such, we can build a copula by starting with the marginal distributions of both X and Y and then imposing a distribution we know to link them.

Consider the case where we are not trying to introduce any dependency at all, i.e. we want X and Y to be independent. The product copula is the only way to express this and it is simply the copula we obtain when the joint distribution of X and Y is simply the product of their CDFs: $J_{X,Y}(x, y) = F_X(x)F_Y(y)$. The following are just a few possible choices:

- The Gaussian copula allows for dependency, but does not show any dependency in the tails.
- The Gumbel copula should be used to emphasize lower tail dependencies (i.e. the downside of the distributions), it only has lower tail dependency.
- The Clayton copula has upper tail dependency.

The Gumbel and Clayton copulas are referred to as asymmetric because they are skewed; in opposite ways, however. The Student-t copula is symmetric in both up and low tail dependency. The main difference between these, and copulas in general, is specifically the section of the distribution on which they show dependency; more so than how much dependency. As such, if one decides to use copulas, the choice of the part of the distribution on which to increase dependency must have a justifiable reason behind it as the copula will stress the dependency in that part.

20.2.3   Gaussian Copula

The Gaussian copula is quite popular in finance – even though it is a symmetric copula and returns among many financial assets exhibit tail dependencies. It was originally applied to finance in the context of credit derivatives to model defaults among multiple corporations, as proposed by Li (2000). Given its symmetric nature, it is perhaps not the best copula to use for modelling defaults, but does have many other applications. Following the above theory, we have two assets, each with its own distribution. The Gaussian copula uses the Normal distribution, which in the two-asset case is the bivariate Normal distribution, and the Gaussian copula is given by

$$C(u, v) = \mathcal{N}_2\left(\mathcal{N}^{-1}(u), \mathcal{N}^{-1}(v)\right) \tag{20.4}$$

where $\mathcal{N}$ is the cumulative Normal distribution. As such, in the Gaussian copula the Normal marginal distributions are made dependent via a bivariate Normal distribution. The correlation

ρ is the only free parameter in the bivariate distribution $\mathcal{N}_2(x, y)$ above, and its value controls the dependency in this copula.

We must be clear on this important point: the Gaussian copula is not modelling two asset prices using a bivariate Normal distribution, it is modelling the dependence between their two distributions using a bivariate Normal distribution. To be precise, it actually models the dependence between the uniform distributions obtained from these. Assume that the two random variables we are correlating via this copula are X and Y, with distribution functions $F_X(x)$ and $F_Y(y)$ respectively. In formula (20.4), the variables u and v are these CDFs, which are the transformed version of X and Y whose result is in $[0, 1]$. We discuss the calibration and simulation of this copula in order to clarify this theory.

Calibrating the Copula

Here we discuss the calibration of copulas, focusing on the case of the Gaussian copula. Assume we have two random variables X and Y for which we have selected a joint distribution that makes financial sense. Our copula takes parametric form from this distribution, and along with marginals of X and Y, must be calibrated to market data. The use of a known parametric form for the joint distribution (the bivariate Normal in the case of the Gaussian copula) becomes important at this step because it will simplify the process of fitting the copula.

Market data will consist of a set of traded options on X, and a separate set of traded options on Y. We can fit the marginals of each to represent the individual implied distributions, and then specify the parameter of the copula, or the marginals and the parameter of the copula can be fitted at the same time.

In the latter, for example, we can compute the density function of the copula. Using the Gaussian copula described here, we have

$$c(u, v) = \frac{\partial^2 C(u, v)}{\partial u\, \partial v}$$
$$= \frac{\partial^2 \mathcal{N}_2 \left(\mathcal{N}^{-1}(u), \mathcal{N}^{-1}(v) \right)}{\partial u\, \partial v}$$
$$= \frac{\Phi_2(\mathcal{N}^{-1}(u), \mathcal{N}^{-1}(v))}{\Phi(\mathcal{N}^{-1}(u))\Phi(\mathcal{N}^{-1}(v))}$$

where

$$\Phi(x) = \frac{1}{\sqrt{2\pi}}e^{-x^2/2}$$

is the Normal (Gaussian) probability distribution function, and

$$\Phi_2(x, y) = \frac{1}{2\pi\sqrt{1 - \rho^2}} \exp\left(-\frac{1}{2(1 - \rho^2)} \left[x^2 + y^2 - 2\rho xy \right] \right)$$

is the bivariate probability density function. This will be fitted to the set of data using a Maximum Likelihood Estimation method.

If we want to capture the skewness and fat tails of the individual marginals, we will need a skew model for each marginal. In this case we can apply the SABR model, specifically because, even though it is a stochastic volatility model, it has been solved to offer a simple form for the prices of European options. Not only do we know the prices of Europeans via a modified function in place of the volatility, enabling us to use Black's formula, but we also have simplified but accurate approximations of the distributions implied by the model. This is also made possible by the fact that we are not constrained in the choice of how to model our marginals, as long as the distribution function used is invertible. Thus, each of our marginals can be set to be a random process defined under the SABR model. See Appendix A, section A.3.2, for more details on the SABR model.

Simulating the Gaussian Copula

If we assume that we know the marginal distributions of two random variables X and Y, given by $F_X(x)$ and $F_Y(y)$ respectively, the following algorithm allows us to simulate the Gaussian copula that introduces the dependency to these two.

1. Simulate a vector of two independent uniform random variables $\{u_1, u_2\}$.
2. Transform these to Normal random variables $\{\epsilon_1, \epsilon_2\}$. This can be done via the Box–Muller transform:

$$\epsilon_1 = \sqrt{-2 \ln u_1} \cos(2\pi u_2), \quad \epsilon_2 = \sqrt{-2 \ln u_1} \sin(2\pi u_2)$$

   These are still independent, and will be standard Normal random variables.
3. Correlate these by multiplying by the decomposed correlation matrix, giving $\{n_1, n_2\}$.
4. Map these back to [0, 1] by applying the Normal CDF

$$\{u, v\} = \{\mathcal{N}(n_1), \mathcal{N}(n_2)\}.$$

5. Apply the inverse marginal distributions to u and v to obtain X and Y as $F_X^{(-1)}(u) = X$ and $F_Y^{(-1)}(v) = Y$.

In the case of standardized random variables, the correlation matrix mentioned in step 3, is the same as the covariance matrix, and is given (in the case of the standard bivariate Normal) by

$$\mathbf{M} = \begin{bmatrix} 1 & \rho \\ \rho & 1 \end{bmatrix}$$

This is decomposed into $\mathbf{M} = \mathbf{L}\mathbf{L}^{\mathrm{T}}$, where $\mathbf{L}$ is a lower triangular matrix, and $\mathbf{L}^{\mathrm{T}}$ its transpose. Given this matrix $\mathbf{M}$, the matrix $\mathbf{L}$ we want is given by

$$\mathbf{L} = \begin{bmatrix} 1 & 0 \\ \rho & \sqrt{1 - \rho^2} \end{bmatrix}$$

The matrix $\mathbf{L}$ is multiplied by the vector $\{\epsilon_1, \epsilon_2\}$ of independent Normal random variables to give a vector of two normally distributed random variables with correlation ρ. Up to step 3, we are essentially just generating random variables from the bivariate Normal distribution. Step 4 maps these back to the interval [0, 1] via the Normal CDF. Finally, the inverse distributions $F_X^{-1}(u)$ and $F_Y^{-1}(v)$ give us back the variables whose marginals we want to combine in the Gaussian copula in the first place. The procedure described allows us to simulate such variables, with their individual marginals intact and, combined via the Gaussian copula, controlled by the correlation ρ. The tractability and relative ease of this simulation process is an important factor in the popularity of the Gaussian copula.

The inverse distributions used in step 5 can be freely specified. They are chosen to be the inverses of the two distributions we want to have as our marginals. So, assuming that our choice of the distributions of each is invertible, we can use the inverse CDF at this step in conjunction with the Gaussian copula to get the required result. The example of the SABR model can be used here; in step 5 the inverse SABR distribution is used. As such the copula will allow for a calibration to the implied skews of the different assets, and allow this to be combined in a Gaussian copula. The copula models the dependency, and this method is particularly useful for hybrid payoffs that are skew sensitive. Caution must be taken because the SABR model works on a forward process, and the result of the simulation in step 5 is a forward.

Multi-variate Case

All the theory presented for the bivariate case extends to the multi-variate case: the existence of the copula in the multi-variate case, and its ability to model dependency among multiple variables. In the Gaussian copula, for example, the same theory holds, only the multi-variate function $\mathcal{N}_n$ replaces the bivariate cumulative Normal distribution $\mathcal{N}_2$ in order to combine the marginals of n different variables instead of two. The simulation process holds, and the calibration process too.

20.2.4   Pricing with Copulas

Other than the possibility of simulating the copula to price various payouts on multiple variables, there are some cases where the copula itself gives us the answer directly.

Bivariate Digitals in Copulas

Consider a digital that pays a coupon if both the price of oil and the S&P 500 index are greater than or equal to their values today in a year's time.

$$\text{Double Digital}_{\text{payoff}} = X\% \times \mathbf{1}_{\{\text{S\&P 500}(T) \geq \text{S\&P 500}(0)\}} \times \mathbf{1}_{\{\text{Oil}(T) \geq \text{Oil}(0)\}}$$

It is important to model the dependency here correctly, and a Gaussian copula should suffice. Referring to the two underlyings as S_1 and S_2, when writing the payoff as an expectation we need to compute the discounted value of the joint probability

$$\Pr\left[\{S_1(T) \geq S_1(0)\}; \{S_2(T) \geq S_2(0)\}\right]$$

More generally, consider the same payoff where the digital pays only if both are above the respective strikes K_1 and K_2, which in this example are today's value of each.

$$\Pr\left[\{S_1(T) \geq K_1\}; \{S_2(T) \geq K_2\}\right]$$

This is in fact closely related to the joint distributions function of the two. Assume that we chose a Gaussian copula and calibrated the copula and both the underlyings to have the marginals consistent with the market of each, then this probability is given by plugging values into the calibrated copula.

Firstly, let P_1 and P_2 be the probabilities of each individually, ending in-the-money. Let $B(T)$ be the price of the relevant risk-free asset (bond) that we know, so

$$\frac{P_1}{B(T)} = \Pr\left(S_1(T) \geq K_1\right), \quad \frac{P_2}{B(T)} = \Pr\left(S_2(T) \geq K_2\right)$$

As such, P_1 and P_2 are the prices of the individual digitals. Sklar's theorem allows us to write the bivariate joint distribution as a copula taking the marginals as arguments (see Cherubini and Luciano, 2002). Thus we can write

$$\frac{Price\,(S_1(T) \geq K_1,\, S_2(T) \geq K_2)}{B(T)} = \Pr(S_1(T) \geq K_1,\, S_2(T) \geq K_2)$$

$$= C\left(\frac{P_1}{B(T)},\, \frac{P_2}{B(T)}\right)$$

The copula allows the bivariate pricing to be broken into the dependency structure, and the marginal univariate distributions. The marginals we obtain from the market as the call spread proxy for each individual digital, including all relevant information regarding the skew. We refer the reader to Cherubini and Luciano (2002) for additional discussions regarding bivariate pricing with copulas.

21

Dynamic Strategies and Thematic Indices

That which is static and repetitive is boring. That which is dynamic and random is confusing. In between lies art.

John Locke

In this chapter we discuss thematic products and dynamic strategies. In these two, the focus is on the underlying, which will be an index of constituents whose weights change through time according to a set of rules. In thematic products, an underlying is constructed on the basis of a theme – for example, emerging markets or green energy. The weights of the constituents of this thematic index are rebalanced at certain time intervals to ensure that it still represents the theme at hand. We describe the key balance that needs to be struck between the ability to create such an index and the ability to structure, price and hedge options with these thematic indices as the underlying.

In a dynamic strategy, one starts with a set of assets, typically from different asset classes, and lays out a set of rules by which the index (the weighted average of these assets) is rebalanced to achieve an investment goal. The ideas behind dynamic strategies come from the theory of portfolio management where one typically balances risky and non-risky assets to achieve target levels of volatility or returns. Examples of these are the cases where one sets a target level for volatility and aims to maximize returns, and the example where one sets a target level for the returns and aims to minimize volatility. The weights are readjusted periodically according to a set of rules and an optimization in order to achieve these goals. We devote a section to the concepts of portfolio management in which we explain the concept of risk versus reward, and using this we move to a discussion of dynamic strategies.

These are grouped together in this chapter because they both fall under the domain of exotic underlyings. For thematic indices and dynamic strategies we discuss the motivation behind investing in such products, the construction process of these indices, how to structure financial products with these as the underlying, and then how to price such options.

21.1 PORTFOLIO MANAGEMENT CONCEPTS

To understand the motivation behind investing in dynamic strategies and their construction, we must familiarize ourselves with the concepts behind portfolio management.

21.1.1 Mean–variance Analysis

Mean–variance theory is a portfolio formation approach based on the idea that the value of investment opportunities can be measured in terms of mean return and variance of return. Harry Markowitz (1952) developed this theory primarily assuming that expected returns, variances and covariances of all asset returns are known, and are sufficient to determine the most suitable portfolio. It is possible to find investment opportunities that generate enormous returns – an example being some emerging market indices – but when these returns come with high levels of risk, measured by volatility, one must consider the risk to reward ratio to determine if it is the correct investment.

The mean–variance approach to portfolio selection is used to allow investors to choose an *efficient* portfolio, which is a portfolio offering the highest expected return for a given level of risk in the portfolio. Here, we assume that all investors are risk averse; they aim to get the highest return and at the same time bear the lowest possible amount of risk. The expected return is approximated by the mean, whereas the investor tolerance for risk is quantified by the portfolio variance of return.

Let's assume that an investor wants to invest in a portfolio composed of n assets $S_1, S_2, \ldots, S_n$. Then the value of the portfolio is computed as follows:

$$\text{Portfolio}_{\text{value}} = \sum_{i=1,\ldots,n} w_i S_i$$

where w_i is the fraction of the portfolio invested in asset i. Note that

$$\sum_{i=1,\ldots,n} w_i = 1$$

For any portfolio composed of n assets, the expected return $E[R_p]$ is

$$E[R_p] = \sum_{i=1,\ldots,n} w_i E[R_i]$$

where $E[R_i]$ is the expected return on asset i. In practice, this quantity is estimated using the mean of returns μ_i computed using historical data

$$\mu_i = \frac{1}{N} \times \sum_{t=1,\ldots,N} \text{Ret}_i(t)$$

and $\text{Ret}_i(t) = S_i(t)/S_i(t-1) - 1$, where $S_i(t)$ is the value of asset i at time t.

On the other hand, the portfolio variance of return σ_p^2 used to measure the risk is computed as described in Chapter 7, for N assets we have

$$\sigma_p^2 = \sum_{1 \leq i \leq N} w_i^2 \sigma_i^2 + 2 \sum_{1 \leq i < j \leq N} w_i w_j \sigma_i \sigma_j \rho_{i,j}$$

where σ_i is the realized volatility of asset i and $\rho_{i,j}$ is the historical correlation between assets i and j.

21.1.2 Minimum-variance Frontier and Efficient Portfolios

When investors quantify their risk tolerance, they seek the portfolio delivering the highest expected return. In order to find an efficient portfolio, one must solve first for the asset weights so that the portfolio variance is the lowest for a given level of expected return. Such portfolios are called *minimum-variance portfolios* and contain efficient portfolios. Here, we first consider the case of portfolios composed of two assets to clarify the method used to draw the minimum-variance frontier. We then generalize to multi-asset portfolios.

Table 21.1 Estimated annualized returns and standard
deviations of two assets.

	Expected return	Standard deviation
Asset 1	18%	27%
Asset 2	7%	11%

Two-Asset Case

Let's take the case of an individual who has decided to invest his retirement plan assets in a
portfolio composed of two assets, asset 1 and asset 2. Then he uses the mean–variance analysis
to determine the fractions of his funds to invest in each asset. Let w_1 and w_2 denote the weights
of asset 1 and asset 2 in the portfolio; note that $w_1 + w_2 = 1$. Assuming that expected returns
and variances can be estimated accurately using monthly historical returns during the last 10
years, he computes the average returns, the variances of returns and the correlation of returns
for the two assets. Table 21.1 shows these historical statistics.

Given these results, one can determine the range of possible expected returns for the portfolio
$E[R_p]$ as well as the associated level of risk, i.e. the variance corresponding to each possible
estimated return. Note that

$$E[R_p] = w_1 E[R_1] + w_2 E[R_2]$$

where $E[R_1]$ and $E[R_2]$ are the expected returns of the individual assets; then

$$E[R_p] = 18\% \times w_1 + 7\% \times (1 - w_1) = 7\% + 11\% \times w_1$$

Here, we can see that the minimum portfolio return is 7% ($w_1 = 0$; case where the funds
are only invested in asset 2) and the maximum portfolio return is 18% ($w_1 = 1$; case where
the funds are only invested in asset 1). So, at this stage of analysis, one specifies a set of
weights for the portfolio assets, computes the portfolio's expected returns, and then quantifies
the portfolio's associated variances σ_p^2 as follows

$$\sigma_p^2 = w_1^2 \sigma_1^2 + w_2^2 \sigma_2^2 + 2 w_1 w_2 \rho \sigma_1 \sigma_2$$

where σ_1 and σ_2 are respectively the standard deviations of asset 1 and asset 2, and ρ is the
correlation between these two assets.

Table 21.2 shows a set of portfolios and the risk/return measures performed on the different
combinations. Figure 21.1 illustrates the minimum-variance frontier over the period covering
the last 30 years by graphing expected returns as a function of variance. This curve shows that
some portfolios provide the same expected return and have different variances. Note that the
variance of the minimum-variance portfolio (the one with the lowest risk) appears to be close to
108 (point M) and is associated with an expected return of 8.10%. This portfolio is composed
of 10% of asset 1 and 90% of asset 2. Therefore, an investor should not choose a portfolio with
less than 10% invested in asset 1 since it would exhibit less return for a higher risk. The portion
of the minimum-variance frontier beginning with point M and continuing above is called the
efficient frontier; portfolios lying there offer the highest expected return for a given level of
risk. In other words, the efficient frontier is the section of the minimum-variance frontier with
a positive slope.

Table 21.2 Relation between risk and returns for different portfolios composed of the two assets described in Table 21.1. A correlation of 5% between the assets is assumed.

w_1	w_2	Expected return	Variance	Standard deviation
0%	100%	7%	121	11%
10%	90%	8.1%	108	10.39%
20%	80%	9.2%	111	10.55%
30%	70%	10.3%	131	11.45%
40%	60%	11.4%	167	12.94%
50%	50%	12.5%	220	14.83%
60%	40%	13.6%	289	17%
70%	30%	14.7%	374	19.35%
80%	20%	15.8%	476	21.82%
90%	10%	16.9%	594	24.38%
100%	0%	18%	729	27%

Moreover, when we look at the portfolio variance formula, we notice that the trade-off between risk and return is not only a function of expected asset returns and variances but also depends on the correlation between the assets. Here, we again see the importance of diversification that is a key concept in asset allocation. Figure 21.2 shows the minimum-variance frontiers for portfolios containing asset 1 and asset 2, assuming four different values of the correlation coefficient. Note that in this case, expected returns are plotted against standard deviation, which doesn't modify the general shape of the curve.

Figure 21.2 illustrates a number of interesting features about diversification. Firstly, when the correlation is equal to 1, this means that the return on one asset is a positive linear function of the return on the other. This leads to the portfolio expected return being a linear function of its standard deviation. For a correlation equal to +1, both assets move in the same way and diversification has no potential benefits. As we lower the correlation coefficient towards −1

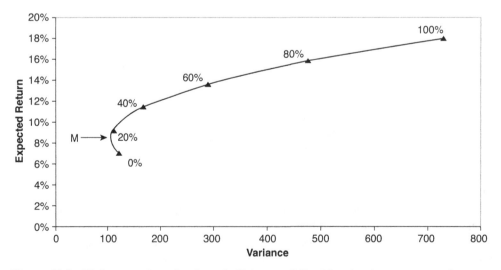

Figure 21.1 Minimum-variance frontier and efficient portfolios. Note that the percentage values next to some graph points represent the weight of asset 1 in the portfolio.

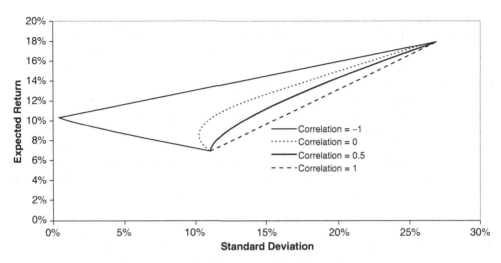

Figure 21.2 Minimum-variance frontier for varied correlations.

and holding all other values constant, we can see that the efficient frontier improves in the sense that it offers a higher expected return for the same standard deviation.

Extension to the Multi-asset Case

Earlier, we considered forming a portfolio of two assets. Typically, however, portfolio managers form optimal portfolios using a large number of assets. Here, we show how to determine the minimum-variance frontier in the multi-asset case. In fact, the idea is to compute the optimal weights w_1, w_2, ..., w_n of the n individual assets composing the portfolio such that its variance is minimum for a specific level of expected return.

Firstly, one determines $R_{\min}$ and $R_{\max}$, the minimum and maximum expected returns possible with the set of assets. One would then need to use some form of optimizer to solve the following problem for specified values of z, $R_{\min} \leq z \leq R_{\max}$,

$$\text{Minimize}: \sigma_p^2 = \sum_{i=1,\dots,n} \sum_{j=1,\dots,n} w_i w_j \text{Cov}(R_i, R_j)$$

$$\text{Subject to}: E[R_p] = \sum_{i=1,\dots,n} w_i E[R_i], \quad \text{and} \sum_{i=1,\dots,n} w_i = 1$$

The resulting weights define the minimum-variance portfolio for a given level of expected return z. Note that, in this case, assets can be sold short since there is no constraint specifying that w_i should be positive. One can add this constraint if he wants to prevent short selling from his set of portfolios.

Adding a Risk-Free Asset

So far, we have considered only portfolios composed of risky securities, i.e. where the standard deviation is not zero. Now, we extend the analysis to the case where an investor decides to hold risk-free assets in his investment portfolio. Here, we assume that investors share identical views about risky assets' mean returns, variances and correlations. The *capital market line* (CML) is the term used to describe the combinations of expected returns and standard deviations available from combining the optimal portfolio and the risk-free asset. Note that the risk-free asset has an expected return equal to the risk-free rate and its standard deviation is equal to zero. Thus the CML must be the line from the risk-free rate that is tangential to the efficient frontier of risky assets described above. Indeed, this line has the maximum slope and provides the best risk–return trade-off. In a state of equilibrium, the tangency portfolio is the market portfolio in which the proportion of all risky assets reflects their market value weights.

Now let's determine the CML equation. If an investor is willing to combine a portion w_m of his tangency portfolio (with expected return $E[R_m]$ and standard deviation σ_m) with a risk-free asset (with expected return R_f and standard deviation σ_f), then the expected return on the entire portfolio $E[R_p]$ is equal to the weighted average of the risk-free asset and the risky portfolio, and is therefore linear:

$$E[R_p] = (1 - w_m)R_f + w_m E[R_m]$$

Since the asset is risk free, portfolio standard deviation is simply a function of the weight of the risky portfolio in the position. This relationship is linear:

$$\sigma_p = \sqrt{w_f^2 \sigma_f^2 + w_m^2 \sigma_m^2 + 2\rho_{f,m} w_f w_m \sigma_f \sigma_m}$$
$$= \sqrt{w_f^2 \cdot 0 + w_m^2 \sigma_m^2 + 2\rho_{f,m} w_f w_m \sigma_f \cdot 0}$$
$$= \sqrt{w_m^2 \sigma_m^2}$$
$$= w_m \sigma_m$$

If we substitute the value of $w_m = \sigma_p/\sigma_m$ back in the equation of the overall expected return, we get

$$E[R_p] = R_f + (E[R_m] - R_f)/\sigma_m \sigma_p$$

The equation above is the capital market line equation. Its slope, $(E[R_m] - R_f)/\sigma_m$, expresses the additional return the investor demands for every 1% increase in the market portfolio standard deviation. The capital market line is illustrated by the solid line in Figure 21.3 and represents the expected returns of only efficient portfolios.

21.1.3   Capital Asset Pricing Model

The *Capital Asset Pricing Model* (CAPM) was introduced in the early 1960s and has played a major role in the development of quantitative strategies since then. In the literature, we see pioneering work by Lintner (1965) among others. Under the same assumptions we mentioned in this section, the CAPM is a theory-based model that describes the relationship between the risk and return on all assets and portfolios, as follows:

$$E[R_i] = R_f + \beta_i(E[R_m] - R_f)$$

where $E[R_i]$ is the expected return on asset i, $E[R_m]$ is the expected return on the market portfolio, R_f is the risk-free rate of return. β_i is the Beta of asset i and is computed as follows:

$$\beta_i = \frac{\sigma_{i,m}}{\sigma_m^2} = \rho_{i,m} \frac{\sigma_i}{\sigma_m}$$

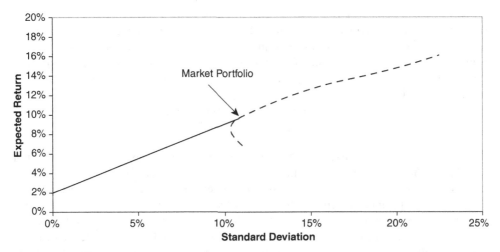

Figure 21.3 Minimum-variance frontier and capital market line. Note that the solid line represents the CML.

The *Beta* of an asset measures its sensitivity to movements in the market. It approximates the overall volatility of a security's returns against the returns of a relevant benchmark. A stock has historically moved $\beta\%$ for every 100% move in the benchmark, based on price level. For instance, if the Beta of an American stock is equal to 1.7, this means that if the S&P 500 index (this index used as the market portfolio for American stocks) performed by 20%, the stock has historically performed by $1.7 \times 20\% = 34\%$. Note that the market portfolio itself has a Beta of 1 since $\sigma_{m,m} = \sigma_m^2$. Also, the β of a risk-free asset is equal to zero since its volatility is null.

The CAPM is an equation describing the expected return of an asset as a linear function of this asset's Beta, which represents the market risk. The term $E[R_m] - R_f$ in this equation is called the market risk premium and describes the excess return on the market compared to the risk-free rate of return. The market risk premium is multiplied by the asset's Beta. Under the CAPM, an asset with a Beta of 1 is expected to earn exactly the expected return on the market portfolio. If an asset has a Beta greater than 1, this means that it exhibits more risks than the market and then earns a higher expected excess return. Conversely, Betas less than 1 indicate lower market risk that makes the expected returns lower than the markets. The CAPM theory has been used primarily to value equities and states that the higher the market risk, the higher the expected return on a specific asset.

21.1.4 Sharpe Ratio

A mean–variance investor willing to put money in one strategy among a set of investment portfolios can use the Markovitz decision rule to make his choice. This rule states that an investment A is better than another one B if it exhibits a higher expected return and a lower variance of returns. In this case, A is said to mean–variance dominate B. A point to note is that when asset allocation has both a higher mean return and a higher standard deviation, the Markovitz decision rule doesn't enable an investor to select a superior portfolio.

Investors search for high returns, but they should also ask how much risk they will have to take in exchange for these returns. This gives rise to the expressions of the risk/reward relationship. Firstly, assume that there is a risk-free rate at which an investor can both lend and borrow, then the *Sharpe ratio* can be used to measure the excess return per unit of risk (risk is measured by the volatility, i.e. standard deviation). The Sharpe ratio is also known as the Sharpe index and the reward-to-variability ratio. In other words, it shows how good the returns of an investment are per unit of risk taken. Sharpe (1994) revisited his 1964 work (see Sharpe, 1964) and the use of the Sharpe ratio (SR) to express the measurement of risk/reward has become standard:

$$\text{SR} = \frac{E[R - R_f]}{\sigma} = \frac{E[R - R_f]}{\sqrt{\text{Var}[R - R_f]}}$$

where R is the asset return, $E[R - R_f]$ is the expected value of the excess of the asset return (over the benchmark return), and σ is the asset return standard deviation.

By using the Sharpe ratio, the investor who seeks to maximize returns at the lowest volatility can quantify two positions in terms of their individual Sharpe ratios in order to decide which is the better investment by selecting the one with the higher Sharpe ratio. Portfolios with a maximal Sharpe ratio are referred to as *locally optimal* portfolios. In the case where the Sharpe ratio of any admissible portfolio is negative, then the money account is the only locally optimal portfolio. By maximizing the Sharpe ratio, an investor targets the highest reward per unit of risk taken.

21.1.5   Portfolio Rebalancing

Portfolio rebalancing involves adjusting the weights of the assets in a portfolio so that it continuously represents the investment strategy. If the investor has an investment goal in mind, based on a fixed time horizon, then as this becomes closer to being realized, the portfolio will typically need to be adjusted. If the desired returns have been realized, then in this situation one may increase the amount of less risky assets, and lower the weights on the riskier ones.

However, if one is not working with a fixed time horizon, and is continuously trying to attain the highest returns at the lowest possible risk, then the portfolio will need to be re-weighted so that it consistently reflects the risk/reward ratio the investor wants to sustain. The need for rebalancing arises because assets change over time (specifically, their volatilities change over time) and the overall portfolio volatility, as computed above, can change resulting in a new risk/reward ratio that is not necessarily in line with the investor's target.

If we are thinking in terms of a portfolio with a specific ratio mix of risky to non-risky assets, a rise in the risky portion of the portfolio can mean that the percentage this part holds is higher than the allowed proportion. For example, assume $100 is invested, $40 in bonds and $60 in equities, giving a 40% to 60% ratio, and equities increase by 15%, meaning that the value of the portfolio will now be $40 (from the bond) plus $69 from the equity. The portfolio is now worth $109, but equities (the risky part) now represent $69/109 = 63.3\%$ of the portfolio. A rebalancing is needed to bring the ratio back to the 40–60 target. Although this is different to the pure Sharpe ratio adjustment to the portfolio, one may only be allowed to invest up to a certain percentage in one part of the portfolio – for example, a constraint on the maximum percentage that can be put into the various possible risky assets. As such one will seek to maximize the Sharpe ratio within the weight constraints.

The rebalancing rules of an asset allocation strategy must be clearly defined. When the portfolio weights are rebalanced on a fixed schedule, e.g. monthly or quarterly, this is referred to as a calendar rebalancing. When the rebalancing is based on an asset's divergence from its allocated target, this is a threshold rebalancing. A calendar rebalancing offers less flexibility but is transparently simple. A threshold rebalancing is more flexible but can involve frequent rebalancing which can be costly in terms of the transaction costs of buying and selling. If it is the volatility of the portfolio that is to be kept at a target, then volatility rebalancing is done by adjusting the underlying weights by selling those assets with higher volatilities and increasing the weights on those with lower volatilities.

21.2 DYNAMIC STRATEGIES

21.2.1 Why Dynamic Strategies?

When high levels of volatility characterize a market environment, spreading across the asset classes (equity, fixed income, commodities, FX) investors wanting to stay involved find themselves taking on a lot of risk. As a result it becomes quite difficult for them to invest large risk premiums in an unstable environment as such. Taking the case of the recent crisis as an example, it was impossible for investors to get returns only by taking a Beta exposure to different asset classes. Also, despite the fact that buying options for speculative purposes can provide investors with the desired leverage, most traded options have a positive Vega, which implies that their premium is quite high in line with the high levels of volatility. Instead, investors are looking for Alpha-generating investments that provide an additional return by outperforming the market benchmarks.

Alpha is the term used as a risk-adjusted measure of the return of an investment. The Alpha of a fund is the term used to describe its performance relative to the risks taken. Alpha can be taken with respect to a relevant benchmark; with Alpha being higher, the better the fund's performance against the benchmark. This is referred to as *Jensen's Alpha*, after Michael Jensen. Investors seeking Alpha traditionally turn to hedge funds or funds of hedge funds in the search for absolute returns, i.e. returns greater than those of the benchmark. Absolute hedge funds would need to accomplish their objective of making profits in the various market environments, specifically, to still perform in falling and/or highly volatile market regimes. In rising markets they would also be expected to perform equally well as their benchmarks and better. The search for Alpha led many investors to hedge funds in recent years; however, hedge funds suffer from several drawbacks, including a lack of transparency, scalability and liquidity. Capital preservation is also a consideration.

To this end, many investment banks, equipped with platforms that can handle cross-asset class risks, have sought to produce in-house *hedge fund strategies*, the goal being the delivery of these as investment solutions to institutional investors seeking Alpha; an alternative to hedge funds themselves. The products, also referred to as dynamic strategies, offer systematic scalable Alpha-generating investments and aim to offer consistent positive performances over set benchmarks at relatively low levels of volatility. The delivery of this strategy to the investor can take many forms including Delta-1, capital protected, etc., and these lend themselves to the standard set of possible wrappers.

A dynamic strategy is essentially a portfolio of assets in which the weights of the various assets are periodically readjusted according to a transparently specified set of criteria. The designer of the dynamic strategy thus plays the same role as the fund manager for an asset management product. Therefore, dynamic strategies are not only based on strong portfolio management and market behaviour concepts, as is the case for hedge funds, but they can also eliminate the aforementioned disadvantages.

From a marketing standpoint, the approach is similar to that used by actively managed funds. If the strategy is formally computed by an independent agent and its performance made available through data providers, then seeing the past performance and doing comparisons with benchmarks makes it easier for the investor, and simplifies its marketing. As such it is typically first marketed as a Delta-1 product with the possibility of offering it as a fund, note or option being an additional feature. By providing investors in such products with regular updates on the weightings and performance of the strategy, one aims for subsequent reinvestments in the strategy, assuming the performance is as required.

When dynamic strategies are structured as an option, these payoffs typically remain simple and do not exhibit a lot of convexities; the exotic nature of the product comes from the non-standard underlying: the dynamic strategy. The simple option structures make these products manageable from a trading standpoint, although it is possible to tailor the option on the strategy at the cost of a more complicated job of hedging. Dynamic strategies capture and emphasize all the benefits of the asset management business. Indeed, the higher the assets under management, the easier it is to make subsequent sales. Also, if a strategy performs well, there would be reinvestments by the investors.

21.2.2   Choosing the Assets

The three most commonly chosen assets are stocks, bonds and cash. Real estate and commodities are among other additional possibilities. Each of these possible assets has its own unique set of risks, and once understood, it is these quite different risks that allow one to combine these assets to achieve an investment goal. Stocks, bonds and cash offer returns that have low historical correlations: economic factors under which one category thrives do not necessarily apply to the others. This means that combinations of these would serve well in a dynamic strategy because it can potentially capture this feature and protect against large losses while also generating consistent returns. Combining various asset classes is a step towards the absolute return objective and should allow for a low correlation to the equity markets among other specific asset classes.

The properties of stocks and bonds have been well discussed in this book and here we briefly review property. As an asset class, property has over the years shown strong performance, and should be considered as a source of capital growth, despite the fact that the crash of 2008 was related to property. Historically, property has a quite low correlation to both bonds and equities, which, along with its potentially high returns, makes it a good candidate as an asset for a dynamic strategy. Accessing the returns of property does not need to involve the actual purchase of real estate (although it could). ETFs that track real estate indices are accessible through equity markets, and there are also fund structures providing access to property.

Last but not least is cash, or near cash, which is the asset class that preserves capital in the short and medium term. Although in some sense cash is more closely related to bonds than the other asset classes, cash has zero (or close to zero) realized correlation with the other asset classes.

21.2.3   Building the Dynamic Strategy

The Specification of a Strategy

Before building the strategy, the rationale identifies the assets that will be used as underlyings for the strategy, depending on market expectations. Also, the dynamic strategy should reflect a specific trading philosophy that will impact the way it will be designed. Two popular trading strategies are the momentum and contrarian strategies.

Momentum trading is based on the observation of trading volumes. Once an asset shows a sudden surge in the traded volume, it is assumed to indicate an institutional interest in this asset. And because of the heavy buying power of financial institutions, the demand for the asset will start growing, thus increasing its value. This move will be noticed by smaller investors who will then start purchasing, which will further increase the asset price. The aim of the momentum strategy is to analyse the trend and understand when and where to enter the market. The idea behind this strategy is to enable the investor to ride the price movements and close the position before the conditions become adverse. The opposite also holds for declining values of an asset's price, which will be followed by a more negative trend.

Contrarian strategies are based on going against the flow. When the market seems to be *crowding* in some aspect, the contrarian sees this as an opportunity to find misprices in the market place and take advantage accordingly. Too much pressure on an asset by market participants, in either direction, can result in the asset being over- or underpriced. The contrarian buys the undervalued assets and sells the overvalued. Such strategies are typically different to those followed by the majority of investors.

The idea behind creating a dynamic strategy is to create a portfolio of assets that is dynamically rebalanced. This means that the weights are recomputed periodically depending on prespecified rules; rebalancing rules that are made available to the investor. Modern dynamic strategies often take the time dimension into account when deciding the asset allocation rules. In doing so, these strategies are also incorporating information about the serial cross-correlation, which is the correlation between one asset's returns during a specific period and another asset's returns during another period of time.

Weight Constraints and Rebalancing

It is imperative that the specification of rebalancing rules is systematic and transparent. To clarify the building process of dynamic strategies, we assume that the strategy is based on n assets. The weights of the assets are changed on a periodic basis to account for the previous m periodical returns of each of the n assets. More precisely, each weight $w_{i,t}$ computed at time t is a linear combination of the previous m periodic returns of each of the n assets with fixed coefficients $\alpha_{i,j,k}$ ($n \times m$ coefficients for each asset composing the portfolio). For $i = 1, ..., n - 1$,

$$w_{i,t} = \sum_{j=1,...,n} \sum_{k=1,...,m} \alpha_{i,j,k} \times R_{i,t-k}$$

where $R_{i,k}$ is the return of asset i at time $t - k$. And since $\sum_{i=1,...,n} w_{i,t} = 1$ at any time t,

$$w_{n,t} = 1 - \sum_{i=1,...,n-1} w_{i,t}$$

The above function is linear but it is important to understand that there are no constraints about the type of formula on which the weights are built. At this stage, the structurer may decide to add a series of constraints depending on the strategy rationale. For example, if one of the assets is an equity index, its weight can be capped to (let's say) 50%. This reduces the maximum equity exposure to 50% of the notional, thus decreasing the risk to equity markets.

The weights of the components can also be floored or even negative, thus implying that the strategy allows short positions on specified assets.

If the coefficients are taken to be positive, the strategy becomes momentum as in the sense that a positive coefficient applied to a positive period's return will increase the weight of the asset in the strategy. A negative return would decrease it. A contrarian strategy results from negative coefficients being applied to previous returns because a positive return of one asset will lower its weighting and vice versa. Specifying a mixture of positive and negative coefficients in the computation of the weights balances between these two strategies.

Most dynamic strategies aim to achieve high returns while keeping the volatility at low levels. For example, the structurer of the strategy can cap the level of volatility to a determined low level, say 10% annually, and maximize the return based on this level of volatility. Another strategy can be based on freezing the expected return (8% annually for instance) and minimizing the volatility. Once all the constraints and the objectives are determined, an optimizer algorithm will need to be utilized to solve for the weights formulas of the assets composing the strategy. Ultimately, dynamic strategies are managed in the same way as funds. There are specific rebalancing dates at which the trader buys/sells specified quantities of the assets in order to adjust the different weights, depending on the rebalancing formula.

The dynamic strategy itself is regarded as an exotic underlying, and the option payoffs structured on dynamic strategies are typically simple in nature. One example is the investor who is bullish on the underlying dynamic strategy, but specifically on its ability to outperform a benchmark index. In this case an outperformance option can be structured on the return of the dynamic strategy versus this benchmark. Another example is the call option where the investor is essentially paying a premium in exchange for a no-downside exposure to the strategy. Note that the seller of a call option on the strategy, who will need to go long Delta in the underlying strategy, must be long $w_i \times \Delta_i$ for each asset i with these weights changing through time. Likewise for the individual Vegas that may need to be dynamically adjusted. If the strategy allows for negative weights, then the cost of shorting the assets, i.e. borrow costs, must also be factored in.

Since most of the strategies present quite low levels of volatility, it is cheap to issue options on such indices, and this makes investing in notes based on dynamic strategies a definite possibility. A management fee is typically charged on an annual basis for providing this exposure to the investor, and is typically a fixed percentage of notional. This will at least cover the transaction costs incurred by the seller and reflect the cost of hedging the exposure to the strategy.

The seller of an option on a rebalancing strategy may be exposed to gap risk, which would be the result of a large move in one underlying followed accordingly by a significant shift in the weights of the index at the next rebalancing date. To price this, one would need to use a model that allows for jumps in the paths of the risky assets of the strategy. This risk can be at least partially hedged using options, possibly short maturity OTM put options in the case of downside jumps. An estimation of the gap risk within the strategy leads to the selection of these hedging options. Cliquet puts can also serve this purpose, with period to period resets matching the rebalancing dates; the cheaper option being cliquet put spreads. Whether this risk is to be hedged or not, it should be estimated and priced into the charge of the management fee.

21.3   THEMATIC PRODUCTS

A thematic product is a financial product whose underlying is constructed on the basis of a specific theme, for example a "green stocks" or "clean energy". An underlying can be constructed to represent these and provide exposure to the theme via equities. Typically this will take on the form of a dynamic index where the selection of the underlying basket is based on a theme, and the (dynamic) weights given by some set of rules. The idea is to strike a balance between providing the investor with the most representative and relevant exposure to the required theme, and at the same time construct an index on which options can be realistically written and hedged.

21.3.1   Demand for Thematic Products

The demand for such a product starts with an investor's view. This may be based on the conclusion of research regarding, for example, the prospects of certain emerging markets, or the increase in the global demand for food, and serve as the investment vehicle to express these conclusions. The reason behind considering a thematic index, compared to a static basket, is that the optimal entry into a basket of assets (whose weights are fixed all the way to maturity) may represent the desired view today, but may not do so in the future. A thematic index can allow for a dynamic allocation that rebalances to ensure consistency with the *theme*. We now consider an emerging markets theme and a green energy theme to illustrate.

Example: Emerging Markets

The term *emerging* generally refers to an economy that is undergoing industrialization and growth at a fast pace. Investing in emerging markets can provide very large returns: recent times have seen some emerging market indices grow by over 60% for some consecutive years. However, this comes at a price: the returns on emerging market indices can be dangerously volatile. Other problems that investors face when trying to access such markets include the lack of transparency in corporate decisions and relatively poor liquidity.

An emerging market index, for example, can be constructed to provide an investor with equity exposure to various emerging economies. The idea behind this thematic index is that as economic factors change, the weights in such an index can be adjusted according to some methodology to reflect these changes. The weights of the countries considered within the index can be selected to reflect factors including political stability, laws and regulations, and economic conditions, in order to provide the investor with a dynamic exposure to an equity basket with lots of potential growth. As these conditions improve (or deteriorate) in a country, its weight in the index can be increased (or decreased respectively). The emerging market's theme provides a good example throughout this section.

Example: Green Energy

Another example is a green energy theme, by which the investor can take a view on a group of equities that are in some way involved in the development of green energy technologies. Green energy refers to energy sources that are environmentally less polluting than traditional energy sources such as oil. The view is that oil is a finite commodity, and environmental concerns and regulations will lead to an increased demand for green energy. This will translate to equity gains in the long run – assuming the product correctly reflects this.

An index with this theme would include firms that are involved in research and development of green energy technologies. To be included, such firms will need to have a minimum percentage (for example 50%) of their revenues being generated from green energy involvement.

Green energy has several subsectors and the index can be structured to balance equally amongst them or possibly focus on some more than others.

21.3.2 Structuring a Thematic Index

Assume we started with a universe of possible assets to create a thematic index, and from these made a selection of a starting basket, with the possibility of adding more from this universe according to some methodology. The weighting in such an index must follow a preset methodology, i.e. a fixed set of constraints, known as the *index methodology*.

For example: assume there are 50 assets that represent the theme, from which we will select 20 to be in our starting basket. The index methodology can, for example, limit the minimum amount of assets to be 10 and the maximum to be 50. The target volatility of the index should stay within the range 15–45% for example. The target equivalent dividend yield on the index can be in the range 1.5–4.5% for example. The weights of the assets should additionally be capped so that no component has more than 15% of the weight of the basket.

In the case of an emerging market index, we have a great deal of uncertainty regarding future dividends and so a broad target range as above would be reasonable to set. The assets are also typically quite volatile, and again a wide range as above would be reasonable. If the index consisted of multiple countries then the weight on any one country should also be capped to ensure that the index is not biased towards one country. The cap will depend on how many countries are to be included; for example, if there are 10, then it is unreasonable to have more than 20% on one country. A thematic index providing equity exposure to Africa cannot have, say, 50% weight on South Africa and still be considered a thematic product for the whole continent. Additionally, the various sectors should also be capped: communication, banking, energy, etc., to again provide some balance. The caps are to ensure that the investor will, throughout the life of the exposure to the thematic index, always gain a balanced exposure to the said theme.

Liquidity is also a concern, especially when emerging markets are involved, and there should also be a liquidity constraint on the assets being considered as constituents in the index. The index methodology should include a minimum requirement of liquidity. If a market were to become more transparent and liquid, then it would again be favoured during the index review. An increased market capitalization of a specific firm within the index will also be considered as a criterion for increasing its weight. We see this below as an important factor when considering pricing options on such an index.

The frequency of the rebalancing of the index will be specified in its methodology. For example, one can have annual or semi-annual index reviews, where the asset constituents are reweighted according to the theme via the methodology. In the case of the emerging market a considerable improvement in the political situation can make one country favourable in terms of potential growth and its weight increased. In the green energy theme, a constituent company may be deriving income from other sources and focusing less on green energy, thus making it unsuitable for inclusion in a green energy theme. Other companies may also have emerged with green energy as a large part of their revenue, and can then be considered for addition to the universe of the thematic index. An unanticipated corporate event can be grounds for making a non-scheduled adjustment to the index, and the creator of the thematic index would typically reserve the right to do so, based on some criteria.

The index can be made into a *composite index*, following the concept behind the composite option of Chapter 20. An emerging market thematic index, which involves equities from various countries denominated in different currencies, can be set to be composite USD, for example (or another currency). The specification of the composite currency will have an impact on how the index looks in a back-test, and can be set according to investors' preferences. Additionally, to make the index more appealing from a marketing perspective, the index methodology can be written in order to make the back-test look optimal. For example, increasing the number of assets by adding de-correlated assets within the theme, if available, to the index will provide a diversification effect and lower the volatility of the index.

21.3.3 Structured Products on Thematic Indices

Once there is such an index we can discuss the products that are possible using it as the underlying asset. In theory any payout is possible, but here we are in the realm of an *exotic* underlying, and the general trend is for relatively simple payouts. The reason is that the underlying should itself encapsulate the investor's view, not a complex payout. By buying an option on a thematic index, the investor gets, in one transaction, exposure to the theme in which they wish to invest, avoiding the time and transaction costs involved in maintaining such an exposure themselves.

Since the derivatives are simple, marketing a simple derivative on such an index is all about the underlying itself, and a back-test reflecting its performance both in absolute terms and comparatively with similar assets is key. Additionally, if the index is formally computed by an independent agent and the results given by data providers, this makes seeing its past performance and doing comparisons easier for the investor, and simplifies its marketing.

A straight exposure to an index can be in the form of a Delta-1 product, or some form of leveraged forward (recall section 3.10). In the simple leveraged forward the investor is long a call option (upside potential) and short a put option (downside risk). These can have the same strike or different strikes reflecting different risk appetites. The participations are not necessarily equal and the investor may only want 50% participation in the downside in order to enhance the participation in the upside. If they are both set at 100% participation, and the strike is ATM, then the investor is exposed with a participation of 100% to both the gains and potential losses in the thematic index. In this case there is no optionality.

The investor who is looking to protect capital and not assume any downside risk can buy a call option on such a thematic index, pay the up-front premium, and from then on only have upside participation in the index. Essentially we have at our disposal in this case all the tools of section 3.10 for structuring the option that best provides the investor with the required exposure, and at a required price. In the case of emerging markets, we generally expect high levels of volatility, making a call option on such an index relatively expensive. Averaging or caps can be used to reduce the prices of these vanilla combinations, and features such as capital protection can be offered by including the option in a note. One can in this case also consider payoffs such as those in section 3.10, where the investor is short volatility.

21.3.4 Pricing Options on Thematic Indices

The above discussion focuses on the investor's point of view and requirements for exposure. One can build a thematic index that genuinely provides the best possible exposure to the theme at hand, and have a methodology by which the investor's view on the theme will be continuously represented through adjusting the weights. Once an option has been specified, taking as underlying a thematic index, the question is how does the seller of an option on such an index price and hedge such a position? The strategy will be to model the index as a single asset, combining the properties of the assets, and accounting for the changes regarding reweighting according to the index methodology.

If we start with a Black–Scholes environment, assuming a log-normal process for the underlying index, we must specify the risk-neutral drift and the volatility of the process. The drift in this case will need to encompass information regarding the risk-free rates in the currencies in which the underlying's constituents are denominated, information regarding the dividend yields of these assets, and additionally any quanto adjustments that are necessary. These inputs will have a large impact on the Delta of the option, but in order to Delta hedge we must ultimately have a minimum amount of liquidity in the assets.

Liquidity

In situations such as the emerging market example, liquidity is a key concern when pricing options on such an index. Delta hedging involves the buying and selling of the underlying assets, and we must be able to sufficiently trade them in order to Delta hedge efficiently. For a stock to be considered *liquid* means that one must be able to buy and sell its stock without moving the price of the stock. In some emerging markets where little volume is traded, it is difficult to buy Delta of stock without moving its price, and so during the construction and subsequent index reviews the seller may impose a minimum amount of liquidity requirement to make pricing possible. This can be done by flooring the daily traded volume at, for example, 10 or 15 million USD, conservatively, and as such there should be sufficient liquidity to Delta hedge. Problems with liquidity come from large bid–ask spreads on certain stocks, and these are generally associated with low volumes, and if such a stock is to be used, one must price a cost into the price, as a cost will be incurred during Delta hedging.

Sometimes companies have shares that are listed on their local market as well as on a foreign market, and the choice of which to include in a thematic index would be the one with the most liquidity. We may be able to find American Depository Receipts (ADRs) for some foreign companies. The holder of an ADR is essentially long a number of shares in a foreign company that is trading on a US exchange. By buying an ADR, compared to accessing a foreign market and buying the stock there, the investor bypasses the transaction costs involved with trading in a foreign market. The ADR's price is in USD and pays dividends in USD. This, and the fact that the ADR is traded through US markets like a local US stock, means that the ADR carries some basis risk, but this can be charged for up front. These can prove particularly useful in the case of some illiquid market products, and if the ADR for a particular stock is more liquid than the stock itself in its local market, then the ADR should be used in place of the stock.

Global Depository Receipts (GDRs) are similar to ADRs but are traded through the London Stock Exchange. Again the holder of a GDR is long a number of shares in a foreign company, and if these are more liquid than the foreign stock, especially in an emerging market, these may be used instead of the stock itself. Additionally to these two, if one is able to trade futures on an index – for example, on the equity index of an emerging market that has constituents in the thematic index – then this adds additional liquidity. As discussed in Chapter 5, futures or other assets can be used in Delta hedging in place of the underlying.

Dividends

Assuming that liquidity in the constituent assets is sufficient to Delta hedge, we must look at the uncertainty in the dividends. Firstly, the index methodology will have a dividend target that should be met, and the rebalancing will take this into account, but especially in the case of emerging markets, there is a large uncertainty surrounding future dividend yields. Problems stemming from tax or regulatory issues in some foreign countries may imply that the holder of a foreign stock may not receive 100% of dividends paid, and because the seller of a call option is long Delta of stock and thus long dividends, one must adjust for this before pricing. One can simply take a haircut on the dividend yield to counter this and the uncertainty coming from the lack of transparency in some emerging market corporate policies. In some cases, for example that of the green theme described above, it may be possible to hedge dividend risks using dividend swaps if the assets are all traded on major exchanges.

Management Fee

If an annual management fee is being charged for maintaining the index, and explicitly for offering an option on such an index, then this must be included in the pricing. Assuming that this is a constant percentage f, typically within the range of 50 bps to 2% per annum, with higher values corresponding to greater complexity in the underlying index, then this can be subtracted from the risk free rate in the drift to make the adjustment. The analogy is an underlying stock that pays an annual dividend of $f\%$, and the impact of this on the pricing is the same as including the annual fee of $f\%$.

Composite Adjustment

A back-test is essentially a time series containing the previous path of the thematic index, and if, when conducting a back-test, the index is to be composite then we must adjust for this. At each stage where returns are considered, generally at the daily close of each stock, then if the index is to be composite USD for example, each stock's price must be changed to its price in USD at this point in time. This is done by simply multiplying each day's closing price by the USD exchange rate with the currency in which the stock is denominated. The composite index will then be adjusted by the volatility of the FX rate.

Volatility

The composite index's time series can then be used to compute the realized volatility of the index. One can consider for example the 100-day realized volatility of the time series, as far back as it can go, with more relevance placed on the more recent period's realized volatility. Even if we had implied volatilities for all the constituent assets, using these to compute the current implied volatility of the index as a basket would require implied correlations that we do not have. As such we need a method for pricing and hedging the volatility of the index.

In many cases, we may be unable to find liquid quotes on the options of the underlying stocks. In this case we find a proxy index or ETF on which we can trade options, and consider a volatility spread between the thematic index and the proxy index, or ETF. We know the time series of the proxy, and thus know its realized volatility. Plotted as a time series against the realized volatility of the thematic index, one can observe the spread between the two. If the proxy is sufficiently related to the thematic index then these two will generally follow similar paths, and, if so, one can consider the average of the difference between the two series. Assuming that this is not too far from the extreme cases, and that the variance of this spread is quite low, one can use this spread to imply the volatility of the thematic index from the proxy ETF or index.

An ETF, or another index, can serve as a Vega hedge proxy for a thematic index, providing we can trade options on it. One compares its realized volatility series with that of the thematic index. If we obtain a spread of 4% between the volatilities, the ETFs (or the indexes) being the higher, then we use the implied volatilities from the options on the ETF (or index) and subtract this spread. This may be particularly relevant if the options on this ETF or index are to be used to Vega hedge an option position in the thematic index. The implied volatility of the option on the proxy used should have a maturity equal to that of the option being priced on the thematic index. From here the volatility to use in pricing is dependent on the nature of the payoff. The payoff governs whether the seller is short or long volatility, and a bid–ask spread is taken around the computed level of volatility accordingly, and as aggressively or conservatively as required.

In the case of an ATM call option, we are not overly concerned about skew, but in the case of a skew-dependent payoff, for example a call spread, we must price this skew. An index's skew is more pronounced than those of single stocks, so if we have an index as a proxy we can use its skew knowing that this is conservative (in the case where the seller is short skew). In the case of the green energy theme this may be possible, especially if the underlying constituents are in some of the major global indices.

Appendices

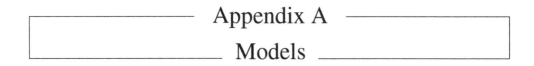

Appendix A
Models

A.1 BLACK–SCHOLES

A.1.1 Black–Scholes SDE

In the Black–Scholes model, the price of the underlying is modelled as a log-normal random variable. The stochastic differential equation (SDE) governing the dynamics of the price is given by

$$dS(t) = r S(t) dt + \sigma S(t) dW_t$$

where r is the risk-free rate, and σ the volatility of the underlying. Like a typical SDE, this equation consists of a deterministic part and a random part. The part $dS(t) = r S(t) dt$ is a deterministic, ordinary differential equation, which can be written as $\frac{dS(t)}{dt} = r S(t)$. The addition of the term $\sigma S(t) dW_t$ introduces randomness into the equation, making it *stochastic*. The random part contains the term W_t, which is Brownian motion; it is a random process that is normally distributed with mean zero and variance t. The assumption of a log-normal price implies that log prices are normally distributed. The log is another way of expressing returns, so in a different way this is saying that if the price is log-normally distributed, then the returns of the underlying are normally distributed.

A.1.2 Black–Scholes PDE

We know the payoff of an option $C(S, T)$ at maturity T, but to know its value at a time $t < T$ we need to understand how C evolves as a function of S and T. The price of the option $C(S, T)$ satisfies a partial differential equation (PDE). If we make Black–Scholes assumptions, then the PDE it satisfies is the Black–Scholes PDE given by

$$\frac{\partial C}{\partial t} + \frac{1}{2}\sigma^2 S^2 \frac{\partial^2 C}{\partial S^2} + r S \frac{\partial C}{\partial S} - r C = 0$$

The parameter r is the continuously compounded risk-free rate of interest, $\sigma > 0$ is the volatility of the stock, and $t > 0$ is the time to maturity of the stock option.

In the case of a call option, the above PDE is satisfied and the following boundary conditions are imposed

- $C(0, t) = 0$ for all t
- $C(S, t) \to S$ as $S \to \infty$
- $C(S, T) = \max(S - K, 0)$

These all make intuitive sense to us. If the spot goes to zero, the call's payout is zero, whatever the time remaining. If the spot gets arbitrarily large, then we know the option is ITM and its price will grow at the same rate as the spot. The third condition is simply the payoff of the call that we want the price to satisfy at maturity. If we solve this PDE using these boundary conditions, then the result is of course the Black–Scholes formula for the price of the call option.

This PDE can be rewritten in terms of the Greeks as

$$\Theta + \frac{1}{2}\sigma^2 S^2 \Gamma + rS\Delta - rC = 0$$

As we have seen before, the assumption of zero rates ($r = 0$) gives the relationship between Θ and Γ.

A.2 LOCAL VOLATILITY MODELS

Local volatility refers to the term $\sigma(S(t), t)$ which appears in the random part of the SDE

$$dS(t) = rS(t)\,dt + \sigma(S(t), t)\,dW_t$$

describing the evolution of a stock price. The case where $\sigma(S(t), t) = \sigma S(t)$, where σ is a constant, is simply the Black–Scholes case. The drift term is the same as the Black–Scholes case, and it contains the risk-free rate r in light of the fact that we are still working in a risk-neutral world.

The first thing to note is that although the function $\sigma(S(t), t)$ can imply various distributions, the local volatility model is still driven by only one source of randomness: W_t, Brownian motion. The idea is to search for this set of coefficients $\sigma(S(t), t)$ so that if we used this diffusion to price European options, we would get back the market data. Finding these coefficients is essentially calibrating the local volatility model.

The PDE satisfied by the price of a call option under the local volatility model is given by

$$\frac{\partial C}{\partial t} + \frac{1}{2}\sigma^2(S(t), t)\frac{\partial^2 C}{\partial S^2} + rS\frac{\partial C}{\partial S} - rC = 0 \qquad (A.1)$$

Given a set of call options of various strikes and maturities, a surface translates to a set of prices of call options $C(T, K)$. The existence of the diffusion coefficients $\sigma(S(t), t)$ that will return these prices was proved by Dupire (1994; see also Wilmott, 2000). In essence, we are asking the question: Is there a distribution such that if we write the payoffs of vanillas as expected values, given this distribution, can it return all the correct prices of vanillas? Dupire's equation states:

$$\frac{\partial C(T, K)}{\partial T} = \frac{1}{2}\sigma^2(K, T; S_0)K^2 \frac{\partial^2 C(K, T)}{\partial K^2} + (r - D)\left(C(T, K) - K\frac{\partial C(K, T)}{\partial K}\right)$$

Writing the equation in terms of the forward to remove the drift terms (Gatheral, 2006), we get

$$\frac{\partial C(F_T, T, K)}{\partial T} = \frac{1}{2}\sigma^2(K, T; S_0)K^2 \frac{\partial^2 C(F_T, K, T)}{\partial K^2}$$

All the terms are known except $\sigma^2(K, T; S_0)$, which can be solved via this equation. To obtain an entire and meaningful distribution, we must have liquid quotes for options of different strikes and maturities. In practice, problems can arise when searching for this distribution, and techniques involving maximum entropy, for example, can be applied.

One debate regarding local volatility is that even though it is a one-factor model that allows for a calibration to implied volatility surfaces, the dynamics implied by these models do not necessarily match those observed empirically. Assuming that we fit an implied skew today, and the underlying moves, how does the implied volatility in the market move, and how does the implied volatility generated by a local volatility model move? This is important from a hedging point of view: the Greeks computed via a model differ depending on the various model assumptions. If an option's price is sensitive to skew, then skew must be included when computing the Delta of an option for example. Delta measures the sensitivity to a move in price, but if the model predicts the skew to move in an opposite manner to that of the market, then the Delta will be wrong. In fact there are cases where a naive non-skew Black–Scholes Delta may be better. Traders will typically adjust the Deltas anyway based on their assumption of whether the skew follows the sticky strike or sticky Delta rules, or some interpolation of these two.

A.3 STOCHASTIC VOLATILITY

Stochastic volatility models are needed when pricing structure with non-trivial Vega convexity – for example, the Napoleon structure of Chapter 14. We use Heston's model as an example and work through some issues.

A.3.1 Heston's Model

Heston's model (Heston, 1993) is a popular stochastic volatility model, particularly for equity derivatives. In Heston, the underlying stock price is modelled as a random process and its variance is also modelled as a random process. In essence this means that the variance is stochastic, but for the majority of our concerns this is acceptable. The two-factor model implies dynamics that are not log-normal and it can generate implied volatility skews and surfaces that are consistent with those observed in the market. The model allows for an arbitrary correlation between the underlying's price process and that of its variance, and additionally, as the title of Heston's paper suggests, there exist semi-closed form solutions for the prices of European options under this model. Having such formulas is what makes calibration to a surface of vanillas tractable.

In its basic form, the Heston model describes the evolution of the two processes according to the following set of SDEs:

$$dS_t = \mu S_t \, dt + \sqrt{v_t} S_t \, dW_t$$
$$dv_t = \kappa(\theta - v_t) \, dt + \sigma \sqrt{v_t} \, dZ_t$$

where v_t is the instantaneous variance, and dW_t and dZ_t are Brownian motions with correlation ρ.

The first feature to note is that the variance is modelled by a mean-reverting process. The term $\kappa(\theta - v_t) \, dt$ in the drift of the variance governs how it reverts: θ is the long-term variance to which this process reverts, and κ is the rate at which it reverts to this mean. Empirical volatilities and variances generally mean-revert over time, and so this modelling assumption is quite realistic.

The term σ is the vol-of-vol term, to be precise it is the vol-of-var, and it governs the volatility of the process for the variance. The correlation ρ is the coefficient that governs joint movements in the stock and its variance. As such we expect that if implemented correctly, then σ will influence the curvature of the implied volatilities: a higher σ will mean more curvature in the implied volatilities. Also, ρ will influence the skew on the implied volatilities – the more negative ρ is, the steeper the skew.

The time t price of a call option $C(S_0, K, v_0, t, T)$, with maturity T, under Heston's model satisfies the partial differential equation (Heston, 1993):

$$\frac{\partial C}{\partial t} + \frac{S^2 v}{2}\frac{\partial^2 C}{\partial S^2} + (r - d)S\frac{\partial C}{\partial S} - (r - d)C$$

$$+ [\kappa(\theta - v) - \lambda v]\frac{\partial C}{\partial v} + \frac{\sigma^2 v}{2}\frac{\partial^2 C}{\partial v^2} + \rho\sigma v S\frac{\partial^2 C}{\partial S\,\partial v} = 0$$

We can immediately see additional terms to the Black–Scholes PDE due to the variance being taken as a random process. Firstly, the term $\frac{\sigma^2 v}{2}\frac{\partial^2 C}{\partial v^2}$ is the Vega convexity term. By allowing for the variance to be stochastic, the pricing PDE that the option prices must involve a Vega convexity term. As such, the model knows about Vega convexity, whereas the local volatility above does not (no terms regarding the volatility or variance appear in equation (A.1)). A similar term will appear in ANY other stochastic volatility.

Additionally, the term $\rho\sigma v S\frac{\partial^2 C}{\partial S\partial v}$ is the Vanna term, which governs the joint movements in both, as is clear from the mixed partial derivative. The correlation term ρ appears in front of this term of the PDE only. In equities, we know that the skew is downward sloping, and this will be reflected in the calibration as we will find a suitable calibrated value for ρ to be negative. This is consistent with what we observe empirically: as the underlying moves down, volatility (or variance) moves up. In the case of FX where we observe a smile, we expect positive values for ρ.

Despite all these parameters, the Heston model, and similar stochastic volatility models, struggle to provide good calibrations to an entire surface. In particular, it struggles to fit both the short end of the skew and the long end simultaneously. This can be remedied with the addition of jumps, discussed below.

Volatility Derivatives in Heston's Model

Heston's model considers the variance of the underlying to be stochastic, satisfying the SDE

$$dv_t = \kappa(\theta - v_t)\,dt + \sigma\sqrt{v_t}\,dW_t$$

It is possible to obtain a closed form for the price of the variance swap of Chapter 16 – computing the fair strike that is. This is given by the expectation of the annualized total variance, which computed to

$$E\,[\text{Annualized Total Variance}] = \frac{1}{T}E\left[\int_0^T v_t\,dt\right]$$

$$= \frac{e^{-\kappa T} + 1}{\kappa T}(\theta - v_0) + \theta$$

This result only involves the drift terms of the variance – not the vol-of-vol or the stock/variance correlation. This makes sense because the price of the variance swap should depend on the prices of European options – not modelling-dependent assumptions. The Delta of the variance swap under Heston is zero, because the underlying spot price does not appear in this equation. Additionally, we can compute the convexity adjustment in Heston's model needed to price volatility swaps. As we saw in Chapter 16 the volatility swap cannot be replicated in a similar fashion to the variance swap. Thus a model is needed, and the price is a function of the model's assumptions.

For a more in-depth discussion of Heston's model we refer the reader to Gatheral (2006), which offers a treatment of all aspects of the model, specifically those relating to volatility derivatives. Implementation and calibration details are discussed by Mikhailov and Nogel (2005). Further details regarding volatility derivatives in the Heston model are found in Sepp (2008), most importantly, analytical formulas for options on realized variance.

A.3.2 The SABR Model

SABR is a stochastic volatility model pioneered in Hagan *et al.* (2002) with the aim of capturing the correct dynamics of the implied volatility smile. The model describes the evolution of a single forward, such as a forward LIBOR rate or a forward FX rate. The volatility of this forward is taken as a random process as well, making it a stochastic volatility model. The forward and its volatility evolve according to the set of SDEs given by

$$\mathrm{d}F(t) = \alpha(t)F^{\beta}(t)\,\mathrm{d}W_t$$
$$\mathrm{d}\alpha(t) = \nu\alpha(t)\,\mathrm{d}Z_t$$

where W_t and Z_t are two correlated Brownian motions, with correlation coefficient $-1 < \rho < 1$.

The first line describes the evolution of the forward process, and this is in fact a local volatility known as the *Constant Elasticity of Variance*, or CEV. The β has the constraint $0 \leq \beta \leq 1$ in the SABR model, and the CEV part, $F(t)^{\beta}$, can be anything between the cases of $\beta = 0$ which is a Normal model, and $\beta = 1$ which gives the log-normal model. In fact, if we take the parameter ν in the second equation to be zero, then the volatility α becomes deterministic; therefore in this case, taking $\beta = 1$ reduces this to the Black–Scholes SDE for a forward. This parameter ν is called the *vol-of-vol* because it is the coefficient in the random part of the volatility.

The volatility in the SABR model is driftless, and is assumed to be log-normal. In contrast with Heston where the variance term has a drift that makes sure it reverts back to the long-run mean, in SABR there is no such mean-reverting drift. This may not make sense at first, that one models volatility as a log-normal process with no mean reversion, especially since we know that volatilities are empirically mean-reverting. However, the SABR model is not trying to capture the dynamics of long-term volatilities. The model is the simplest extension of the Black–Scholes model that knows about volatility smiles and skews, and gives correct smile dynamics. The model's simplicity allows for a quite *accurate*, *intuitive* and *closed-form* solution (given in section 17.1.8) that is perhaps its greatest strength.

The SABR formula is derived by solving the PDE associated with the price of a call option under the SABR model. The PDE is simpler than Heston's because of the absence of drift terms. The method used to solve the PDE is an asymptotic method, which means that the solution is not exact, but is quite accurate for certain conditions. In the SABR model this condition is that $\nu^2 t$ (vol-of-vol squared × time to expiration) is small. The result of the asymptotic expansion is a volatility that can be used in conjunction with Black–Scholes formula. This volatility involves all the parameters of the model: β, ρ, ν, the initial values we know from the market for F_0 and α_0, and the strike of the option. When used as the volatility in the Black–Scholes model, it returns the SABR price of an option. The fact that the model is solved in terms of the implied volatility generated by the model, means that calibration to implied volatilities in the market can be done directly. Additionally, useable formulas for the probability distribution in the SABR model have been derived, making it relatively easy to use the model in a copula. For useable formulas and derivations of the probability distribution of the SABR model, we refer to Hagan *et al.* (2005).

The SABR formula is an excellent approximation in the case of ATM options, but its accuracy deteriorates as we go to deep OTM call options. The reality is that these options, in the case of CMSs for example, must be priced correctly. The SABR volatility formula can diverge as we go deep OTM when in reality the implied volatilities of these options should converge to a constant. Nonetheless, these problems in the wings can be remedied, possibly by reparameterizing the implied volatility formula of SABR to be constant beyond certain levels of strikes.

A.4   JUMP MODELS

As we know, the returns in equity markets exhibit fat tails. The assumption of log-normality is not observed and we seem to have an equity skew. One way to explain this is to consider jump models. A jump component can be added to some of the models we know in order to make them more realistic by allowing the underlying's price to *jump*. The inclusion of jumps helps to explain the short end of the skew and allows models to be better calibrated to this end of the skew. Recall the discussion in Chapter 4.

Merton's jump-diffusion system (see Merton, 1976) models the asset's price by a Brownian motion with drift, as in the case of Black–Scholes, but additionally with a compound Poisson process to model the jumps. The corresponding SDE, in a jump-diffusion setting, is

$$\frac{\mathrm{d}S}{S} = (\alpha - \lambda k)\,\mathrm{d}t + \sigma\,\mathrm{d}W_t + \mathrm{d}q_t$$

Here α is the instantaneous expected return on the asset price, S; σ is the instantaneous variance of the return when the Poisson event does not occur; $\mathrm{d}W_t$ is a standard Brownian motion; and q_t is the independent Poisson process. The diffusion part models small movements in the underlying, and the jump portion adds randomly occurring large movements, i.e. jumps. Market crashes are often characterized by large downward jumps, which must be modelled by a jump process as these large moves are not typical of standard diffusions.

Bates's model (see Bates, 1996) is essentially a Heston model plus jumps similar to those of Merton. As such, it allows for both stochastic volatility and jumps. The result is that the Bates model can be much better fit to an entire surface: the jumps are used to explain the short maturity skew, and the stochastic volatility the longer end of the skew. Separately, either of these models would struggle – the stochastic volatility model to fit the short end and the jump model to explain the long end – but combined they complement each other well.

A.5   HULL–WHITE INTEREST RATE MODEL AND EXTENSIONS

One popular short-rate model, as mentioned in Chapter 20 in the context of interest rate models, is the Hull–White model (see Hull and White, 1990). The original Hull–White model is also known as the "extended Vasicek" because it models the short rate with a (modified) Vasicek process:

$$\mathrm{d}r(t) = (\theta(t) - \kappa(t)r(t))\,\mathrm{d}t + \sigma(t)\,\mathrm{d}W(t)$$

Firstly, notice that the drift term is similar to that of the variance in Heston's model: it is mean-reverting. Again this is a valuable property of the model because interest rates are generally mean-reverting, and if one has to assign a drift, this is a reasonable choice. The drift $(\theta(t) - \kappa(t)r(t))\,dt$ can be written as

$$\kappa(t)\left(\frac{\theta(t)}{\kappa(t)} - r(t)\right)dt$$

and the interpretation of the parameters of long-run mean and reversion rate are clear.

It is the addition of these time-dependent parameters in the process that generalizes the Vasicek process, and in fact makes the model more applicable. The time-dependent drift function $\theta(t)$ is typically chosen so that the model gives an *exact* fit to today's observed yield curve. Closed forms for bond prices are given in terms of this function and the rest of the model parameters, see Hull and White (1990). The parameter $\sigma(t)$ is taken to be time dependent so that the model has more flexibility to also fit the implied volatilities of swaptions or caplets.

From an implementation standpoint, the fact that this model can be placed onto a pricing tree or lattice makes it particularly useful for products such as Bermudan swaptions whose pricing requires some form of backward induction. As neat as this may be, the model suffers from the problems mentioned in Chapter 20 in that the forward rates are perfectly correlated in these models. This makes them unsuited for pricing applications that have sensitivities to the correlation between forward rates. One possible way around this, and a method of allowing the model to offer a much richer volatility structure, is to make it into a two-factor model.

Two-Factor Short-Rate Models

The two-factor Hull–White model results from adding a second process to the model as described above (see Hull, 2003). Consider the model dynamics

$$df(r(t)) = [\theta(t) + u - \alpha(t)\,f(r(t))]\,dt + \sigma_1(t)\,dW_1(t)$$
$$du = -bu\,dt + \sigma_2(t)\,dW_2(t)$$

where the function f generalizes the Hull–White model, allowing the above process to represent a function of the short rate, giving greater calibration potential. The additional factor u is itself a mean-reverting process with a long-run mean of zero (it also has an initial value of zero).

As such, instead of taking the volatility of the short rate to be stochastic, the authors have allowed for a more elaborate drift term. This part of the equation controls how the yield curve is captured and it allows for a rich set of shapes to be calibrated with much less time dependence than the one-factor case. Additionally, closed form prices for bonds exist in the two-factor case, making calibration quick.

Appendix B

Approximations

B.1 APPROXIMATIONS FOR VANILLA PRICES AND GREEKS

In section 5.9 of Chapter 5 concerning the Greeks, we saw some approximations that can be used for quick mental computation of prices and Greeks. Here we give their derivations.

Firstly, we need to approximate the Normal probability density function $\phi(x)$, which is also referred to as the derivative of the Normal CDF $\mathcal{N}'(x)$

$$\phi(x) = \frac{1}{\sqrt{2\pi}} e^{-\frac{x^2}{2}}$$

$$= \frac{1}{\sqrt{2\pi}} \left(1 - \frac{x^2}{2} + \cdots \right)$$

which is just a standard Taylor series expansion of the exponential function. The Vega of both call and put options under Black–Scholes is given by $\mathcal{V} = S\mathcal{N}'(d_1)\sqrt{T}$. In the case where the option is ATM, d_1 reduces to $d_1 = \sigma\sqrt{T}/2$, and the Vega of the ATM vanillas can be approximated, using the above formula, as

$$\text{Vega} = S\sqrt{T}\mathcal{N}'(d_1)$$

$$= S\sqrt{T}\frac{1}{\sqrt{2\pi}} \left(1 - \frac{d_1^2}{2} + \cdots \right)$$

$$= S\sqrt{T}\frac{1}{\sqrt{2\pi}} \left(1 - \frac{\sigma^2 t}{8} + \cdots \right) \tag{B.1}$$

If we take only the zeroth order of this series expansion we get

$$\text{Vega}_{\text{ATM}} \approx \frac{S\sqrt{T}}{\sqrt{2\pi}}$$

The price of an ATM call option can then be approximated knowing that the ATM call is linear in volatility (no Vega convexity, assuming zero rates). We get

$$\text{Call}_{\text{ATM}} \approx \frac{S\sigma\sqrt{T}}{\sqrt{2\pi}}$$

The price of the call option can alternatively be approximated directly from the Black–Scholes formula

$$C = S\mathcal{N}(d_1) - Ke^{-rT}\mathcal{N}(d_2)$$

and approximating the Normal CDF $\mathcal{N}(x)$. The result for the approximation of the call option's price can be found in the literature in Brenner and Subrahmanyam (1988).

We now approximate the Normal CDF to use below. Starting from the definition of the Normal CDF and using the above approximations based on Taylor series of the exponential, plus some tricks regarding the CDF, we get

$$\mathcal{N}(x) = \frac{1}{\sqrt{2\pi}} \int_{-\infty}^{x} e^{-\frac{s^2}{2}} ds$$

$$= \frac{1}{\sqrt{2\pi}} \int_{-\infty}^{0} e^{-\frac{s^2}{2}} ds + \frac{1}{\sqrt{2\pi}} \int_{0}^{x} e^{-\frac{s^2}{2}} ds$$

$$= \frac{1}{2} + \frac{1}{\sqrt{2\pi}} \int_{0}^{x} \left(1 - \frac{s^2}{2} + \cdots \right) ds$$

$$= \frac{1}{2} + \frac{1}{\sqrt{2\pi}} \left(x - \frac{x^3}{6} + \cdots \right)$$

The closer x is to zero, the more accurate this approximation. If rates are zero, and the call is struck ATM, then substituting this approximation for the CDFs into Black–Scholes gives the same zeroth-order approximation to the price of the call option as above. To make both these more computable in the head, we note that the fraction $1/\sqrt{2\pi}$ is approximately equal to 0.4.

Moving on, the Delta of a call option is given by $\mathcal{N}(d_1)$ under Black–Scholes, and we approximate this also using the above formula.

$$\Delta = \mathcal{N}(d_1)$$

$$= \frac{1}{2} + \frac{1}{\sqrt{2\pi}} (d_1 + \cdots)$$

$$\approx \frac{1}{2} + \frac{d_1}{\sqrt{2\pi}}$$

$$\approx 0.5 + 0.4 d_1$$

where we have just plugged d_1 into the above approximation of $\mathcal{N}(x)$, and taken this expansion to the zeroth order only. We already know that the d_1 of an ATM option is given by $\sigma\sqrt{T}/2$, so the zeroth-order approximation to the Delta of an ATM option is $0.5 + 0.2 \times \sigma\sqrt{T}$.

The approximation for Gamma also follows from similar approximations:

$$\text{Gamma} = \frac{\mathcal{N}'(d_1)}{S\sigma\sqrt{T}}$$

$$= \frac{1}{\sqrt{2\pi}\, S\sigma\sqrt{T}} \left(1 - \frac{d_1^2}{2} + \cdots \right)$$

$$\approx \frac{1}{\sqrt{2\pi}\, S\sigma\sqrt{T}}$$

$$\approx \frac{0.4}{S\sigma\sqrt{T}}$$

B.2   BASKET PRICE APPROXIMATION

The approximate formula used for portfolio variance, and also to approximate the volatility of a basket, is given by

$$\sigma_B = \sqrt{\sum_{i=1}^{n} \sum_{j=1}^{n} w_i w_j \sigma_i \sigma_j \rho_{i,j}}$$

where the sums are over all assets in the basket/portfolio. Assuming log-normality of the underlying assets, this formula is not exact. It follows from the approximation that

$$\mathcal{B} = \sum_{i=1}^{n} w_i S_i \approx \prod_{i=1}^{n} S_i^{w_i}$$

where the basket, defined as a sum of assets, is approximated by a product. See De Weert (2008).

A consequence is that if we assume zero rates as dividends, then the price of the call option on the basket is given by

$$C_B = \mathcal{B}(0) \mathcal{N}(d_1) - K \mathcal{N}(d_2)$$

where d_1 and d_2 are given by the usual formulas now using σ_B for the volatility term, and in all places $\mathcal{B}(0) = w_1 S_1(0) + w_2 S_2(0)$ replaces the spot S in the Black–Scholes formula.

B.3   ICBC/CBC INEQUALITY

In section 9.2.2 we saw the inequality

$$\text{ICBC}_{\text{payoff}} < \text{CBC}_{\text{payoff}}$$

where

$$\text{ICBC}_{\text{payoff}} = \max \left[0, \frac{1}{N} \sum_{i=1}^{N} \min \left(\text{Perf}_i, \text{Cap} \right) \right]$$

$$\text{CBC}_{\text{payoff}} = \max \left[0, \min \left(\frac{1}{N} \sum_{i=1}^{N} \text{Perf}_i, \text{Cap} \right) \right]$$

Not to complicate things, let's do this for the case of two assets, although it can be proved for general N. For two assets we have

$$\text{ICBC}_{\text{payoff}} = \max \left[0, \tfrac{1}{2} \min \left(\text{Perf}_1, \text{Cap} \right) + \tfrac{1}{2} \min \left(\text{Perf}_2, \text{Cap} \right) \right]$$
$$= \tfrac{1}{2} \max \left[0, \min \left(\text{Perf}_1, \text{Cap} \right) + \min \left(\text{Perf}_2, \text{Cap} \right) \right]$$
$$\text{CBC}_{\text{payoff}} = \max \left[0, \min \left(\tfrac{1}{2}(\text{Perf}_1, \text{Cap}) + \tfrac{1}{2}(\text{Perf}_2, \text{Cap}) \right) \right]$$
$$= \tfrac{1}{2} \max \left[0, \min \left(\text{Perf}_1 + \text{Perf}_2, 2\text{Cap} \right) \right]$$

so essentially we only need to compare

$$\min \left(\text{Perf}_1, \text{Cap} \right) + \min \left(\text{Perf}_2, \text{Cap} \right)$$

and

$$\min\left(\text{Perf}_1 + \text{Perf}_2, 2\text{Cap}\right)$$

An analysis of the only four possible outcomes, $\text{Perf}_1 > C$ and $\text{Perf}_2 > C$, $\text{Perf}_1 > C$ and $\text{Perf}_2 < C$, $\text{Perf}_1 < C$ and $\text{Perf}_2 > C$, $\text{Perf}_1 < C$ and $\text{Perf}_2 < C$, shows that in each case

$$\min\left(\text{Perf}_1, \text{Cap}\right) + \min\left(\text{Perf}_2, \text{Cap}\right) \le \min\left(\text{Perf}_1 + \text{Perf}_2, 2\text{Cap}\right)$$

so the result holds.

B.4   DIGITALS: VEGA AND THE POSITION OF THE FORWARD

The goal of this section is to derive a formula that allows for a speedy mental check for the seller of a digital to assess whether they are long or short volatility based on the position of the forward.

We know that the price of a digital is given by the limit of a call spread. Under Black–Scholes the digital call's price is given by $D(K) = \mathcal{N}(d_2)$, which is essentially the derivative of the Black–Scholes formula for a European call option w.r.t. the strike of the option. Firstly, we write d_2 in terms of the forward F

$$d_2 = \frac{\ln\left(F/K\right) - \sigma^2 t/2}{\sigma\sqrt{T}}$$

now write $\mathcal{N}(d_2)$ as its definition as a CDF:

$$\mathcal{N}(d_2) = \frac{1}{\sqrt{2\pi}} \int_{-\infty}^{d_2} e^{-\frac{x^2}{2}}$$

Then the Vega of a digital is given by the derivative of this integral w.r.t. the volatility σ:

$$\begin{aligned}
\frac{\partial D(K)}{\partial \sigma} &= \frac{\partial}{\partial \sigma}\left[\frac{1}{\sqrt{2\pi}}\int_{-\infty}^{d_2} e^{-\frac{x^2}{2}}\right] \\
&= \frac{1}{\sqrt{2\pi}}\left[e^{-\frac{d_2^2}{2}} \times \frac{\partial d_2}{\partial \sigma}\right] \\
&= \frac{1}{\sqrt{2\pi}}e^{-\frac{d_2^2}{2}} \times \left[\frac{-\ln\left(F/K\right) - \sigma^2 t/2}{\sigma^2\sqrt{t}}\right]
\end{aligned}$$

where moving to the second equality we used the fact that only d_2 depends on σ. The last equality involves simply computing the derivative of d_2 given above by the volatility σ.

So, in essence, the Vega of the digital is positive (i.e. the seller of the digital is short volatility) only if

$$-\ln\left(\frac{F}{K}\right) - \frac{\sigma^2 t}{2} > 0$$

because all the other terms are positive. For this to be satisfied we need

$$F < K \times e^{-\sigma^2 t/2}$$

for reasonable volatility σ and time to maturity t the term $\sigma^2 t/2$ is small and the exponential can be approximated as a series giving the inequality

$$F < K \times \left(1 - \frac{\sigma^2 t}{2}\right)$$

The opposite holds in that if

$$F > K \times \left(1 - \frac{\sigma^2 t}{2}\right)$$

then the above digital Vega will be negative and the seller of the digital is long volatility.

So, as a first check, if the forward F is greater than the strike K then the second inequality is immediately satisfied and the seller is long volatility. An equality (instead of either of these inequalities) refers to the case where the seller is flat on volatility. This approximate inequality serves as a good mental check for the seller of a digital to see if they are long or short volatility.

Postscript

Dear reader, if you are reading this then it is fair to assume you have read at least part of the book. We would like to thank you for being our reader, and we truly hope you have benefited from the work. We would be delighted to hear any thoughts you have regarding this text; the more feedback we have from our readers the more we can improve the work.

Our best regards.

The authors

Bibliography

Alexander, C. (2001) *Market Models: A Guide to Financial Data Analysis*. John Wiley & Sons Ltd, Chichester.

Allen, P., Einchcomb, S. and Granger, N. (2006) *Conditional variance swaps*. Product note. JP Morgan.

Bates, D.S. (1996) Jumps and stochastic volatility: Exchange rate processes implicit in deutsche mark options. *Review of Financial Studies*, **9** (1), 69–107.

Bergomi, L. (2004) Smile dynamics II. *Risk* (September).

Black, F. (1976) The pricing of commodity contracts. *Journal of Financial Economics*, **3**, 167–179.

Black, F. and Scholes, M. (1973) The pricing of options and corporate liabilities. *Journal of Political Economy*, **81**, 631–659.

Bossu, S. (July 2005) *Arbitrage Pricing of Correlation Swaps*. Equity Derivatives Group, JP Morgan Securities Ltd.

Bossu, S., Strasser, E. and Guichard, R. (2005) *Just What you Need to Know About Variance Swaps*. Equity Derivatives Group, JP Morgan Securities Ltd.

Brace, A., Gatarek, D. and Musiela, M. (1997) The market model of interest rate dynamics. *Mathematical Finance*, **7**.

Breeden, D. and Litzenberger, R. (1978) Prices of state-contingent claims implicit in option prices. *Journal of Business*, **51**, 621–651.

Brenner, M. and Subrahmanyam, M.G. (1988) A simple formula to compute the implied standard deviation. *Financial Analyst Journal*, **5**, 80–83.

Brigo, D. and Mercurio, F. (2006) *Interest Rate Models: Theory and Practice with Smile, Inflation and Credit* (2nd edition). Springer-Verlag.

Brigo, D., Mercurio, F., Rapisarda, F. and Scotti, R. (2004) Approximated moment-matching dynamics for basket-options pricing. *Quantitative Finance*, **4**, 1–16.

Broadie, M., Glasserman, P. and Kou, S. (1997) A continuity correction for discrete barrier options. *Mathematical Finance* (October).

Broadie, M., Glasserman, P. and Kou, S. (1998) Connecting discrete and continuous path-dependent options. *Finance and Stochastics*, **2**, 1–28.

Carr, P. and Lee, R. (2007) Realized volatility and variance: Options via swaps. *Risk* (May).

Carr, P. and Lewis, K. (2004) Corridor variance swaps. *Risk*, **17** (2).

Carr, P. and Madan, D. (1998) Towards a theory of volatility trading. In R. Jarrow (ed.), *Volatility* (pp. 417–427). Risk Publications.

Carr, P. and Madan, D. (2005) A note on sufficient conditions for no arbitrage. *Finance Research Letters*, **2**, 125–130.

Carr, P. and Wu, L. (2006) A tale of two indices. *Journal of Derivatives* (Spring).

Carr, P. and Wu, L. (2007) Stochastic skew in currency options. *Journal of Financial Economics*, **86**, 213–247.

CBOE (2006) *VIX Futures White Paper*. Chicago Board Options Exchange.

Cherubini, U. and Luciano, E. (2002) Bivariate option pricing with copulas. *Applied Mathematical Finance*, **9** (2), 69–85.

Cherubini, U., Luciano, E. and Veccahiato, W. (2004) *Copula Methods in Finance.* John Wiley & Sons Ltd, Chichester.

De Weert, F. (2008) *Exotic Options Trading.* John Wiley & Sons Ltd, Chichester.

Deacon, M., Derry, A. and Mirfendereski, D. (2004) *Inflation-Indexed Securities: Bonds, Swaps and Other Derivatives* (2nd edition). John Wiley & Sons Ltd, Chichester.

Demeterfi, K., Derman, E., Kamal, M. and Zou, J. (1999) More than you ever wanted to know about volatility swaps. *Quantitative Strategies Research Notes.* Goldman Sachs.

Derman, E. (1992) *Outperformance Options.* Goldman Sachs.

Derman, E. (1999) Regimes of volatility. *Risk,* **12** (4), 55–59.

Derman, E. and Kani, I. (1994) Riding on a smile. *Risk,* **7**, 32–39.

Derman, E. and Kani, I. (2004) *The Volatility Smile and its Implied Tree.* Goldman Sachs.

Dupire, B. (1994) Pricing with a smile. *Risk,* **7** (1), 18–20.

Garman, M. (1989) Recollection in tranquility. *Risk,* **2** (3), 16–19.

Garman, M.B. and Kohlhagen. S.W. (1983) Foreign currency option values. *Journal of International Money and Finance,* **2**, 231–237.

Gatheral, J. (2006) *The Volatility Surface: A Practioner's Guide.* John Wiley & Sons Ltd, Chichester.

Geman, H. (2005) *Commodities and Commodity Derivatives: Modeling and Pricing for Agriculturals, Metals, and Energy.* John Wiley & Sons, Inc.

Gibson, R. and Schwartz, E.S. (1990) Stochastic convenience yield and the pricing of oil contingent claims. *Journal of Finance,* **45** (3), 959–976.

Giese, A. (2006) On the pricing of auto-callable equity structures in the presence of stochastic volatility and stochastic interest rates. *Frankfurt MathFinance Workshop* (March).

Goldman, B., Sosin, H. and Gatto, M.A. (1979) Path-dependent options: Buy at the low, sell at the high. *Journal of Finance,* **34**, 1111–1127.

Hagan, P.S. (2003) Convexity conundrums: Pricing CMS swaps, caps, and floors. *Wilmott Magazine,* pp. 38–44.

Hagan, P.S., Kumar, D., Lesniewski, A.S. and Woodward, D.E. (2002) Managing smile risk. *Wilmott Magazine* (September).

Hagan, P.S., Lesniewski, A.S. and Woodward, D.E. (2005) *Probability distribution in the SABR model of stochastic volatility.* Working Paper.

Haug, E. (2006) *The Complete Guide to Option Pricing Formulas* (2nd edition). McGraw-Hill.

Heston, S.L. (1993) A closed-form solution for options with stochastic volatility with applications to bond and currency options. *Review of Financial Studies,* **6** (2), 327–343.

Higham, N. (2002) Computing the nearest correlation matrix: A problem from finance. *IMA Journal of Numerical Analysis,* **22**, 329–343.

Hughston, L.P. (1998) *Inflation derivatives.* Working Paper, King's College, London.

Hull, J. (2003) *Options, Futures, and Other Derivatives* (5th edition). Prentice Hall: Upper Saddle River, N.J.

Hull, J. and White, A. (1990) Pricing interest-rate derivative securities. *Review of Financial Studies,* **3** (4), 573–592.

Hunter, C. and Picot, G. (2005) Hybrid derivatives: Financial engines of the future. In L. Nicholson (ed.), *The Euromoney Derivatives and Risk Management Handbook, 2005/2006.* Euromoney Books.

Jamshidian, F. (1997) LIBOR and swap market models and measures. *Finance and Stochastics,* **1**, 293–330.

Jeffery, C. (2004) Reverse cliquets: End of the road? *Risk,* **17**, 20–22.

Johnson, H. (1987) Options on the minimum or maximum of several assets. *Journal of Financial and Quantitative Analysis,* **22** (3), 277–283.

Kemna, A. and Vorst, A. (1990) A pricing method for options based on average asset value. *Journal of Banking and Finance* (14 March).

Lee, R. (2008) *Gamma swap.* Working Paper, University of Chicago (August).

Li, D. (2000) *On default correlation: A copula function approach.* Working Paper, RiskMetrics Group, New York.

Lintner, J. (1965) The valuation of risk assets and the selection of risky investments in stock portfolios and capital budgets. *Review of Economics and Statistics,* **47** (1), 13–37.

Margrabe, W. (1978) The value of an option to exchange one asset for another. *Journal of Finance,* **33** (1), 177–186.

Markowitz, H. (1952) Portfolio selection. *Journal of Finance*, **7** (1), 77–91.

Merton, R.C. (1973) The theory of rational option pricing. *Bell Journal of Economics and Management Science*, **4**, 141–183.

Merton, R.C. (1976) Option pricing when underlying stock returns are discontinuous. *Journal of Financial Economics*, **3**, 125–144.

Mikhailov, S. and Nogel, U. (2005) Heston's stochastic volatility model implementation, calibration and some extensions. *Wilmott Magazine.*

Nelsen, R.B. (1999) *An Introduction to Copulas.* Springer-Verlag Statistics, New York.

Neuberger, A. (1990) *Volatility trading.* Working Paper. London Business School.

O'Kane, D. (2008) *Modelling Single-name and Multi-name Credit Derivatives.* John Wiley & Sons, Ltd, Chichester.

Overhaus, M. (2002) Himalaya options. *Risk*, **15** (3), 101–104.

Overhaus, M., Bermudez, A., Buehler, H., Ferraris, A. and Jordinson, C. (2007) *Equity Hybrid Derivatives.* John Wiley & Sons, Ltd, Chichester.

Quessette, R. (2002) New products, new risks. *Risk*, **15** (12).

Rebonato, R. (2002) *Modern Pricing of Interest-Rate Derivatives: The LIBOR Market Model and Beyond.* Princeton University Press.

Rebonato, R. (2007) *A time-homogeneous, SABR-consistent extension of the LMM: Calibration and numerical results.* Working Paper. Tanaka Business School.

Rubinstein, H. (1995) Somewhere over the rainbow. *Risk*, **8** (11), 63–66.

Schmidt, T. (2007) *Coping with copulas.* Working Paper. Risk Books.

Schofield, N.C. (2007) *Commodity Derivatives: Markets and Applications.* John Wiley & Sons Ltd, Chichester.

Sepp, A. (2008) Pricing options on realized variance in the Heston model with jumps in returns and volatility. *Journal of Computational Finance*, **11** (4), 33–70.

Sharpe, W.F. (1964) Capital asset prices: A theory of market equilibrium under conditions of risk. *Journal of Finance*, **19** (3), 425–442.

Sharpe, W.F. (1994) The Sharpe ratio. *Journal of Portfolio Management*, **21** (1), 49–58.

Sklar, A. (1959) Fonctions de repartition en dimensions et leurs marges. *Publications de l'Institut de Statistique de l'Université de Paris*, **8**, 229–231.

Stulz, R.M (1995) Options on the minimum or the maximum of two risky assets: Analysis and applications. *Journal of Financial Economics*, **10** (2), 161–185.

Taleb N. N. (1997) *Dynamic Hedging: Managing Vanilla and Exotic Options.* John Wiley & Sons Ltd, Chichester.

Trivedi, P.K. and Zimmer, D.M. (2007) Copula modelling: An introduction for practitioners. *Foundations and Trends in Econometrics*, **1** (1), 1–110.

West, G. (2005) *Calibration of the SABR model in illiquid markets.* Working Paper.

Wilmott, P. (2000) *Paul Wilmott on Quantitative Finance.* John Wiley & Sons Ltd, Chichester.

Wilmott, P. (2002) Cliquet options and volatility models. *Wilmott Magazine.*

Wystup, U. (2002) How the Greeks would have hedged correlation risk of foreign exchange options. In *Foreign Exchange Risk* (pp. 143–146). Risk Books.

Wystup, U. (2007) *FX Options and Structured Products.* John Wiley & Sons Ltd, Chichester.

Index

Index compiled by Indexing Specialists (UK) Ltd